The InfoSec Handbook

An Introduction to Information Security

Umesh Hodeghatta Rao
Umesha Nayak

Apress
open

The InfoSec Handbook

Umesh Hodeghatta Rao and Umesha Nayak

Publisher: Heinz Weinheimer
Lead Editors: Saswata Mishra (Apress), Steve Weiss (Apress), Stuart Douglas (Intel)
Development Editor: Kenyon Brown
Technical Reviewer: Jeremy Frady
Coordinating Editor: Mark Powers
Cover Designer: Anna Ishchenko

Distributed to the book trade worldwide by Springer Science+Business Media New York, 233 Spring Street, 6th Floor, New York, NY 10013. Phone 1-800-SPRINGER, fax (201) 348-4505, e-mail orders-ny@springer-sbm.com, or visit www.springeronline.com.

For information on translations, please e-mail rights@apress.com, or visit www.apress.com.

About ApressOpen

What Is ApressOpen?

- ApressOpen is an open-access book program that publishes high-quality technical and business-information texts.

- ApressOpen eBooks are available for global, free, noncommercial use.

- ApressOpen eBooks are available in PDF, ePub, and Mobi formats.

- The user-friendly ApressOpen free eBook license is presented on the copyright page of this book.

Umesh H R : I dedicate this book to my mother who was always supportive and encouraging in all my pursuits in life.

Umesha Nayak: I dedicate this book to my mother and my wife, both of who have supported me in different phases of my life.

Contents at a Glance

Contents

About the Authors

Professor Umesh Hodeghatta Rao is on the faculty at Xavier Institute of Management, Bhubaneswar, in the area of Information Systems. He has more than 20 years of work experience and has held technical and senior management positions at Wipro Technologies, McAfee, Cisco Systems, and AT&T Bell Laboratories, USA. He has published journal articles in international journals and conferences. He graduated with a master's degree from Oklahoma State University, USA (MSEE) and is pursuing a PhD at the Indian Institute of Technology, Kharagpur. He is a senior member of the IEEE.

Umesha Nayak is a director and principal consultant of MUSA Software Engineering Pvt. Ltd. which focuses on systems / process / management consulting. He has 32 years' experience, of which 11 years are in providing consultancy to IT / manufacturing and other organizations from across the globe. He is a Master of Science in Software Systems; Master of Arts in Economics; CAIIB; Certified Information Systems Auditor (CISA), and Certified Risk and Information Systems Control (CRISC) professional from ISACA, US; PGDFM; Certified Ethical Hacker from EC Council; Certified Lead Auditor for many of the standards; Certified Coach among others. He has worked extensively in banking, software development, product design and development, project management, program management, information technology audits, information application audits, quality assurance, coaching, product reliability, human resource management, and consultancy. He was Vice President and Corporate Executive Council member at Polaris Software Lab, Chennai prior to his current assignment. He also held various roles like Head of Quality, Head of SEPG and Head of Strategic Practice Unit - Risks & Treasury at Polaris Software Lab. He started his journey with computers in 1981 with ICL mainframes and continued further with minis and PCs. He was one of the founding members of the information systems auditing in the banking industry in India. He has effectively guided many organizations through successful ISO 9001/ISO 27001/CMMI and other certifications and process/product improvements.

Acknowledgments

We are extremely thankful to all the readers of this book. Without the readers, this book is of no value. We have made a sincere effort to present the material in lay terms so that it is easy for readers to understand. We hope that readers find it to be so. We also hope the necessary material has been covered in this book. We will be very happy to receive any feedback from the readers and we assure all the readers that we will sincerely consider the feedback and use it during the future revisions of this book.

We would like to sincerely thank Rekha Umesh for reviewing the book. Also thanks to our families for supporting us throughout the development of this book.

Introduction

This book explains information security concepts in lay terms. The target audience is beginning users. At the same time, we also describe some of the concepts in detail in order for the content to be of interest to people in the information security field.

With the increasingly connected world revolving around the revolution of internet and new technologies like mobiles, smartphones, and tablets, and with the wide usage of wireless technologies, the information security risks have increased. Any information security vulnerability is possible to be widely exploited by the hackers and crackers who are looking for such opportunities. Both individuals and organizations are under regular attacks for commercial or non-commercial gains. The objectives of such attacks may be to take revenge, malign the reputation of a competitor organization, understand the strategies and sensitive information about the competitor, simply have fun of exploiting the vulnerabilities through new means and claim superiority, misuse of information like credit card details, banking account details for monetary gains, and so on. Over a period of time exploitation from the perspective of making monetary gains has increased. While objectives may vary from attack to attack, the impact can be very severe in terms of reputation loss to business loss to monetary loss to loss of sensitive information of strategic / competitive value, or loss of intellectual property rights. The hackers are constantly looking for vulnerabilities in the software applications, protocols, and infrastructure. Hence, the need to protect information assets and ensure information security receives adequate attention.

This book considers various important aspects of relevance to information security both from the perspective of individuals and organizations. As assured at the beginning of this book we maintain the simplicity of the explanations without using high-tech jargons so readers can understand. We also provide a significant number of tips to the readers which they can follow to avoid them getting into the trap of attackers and becoming prey to the attacks.

Our book is organized in five sections:

- Part I: Introduction

  We start the book with an interesting discussion on the need for security and highlight the value of information security programs to all the employees and relevant personnel like contractors and vendors. We then explore the history of information security and highlight what some of the major hackers / crackers did to circumvent the system and exploit them.

- Part II: Key Principles and Practices

  We cover major aspects of information security, including fundamental concepts underlying information security like confidentiality, integrity, and availability. We explore the importance of having appropriate access control applied to all the stakeholders and discuss various access control models including the role-based access control model and attribute-based access control model. We then explore important aspects of information systems management like risk management, incident response, disaster recovery, and business continuity planning.

- Part III: Application Security

  We examine application security-related issues including web application security issues. We also explore the approach to be taken by the organizations to avoid these application security issues. We then explore the issues of malicious software like adware, spyware, viruses, worms, and Trojans. In this context we discuss the value of anti-virus software and provide details of some of the commercially available useful anti-virus software. We then explore the world of encryption and Cryptography. We describe Symmetric Key Cryptography and Asymmetric Key Cryptography.

- Part IV: Network Security

  We explore network security, the fundamentals of networking, and the vulnerabilities related to network security and what needs to be done to ensure network security. We then describe Firewalls, Intrusion Detection and Prevention Systems, and Virtual Private Networks. We also touch upon data backups and cloud security.

- Part V: Physical Security

  We discuss physical security, and explain important physical security related issues and how they can be handled effectively. In this context we discuss the role of biometrics and various biometric systems. We explain the social engineering aspects and how individuals and organizations can be impacted because of this. We also describe what individuals and organizations have to do to ensure that they do not become prey to the social engineering attacks.

What to Take From This Book?

This book is primarily intended to open up and make clear the aspects of information security to beginners in the field of information security. However, this book also brings in a newer perspective and the latest trends of interest to those who have a good understanding of the information security field, like the information security professionals who may be information security auditors, information security consultants, and information security officers. This book is intended to give a clear understanding of concepts and related information in simple terms rather than through complicated jargon and abstract theories. The approach used in this book is practical and straightforward, and clarity is the main focus of this book. Wherever possible, various aspects are demonstrated through the situational scenarios. The intention is not to get too technical, but as far as possible to elaborate on technical aspects in common terms so that most intended readers of this book can understand what is being conveyed.

As most of you are aware, technological advances are happening at a high speed and we cannot claim that we are the masters of a particular technology, or that we understand the intricacies of each technology. Everyone, including us, is exploring every day; learning either a new concept or getting more clarity on existing concepts. Hence, as learning is an everyday process, we proceed with our knowledge of information security and bring to you as many concepts as possible regarding information security in simple and clear terms.

How to Read This Book?

Although we suggest that you read the chapters in sequential order, from the introduction to the last chapter as concepts are built on each other, readers are free to go through any chapter of their liking as we have also made an effort to ensure that each chapter can be read independently. If readers are already well versed in information security, then we suggest that they go through the chapters of their own interest.

Chapter 1 focuses on the need for security in general and information security in particular. We also discuss the value of and need for security programs. We then offer potential scenarios in which we do not care about security with examples from the current world. We then explore the information security scenario today. We conclude with information about some of the applicable standards and certifications such as ISO27001:2013, PCI DSS by PCI Security Standards Council, and COBIT from ISACA.

Chapter 2 focuses on the history of computer security, including the purpose as to why computer security evolved, the role of the world wars in its evolution, the initial forms of security of communication, including initial cipher usage like the Caesar cipher and initial cipher machines like Enigma and the greatest hackers and crackers in the field of computer security.

Chapter 3 focuses on key concepts behind information security, such as confidentiality, integrity, availability, possession or control, authenticity, and utility as well as the principles of information security to be applied at the organization level, including key responsibilities and accountability. We also deliberate the role of processes, people, and technology in meeting information security needs.

Chapter 4 focuses on the important aspects of access controls, the need for those controls, the importance of control, and various access control models.

Chapter 5 focuses on aspects of information systems management such as risk management, incident response, disaster recovery, and the business continuity.

Chapter 6 focuses on software application security and web security. We also discuss the web browser, web server, and web applications related information security issues. We also provide the best practices to protect the individuals / organizations from such information security issues.

Chapter 7 focuses on an in-depth analysis of discussion on malicious software, different types of malicious software, how they propagate, and the historical aspects of malware. We also discuss what an anti-virus is, what its benefits are, and how to manage most effectively the anti-virus software and common anti-virus platforms that are used in the industry.

Chapter 8 focuses on cryptography, one of the important ways of preserving the confidentiality of the message or communication and also its authentication. In this chapter, we also focus on what is meant by cryptography, encryption, cryptoalgorithm, and encryption/decryption keys. We also discuss symmetric cryptography and asymmetric cryptography. In this context we discuss on public key infrastructure. We also discuss how these cryptography aspects are used, the value of the certificates like digital certificates and digital signature in the field of cryptography, various hashing algorithms, and the disk/drive encryption tools that are used.

Chapter 9 focuses on an introduction to basics of networking, communication concepts, networking models like OSI and TCP/IP models, comparison between them and the protocols used by different layers. We also discuss the information security issues related to networking.

Chapter 10 focuses on firewalls which are essential in today's world to protect organizations. This chapter covers the basics of firewalls and their functionality, the importance of the firewalls, the types and different generations of firewalls, and how the firewalls are used. We also discuss best practices.

Chapter 11 focuses on an introduction to intrusion detection and prevention systems (IDS/IPS), their purpose and uses, various detection methodologies employed by these systems, types of IDS/IPS methodologies that are available and popular, and the typical responses by these.

Chapter 12 focuses on the introduction to the Virtual Private Network (VPN), their uses, types of VPNs, and the protocols used to make the VPNs effective.

Chapter 13 focuses on the importance of data backups, the benefits of using a backup, the dangers of not having backups, and various types of backups. This chapter also covers the current hot topic of cloud computing and related models, and issues of privacy and compliance that are related to them.

Chapter 14 focuses on physical security in general including fire safety and one of the important aspects of physical security: biometrics. This chapter introduces biometrics, why it is gaining popularity, its functionality, the multi-modal biometric systems, issues, and controversies pertaining to biometric systems.

Chapter 15 focuses on another important topic in the current world: social engineering. This chapter covers the introduction to social engineering, how social engineering attacks are made possible, and typical social engineering scenarios, We also discuss various techniques that are used in the field of social engineering, such as pretexting, phishing, baiting, and tailgating and the steps to be taken to avoid falling prey to social engineering.

Chapter 16 focuses on two of the current and important trends in information security: wireless security and mobile security. We also cover bluetooth security.

PART I

■ ■ ■

Introduction

This section introduces the concept of security in general and information security in particular. The intention was also to provide a historical perspective about information security.

Chapter 1, "Introduction to Security," highlights three examples of information security breaches recently published on the internet. The first example explains how the encrypted messages can be read by injecting plaintext into HTTPS request and measuring compression changes. The second example explains how the NSA was provided direct access to the networks of some of the big corporations like Google, Yahoo, and Microsoft and how the tapping of information from undersea cables where the information moves unencrypted was carried out. The third example explains the breach of 40 million credit and debit cards, which happened during the busy Christmas season at Target. We then generally describe what security is and describe it as protecting what one has. We also look into the fact that security not only applies to physical assets, but also non-physical assets like confidential information, research information with high value realization potential, intellectual property rights, and security of customers. We also highlight the role of terrorists and disgruntled employees in the breach of security. We then explore why security is important. In this context we look into how every individual and organization wants to preserve its societal status and how the compromise of information security can lead to misuse of the information at the wrong hands. We then look into the importance of protection of business information of value and protection of customer data and that information security should not be implemented for the sake of implementing it, but with all the serious consideration it requires. We also highlight how new technologies, new products, and new applications can also bring new security threats to the fore. We then discuss what happens if we do not care about security with examples from the current world. We then discuss the history of computers and information security. We then explore the information security scenario today. We also discuss how prevention is better than cure and explain the need to build in appropriate controls through risk assessment of what can go wrong. We conclude with information about some of the applicable standards and certifications like ISO27001:2013, PCI DSS by PCI Security Standards Council, and COBIT from ISACA.

Chapter 2, "History of Computer Security," starts with the history of exploiting security started with the tapping of telephone lines and how the telephone operators intentionally misdirected the calls and eavesdropped on the conversations. We also look into the role of "phreakers" like John Draper. Next we look into how bulletin boards became the target of hackers as the people started sharing passwords, credit card numbers thereon. Then we look into Ian Murphy's breaking into AT&T's computers and Kevin Mitnick's stealing of computer manuals of Pacific Bells's switching center. Then we look into how Computer Emergency Response Team (CERT) was formed by government agencies in charge of ARPANET to counter increasing threats to security. We then look into how the 1990s saw more hacking activities such as the "Michelangelo" virus, the arrest of notorious hacker Kevin Mitnick for stealing credit card data, and the 1998 Solar Sunrise attack targeting Pentagon computers by Ehud Tenebaum. We look into the growth of the Internet and how business-related information became available on the Internet and with the increasing threats the technologies like firewalls, antivirus programs came into existing while on the other hand the viruses, Trojans, and worms were proliferating. We then explore the history of communications and in the context discussed Caesar cipher. We also highlight how the need for secure communications in the context of military information exchange led to cryptography.

We then discuss the role of world wars in the development of coding to exchange the information secretly. In this context we discuss Enigma machine and how Alan Turing succeeded at Bletchley Park in decoding the messages coded through Enigma machine and how this led to the shortening of World War II. We then discuss some of the greatest phreakers and hackers like John Draper and Kevin Mitnick and discuss in today's context of the Internet the role of people like Julian Assange of WikiLeaks and whistleblowers like Edward Snowden in the context of the role of the NSA in the breach of information security.

CHAPTER 1

■ ■ ■

Introduction to Security

Scenario 1: A post on `http://threatpost.com`, Threatpost, the Kaspersky Lab Security News Service, dated August 5th, 2013 with the title "BREACH Compression Attack Steals HTTPS Secrets in Under 30 Seconds" by Michael Mimoso, states[1]:

> "A serious attack against ciphertext secrets, buried inside HTTPS responses, has prompted an advisory from Homeland Security.
>
> The BREACH attack is an offshoot of CRIME, which was thought dead and buried after it was disclosed in September. Released at last week's Black Hat USA 2013, BREACH enables an attacker to read encrypted messages over the Web by injecting plaintext into an HTTPS request, and measuring compression changes.
>
> Researchers Angelo Prado, Neal Harris, and Yoel Gluck demonstrated the attack against Outlook Web Access (OWA) at Black Hat. Once the Web application was opened and the Breach attack was launched, within 30 seconds, the attackers had extracted the secret."

Scenario 2: A post on `http://threatpost.com`, Threatpost, the Kaspersky Lab Security News Service, dated December 30th, 2013 with the title: "Most Surprising NSA Capability: Defeating the Collective Security Prowess of the Silicon Valley" by Dennis Fisher, states as follows[2]:

> "Some of the earliest leaks to emerge from the Edward Snowden cache described a program called PRISM that granted the NSA "direct access" to networks run by Google, Yahoo, Microsoft, and many other companies. That direct access was quickly interpreted to mean that those companies were giving the agency data links to their servers through which the NSA could collect traffic information on targets. The affected companies quickly denied this; only later was it revealed that "direct access" came in the form of tapping undersea cables that carry unencrypted traffic between data centers around the world. The revelation triggered an immediate response from Google, Microsoft, and Yahoo, who said that they would be encrypting that traffic in the near future. In addition, some Google engineers had some choice words for the NSA's in-house hackers. In the words of Google's Mike Hearn, "The traffic shown in the slides below is now all encrypted and the work the NSA/GCHQ staff did on understanding it is ruined.""

What is Security?

The events above are a few of the security breaches that were reported during 2013. There are many security breaches reported every year from different quarters of the world. Some of these may be accidental and some intentional. Some may not be with the intention of making money, while others are done purely with the intention of making money. Some events may be done for one-upmanship or merely for the thrill of breaking the system. With more computers and people interconnected and in turn, connected by the internet, the role of computer security in general and information security in particular, with special emphasis on cybersecurity, is gaining momentum. With technological advances and the spread of technological know-how, information security is certainly a humongous task for everyone! That is, all computer users including the non-technical ones.

Our intention here is not to define the term "security," but to explore the term so that it becomes crystal clear to the readers as to what it really means. A basic animal instinct is to ensure one's own "safety." Every animal, including a human, will fight for its safety. Everyone wants to be safe and preserve whatever they have with them whether that be assets, money, or otherwise. The security of the individual, company, assets, or security of their information and many more similar things are expected and seem to be quite in sync with nature's laws. Security, in simple terms, is protecting what you or others have. This same idea applies to entities like government departments, agencies, companies, institutes, and so on, irrespective of their size or function.

The security of not only physical assets, but of non-physical assets as well are important and necessary. Some of these non-physical assets include confidential information and data; intellectual property; research data with the potential of high value realization and high investment; and the security of your customers or end users when at your facility or while using your systems. The security of the installations with high defense or strategic value, like nuclear installations, nuclear sources, chemical and biological laboratories, and areas with high-level political and administrative dignitaries, are of significance. Most terrorist threats are guided (or misguided) by so-called ideals or ulterior motives, making the security more important. Security is even more important with the recent rise in widespread use of technology such as mobile phones, the internet, tablets, and other mobile devices. Disgruntled or unhappy employees are also achieving significance by leaking information that is of strategic importance, either for exacting vengeance or for profit.

Why is Security Important?

Earning is difficult, but losing is extremely easy. You have to earn with your efforts, but you can lose because of others' efforts. No individual or entity wants to lose what they have earned through hard work (or even otherwise!). If you lose what you have, you have to start over again, which is hard for anyone. Again, by nature, everyone wants to preserve their energy and secure their future for themselves and their children. Every organization wants to secure its bright future. Securing what you have and not losing it, while getting more of it, is important for societal status. Every individual or organization is a "social animal" and is conscious about their status. Status is what makes one distinct or different from others. Organizations or governments have a lot of information at their fingertips which is of strategic importance to them. They invest a lot in carrying out research in areas of strategic, military, or competitive significance to them. The loss of this information to a third party with the same interests may lead to their strategy being a complete waste, thereby leading to the waste of entire investments and years of effort. This may require them to restart their efforts, possibly using a new way of thinking. Information may be required by those who want it for the value of it, or who want to show their heroism. Some of the current generation of so-called computer hackers may just want to satisfy their ego or show their supremacy over the technology and may steal useful and valuable information and publish it to others. Others may want to mine for data of value so that they can sell the same to others, who want the information to either harm others or make commercial gains from it. Terrorists may want the information to either destroy the strategic or military capability of a country, or to threaten the economy of a country by using the information they steal. Also, 3D printers present a new possible threat by potentially being used by terrorists to create weapons! The primary reason for information security is the threat of information being misused if it lands in the wrong hands.

Some people feel that the need for information security is "hyped." However, we in technology security do not think so. It is possible to think of information security as "hyped" only if our focus is on information security just for the sake of information security, and not based on the risks to the business of any information leakage, breakage, or loss. The protection of business information of value is the primary reason for information security. We must ask ourselves, "Can we risk the leakage of customer data held by us or to which we have access?" If the answer is "no," then we have used basic Risk Management to justify a need for security because the leakage of customer data can only be at our own peril.

Furthermore, the pace at which we are coming up with new technologies is also of concern to security. New technology, new products, and new applications are brought to the market with such speed that inherent security issues may not be known yet and it may not have been possible to be tested thoroughly before launch. Once new technologies are in the market, there is a possibility that somebody may accidentally or intentionally break through any of the inherent security flaws in the technology, product, or application. It is necessary that entities or individuals have the capability to be able to respond at such a speed that the chances of an exploitation of a security flaw are very minimal. Many times, it may not be possible to do so because of design or technical issues behind the flaw, or because of the extent to which the solution is required, sometimes across multiple systems and by multiple users. This means that some of the entities or users are open to the exploitation of such a security flaw. Oftentimes, users and entities may not apply the corrective actions immediately, either because of a lack of appreciation of the gravity of the issue, because of ignorance, or because of other priorities. This is very much true when there are deadlines to be met and many of the compulsory checks get skipped due to lack of time or personnel to perform those checks.

Science and technology provide many tools which are at the disposal of entities and people that can be used for either good purposes or bad purposes. Bad guys can always use such facilities or tools for bad purposes. For example, a security tool like Metasploit or Nessus or nMap, if placed in an auditor's hands, can harden infrastructure, whereas in a cracker's hands they become the go-to tools for criminal activity. A proper focus on information security allows only the required details about the entity or person to be known to the outside world. If any entity or person wants "peace of mind" in today's connected world, information security is a MUST.

■ **Note** Sometimes the book might appear to use the terms "cracker" and "hacker" interchangeably. However, they are different. A cracker is the name given to a hacker who breaks into computers for criminal gain. A hacker, however, can also be an internet security expert who is hired to find vulnerabilities in systems.

What if You Do Not Care About Security?

If you think you don't need to care about information security, you are creating more risk than you bargained for. With advanced technologies at the disposal of many people, it is only a matter of time until you are robbed or your reputation is tarnished. Hence, at this time, no person or entity can ignore or take its own security lightly, making it hard to sleep at night! For example, you could find that if you doze off, and ten minutes have passed, your debit card could be stolen by someone and already, all the money in your account could be swindled by someone. Maybe your laptop is stolen and the new proposal of millions of dollars you have been working on quite painstakingly is already in the hands of your competitors. Maybe the innovative concept you have been discussing over the phone is overheard, recorded, and patented by someone else. There are unlimited possibilities as to what can go wrong. If you do not care about security, your existence itself will be at risk. Beware of this!

There are instances of Automated Teller Machines (ATMs) being towed away or otherwise hacked by thieves. There are many instances where information has been stolen from emails, laptops, or cell phones and used to blackmail the owners.

There have been instances of weak encryption being substituted by strong encryption, and entities/people have been blackmailed have had to shell out significant amounts of money to get the data decrypted. There have been instances where passwords have been changed or servers have been overtaken by others and then thieves demand a ransom to restore access. There have been instances where software applications have been pirated by overcoming built-in controls and thus, the entity that created the software loses a significant amount of revenue.

There have also been instances of identity theft, which can lead to huge losses. There have been instances where the data of strategic and military importance has been stolen physically or through logical means of hacking. There have been instances of gaining physical entry into secure areas and destroying crucial assets, including information assets. There have been instances where the data has been compromised, either by luring the people or by other means, which leads the party to huge losses. We cannot even fully imagine the kind of possibilities that are out there. Perhaps, the hacker is even able to intervene with the navigation system of an airplane or a missile and bring it down or make it strike somewhere else! The possibilities are endless, and we do not know the extent of damage information in the wrong hands could potentially cause. We can continue citing examples, but we hope to bring as many instances as possible to your attention as we write this book.

We have seen or heard of instances of hacking into banking accounts and initiating transactions or hacking into systems and obtaining credit card or debit card related information or credentials such as PIN or Telephonic PIN and misusing them. Phishing attacks are common as are instances of credit cards or debit cards being cloned. There have been instances of identity theft and fake profiles created on social media. Social engineering attacks, where attackers befriend persons and later misuse the information or relationship obtained, are becoming common.

Malicious software attacks through links or attachments in emails, through add-ins to the browser, or through the download of free applications or games is common. Tracking or hacking through mobile devices is a recent phenomenon that must be monitored. Exploiting the technical vulnerabilities of the applications, protocols, web browsers, web servers, or utilities is also a known phenomenon.

Eavesdropping on wireless communications or misusing wireless connections is on the rise. The rogue wireless access points set up by attackers attract many users which leads to the compromise of important information like login credentials.

In addition to the above, ineffective maintenance of the systems or utilities such as UPS or electrical cables can lead to system failure, thus reducing productivity.

There have also been instances of misuse of surveillance cameras, remote connection utilities used to hack into someone else's system, and application errors not known or not fixed by the vendor organizations.

With a lot of information getting distributed easily across the globe because of Web and Cloud technologies, there are a lot of challenges to ensure that data and information of value are well protected so that they are not compromised.

The Evolution of the Computer and Information Security

If you glance through the history of computer security, you will find that the initial need was to physically protect the mainframe computers, which were used to crack the encrypted messages used during the world wars. Physical security was provided through security guards, identification cards, badges, keys, and other means. These regulated the access to sites and locations where the mainframe computers were hosted and were essential for protecting them from theft and destruction. This was the main scenario during the 1950s and 1960s.

ARPAnet, the precursor to the Internet, was started with the intent of sharing data between remote locations. With the primary intention of ARPAnet being a provision of connectivity across various locations and systems, information security does not seem to have been given much importance. However, as the days progressed and more data and more people came on to ARPAnet, linking many computers, the need for information security increased.[5]

The MULTICS, multi-users, and timesharing operating systems increased the need for information security. MULTICS (Multiplexed Information and Computing Services) operating system, true to its name, facilitated many different users to access the system simultaneously. The MULTICS was a research project started at MIT in 1964 and sponsored by Honeywell, GE, and MIT that allowed multi-user capability serving thousands in academic and research communities. This operating system provided much-needed focus on computer security and was built into the requirements for computer security. Honeywell then dropped out of the consortium to develop its own product. MULTICS systems were eventually sold for commercial use by Honeywell, with both the security and services.

Multi-user systems allow hardware and software applications to be accessed by multiple users. Multiple users can access the single system from the same location or a remote location using different computer terminals with different operating systems. These terminals are connected through wires and telephone networks. Since systems were shared by users who might not trust each other, security was of major concern and services were developed to support security features for file sharing via access control. MULTICS machines were developed to protect data from other users. Information co-existed on the same machine and the data was marked as 'Confidential', 'Classified', etc. Operating systems were designed to ensure that the right data is accessed by the right user.[6]

Ken Thomson from Bell Labs liked the MULTICS system but felt it was too complex and the same idea could be implemented in a simpler way. In 1969, he wrote the first version of Unix, called UNICS (Uniplexed Operating and Computing Systems). In 1973, Ken Thomson and Denise Ritchie wrote the first C compiler and rewrote Unix in C. The following year, Unix was licensed to various universities. University of California Berkley modified UNIX and called their version "BSD" Unix, and Bell Labs continued to use Unix under the name "System V-+" Unix. Eventually, there were two types of Unix operating systems: BSD and System V. The biggest advantage Unix had was its networking capabilities.

Unix became an ideal operating system for connecting different systems and providing e-mail services. It supported the TCP/IP protocol for computer communication. It also provided security features like user authentication mechanisms through user ID and password, different levels of access, and restrictions at the file level.[6]

In the mid 1970s, the invention of microprocessors led to a new age of computing with the introduction of Personal Computers (PCs). The 1980s gave rise to wider computer communication through the interconnection of personal computers, mainframe computers, and mini computers. This enabled resources to be available to all users within a networking community and led to the need for complex information security. As the popularity of PCs grew, networks of computers became more common as did the need to connect these computer systems together. This gave rise to the birth of the Internet. In the 1990s, the Internet was made available to the general public. The Internet virtually connected all computers over a pre-existing telephone infrastructure. After the Internet was commercialized, the technology became pervasive, connecting every corner of the globe. However, initial days of internetworking experienced many issues because of factors like incompatibility of the proprietary protocols not allowing proper communications between two systems/networks, different vendors using different technologies to ensure their stronghold on the technology, and difficulties in ensuring that the message intended reaches only the destination device. Routing technologies, standardization efforts on the protocols, and standardization of computer systems and logical addressing systems like IP changed the scenario over time and enabled easy communication between various devices on the internet.

Tim Berners Lee wrote the first web page and the first web server.[7] He designed the World Wide Web (WWW) to link and share news, documents, and data anywhere in the network. By 1991, people outside CERN joined the web community and in April 1993, World Wide Web technology was made available to the public. Since that time, the web has changed the world. It has become the most powerful communication medium today. More than 30% of people in the world today are connected to the web. The WWW has changed the way we communicate with people, the way we learn new things, the way we do business, the way we share information, and also the way we solve problems. It has allowed everyone to not only be connected to one another, but also enables the sharing of information widely across the globe.[8]

The growth of the web has been phenomenal. There are more people communicating online today than any other medium. More shoppers buy and sell online today than in any other retail store. The rapid growth of the web and web usage has brought about many innovative developments. The web has several layers of technologies that all work together to deliver communication to the user. Today, the Internet has connected millions of "unsecured" computers together. This has been enabled through the growth of networking technologies and equipment like switches, multi-layered switches, and routers coupled with standardization of various protocols used. The switches enable connecting many machines within an organization and ensuring the frames are passed on appropriately to the intended destination computer whereas routers play a large role in routing the messages/communications from one network to the other and also connect to the internet. Routers are intelligent equipment and route the messages/communications efficiently from the source to the destination and connect to the internet. Also, many of the routers are now built with firewall capabilities. Advanced routers may act as switches as well as router. DHCP, NAT, and DNS have made the configuration and routing easy.

The vulnerability of information on each computer depends on the level of security provided by each system and to the system to which it is connected. Recent cyber threats have made organizations and governments realize the importance of information security. Information security has now become one of the major technologies to support the smooth operation of the Word Wide Web and Internet.

With the invention of the World Wide Web and the Internet, millions of users are connected and communicating with each other. This has raised several concerns regarding the integrity of the user, confidentiality of data, types of data that are being shared in the system, who is accessing the data, who is monitoring the information that is being sent on the Internet, and many more concerns related to information security. With the advancement of technologies such as wireless and cellular, users are always connected and networked computing has become the prevailing style of computing. As information became more exposed to the outside world, securing information has become a major challenge in the era of Inter-networking.

Information security is meant to protect information and information systems from unauthorized users accessing, using, modifying, or destroying the information. According to the standards defined by the Committee on National Security Systems, information security is the protection of information and its critical elements, including systems and hardware that uses, stores, and transmits that information. Security is achieved by implementing policies, guidelines, procedures, governance, and other software functions. Information security consists of three main components: hardware, software, and a communication system.

Various tools are developed daily to combat the compromise of information security. Several standards and guidelines have been implemented to reduce the propensity for information security breaches. However, in a constantly evolving world, information security will always be a matter of concern that will need to be addressed for the good of the world!

Information security also spans to physical aspects like hardware and infrastructure, the operating system, networks, applications, software systems, utilities, and tools. Other important contributors (favorable or adverse) to the field of information security are human beings, particularly employees, contractors, system providers, hackers, and crackers.

Information Security Today

Let's explore information security in today's context. Information security is a matter of concern for organizations and individuals alike. Modern hackers are equipped with technological knowledge and tools to infiltrate the accounts of individuals and their credit and debit cards.

Thieves and the authorities are constantly at odds. Most often, thieves are beating the authorities. Many times, the police learn a new technique only after thieves have used it. Similarly, in the field of information, there is always a race between hackers and crackers and the information security personnel. With widespread use of Information Technology and related tools, particularly with the advent of the Internet, it has become a challenge for organizations and their employees to prevent the misuse of information.

Information in lay terms is anything that is communicated in any form, public or private. Any compromise of private information to others can have a significant impact on the parties involved, including the loss of reputation, finances, or other consequences depending upon the nature of the information. All forms of technology, including the Internet, credit cards or debit cards, ATMs, bank web portals, and so on, are all under attack; most times intentionally, sometimes accidentally.

Cloud computing is the popular buzz word today and has many benefits but also presents many new risks. A contextual illustration of this scenario is given in Figure 1-1. The rise in the use of electronic chips in everything from automobiles to refrigerators to TVs is another cause for concern. Theories of such attacks are emerging every day. This possibility is illustrated in Figure 1-2.

Figure 1-1. *Mistrust on "Cloud" and its security*

SCENARIO OF THE FUTURE?

Figure 1-2. Is this the future state of security?

Information security is an extension of computer security and extends beyond physical control to logical control, control over media, and control over a medium of communication. Information security should be one of the most important goals of everyone, including employees, contractors, suppliers/vendors, and other service providers. Even though there is growing recognition of this fact, there is still a lot more that needs to be understood and implemented by all the stakeholders involved.

In this fast-paced world, where information is an asset and the achievement of business objectives is everybody's responsibility, ensuring that the information security risks are minimized with the appropriate controls in place, has become a top priority. Of course, it is not always possible to eliminate all the vulnerabilities and consequential threats, but it is necessary to identify the risks to minimize the overall risk to the organization. It is also necessary that organizational management understands the residual risks created by the controls they have put in place. A proper and appropriate risk assessment and management methodology is one of the prime necessities of an information security framework.

As the old adage goes, "An ounce of prevention is worth a pound of cure." It is always better to put on our critical thinking caps and consider what can go wrong and have the appropriate solutions in place than to worry after an incident has taken place and cost us our reputation or significant monetary loss, either in terms of penalty or in terms of consequential damages.

Even with the utmost sincerity and tremendous efforts, it is not possible to have 100% foolproof information security, because while there may be many known issues, there may also be an equal number of hidden ones. However, if we do not make sincere efforts to at least contain known security flaws or security issues which are applicable to our organization, we do an injustice not only to ourselves and to our customers, but also to the world at large.

Customers have also started explicitly looking for information security being implemented whenever they purchase a system, software, or application. They will not be inclined to purchase any product with known security flaws. As such, product companies, as well as service companies, are required to focus more on information security. What better place to start information security than right at the requirements phase and carry it through during the design, development, testing, and deployment phases? Secure coding practices are gaining momentum and are going to be one of the focus areas of the future.

The following information sheds light on the current information security environment:

"The Norton Report[3] (for 2013), now in its fourth year, is an annual research study, commissioned by Symantec, which examines consumers' online behaviors, attitudes, security habits, and the dangers and financial cost of cybercrime." The Norton Report highlights the following information[3]:

- Consumers are more mobile than ever, but are leaving security behind. Despite the fact that 63% of those surveyed own smartphones and 30% own tablets, nearly one out of two users don't take basic precautions such as using passwords, having security software, or backing up files on their mobile device.

- Cybercrime continues to be a growing global concern. Both the total global direct cost of cybercrime (US $113 billion; up from $110 billion) and the average cost per victim of cybercrime ($298; up from $197) increased this year.

- As people are now constantly connected, the lines are blurring between their personal and work lives, across multiple devices and storage solutions. Nearly half (49%) of the respondents report using their personal devices (PCs, laptops, smartphones, tablets) for work-related activities."

Information security is often not given adequate attention primarily based on the false theory that the risk is low. It is also possible that many times, we try to use complex solutions rather than simple solutions. Whatever the method of implementation, information security has become imperative.

Applicable Standards and Certifications

In order to ensure information security, various efforts have been made by the industry in the form of standards and certifications. Some of the popular ones are ISO/IEC 27001:2005[4] (revised in 2013) — Information Systems Security Management System — Requirements by the International Organization for Standardization (based on ISO/IEC 27002), Payment Card Industry Data Security Standard (PCI DSS) by PCI Security Standards Council, Payment Application Data Security Standard (PA-DSS) by the PCI Security Standards Council, Control Objectives for IT and related Technology (COBIT) by Information Systems Audit and Control Association, ISO 20000-1:2011[4] i.e. Information technology — Service Management — Part 1: Service management system requirements. These are the standards against which an organization or an application can get certified (as appropriate) to or adapted by an organization to improve itself and provide a base for the compliance check for others.

Some of the other related regulations/framework of importance are: Sarbanes-Oxley Act of 2002 also known as SOX, Committee Of Sponsoring Organization of the Treadway Commission (COSO) framework, the Health Insurance Portability And Accountability Act (HIPAA) of 1996, Federal Information Security Management Act (FISMA) of 2002, Federal Information Processing Standards (FIPS) released by the National Institute of Standards and Technology (NIST), just to name a few.

Some of the other standards of relevance are: ISO/IEC 15408-1:2009 - Information technology — Security techniques — Evaluation criteria for IT security — Part 1: Introduction and general model[4]; ISO/IEC 15408-2:2008 - Information technology -- Security techniques — Evaluation criteria for IT security — Part 2: Security functional components[4]; ISO/IEC 15408-3 - Information technology — Security techniques — Evaluation criteria for IT security — Part 3: Security assurance components[4]; ISO/IEC 18405:2008 - Information technology — Security techniques — Methodology for IT security evaluation[4]. The International Organization for Standardization has also published many more guidelines for security professionals[4]. Furthermore, organizations like Information Systems Audit and Control Association in the U.S. have published many useful models and papers on information security.

We will elaborate on the above as it becomes relevant in subsequent chapters of this book.

The Role of a Security Program

Typically, a lack of awareness is one of the prime reasons for not adhering to requisite security guidelines and consequential security breaches. For instance, when a person ignores an advisory about how laptops left visibly in cars can be stolen or a travel advisory warning against travelling by taxi or other unknown vehicle, there is an increased risk for information security breach. Similarly, failure to create a strong password on your work computer can result in information security breaches at many levels, endangering you and your organization's reputation.

Awareness is the number one step in ensuring security, both physical security and information security. Awareness ensures that the chances or risks of vulnerability and threats to security are reduced considerably. Toward this end, it is essential to provide organizationwide security awareness programs to all employees (permanent or temporary), contractors, suppliers/vendors, customers, and all other relevant stakeholders who have access to the organization or its information. In order to achieve this, organizations need to ensure regular security awareness programs spanning various aspects of their life in the organization, clearly explaining what can go wrong. However, to ensure that all these stakeholders understand why security is important, it is essential for the success of any security program. Still, as the saying goes, "Knowing but not doing is equivalent to not knowing at all", and it is up to the individual participants of these programs to take the message and content of these programs seriously and implement them in letter and in spirit.

It is not enough that such a security program is in place and is conducted only once for the entire organization. This has to be an ongoing process to ensure that any new stakeholders, including new employees, are trained invariably. In addition, the organizational structure and environment (internal and/or external) may undergo changes which may lead to different vulnerabilities and threats. Hence, it is necessary that these programs are regularly reviewed, updated, and all the relevant stakeholders are trained on the changed scenarios and made aware of new risks.

All programs should take into account the risks the organization is currently undertaking and the controls they have painstakingly put in place for any security violation which defeats the very purpose of such controls. Involving each and every person is important for the success of any Security Program. Any person who is not aware of the security requirements, like a new security guard, employee, system administrator, or a new manager, can endanger the entire organization.

Moreover, in addition to the regular security programs as mentioned above, strong audits/assessments/compliance checks to ensure compliance to the policies, processes, and instructions of the company towards its security are to be adhered to without fail. A good execution is required to ensure the success of any well-intended program. However, execution is possibly the weakest link when it comes to most of the entities as well as most countries. Hence, regular checks carried out by competent and independent personnel of the organization or external agencies who do it not for the sake of just checking, but carry them out with the true intention and goal of bringing out any compliance weaknesses to the fore, is essential. Many times, reports of such compliance checks are beautifully made and wonderfully presented to the management but more often are totally forgotten, which could eventually lead to these documents creating liabilities when the suggested resolutions are not acted upon. Any compliance check with actions not being taken seriously on weaknesses found during the check is as good as a compliance check not being carried out in the first place! The better the compliance check carried out with extreme focus by the competent personnel and with extreme focus on the actions to be taken (and actually taken), the better the entity will be!

■ ■ ■

CHAPTER 2

History of Computer Security

Introduction

The first events in the history of exploiting security date back to the days of telephony. Telephone signals were sent via copper cables. Telephone lines could be tapped and conversations could be heard. In the early days of telephone systems, telephone operators intentionally misdirected calls and eavesdropped on conversations. In the 1970s, a set of people known as phreakers exploited the weakness of digital switching telephone systems for fun. Phreakers discovered the signal frequency at which the numbers are dialed and tried to match the frequency by blowing a whistle and fooling the electronic switching system to make calls for free. Among these phreakers, John Draper found that he could make long-distance calls for free by building an electronic box that could whistle different frequencies.

During the 1960s and 1970s, telephone networks became the dominant mode of communication, connecting millions of users. Given the increasing importance of computers and the advent of time shared systems, it was natural to consider linking the computers on the telephone networks so that information could be shared among geographically distributed networks. Since telephones were analog and computers were digital, modem (modulator and demodulator) devices were used to connect computers over the telephone network. Connecting computers and sharing information was of major interest during the early days of network computing and the security of the information became weak. Since people already knew how to break and tap into the phone systems, it became a game for them to break into the computer system, which was connected over the telephone networks.

With the creation of Advanced Research Projects Agency Network (ARPANET), a limited form of a system break-in to the network began. ARPANET was originally designed to allow scientists to share data and access remote systems. E-mail applications became the most popular application to allow scientists to collaborate on research projects and discuss various topics over the network. Soon, a bulletin message board was created where people could post a topic and discuss various research topics together. Bulletin boards became the venue of choice for discussing a wide range of topics, including passwords, credit card numbers, and trade tips, which encouraged the bad guys to hack into the system. Some famous bulletin boards include Sherwood Forest and Catch-22.

WHAT IS ARPANET?

The predecessor of the Internet, the Advanced Research Projects Agency Network (ARPANET) was a large wide-area network created by the United States Defense Advanced Research Project Agency (ARPA). Established in 1969, ARPANET served as a testing ground for new networking technologies, linking many universities and research centers. The first two nodes that formed the ARPANET were UCLA and the Stanford Research Institute, followed shortly thereafter by the University of Utah. Some of the reasons for creating ARPANET include making it easier for people to access computers, to improve computer equipment, and to have a more effective communication method for the military.

In the 1980s, the TCP/IP network protocol Transmission Control Protocol (TCP) and the Internet Protocol (IP), and Personal Computers (PC) brought computing to homes where more and more people connected to the Internet. The 1983 fictional movie, "War Games," was watched by millions of people and popularized hacking and made it glamorous. In 1981, Ian Murphy broke into AT&T's computers and changed billing rates of meters. He was later convicted.[1] Kevin Mitnick stole computer manuals of Pacific Bells' switching center in Los Angeles, California, and was prosecuted for this crime.[1] Bill Landreth was convicted for breaking into NASA's Department of Defense computers through GTE's e-mail network. In 1988, Kevin Mitnick was held for stealing software that was worth $1 million, and also caused damages of around $4 million.

With increasing threats to security, government agencies in charge of ARPANET came up with the Computer Emergency Response Team (CERT): the first network security organization in 1988.[2] The purpose of CERT is to spread security awareness among users and find ways to mitigate security breaches. As the Internet became popular, with more and more users becoming active, it became an appealing target for the "hackers" around the world. The 1990s saw more hacking activities such as the "Michelangelo" virus and the arrest of notorious hacker Kevin Mitnick for stealing credit card data, and the 1998 Solar Sunrise attack targeting Pentagon computers by Ehud Tenebaum.[3]

Today we are living in the Internet and World Wide Web (WWW) era, where everyone is connected. The Internet has changed the way we communicate with each other. The Web allowed information to be accessed instantly from anywhere in the world. First-generation web 1.0 was just a static web. Web 2.0, called interactive web, allowed the users to communicate by emphasizing online collaboration. Web 3.0 technology called 'the intelligent Web' emphasized machine-facilitated understanding of information to provide a more intuitive user experience. The Web has become a social medium where we can interact with one another, which has unfortunately resulted in many threats and vulnerabilities and an increasing number of security breaches. Some of the popular attacks include "Mellisa, the love bug," the "killer resume," and "The code red."

Communication

Communication is about conveying messages to the other party or to a group. These messages carry certain information. The medium through which information is communicated can be words or signs. The basic need to communicate has evolved languages, and language is used as a medium to share information, ideas, and feelings. There are three main types of communication: oral communication, written or verbal communication, and non-verbal communication.

During oral communication, parties communicate through voice as a medium. The parties involved in the oral communication are expected to be able to convey the message, which clearly expresses all their feelings, needs, wants, values, beliefs, and thoughts. Again, both the sender and the receiver use the same language so that both can understand. The sender can speak and the receiver can listen and vice versa, in order to exchange information. The tone of voice or the gap of silence makes a huge difference in oral communication.

During non-verbal communication, the communication is through the use of body language, gestures, facial expressions, and signs. These expressions may be well structured or unstructured. The semaphores that were used by military, sign language used by deaf persons, and gestures, postures, facial expression, and eye contact used by humans are a few of the examples. Semaphore Flags are the telegraphy system that conveys information at a distance by means of visual signals with handheld flags, rods, disks, paddles, or occasionally bare or gloved hands. Information is encoded by the position of the flags and is read when the flag is in a fixed position. Semaphores were adopted and widely used (with hand-held flags replacing the mechanical arms of shutter semaphores) in the maritime world in the nineteenth century. It is still used during underway replenishment at sea and is acceptable for emergency communication in the daylight or while using lighted wands instead of flags at night. Even verbal communication may have underlying non-verbal signals like stress, rhythm, and intonation, which may convey a different meaning to the person tuned to such signals or intended recipients of such signals. Non-verbal communications can be considered coded and may have different meanings to different recipients. Many times, non-verbal communication or gestures complement or negate the words spoken and may emphasize the words spoken or give them a different meaning than the meaning of the words spoken. Strong observation and hearing is required to understand the non-verbal communications, particularly if they are embedded with secret signals.

Sometimes, information needs to be communicated to only a few people and understood by only a few people, like the messages sent by kings, military commanders, diplomats, and other military people. Since the early days of writing, kings and commanders in India used secret codes to send messages to other kings and commanders outside the state. During war time, secret messages were sent by a network using simple alphabetic substitutions often based on phonetics. The ancient Chinese used the ideographic nature of their language to hide meanings of words. In the past, sensitive messages were transported through trusted persons, were guarded and were stored in a secure environment, thus ensuring the security of information. Julius Caesar (50 B.C.) is credited with the invention of cipher code to protect the confidentiality of information in order to prevent secret messages from being read by others. The Caesar cipher is named after Julius Caesar, who used simple coding techniques to protect messages of military significance. Caesar used a simple technique of replacing each letter in the plaintext by a letter shift of 3. He used this method for all his military communications.[4]

It is unknown how effective the Caesar cipher was at that time, but there are incidences in the nineteenth century where the personal advertisements section in newspapers would sometimes be used to exchange messages encrypted using simple cipher schemes. According to Kahn (1967), there were instances of lovers engaging in secret communications coded in Caesar cipher in *The Times* personal ads. More complicated Caesar cipher also in use by the Russian army during war times because it was difficult for their enemies to decipher.[5]

The need for communication not only helped in the development of many languages, but also the basic need to communicate with those at a distance resulted in the invention of telegraphs and telephones. The telegraph is a communication system invented by Samuel Morse (1791–1872), in which information is transmitted over a wire through a series of electrical pulses called Morse code. Morse code is a series of dots and dashes.[6] The pattern of dots and dashes were assigned to letters of the alphabet, numerals, and punctuation marks. Telegraph operators used Morse code to code the plain text messages before transmission over the electric cable and at the receiving end, where operators translated the Morse code back to plain English. The electric telegraphs transformed how wars were fought, and how military commanders sent their messages to distant soldiers and commanders. Rather than taking weeks to deliver messages by horse carriages and trusted messengers, information could be exchanged between two telegraph stations almost instantly. There are records of using telegraph systems during the Crimean war of 1853–1856. In the 1860s, the Russian army used telegraphs for communication between field officers and headquarters. After the telegraph, further inventions led to distance-based communication, such as radio and telephone.

During the early days of distance-based communications, messages were disguised to protect the confidentiality and to avoid them being revealed to others. It is natural that the messages sent through the telegraph, telephone, and eventually the radio, were also expected to be disguised in the form of codes. With the advent of distance communication methods using radio signals, the use of cryptography became very important, especially for coordinating military operations. Historically, we know that the French, American, and German armies were actively using various kinds of cipher methods during World War I.

World Wars and Their Influence on the Field of Security

There is no doubt that the world wars had significant influence on the field of security. As the adage goes, "Necessity is the mother of invention." In the interest that secrets are preserved and conveyed safely, new ways of securing the information were explored, invented, and practiced. These efforts have provided many solutions to today's problems and had set things in the right direction for further invention and innovation. Many of today's security practices originated somewhere during the world wars.

Cypher Machine: Enigma

Telegraphs, telephones, and radios have changed the meaning of communication. The demand for these services came from the railroads, the press, business and financial sectors, and private citizens. However, it became even more important for military communication. The telegraph led to considerable improvements in the commanding of troops, but it also required qualified specialists. The invention of the telephone by Alexander Graham Bell in 1876 opened a new sphere of communication. Telephone connections required a significant amount of cabling, power, and time for laying, and the same cable could not be used for both a telephone and telegraph. The invention of the radio became one of the greatest inventions in world history. Guglielmo Marconi was an Italian inventor who invented radio communication in 1895 which changed the world of communication, particularly in the military. However, messages sent through these devices were not protected and could be overheard by others. Messages sent over a telegraph line or radio link cannot be packed in an envelope and anyone who has access to the lines or a radio receiver could intercept messages and read everything without being identified. Thus emerged the need for secure communication for the military as well as civilians and has become essential that even when messages are heard, nobody other than the intended listeners should make out the contents.

Most pre-World War II military communication relied on the simple shuffling of words or a number representation for each word. Other methods were easily decipherable using frequency analysis. During this time, Enigma emerged as a means of communication due to its complex encryption methods.

In 1919, Dutchman Hugo Alexander Koch constructed one of the world's first electromechanical rotor machines for encrypting and decrypting messages called the Enigma. Initially, he thought he could sell these machines to banks to make secure transactions over regular telephone and telegraph channels. But neither banks nor the government showed any interest. After a few years, the patent went to Arthus Scheribus, who sold these machines to the German government.[7]

The strength of the Enigma, shown in Figure 2-1, gave Germans complete confidence in the security of their messages during military operations. In fact, Germans changed the coding keys every three months until 1935, and then monthly until 1936. During the war in 1943, keys were changed every eight hours. The "invincible" German secret machine was one of the most important milestones of World War II. Without breaking Enigma, World War II would have taken a different course and would have been extended for a few more years.[7,8]

Figure 2-1. *The German Wehrmacht Enigma (Copyright © 2014 Dirk Rijmenants)*[9]

During war time, Germans used Enigma to encode military commands over the radio. Enigma is an electromechanical device where you can set the rotor to a certain position and type the message just like a typewriter, for a mechanically encoded message. The intended receiver needed to know the exact position of the rotor in order to decode the message. The basic three-rotor Enigma with a 26 X 26 X 26 had 17,576 possible combinations of rotor states. The Enigma had three normal rotors and one reflector that could be set in one of 26 positions. For ten pairs of letters connected to each rotor and six wheels, there could be as many as 150,738,274,937,250 possible states. This gave the Germans a huge advantage in the war. Each time the messages were generated using a different set of combinations and with billions of combinations, the German military thought that the Enigma messages would remain unbreakable.[7]

Bletchley Park

After Hitler was appointed Chancellor of Germany on January 30, 1933, the Nazi Party began to consolidate their power by conquering neighboring countries. Hitler invaded Poland in September 1939 and thus launched World War II in Europe. Germany conquered most of Europe by 1940, and then threatened Britain next. Britain and her allies were unable to understand the military strategy of Hitler and worried about the use of Enigma and the problem posed by this machine. Breaking the Enigma continued to be a major challenge during World War II. Even the early mainframe computers were put to use to try and break the Enigma code.

The Germans thought that the Enigma code was impossible to break because of the many key combinations. However, Poland's Biuro Szyfrow, based on the Enigma codebook sold by the German spy Hans-Thilo Schmidt, attempted to break the Enigma messages. Three Polish mathematicians – Marian Rejewski, Henryk Zygalski, and Jerzy Rozicki – were convinced that they could break the Enigma. They also developed an electro-mechanical machine, called the Bomba, to break the Enigma code. During this process, they found two major flaws in the design. When Germans invaded Poland, the Polish Biuro Szyfrow passed on all the details and Bombe machines to the troubled French and British intelligence.

Alan Turing, widely known as the father of computer science and artificial intelligence, joined the British Government Code and Cypher School (GC &CS) and set up a secret code-breaking group called "Ultra" at Bletchley Park to break the Enigma code.[10]

Figure 2-2. *Alan Turing (photograph by Colin Smith)*[11]

Turing designed "Bombe" machines that were used to decipher Enigma. The Turing Bombe searched for the enigma settings for a given piece of plain and cipher text. Turing used his mathematical skills to decipher the Enigma codes. Initially, Turing and his colleagues relied on guessing the content based on external information. This helped them to reduce the strength of the key and finally they were able to break the Enigma codes. The Turing machine is one of the major inventions during the world war apart from atom bombs. It is estimated that this work by GC & CS shortened World War II by two years and Turing received the Appreciation Order of the British for the crucial role he played.

Code Breakers

The development of security has a military origin. Since the early days of World War II, breaking into any information is considered another technological challenge. As we described in earlier paragraphs, the German military relied on Enigma to encrypt all military communications in World War II, and to win the war, it became absolutely necessary for the allies to break the Enigma coded communication. The allies finally broke into it under the leadership of Alan M. Turing in Bletchley Park, who expanded further on the work done by the Polish mathematician and cracked the Enigma coded messages using a new machine designed by them known as "Bombe". After winning the war, Winston Churchill reportedly said to George VI: "Thanks to Ultra that we won the war".[12] It was also believed that the war was shortened by two years because they were able to break the Germans' military codes and spoil their strategies. The work done by Turing and his colleagues in Bletchley Park brought a new dimension to cryptography in the modern world. Cryptography required an understanding of logic, statistical theory, information theory, and advanced technology.

In the early days of computers, security was concerned only with the physical device and access to it. Early mainframe computers were used to store government records, personal information, and transactional processing. The security was to safeguard the data stored in the computers. Hence, physical access to the location was guarded and very few personnel had access to this location. Access was only achieved by authorized photo identification. The entry and exit to the computer rooms were monitored to ensure that the device, as well as the data stored in the device, was secured.

The security concerns increased as the technology advanced from single user mainframes to multiuser systems. The UNIX operating system evolved from MULTICS systems, which were originally designed for multi-user access.[13] UNIX is a multi-user, multi-tasking operating system, which allowed multiple users to access the system remotely (multi-user), and each user can run multiple applications simultaneously (multi-tasking). UNIX brought in the concept of authentication for secure access of files and data in a shared environment. The UNIX system was designed to provide the security for accessing files with user IDs and group IDs using sophisticated security programs. However, the system needed to be configured properly. Misconfiguration of the system could lead to the exposure of data and files to other unintended users, thus creating security holes. Much of the UNIX system was developed by students as a research project by including many of networking utilities and protocols. Since these programs were not written with proper design and are not formally tested, earlier versions of UNIX were buggy and could be exploited easily.

Mini computers, Personal Computers (PCs), Client Server architecture and Transmission Control (TCP), and Internet Protocol (IP) revolutionized computer communication. Mainframe computers were connected on the telephone network based on a "circuit switching" of protocols. In 1973, the U.S. Department of Defense, as a part of a research initiative, allowed universities and research organizations to connect to their network using the ARPANET protocol, a "packet switching" protocol. The objective of this project was to develop a communication protocol that would allow computers to communicate transparently across different geographies. This research initiative of ARPANET led to the development of a new protocol, based on packet switching, called TCP/IP (transmission Control protocol) and Internet Protocol. While the ARPANET protocol started as connecting just universities, the TCP/IP protocol opened to the public allowed the connection of millions of users and millions of computers resulting in the Internet – the Internetworking of computers. Today, billions of users are connected across the globe on the Internet which continues to grow exponentially.

The basic need of a computer network is to share information on the network. The TCP/IP protocol suite connects the computers; however, many utilities such as file transfer, remote login, remote shell, telnet, and send mail developed on top of the TCP/IP protocol support information sharing on the Internet. A File Transfer Protocol (FTP) allows files to be transferred from one remote computer to another. A Sendmail protocol allows for the sending and receiving of e-mails from one system to another. With the World Wide Web (WWW) and HTTP protocols, the Internet exploded beyond the sharing of information to doing business on the Internet. Today, the WWW has changed the way we live, how we interact with others, share information, how we buy and sell goods and do business. On the WWW, you can share texts, pictures, images, video, and audio files. To support different applications on the web, multiple utilities and protocols have been developed. With the rise in e-commerce, not only the good guys transact on the web, but we also find many bad guys out there attempting to steal information and make a profit. In response, expectations of information security have changed. Security is no longer just about protecting a physical device, it has now expanded to ensure confidentiality, integrity, authenticity, and availability.

Some Historical Figures of Importance: Hackers and Phreakers

While a set of scientists work toward securing the network and the information that flows on the network, there is another set of phreaks who challenge the scientists by breaking into the network and the information by cracking the security codes. Hackers are intruders who are as capable and knowledgeable as the scientists, but instead of securing the system, they break into the system, thus undoing all the hard work that the scientists have put in. However, there is a new category of security professionals known as ethical hackers, who try to help the industry and governments to unearth the security risks. These are the good guys and are known as the "white hats," whereas the bad guys are typically known as the "black hats."

The early days of telephone networking witnessed hackers making long-distance calls without actually paying. Hackers used electronic devices to crack into the telephone network to make long-distance calls (Figure 2-3). The telephone network hackers became popularly known as phreakers. During the same time, the term "cracker" originated as a name for people who crack the system's security, often by cracking the system's password.

Figure 2-3. *Hackers cracked into telephone networks*

Among the Phreakers, John Draper became famous because of a simple discovery. Earlier telephone systems used in-band signaling for sending control information such as dial tone, busy tone, receiver off-hook, and routing address to the switch in the same channel where the user's voice was being transmitted. Table 2-1 shows the frequency of different control signals. These signals are generated by the Central Office (CO) switch. Subscribers are connected to the CO, and when the phone is off the hook, the CO transmits a 350 and 440 Hertz signal to the subscriber which is the dial tone. A 2600 Hertz frequency tone generates a call over signal and provides control over other signals to make another call again. Similarly, the CO transmits other control signals to the subscriber, which was made public in the Bell Systems Technical Journal.[14,15]

Table 2-1. *Network Call Progress Tone Frequencies*

Tone	Frequency (hz)	On Time	Off Time
Dial	350 + 440	Continuous	
Busy	480 + 620	0.5	0.5
Ringback, Normal	440 + 480	2	4
Ringback, PBX	440 + 480	1	3
Congestion(Toll)	480 + 620	0.2	0.3
Recorder (local)	480 + 620	0.3	0.2
Receiver Off-hook	1400+2060+2450+2600	0.1	0.1

John Draper, shown in Figure 2-4, was discharged from the military because he had knowledge about the telephone systems. After the telephone companies made the control signals public, Draper was anxious to break into the telephone systems. One day, he found out that packaged boxes of Cap'n Crunch cereal could emit a tone precisely at 2600 Hertz. Using Cap'n Crunch boxes, John would blow the whistle to make long-distance calls. This whistle experiment led him to come up with an electronic device called the Blue Box, which would generate different control tones used by the phone company. He succeeded in making long-distance calls from a public telephone without actually ever paying for the calls.[15]

Figure 2-4. *John Draper (Copyright © 2014 The Porticus Centre, Beatrice Technologies)*[16]

Draper popularized this device and became infamous for hacking into telephone systems. He was arrested in May of 1972 for toll fraud charges and was sentenced to a five-year probation. In 1976, he was arrested again for wired fraud charges and spent four months in prison.

Kevin Mitnick

By the 1980s, technology advancement in computers shifted the attention of hackers from phones to computers. With mini-computers, PCs gained popularity and the Internet became a key invention for sharing information. Bulletin Board Systems (BBS) made its appearance where people could post messages on any topic. The BBS became a platform for hackers for their hacking activity. Hackers got into the BBS as normal users and collected users' discussion information, such as credit card numbers, telephone numbers, and e-mail IDs, and pass it on to the hacking community. The BBS was also used by hackers to discuss how to use stolen credit cards, guess computer passwords, and share other users' passwords. In 1986, the government realized the threats to information security and passed the Computer Fraud and Abuse Act, making computer-related abuse a crime across the United States of America.

During the days of ARPANET (before the Internet), users shared jokes and annoying messages with each other, which was not considered a major security issue. Also, the network was small and users knew and trusted each other. Even connecting to the remote system was not considered a major security risk until 1986 when Cliff Stoll published his experience in a book, called *The Cuckoo's Egg*, which described how he connected to a remote computer and copied data from the remote machine without having authorized access. This was the first ever security incident that was formally reported upon. In 1988, Robert T. Morris wrote a computer program that could connect to a remote machine and copy data to another computer and repeat this action over the network. This self-replicating tool, now popularly known as the Morris Worm, exploded on the ARPANET. The worm used up the CPU and system resources of the victim's computer, which after the hack, could not function properly. As a result of this widespread worm, nearly 10% of the computers on the network stopped functioning at the same time. The damage of this worm initiated the Defense Advanced Research Project Agency (DARPA) to form a team to handle computer emergencies called CERT (Computer Emergency Response Team) in 1988. Morris was reprimanded by the U.S. government, was fined $10,000 for damages, put on probation, and was sentenced to community services.

In the 1990s, the Internet gained momentum. The Department of Defense and DARPA made the ARPANET public. A version of the ARPANET protocol, called the TCP/IP, has evolved and the ARPANET became the Internet, connecting thousands of users. After the Internet became public, millions of users and many organizations, universities, and commercial entities became connected to the Internet as well. As the number of Internet users grew, it became difficult for users to trust the network. Resources shared data on the network with other users, thus causing the Internet to become vulnerable to attacks.

Kevin Mitnick, wrote his first hacking program when he was in high school. When a teacher asked the class to write a program to print the Fibonacci number, Kevin wrote a program that could get the passwords of students. His teacher gave him an A for writing this program. His passion for writing programs to crack computers continued. He cracked the computer systems of many companies, such as Digital Equipment Corporation, Motorola, and SUN; all mostly for fun. However, when companies found out that he hacked into their computer systems without authorization, he became a wanted man by the U.S. government. In 1988, he was convicted of copying software from a Digital Equipment Corporation (DEC) and was sentenced with twelve months imprisonment and three years of supervised parole. While he was on parole, he hacked into several computer systems, including Pacific Bell system's voicemail server - the largest telephone network - and stole computer passwords and broke into e-mail servers. After a warrant was issued to arrest him, he fled and became a fugitive for 2 ½ years. Finally, he was arrested in 1995. In 1999, Mitnick confessed to computer fraud and illegally intercepting the communication network and was sentenced to almost four years in prison.[17]

Though Mitnick claimed he did not hack the computer systems for monetary gain, it was still considered illegal according to the U.S. government. Despite his run-ins with the law, Mitnick has influenced modern-day hackers, including WikiLeaks. Today, he spends his time advising companies about the security vulnerabilities in their networks.

Today, the Internet and World Wide Web (WWW) has changed the way we live. According to the latest statistics, more than 3 billion users are on the Internet. Web technologies (Web 2.0) provide many applications and tools that have enabled how we interact on the Internet. Originally just a means of e-mail communication, the Internet is now used for buying, selling, marketing, advertising, channel for B2B, B2C, and many more. This also means the Internet now has different kinds of users connected: trusted or untrusted, good intentioned or bad intentioned. That means the Internet has become more vulnerable to attacks. More and more security incidences are reported at CERT every day. Thousands of intruders are on the Internet and they can:

- Probe: Monitor the network and its users by using tools and tapping the wires.

- Scan: Scan the network and its devices for vulnerabilities, using probing and similar tools.

- Write malicious code: A program or an application that contains harmful code. By installing such an application, your system can be compromised and without your knowledge, it can send your personal data to the remote user. Programs like viruses, worms, and Trojan horses, are a few examples of malicious code.

- Denial of Service: All your system resources could be exhausted or stopped temporarily.

- Gain Access: Gaining unauthorized access to a network, system, and their resources.

In the early days of the Internet, the user groups were relatively small. Intruders exploited relatively simple weaknesses, such as passwords or default configurations of the system. The technique was relatively simple and it worked. During those times, organizations did not have the expertise in configuring systems or tools to monitor the security of the network. Awareness of the scope of the problem was also limited. Today, the importance of security and its awareness has increased among people and networks have become more secure. Consequently, the intruders also have become smarter. Many sophisticated tools have been developed by them and made available to the public. This has become a day-to-day challenge between the good guys and the bad guys.

Today, the most controversial topic related to security is WikiLeaks. WikiLeaks, founded by Julian Assange, is a non-profit organization that is reporting important and confidential news and information to the public on digital media. WikiLeaks provides the evidence, along with the news. The news piece is generally political and is of significant value to society. WikiLeaks has published a number of confidential and classified information. Some of the famous WikiLeaks stories are listed below:

- E-mail contents of Sarah Palin's account (U.S Republican Vice Presidential candidate) in 2008

- Contributors to the Norm Coleman Senatorial campaign (March 2009)

- Communications related to the tax avoidance by Barclays Bank (March 2009)

- Nuclear accident in Iran (2009)

- U.S. Department of Defense Counter-intelligence Report (March 15, 2010)

- "The Global Intelligence Files", containing more than 5 million e-mails from Stratfor, dating from July 2004 to December 2011

- Bradley Manning exposed the truth about America's wars in the Middle East and how the United States conducts foreign policy

WikiLeaks allows any user to upload information anonymously. Users can electronically submit the information without revealing their identity. WikiLeaks uses highly sophisticated technology by providing electronic drop boxes fortified by cutting-edge cryptographic information technology. The site also provides maximum security to the information and their sources.

Bradley Manning, a military personnel, leaked documents to WikiLeaks related to America's wars in the Middle East in 2010 which sparked a global debate about U.S. foreign policy. While Manning was deployed in Iraq, he accessed secure intelligence networks to gather secret military and diplomatic files which he downloaded and passed on to WikiLeaks. This information was published by WikiLeaks and read by millions of people across the world. Manning was caught when he openly admitted the leaks. According to the U.S. government, he is a traitor who revealed military secrets and put the lives of his comrades-in-arms in danger. Prosecutors argued throughout the trial that the published secret information had directly benefited Al-Qaeda. Manning is facing a 35-year jail term for leaking over 750,000 military and security documents to WikiLeaks.[18]

In June 2013, Edward Snowden a former member of the U.S. National Security Agency, exposed documents and information about both the Internet and phone surveillance by U.S. intelligence on WikiLeaks.[19,20] The documents contained vast information about the domestic surveillance of millions of American citizens under the U.S. government program called PRISM. Though his argument is that the "U.S. government destroys privacy, Internet freedom, and basic liberties for people around the world with this massive surveillance machine they're secretly building," the U.S. government has charged Mr. Snowden with theft of government property, unauthorized communication of national defense information, and willful communication of classified intelligence. Each of the charges carries a maximum of 10 years in prison. Snowden is currently in Russia on temporary asylum.

According to the WikiLeaks web site, WikiLeaks claims that it is working for transparency based on Article 19 of the Universal Declaration of Human Rights. The WikiLeaks web site further defines "principle leaking" as necessary to fight corruption, to uphold individual rights and good governance. In recent days, WikiLeaks has come under severe attack by many governments, particularly the United States, for publishing confidential information on its web site. WikiLeaks has been questioned on the impact of such leaks.

The most high-profile documents published by WikiLeaks are either U.S. government related documents or U.S. government actions against other countries, such as hidden war crimes, prisoner abuse, or individual privacy. After the leak of the content of U.S diplomatic cables and PRISM, the U.S. reaction has been more harsh and the White House Attorney General Eric Holder asserts that WikiLeaks is an increasing threat to national security, America's economy, and is undermining U.S. national security and needs to be stopped. Stephen Aftergood, the director of the Federation of American Scientists Project on Government Secrecy explains that, "It has invaded personal privacy. It has published libelous material. It has violated intellectual property rights. And above all, it has launched a sweeping attack not simply on corruption, but on secrecy itself. And I think that's both a strategic and a tactical error. It's a strategic error because some secrecy is perfectly legitimate and desirable. It's a tactical error because it has unleashed a furious response from the U.S. government and other governments that I fear is likely to harm the interests of a lot of other people besides WikiLeaks who are concerned with open government. It may become harder to support protection for people who disclose and publish classified information after WikiLeaks."

Chapter Summary

- We explored security issues from the days of telephony and discussed how a class of people known as the "phreakers" tried to exploit the weaknesses in telephone systems. We also discussed how the telephonic lines allowed the computers to be connected with each other and how those who could exploit the telephone lines continued to hack into computers with this knowledge. We also looked at how bulletin boards and the information on these bulletin boards were misused. We made a passing reference to some of the legendary hackers and how the increasing threats to computer security led to the CERT initiative.

- We also explored both verbal communication and non-verbal communication. We looked at how secret communications were being conveyed through a coded language using Caesar cipher from the days of Julius Caesar. We also discussed how, with the advent of telegraphs and radio, the need for coding these messages was necessary to protect the confidentiality of these messages.

- We briefly touched upon how the world wars necessitated the securing of messages being relayed and mentioned that most of the current security practices have had their base on the security practices commenced during the world wars. We further explored how the Enigma cipher machine helped Germans in World War II to encode their military messages securely and how the breaking of the Enigma code led to the shortening of World War II.

- We introduced the code breakers and discussed how a great Polish mathematician by the name of Alan M. Turing broke the Enigma code, thus shortening World War II.

- We discussed two famous categories of computer hackers: the "phreakers" and the "hackers". We introduced one of history's famous phreakers, John Draper, who was an expert at hacking and misusing telephone lines. We also discussed one of the most famous hackers, Kevin Mitnick, who could break into almost any computer, including those of big names like DEC, Motorola, and SUN. Additionally, we discussed WikiLeaks, which is a recent phenomenon in the field of computer security and we explained how WikiLeaks brought to the forefront many political secrets.

PART II

■ ■ ■

Key Principles and Practices

This section discusses the key principles and practices related to information security.

Chapter 3 "Key Concepts and Principles," starts by explaining that every organization exists for achievement of its objectives. In this regard, we mention that information security has to be implemented keeping in mind an organization's business objectives and business requirements, such as how the information technology has to enable information security which, in turn, will protect its business, its customers, its partners, its systems including its people, infrastructure (including its networks), and applications. We then highlight that information security refers to the processes and methodologies that are designed to protect sensitive information or data from unauthorized access, use and misuse, disclosure, modification, destruction, or disruption. We also mention that it has to ensure the validity of the genuineness of the information and rejection of false information. We then highlight that over the years information security has moved further from primarily physical security to network, software security, and human/personnel security.

We then elaborate upon various threats with examples and differentiate between internal and external threats. We also categorize various threats under each of the layers of security. We then explain various layers of security in the layered approach to information security, including host/platform security layer, network security layer, application security layer, access control layer, and physical security layer. We also discuss how each layer complements the other layers and also highlight some of the significant issues pertaining to each layer. We then look into various security frameworks provided by various standards or models or methodologies like ISO 27001:2013 (i.e., Information Security Management Systems - Requirements); NIST's special publication 800-39 (i.e., Managing Information Security Risk: Organization, Mission, and Information System View complemented by 800-53 Revision 4 (i.e., Security and Privacy Controls for Federal Information Systems and Organizations)and SABSA©. We explore each of these in detail. We then look into various Pillars of Information Security (i.e., policies and processes, people, and technology). We then highlight under the pillar "People" how organization of information security has to be carried out, the need for independence among various roles, the clear definition of specific roles and responsibilities related to information security, and authority for information security enforcement. We similarly highlight under the pillar "Policies & Processes" and "Technology" some of the important aspects to be borne in mind. We then discuss in detail the confidentiality, integrity, and availability aspects of information security as per the traditional CIA triad. Further, we explore some of the complementary aspects like possession or control, authenticity and utility and also highlight some of the subtle variations with respect to integrity and availability as professed by Parkerian Hexad. Finally, we elaborate upon the typical implementation cycle of information security. Then we explain some of the key principles of information security as specified by NIST.

In Chapter 4, "Access Control," we mention at the outset that any type of access to information needs to be protected, whether the access is physical, meaning accessing CPUs and hard disks, or logical, meaning accessing the system directly or remotely. We then mention that access control has two components: Authentication and Authorization. Authentication is verifying the identity of a user or a host that is accessing the system or network resource. Authorization is permitting or restricting access to the information based on the type of users and their roles: employee, contractor, administrator, or manager. We then highlight how access control provides for confidentiality and integrity of data.

We then mention that Access controls are security features that control access to systems and resources in the network. The goal of access control is to protect information from being lost, stolen, deleted, or modified either intentionally or accidently by those who are not authorized to access it. Next, we discuss three types of access controls, that is, network access, system access, and data access. Three layers of access control: administrative controls, technical controls, and physical controls are discussed in detail. Under administrative controls we discuss access control policies; personnel-related jobs, responsibilities and authorities; segregation of duties; supporting policies and procedures; and control over information access to trade restricted persons. Technical (Logical) controls include passwords, smartcards, encryption, network access, and system access. Physical controls include network segregation, perimeter security, security guards, badge systems and biometric access controls. Then we explore various access control strategies, including discretionary access control, mandatory access control, role-based access control, and attribute-based access control. Then we discuss how effective implementation of access controls is ensured through access control lists; AAA Framework including RADIUS and TACAS+; LDAP and Active Directory; and IDAM.

In Chapter 5, "Information Systems Management," we discuss that in order to ensure information security, we need to act proactively. When proactiveness does not stop the breaches we need to react effectively and efficiently to them and when breaches cannot be avoided we need to recover the businesses as fast as possible to provide continued services to the customers or even to offer continued services during the breaches even if at a reduced level.

Risk Management when applied with the right intention, with the deployment of the right methodology, with the involvement of the right people, with the application of right thinking, and with the execution of the actions effectively, can provide a reasonably good proactive approach to ensure that there is a high chance of avoiding information security breaches or incidents. In spite of being proactive we cannot be assured that security breaches cannot happen as this evolving world provides many opportunities and ways to breach the system. Incident response provides such a reactive response to ensure that the breaches are handled, contained, and recovered from effectively. In spite of effective risk management and incident response systems in place you cannot rest assured of continuity of business or speedy recovery when the organization is affected by severe security breaches or disasters. Hence, there is a great need for an effective disaster recovery and business continuity system to be put in place which is again a proactive as well as reactive system to ensure that the business can still continue in spite of disasters or severe security incidents and that there is a high probability of a speedy recovery. We define in lay terms the important terminologies like risk, incident, disaster, disaster recovery, and business continuity.

We then explain how to carry out effective risk management. We then describe how incident response mechanisms are effectively implemented by the organization. We further explore the disaster recovery and business continuity plans, their essential contents, and how they need to be validated, tested, and maintained.

CHAPTER 3

■ ■ ■

Key Concepts and Principles

Introduction

Every organization or enterprise exists to achieve its objectives, both business objectives and social objectives. Its existence or continued existence is of no use unless it is able to achieve its objectives. For the continued existence of any organization, information security has become a non-negotiable necessity. However, the acceptability for information security is very low in an organization because of its arbitrary implementation. Information security will be appreciated by everybody if it is implemented, keeping in mind an organization's business objectives and business requirements. Furthermore, information technology has to enable information security which, in turn, will protect its business, customers, partners, and systems, such as its people, infrastructure (including its networks), and applications. This in turn means that all the strategies of the organization – business strategies, IT strategies, and information security strategies – have to complement each other and are to be balanced.

Information security refers to the processes and methodologies that are designed to protect sensitive information or data from unauthorized access, use and misuse, disclosure, modification, destruction, or disruption. In addition, it also covers the validity or genuineness of the information and rejection of false information received from others. The terms "information security," "computer security," "data security," and "information assurance" are frequently used interchangeably. Though there are subtle differences between these different terms, their common goal is to protect the Confidentiality, Integrity, and Availability (CIA) of data.

The objective of information security is to protect information and its critical assets including people, systems, and hardware that use or process, store, and transmit the data. To protect the information and its related systems, organizations have technology and tools, policies and processes, and also the necessary training and awareness programs, and also rewards for abiding by the security policies and processes and penalties for any security breaches. Many organizations have disciplinary processes instituted that consider and investigate the security breaches. Intentional security breaches normally lead to the termination of the employee / contractor or disengagement of the supplier. Unintentional or accidental security breaches may be considered leniently but organizations should still warn the employees in such cases. Reporting of the security breaches or incidents is appreciated by many organizations and is rewarded in kind or cash.

The requirements of information security have undergone major changes in the last few decades. Before the widespread use of computers and the Internet, information security was primarily restricted to physical access, such as a guarded room and locked security cabinets to store sensitive confidential information. With technological innovations and the introduction of computers and TCP/IP communication, automated tools became a necessity for protecting data stored on a computer system. The need for computer security became even more evident with the advent of the Internet where the systems and data are accessed and transmitted over the public telephone and data network. **Physical Security** is still a significant part of any security system and cannot be ignored as it is an important line of defense for most organizations. **Hardware Security** can be primarily considered under Physical Security, even though some of the components of the hardware can be considered under other securities such as Network Security.

TCP/IP is the underlying protocol for computer communication that facilitates distributed connectivity and communication facilities for sharing data between two computers present at different locations. TCP/IP is the underlying protocol that resulted in the invention of the Internet and the World Wide Web (WWW). As information is now being shared by millions of users on the Internet, **Network Security** became extremely essential to protect the data that is being transmitted and guarantee that the data is not tampered with during the transmission. **Communications Security,** that is, securing communications through the use of various mechanisms, can be considered broadly as a part of Network Security. Secure routing mechanisms, secure session mechanisms, and secure encryption mechanisms may be considered as part of Communications Security.

Another important layer of security is **Software Security**, which broadly deals with the Operating System Security, the Application Security, and the security of software utilities/tools, including the security of tools used to provide information security. Operating systems provide many of the functionalities required for the servers and computers to work effectively, including communication capabilities with other systems, processing of information, and effective functioning of applications. Recently, with the increased use of mobile phones and tablets (which are also used for significant official work) and with such diverse operating systems like Android, iOS, Symbian, and BlackBerry, many more possible security issues have opened up. Recent years have also seen a huge growth in the number of applications developed and deployed on these products. It is not yet clear to what extent secure practices are being used during their design, development, and deployment. As seen in practice, secure design, development, and deployment is lagging behind significantly, even on stable and best in class operating systems, thus opening up several avenues for security flaws and providing entry points for malicious attackers. This may also provide unintended entry points for the insiders with malicious intent.

Human or personnel security is another important layer. Keeping personnel motivated, making them aware of the information security risks, and involving them in the implementation of the same is an important aspect of information security which cannot be forgotten at any cost. Employees (permanent or temporary), contractors, and suppliers are all significant in this regard.

All of the important layers that have been discussed (supported by policies, procedures, and processes to plan, implement, monitor, audit, detect, correct, and change of any of the components of all the above layers) constitute a layered approach to information security. Appropriate coordination between the various layers, and the distribution of risks and opportunities to different layers, will vary, depending on the cost effectiveness and ease of use, and the impact on the efficiency and effectiveness of information security.

Figure 3-1 illustrates the context diagram of various layers of information security interacting with each other and providing a robust security architecture.

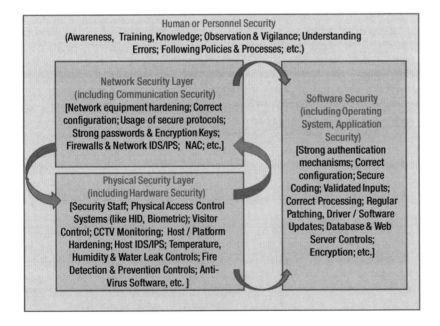

Figure 3-1. Primary layers of information security

An effective Information Security Architecture should consider all the layers without omitting any of them. It should also consider the effectiveness and have an integrated view of all of them, rather than a secluded and narrow view of any one business, unit, equipment, component, tool, or utility. Before beginning the discussion of an effective Information Security Architecture, we will look into various threats that are normally considered under these layers.

Security Threats

The word 'threat' in information security means anyone or anything that poses danger to the information, the computing resources, users, or data. The threat can be from 'insiders' who are within the organization, or from outsiders who are outside the organization. Studies show that 80% of security incidents are coming from insiders.

Security threats can be categorized in many ways. One of the important ways they are categorized is on the basis of the "origin of threat," namely external threats and internal threats. The same threats can be categorized based on the layers described above.

External and Internal Threats

External threats originate from outside the organization, primarily from the environment in which the organization operates. These threats may be primarily physical threats, socio-economic threats specific to the country like a country's current social and economic situation, network security threats, communication threats, human threats like threats from hackers, software threats, and legal threats. Social engineering threats like using social engineering sites to gather data and impersonate people for the purpose of defrauding them and obtaining their credentials for unauthorized access is increasing. Theft of personal identifiable information, confidential strategies, and intellectual properties of the organization are other important threats. Some of these physical threats or legal threats may endanger an entire organization completely. Comparatively, other threats may affect an organization partially or for a limited period of time and may be overcome relatively easily. Cybercrimes are exposing the organizations to legal risks too.

Some of the important external threats are illustrated below in Figure 3-2.

Figure 3-2. *External threats*

Internal threats originate from within the organization. The primary contributors to internal threats are employees, contractors, or suppliers to whom work is outsourced. The major threats are frauds, misuse of information, and/or destruction of information. Many internal threats primarily originate for the following reasons:

- Weak Security Policies, including:

    - Unclassified or improperly classified information, leading to the divulgence or unintended sharing of confidential information with others, particularly outsiders.

    - Inappropriately defined or implemented authentication or authorization, leading to unauthorized or inappropriate access.

    - Undefined or inappropriate access to customer resources or contractors/suppliers, leading to fraud, misuse of information, or theft.

    - Unclearly defined roles and responsibilities, leading to no lack of ownership and misuse of such situations.

    - Inadequate segregation of duties, leading to fraud or misuse.

    - Unclearly delineated hierarchy of "gatekeepers" who are related to information security, leading to assumed identities.

- Weak Security Administration, including:

    - Weak administrative passwords being misused to steal data or compromise the systems.

    - Weak user passwords allowed in the system and applications, leading to unauthorized access and information misuse.

    - Inappropriately configured systems and applications, leading to errors, wrong processing, or corruption of data.

    - Non-restricted administrative access on the local machines and/or network, leading to misuse of the system or infection of the systems.

    - Non-restricted access to external media such as USB or personal devices, leading to theft of data or infection of the systems.

    - Non-restricted access to employees through personal devices or from unauthenticated networks and the like, leading to data theft.

    - Unrestricted access to contractors and suppliers leading to theft or misuse of information including through dumpster diving or shoulder surfing.

    - Unrestricted website surfing, leading to infections of viruses, phishing, or other malware.

    - Unrestricted software downloads leading to infection, copyright violations, or software piracy.

    - Unrestricted remote access leading to unauthorized access or information theft.

    - Accidentally deleting data permanently.

- Lack of user security awareness, including:

    - Identity theft and unauthorized access due to weak password complexity.

    - Not following company policies, such as appropriate use of assets, clean desk policy, or clear screen policy, leading to virus attacks or confidential information leakage.

    - Divulging user IDs and/or passwords to others, leading to confidential information leakage.

    - Falling prey to social engineering attacks.

    - Falling prey to phishing and similar attacks.

    - Downloading unwanted software, applications, or images or utilities/tools leading to malware, viruses, worms, or Trojan attacks.

    - Improper e-mail handling/forwarding leading to the loss of reputation or legal violations.

    - Improper use of utilities like messengers or Skype and unauthorized divulgence of information to others.

    - Inappropriate configuration or relaxation of security configurations, leading to exploitation of the systems.

    - Entering incorrect information by oversight and not checking it again or processing the wrong information.

    - Ignoring security errors and still continuing with transactions, leading to the organization being defrauded.

Some of the important external and internal threats are collated in Table 3-1 for easy reference.

Table 3-1. *External and internal threats*

External Threats	Internal Threats
Physical Threats	**Human Threats**
Natural disasters like cyclones, hurricanes, floods, earthquakes, etc.	Frauds, misuse of assets or information
Fire	Errors or mistakes by the employees
Terrorist threats like bombs, hostage situation	Espionage, Shoulder surfing
Hardware destruction	Social Engineering by the employees
Physical intrusion	Exploitation of lack of knowledge or ignorance of fellow employees
Sabotage	Use of weak administrator passwords or passwords of others and gaining unauthorized access
Theft of the assets and Intellectual Property sensitive assets/information	Theft
Network Threats	Policies not executed or followed
Sniffing or Eavesdropping	Improper segregation of duties leading to fraud or misuse
TCP/IP issues like snooping, authentication attacks, connection hijacking	Malware infection threats due to infected media usage or unauthorized software downloads
Spoofing	**Internal Application Issues**
Man in the middle attack	Invalidated inputs
Denial of service attacks	Misconfigured application leading to errors or wrong processing
SQL injection	Inappropriate error or exception handling leading to issues
Exploitation of default passwords on network equipment being unchanged	Parameter manipulations; Manipulation of Buffer Overflows
Exploitation of weak encryption	Unauthorized access
Software Issues	**Other Issues**
Defects leading to errors	Unrestricted access to USB leading to pilferage of information
Defects being exploited	System or data corruption may be due to power surges, temperature control failure or for other reasons
Malware like Viruses, Worms, Trojans, Back doors	Hardware failure due to malfunctioning
Bots or Botnets	Infrastructure like UPS failure due to improper maintenance
Invalidated inputs	
Authentication attacks	
Exploitation of misconfigurations	

(*continued*)

Table 3-1. (*continued*)

External Threats	Internal Threats
Session Management related issues	
Inappropriate error handling or exception handling by the applications	
Buffer overflow issues	
Cryptography wrongly handled by applications	
Parameter manipulations	
Operating system related issues – security flaws in the operating system	
Human Threats	
Social engineering	
Attack by hackers/man in the middle	
Blackmail, extortion	
Espionage	
Compliance Threats	

Note: The legal requirements pertaining to information and communication can lead to closure of the organization or huge penalties

Information Security Frameworks and Information Security Architecture

Information security framework provides guidance for the effective implementation of information security in the organization and development of an effective information security architecture, which in turn, provides assurance that information security has been effectively employed in the organization. One word of caution here: "Whatever the level of implementation, you cannot be 100% assured of information security". However, if you have implemented security measures effectively, this will enable you to control many of the security threats and prepare you to be quick in providing reactive responses to the threats. Organizations can only be defensive in their approach as an offensive strategy is illegal. Such framework or architecture enables you to either prevent or detect and react to attacks or to recover from attacks.

In order to protect information and data from the above threats, organizations typically have "layers of protection." This practice of layering defenses improves an organization's overall security posture. Successful organizations have layers of security, as shown in the Figure 3-3.

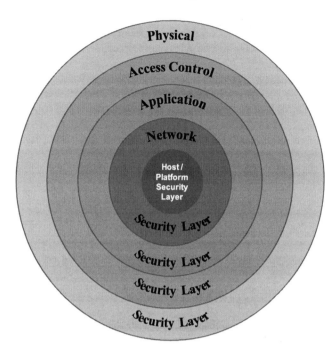

Figure 3-3. *A layered approach to security*

As you can see in Figure 3-3, these five layers of security support and complement each other. While the Access or User Layer ensures clear authentication and authorization, the security clearance through appropriate controls, the Application security layer ensures effective controls over web servers, databases, and applications through various controls like encryption and identity management. The Network security layer provides protection through controls like the firewall, IDS/IPS while the Platform/Host security layer ensures controls like Host IDS/IPS, and anti-virus software, whereas the Physical security layer ensures controls like secured access, asset control, and fire protection.

The Platform/Host Security is ensured primarily through the hardening of the servers. Root / administrator passwords are changed from the default passwords to strong passwords and are tightly controlled. Furthermore, the anti-virus solutions of repute when installed on the servers provide significant protection for them from malware or spyware infections. Security patches are released by most of the operating system vendors periodically. The timely application of these to the concerned server after testing the impact of them on the applications working on such platforms/hosts ensures that these servers are well protected. Similarly, drivers need to be maintained and updated as needed. Periodic preventive maintenance of these hosts to clean up space, remove unwanted files, archive unwanted data, defragment disks, ensure up-to-date and relevant patch updates, and software or driver upgrades, will ensure continued performance. Otherwise, there may be a performance degrade which impacts availability and increases security threats. Similarly, the maintenance of facilities and utilities, such as temperature controls in the server room/data center, humidity controls in the server room/data center, and preventive maintenance of UPS, help ensure secure systems. Weak administrator passwords can also put the servers at risk.

As we saw earlier in this chapter, network security is the next protective layer that connects the hosts/platforms to others. Some aspects that need to be ensured here are that the network equipment is hardened, default passwords are invariably replaced with stronger passwords, all the network equipment such as routers are configured correctly, and protocols are used appropriately depending upon the infrastructure and organizational needs. Firewalls and IDS/IPS need to be set up appropriately with relevant configurations and policies so that they are able to detect, alert, or prevent some of the attacks. Weak administrator passwords, weak or unprotected encryption keys, or misconfigurations can be exploited and can place the organizations and its business at risk. Networks are prone to other types of attacks such as spoofing, man in the middle attacks, sniffing, or eavesdropping, leading to impersonation or loss or misuse of data. Networks are also prone to such vulnerabilities like session hijacking and denial of service attacks.

Application security is a major issue worldwide. Web servers and databases need to be secured by appropriate installations and configurations. In this fast-paced world, the focus on completion of software development and its delivery has become more important than its security. Surprisingly, most of these applications are not tested for security. These applications can be prone to attacks like SQL injection, buffer overflows, and invalidated data inputs which can eventually lead to the compromise of the host systems on which they are running. Similarly, ineffectively tested or misconfigured applications may lead to processing errors or not validating the errors, leading to the loss of integrity of the data. Weak authentication and authorization mechanisms built into these applications or misconfiguration of these applications may lead to unauthorized access or other issues like corruption of data and the like. Defects in applications can not only lead to errors in data but such defects related to security can lead to security breaches. Applications not patched on a timely basis may be prone to viruses or the exploitation of such security flaws or errors. It is also possible that the interface between two applications is weak, which leads to an insecure transfer of data between these applications, and subsequent exposure of this data to others.

Access to systems is regulated by the access control layer. Access control layers have to be set up as per the organization's access control policy. Some of the access control models of interest are mandatory access control, discretionary access control, and non-discretionary access control models. Some of the access control administration models are the centralized administration model, decentralized administration model, and the hybrid administration model. Both the internal and external access controls and external need to be appropriately handled. Authentications and authorizations have to be set up appropriately. Primary threats due to an improperly configured access layer are unauthorized or have incorrect access or denial of appropriate access. Over time, it has been observed that single authentication mechanisms are broken relatively easily, making multiple authentications preferable for maximum security.

The other important layer is the physical security layer. Traditionally, security guards and locks were the primary means of physical security. Because of the human element involved where negligence or ignorance lead to security threats, complementary security controls like biometric access (finger prints, iris scan, etc.), access through smart cards coupled with passcodes, and the like, are implemented. Selection of an appropriate location for the organization protects it from potential natural hazards like floods. Having secured electrical wiring with the appropriate safety mechanisms like well-maintained earth pits, UPS for regulated power, trippers, and fuses provides substantial security from electrical fires. Good practices like not storing flammables like diesel, petrol, other chemicals in the premises, and not storing easily flammable materials like empty cartons or huge quantities of old papers reduce the threats of fire. Proper visitor control mechanisms and control over the entry and exit points can reduce the propensity for physical intrusion or unauthorized physical access or sabotage, vandalism, espionage, theft, and destruction of systems. Policies not followed by employees can allow such threats due to tailgating which is a very common issue at most organizations. Ignorance and incompetence, and a lack of awareness and training can lead to mistakes.

Layers of security provide complementary controls which mean that a threat not controlled by one layer is controlled by other layer and vice versa. Some of the threats may be controlled by multiple layers also. Thus, a layered approach, which is an integrated approach, provides better protection to the organization than a single layered approach. The controls built through the layered approach normally defend the organization against most threats. This effectively means that the threat has to percolate multiple layers before it is effective.

"Defense-in-depth" builds over a layered security approach and complements it through additional mechanisms, especially for monitoring, alerting, and emergency response, including disaster recovery, as applicable. This normally includes forensic analysis and criminal activity reporting. This is also complemented where required by authorized personnel activity auditing.[1] Normally, the defense-in-depth strategy monitors current activities, and alerts you to imminent threats, thus enabling you to counter such threats through an emergency response or quick recovery, whereas multi-layered security control strategy delays the threat and provides ample time to react. For defense-in-depth to be effective at monitoring the speed at which the traffic/data is monitored and analyzed, and for the alerts to be communicated to the relevant tools or experts for further action, the analysis should be very high for such emergency responses to be effective.[1] Furthermore, such tools should have the capability to provide zero or very limited false alerts. Also, a team of experts like the Computer Emergency Response Team (CERT) should be formed and trained to handle such alerts and deal with emergency responses. Sometimes, it is impossible to avoid or counter an attack, but alerts need to be investigated immediately. This requires a forensic analysis capability in the organization. As organizations cannot carry out a counter-offensive in response to an attack because of legal restrictions, particularly in the case of such attacks where the solution is not immediately known, it is advisable to involve agencies like internet service providers or government security agencies (as appropriate to the gravity of the situation) so that the appropriate responses or corrective mechanisms may be identified and implemented at the earliest possible time.

There are various Security Frameworks that are provided by various standards or models or methodologies. Some of these are:

- An Information Security Management Systems Framework provided by Information Technology – security techniques – information security management systems – requirements (ISO/IEC 27001:2013) supported by Information Technology – security techniques – code of practice for information security controls (ISO/IEC 27002:2013) and related standards.

- NIST Special Publication 800-39: Managing Information Security Risk: Organization, Mission, and Information System View complemented by 800-53 Revision 4: Security and Privacy Controls for Federal Information Systems and Organizations.

- SABSA® (SABSA® is a registered trademark of The SABSA Institute which governs and co-ordinates the worldwide development of the SABSA Method.)

None of them use the same layers, but all have core layering concepts in common either depicted directly or indirectly through means such as the control objectives.

Information Security Management Systems Framework Provided by ISO/IEC 27001:2013

The framework suggested in this standard, i.e., information technology, security techniques, information security management systems, and requirements (ISO/IEC 27001:2013) is complemented by the guidance provided in the code of practice for information security controls (ISO/IEC 27002:2013).[2] This standard suggests that the security issues related to an organization have to be understood both in external and internal contexts and based on the needs and expectations of the interested parties. A risk assessment is necessary whereby the level of a risk is understood, the quantified risk has to be compared with acceptable risk as per the acceptance criteria of an organization and where appropriate, risk treatment options have to be identified, planned, and enacted.[2] The standard does not dictate any specific risk assessment methodology to be used. Where risks need to be mitigated, additional controls can be identified from various sources or from the list of controls provided in the standard.[2]

This standard 27001:2013 does not suggest any specific layers or a layered approach, but it provides guidance as to various structural elements for an effective information security implementation, through control clauses. The control clauses are Information Security Policies, Organization of Information Security, Human Resources Security, Asset Management, Access Control, Cryptographic Controls, Physical and Environmental Security, Operations Security, Communications Security, System Acquisition, Development and Maintenance, Supplier Relationships, Information Security Incident Management, Information Security aspects of Business Continuity Management, Compliance.[2]

However, 35 control objectives and 114 controls are explicitly suggested here and the explanations to those are clearly provided for effective guidance in ISO/IEC 27002:2013. If an organization applies the risk management effectively and comprehensively at the organizational level (not in silos at the functional level) using this standard, there is a good chance that the organization will be able to face the information security threats quite effectively.

NIST Special Publication 800-39 complemented by 800-53

The NIST special publication 800-39: Managing Information Security Risk: Organization, Mission, and Information System View, provides guidance on integrated organization-wide risk management.[3] Chapter Two of this special publication describes:

- The components of risk management

- The multi-tiered risk management approach

- Risk management at the organization level (Tier 1)

- Risk management at the mission/business process level (Tier 2)

- Risk management at the information system level (Tier 3)

- Risk related to trust and trustworthiness

- The effects of organizational culture on risk

- Relationships among key risk management concepts

Chapter Three describes a life cycle-based process for managing information security risks including:[3]

- A general overview of the risk management process

- How organizations establish the context for risk-based decisions

- How organizations assess risk

- How organizations respond to risk

- How organizations monitor risk over time

As you can see from the above, the risk management process is focused on three specific layers – the organization level (Tier 1), the mission/business process level (Tier 2) and the information system level (Tier 3).

The NIST special publication 800-53 Revision 4: Security and Privacy Controls for Federal Information Systems and Organizations, provides guidance on assignment of effective security controls during the multi-tiered risk management approach.[3]

Chapter Two describes the fundamental concepts that are associated with security control selections and specification including:

- Multi-tiered risk management

- The structure of security controls and how the controls are organized into families

- Security control baselines as starting points for the tailoring process

- The use of common controls and inheritance of security capabilities

- External environments and service providers

- Assurance and trustworthiness

- Revisions and extensions to security controls and control baselines

Chapter Three describes the process of selecting and specifying security controls for organizational information systems including:[3]

- Selecting the appropriate security control baselines

- Tailoring the baseline controls, including developing specialized overlays

- Documenting the security control selection process

- Applying the selection process to new and legacy systems

The application of SP 800-39, complemented with SP 800-53, provide a good foundation for any organization. Furthermore, other NIST special publications like SP 800-30 Rev 1 Guide for Conducting Risk Assessments give a detailed guideline on each of the steps of risk assessment.[3]

SABSA®

SABSA® is an open, generic, scalable methodology for formulating information security architecture and information assurance architecture, from The SABSA Institute. The beauty of the SABSA methodology is that it bases its information security architecture on business requirements, technology enablers required for business, and business requirements for information security.[4] As such, the usual conflict of business users being adversely impacted or not happy with information security is avoided and thus, the usual resistance for information security from the business users.

SABSA specifies a six layered architecture for information security with five vertical layers, namely the Business View or Contextual Security Architecture Layer, the Architect's View or Conceptual Security Architecture Layer, the Designer's View or Logical Security Architecture Layer, the Builder's View or Physical Security Architecture Layer, and the Tradesman's View or Component Security Architecture Layer and a horizontal layer supporting all the layers, i.e., Service Security Management Architecture Layer.[4] The SABSA layered structure is depicted for easy reference in Figure 3-4.

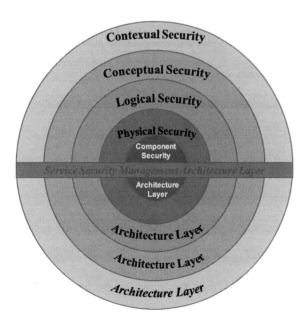

Figure 3-4. *SABSA information security architecture*

On the Contextual Security Architecture Layer, Business Users provide the business requirements that must be met by the architecture. At the Conceptual Security Architecture layer, an architect provides the overall context by which the business requirements of the organization are to be met. On the Logical Security Architecture layer, the Designers provide a systems engineering model which views the business as a system and delineates it in terms of a system of systems through various sub-systems. On the Physical Security Architecture layer, the builder provides physical security mechanisms and the servers that will be required to provide these services. On the Component Security Architecture layer, the tradesmen work on specifications provided by the builder and work with specialist products and system components which together, build what was expected by the builder. On the Service Security Management Architecture layer, the service manager deals with the system operations and service management work. Each subsequent layer builds on the output of the earlier layer, whereas the sixth layer, i.e. the Service Security Management Architecture layer, provides support to the other five layers. The security layers are described in Table 3-2.[4]

Table 3-2. *The SABSA® Information System Architecture layers*

Security Layer	Description
Business View or Contextual Security Architecture	The goals the business wants to achieve; the functional description of the same; the users, their requirements, their numbers, etc.; locational requirements and dependencies; usage patterns over time, etc. Primary considerations are: the business and its assets which need to be protected and the business needs for information security; business risks expressed in terms of business opportunities and the threats to business assets; business processes that require security; structural aspects of business security including external support structures; business geography and location-related aspects of business security; the time-related aspects of business security.
Architect's View or Conceptual Security Architecture	What needs to be protected expressed in terms of SABSA Business Attributes; the importance of protection in terms of controls and enablement objectives; how to achieve this protection through high-level technical and management security strategies, business process mapping framework; who is involved in the security management in terms of roles and responsibilities; where the architect wants the protection to be conceptualized in terms of security domains; when the protection is relevant in terms of a business time-management framework.
Designer's View or Logical Security Architecture	The business information that needs to be secured; security and risk management requirements for securing the business related information; specifying the logical security services and how they fit with each other; specifying the entities, their inter-relationships, their attributes, authorized roles and privilege profiles, etc.; specifying the security domains and inter-domain relationships; specifying the security related calendar and time-frames, etc.
Builder's View or Physical Security Architecture	Specifying the business data model and the security related data structures; specifying the rules that drive the logical decision making within the system; specifying the security mechanisms including the physical applications, middleware, servers, etc.; specifying people dependency in terms of human interface and access control systems; specifying the physical layout of the security technology infrastructure, etc.

(*continued*)

Table 3-2. (*continued*)

Security Layer	Description
Tradesman's View or Component Security Architecture	ICT components including data repositories and processors; risk management related tools; process tools and standards; personnel management tools and products; locator tools and standards; step timings and sequencing tools, etc.
Service Manager's View or Service Security Management Architecture	Service delivery management; operational risk management; process delivery management; personnel management; environment management; schedule management.

Table 3-3 summarizes the three frameworks.

Table 3-3. *Advantages and disadvantages of IS frameworks*

Framework	SABSA®	NIST SP 80-39 & 80-53	ISO/IEC 27001:2013
Advantages	1. Business focused 2. Consideration zone is enterprise. 3. Multi-Layered approach covering essential aspects. 4. Steps provided to clearly guide the implementation of infrastructure security architecture. 5. Compulsorily involves different views. 6. Various stakeholders including business users are involved in arriving at the information security architecture.	1. Business focused 2. Consideration zone is organized 3. Well-focused risk identification, management and control framework built in–multi-tiered risk assessment.	1. Consideration zone is normally organization. 2. Well-focused risk identification, management and control framework. 3. Several controls which can be useful are suggested 4. Each control has been explained in detail in ISO/IEC 27002:2013. 5. There are many guidelines by ISO which support the above like ISO/IEC 31000:2009, etc.
Disadvantages	1. Some risks may not be considered if the risk assessment methodology used is not robust, as the focus is more on business enablement and business considerations may out-focus the risks.	1. Success depends upon the involvement of relevant stakeholders with appropriate knowledge, experience and expertise and on identifying the risks appropriately.	1. No layered focus specified directly but only specified indirectly through the control clauses. Success depends upon involvement of all relevant stakeholders and the expertise in proper risk assessment and risk treatment.

Pillars of Security

Security is a continuous process. It involves people, policies, procedures, processes, and technology. These three categories can be considered the pillars of information security. These pillars of security and their interconnections are depicted in Figure 3-5.

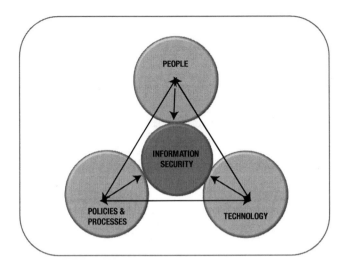

Figure 3-5. *The People, Processes, and Technology triad for information security*

As we saw in the foregoing paragraphs, people are an important, unforgettable part of information security. Effective information security involves the assignment of clear roles and responsibilities of people in any organiztion.

People

Without people there is no need for or possibility of any information security. People are the strongest pillars of the information security on the one side. But, they may sometimes tend to be the weakest pillars because of the lack of awareness or bad motives. They are easily prone to social engineering attacks or other malicious attacks. Hence, for strong information security their awareness, vigilance, and positive involvement must be increased and ensured.

Organization of Information Security

Every organization creates its structure from a functional and administrative point of view. This is very important from the perspective of the efficiency and effectiveness of work, which allows an organization to grow. However, with the widespread use of computers, the Internet, reliable connectivity, new technologies, and awareness of these new technologies among children to adults, it has become increasingly important to assign roles and responsibilities from the perspective of information security. Effective implementation of information security provides the customers, the management of the organization (including the shareholders), the employees of the organization, and all other related stakeholders the requisite assurance about an organization.

In the context of an organization, it is not enough that only the top management is concerned about information security, but it is important to involve everybody down the line, including the receptionist, the security staff, and the housekeeping staff. This requires commitment from all levels of an organization to ensure the effectiveness of implementation of information security. As it is said, "The strength of a chain is only as good as its weakest link."

With every passing day, organizations are acquiring more information processing facilities, off the shelf software, and customized software, and we know that our dependency on IT is only going to increase significantly in the coming years. Hence, it is necessary that we are proactively organized to plan and implement information security to protect ourselves, our customers, our partners, our suppliers, and other relevant stakeholders. We also need to organize ourselves to avoid, deter, prevent, detect, investigate, and overcome the issues related to information security or information security breaches.

The Need for Independence

Technology within an organization is normally headed by a Chief Technology Officer (CTO) or a Chief Information Officer (CIO). He is supported by others like IT Managers and operations staff such as system administrators, database administrators, network administrators; development staff such as programmers and support staff; and others, as relevant. Many organizations also provide information security responsibility for the same role as a CTO/CIO. It is possible in some organizations that this may not create any significant conflict of interest or issue because of the maturity of such a person, the size of the organization, or because of the maturity of others in the organization. However, it is possible in many organizations because of a conflict of interest primarily due to a lack of adequate maturity in such a person, that he may not give adequate attention to information security either because of "confirmation trap or functional fixation".[5] He may also find the need to cover up or not to publicize information security incidents in order to save himself, his personnel, or to increase the investment in information technology tools, rather than on information security related aspects. We strongly feel that there should be a clear segregation of duties between IT and information security. We strongly advise that there should be a role similar to Chief Information Security Officer (CISO) or Information Security Officer (ISO) in any organization to ensure effective independence and a non-biased view on information security. In our opinion, as the organizations and their interfaces with the external world increase in complexity, the segregation of duty in information security is also important like in any other functional areas, including finance and human resources. This segregation of duties also provides an additional view point on the same aspect.

Specific Roles and Responsibilities

Ideally, for successful implementation of the information security, it should follow a top-down approach with a clear commitment from the top, including the board of directors. If this is not the case, information security may only be seen as implemented or being implemented on paper without much success at the ground level. Even though there is no uniformity of approach as far as how various organizations have organized the information security related roles, many organizations who are serious about the implementation of information security with real intentions (not to just show the outside world or to get the certification) will have clearly assigned specific roles which handle information security in earnest.

Audit Committee or Information Security Committee at the Board Level

If we take the top-down approach, we should have at the board level, either as a part of an audit committee or as a part of a separate information security committee, a person from the board responsible for looking into information security implementation at the organization level. She should be such a person who need not be a technological expert, but who has her ears and eyes open to the external world and assimilates all issues related to information security at the global and various organizational levels. She should be a person who is actually interested in information security, and asks the tough questions on any proposal for new information processing facilities, modifications to the existing information processing facilities, new acquisitions of critical pieces of software of significant influence on the business, or of any information security aspects. These questions should not be asked just for the sake of asking them, but with all the seriousness of really understanding what the information security risks that an organization is undertaking/undergoing at any point of time or is likely to undergo in the future. She should advocate for and be the representative at the board meeting for the need for information security and convince other board members on filling the gaps related to information security.

Information Security Sponsor or Champion

The CEO or the president of the organization himself has to demonstrate commitment to information security by being the sponsor or champion of information security. This ensures that information security gets automatic buy-in in the organization when it is publicized that the CEO or the president himself is the champion of information security and he takes it very seriously. It is not enough that such a person only becomes a champion by designation or nomination, but also that he takes information security seriously and demonstrates it by his practice. It is necessary that such a role leads by example. The role of such a CEO or president as the information security champion or sponsor is primarily to:

- Promote the culture of information security in the organization

- Communicate strongly and sincerely the need for information security

- Appoint/assign other such roles so as to effectively implement information security within the organization

- Support the funding of information security projects

- Demonstrate a high commitment to information security

Chief Information Security Officer or Information Security Officer

There should be a senior person at the top management level, well empowered by the board, CEO, or the president of the organization, to head the information security cell, that is, a Chief Information Security Officer or an Information Security Officer. Ideally the role of such a person is to:

- Understand the information security risks to the entire organization, including to the business, information processing facilities, IT environment, and physical environment, both from the external and internal perspective

- Ensure that the risk assessment is carried out and the risk mitigation plans are put into effect when necessary

- Guide the entire organization on the need for information security

- Determine appropriate policies in the context of various areas of relevance to information security

- Determine and publish various procedures or work instructions to implement the policies of relevance to information security

- Educate and motivate internal and external stakeholders, including the suppliers and contractors to effectively implement information security requirements

- Analyze information security incidents and take the corrective actions as appropriate to information security related incidents

- Ensure that personnel of the organization, suppliers, contractors, and customers as necessary are educated or are made aware of the means of ensuring information security

- Coordinate with external agencies/forums to understand the prevailing or possible information security issues

- Report the status of information security in the organization to the CEO, the president, or the Board, as required

In the interest that information security is successfully implemented in the organization, the CISO/ISO has to consult with and involve other functional heads, including IT personnel, suppliers, contractors, and others. The greater the extent of involvement of various people on all levels, the greater the success of the implementation of information security in any organization. Periodic risk assessment, ongoing diligence, regular training of the staff on information security, and motivating staff and others to bring information security events to the organization's knowledge are very important in the entire list of responsibilities. He should have a good reporting mechanism of the various security events or incidents, so that they get his requisite attention and appropriate corrective actions can then be determined.

Information Security Forum

We have seen that in many organizations, there is a forum created, usually known as the Information Security Forum, consisting of the CTO, the CISO, the Business Representatives and department/functional heads to ensure that there is always an exchange of information and discussion on the implementation of different action plans related to the information security risks that the organization is facing at that point in time or is exposed to in the future. Business representatives are important constituents of this forum as they provide the business goals, how the technology needs to enable business, and business requirements of information security, thus providing the mandatory piece of information for planning and the implementation of any effective information security system. Such a forum can be both educational and action oriented. Having such a forum at the organization increases the buy-in factor for information security projects or information security related action plans in the organization and provides a better, more positive push in the direction of information security implementation. We strongly feel that such a forum needs to be created in every organization.

Information Security Specialists

The CISO/ISO should be assisted by either independent security specialists from outside or inside the organization. It is necessary that their views are heard with attention, considered adequately, and are acted upon where found relevant, applicable, and useful. If their recommendations are not implemented, the CISO/ISO should be informed. They should be encouraged to come up with their own views and bring them to the table. They should be motivated to speak of current or potential issues. With them being active on various relevant forums, they can bring up any new issues or which are being discussed as potential issues to the organizational CISO/ISO's knowledge, so that depending upon the relevance and severity of such issues, the organization can proactively decide on the actions to avoid, deter, prevent, detect, research, investigate, and eliminate. They also advise the CISO/ISO on technologies and products related to information security. Some of them can take roles like security architects, security designers, or security auditors.

Project Managers

Each project manager in the organization, whether he manages an infrastructural project, an IT project, a software development project, or any other type of project, should always look for the kind of information security risks he may be leading the organization to and take any necessary risk mitigation action that's necessary. Thinking of information security risks should be an integral part of project management from the initial planning stage and should continue to be considered throughout the life cycle and through design and development phases – until the successful completion of the project. Interestingly, this is one of the controls that was newly brought in by the recent revision of information security management systems – Requirements (ISO 27001:2013 – Control number A.6.1.5).[2] The need for this change was amplified in the Frost & Sullivan Market Survey (sponsored by (ISC)[2] and prepared by Robert Ayoub, CISSP Global Program Director) on information security, which claims that 73% of application vulnerabilities are one of the top security issues.[11]

Data Owners

Data owners should decide who needs access to which data. Restriction from or access to data may arise from an agreement with concerned customers. Data owners should regularly review access that is granted to users and check for the continued relevance of such access to ensure that the applications accessing the data, modifying the data, or deleting the data do so appropriately as per the business requirements.

Data Custodians

Data custodians are not owners of the data, but by their job roles, they are designated as the custodians of the data, such as database administrators. They have access to the entire set of data, but have to be very careful to ensure that such access is utilized only as per their role and primarily should be used to preserve the confidentiality, integrity, and availability of the data to the rightful and authorized persons. They should act on authorization requests based on the approval of the data owners. They should also exercise caution and due diligence in all their activities.

Users of the data

Users of the data have a huge onus in protecting and ensuring information security. They should be guided by their terms of access and the need for access. They should access only such data which is of relevance to them in completing their assigned roles and responsibilities. They should follow all the policies, procedures, work instructions, and guidelines to ensure that they protect information security. They should take information security seriously and be vigilant to ensure that even others do not violate these policies, procedures, work instructions, and guidelines. Some roles and important responsibilities are described in Table 3-4.

Table 3-4. *Important information security roles and responsibilities*

Role	Responsibility
Audit Committee of the Board	• An advocate of information security at the board level and convince other board members of the importance of information security • Bring sufficient focus on information security aspects in various decision making processes
Information Security Champion or Sponsor	• Promote the culture of information security within the organization • Assign/appoint appropriate roles to effectively support information security • Promote strongly and sincerely the need for information security
CISO	• Ensure proper risk assessment and determination of appropriate controls • Ensure the definition of appropriate policies, procedures, and processes • Coordinate with other agencies and forums to understand threats to information security • Report the status of information security to the management • Motivate and train employees, contractors, and suppliers on information security do's and don'ts
Information Security Forum	• Ensure collaboration across all functions/departments-including business • Ensure a focus on the execution of information security across the organization
Information Security Specialists	• Provide an unbiased and frank opinion on current or potential risks related to information security • Assist the CISO in an effective understanding and implementation of information security requirements, risks, architecture, products, and technology

(*continued*)

Table 3-4. (*continued*)

Role	Responsibility
Project Managers	• Consider information security related risks and mitigate them throughout the project life cycle
Data Owner	• Understand the characteristics and sensitivity of the data and provide the appropriate access/restrict access
	• On a periodical basis, review the access granted to ensure its continued appropriateness
Data Custodian	• Ensure the safety of the data and act as per the directions of the data owners
Users of the Data	• Ensure that data is used only for the purposes for which it is intended
	• Follow all the policies, procedures, and processes diligently to ensure the security of information assets

Authority for Information Security

Empowerment or authority should be vested as appropriate in each of the above roles in order for them to be effective. Definitely the CISO or the ISO should have the authority to stop any activity which is going to lead the organization into severe information security lapses or issues. Everyone in the information security forum should have the authority to demand information security primarily to protect the business, its customers, and its partners. Information security specialists in the organization should have the authority to demand that they be heard. Such an authority should be vested in such roles by the board, CEO, or the president of the organization and make it clear across the organization.

Policies, Procedures, and Processes

Information security is incomplete without clearly defined policies which guide employees, contractors, and suppliers. Policies provide guidance to everyone and depict the commitment of management to them. The following are some of the policies that are important to most of the organizations, as per ISO/IEC 27001:2013:[2]

- Information Security Management Systems Policy
- Access Control Policy
- Information Classification and Handling Policy
- Physical and Environmental Security Policy
- Acceptable Use of Assets Policy
- Clear Desk and Clear Screen Policy
- Privacy and Protection of Personally Identifiable Information Policy
- Mobile Devices and Teleworking Policy
- Backup Policy
- Restrictions on Software Installations and Use Policy
- Protection from Malware Policy
- Management of Technical Vulnerabilities Policy

- Information Transfer Policy

- Communications Security Policy

- Cryptographic Controls Policy

- Policy on Supplier Relationships

Some of the other standards like Information technology – Service management – Part 1: Service management system requirements (ISO/IEC 20000-1:2011) call for more policies.

Procedures and processes describe how the intent of the policies is to be implemented. They detail step-by-step instructions on how to carry on the work so that the intentions of these policies are adhered to. Training the employees, contractors, and suppliers on the relevant policies, procedures, and processes is a must in order to ensure that these are understood. With the ever-evolving business environment, challenging risks, and changing technologies policies need to be reviewed and kept current. Thus, the training process should be ongoing and continual.

Technology

Technology is another important pillar. There are many good and competing technologies available to protect information security. All these technologies need to be explored within the entire context of the organization to ensure they seamlessly integrate with the overall fulfilment of both business and information security requirements. Technology should fulfil the requirement of information security architecture. Business and its risks and opportunities should be the main focus and technology should be an enabler rather than the end to meet the same.

Some of the important technologies available are auto monitoring and alerting systems, logging systems, detecting systems, preventive systems, and recovery systems. Examples are firewalls, IDS/IPS, and anti-virus software.

Information Security Concepts

What constitutes information security? What are we protecting through information security? This requires sufficient consideration if the field of information security is to be better understood. The following discussion sheds light on the important aspects or constituents of information security.

CIA Triad

The compromise of information security is one of the biggest issues faced by the IT and IT enabled industry, which is almost every industry these days. Some of the scenarios of the possible compromise of information security are depicted in Figure 3-6. Figure 3-7 depicts one of the important models of information security popularly known as CIA Triad.

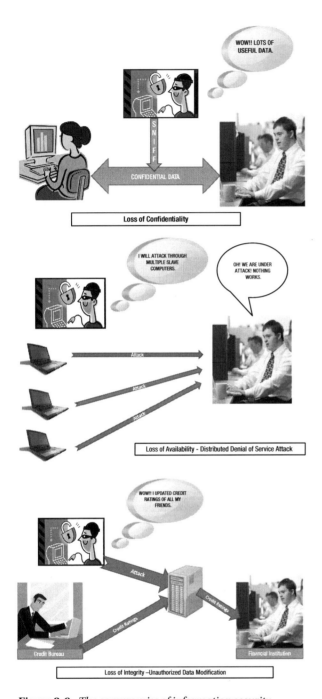

Figure 3-6. *The compromise of information security*

Figure 3-7. *CIA triad*

■ **Note**   As mentioned in the introduction to this chapter, the CIA triad is one of the most important models of information security which specifies the important properties or characteristics of information assets, without which, an understanding of information security is not possible. However, the importance of the CIA triad has increased in recent years because of the way we input, transfer, or store the information. Mainly, "confidentiality" has taken a bigger beating compared to the other properties.

Traditional definitions/views on "confidentiality", "integrity," and "availability" came from the National Institute of Standards and Technology (NIST)/U.S.Code and are the most referred and used ones. However, if you look at the definitions from various organizations or standards organizations active in the field of information security, you will be quick to realize that each definition varies from the other and hence, these definitions may not be all pervasive and comprehensive. Some of the popular definitions are reviewed in the following sections.

Confidentiality

Some information is secret, sensitive, or needs to be restricted as a disclosure to unintended sources can create such things as the compromise of a nation's security or strategic installations, the loss of business opportunities, a first mover advantage, intellectual property rights, and privacy. Such information is considered in general terms as "confidential" and needs to be protected zealously by appropriate authorization or restrictions. Consider the following scenarios to fully understand:

- You have decided on a business strategy to counter a competitor and it is leaked to others accidentally or by an aggrieved senior management person who just left the organization.

- You have innovated a new technological idea and want to patent it. But, before you patent it, the same idea is copied by someone and further passed on to someone else and is patented by them instead.

- The patient information and medical records of the patients you have stored have been stolen and made public.

- You find that one of the administrative passwords is compromised and significant data of confidential nature has been stolen.

Chapter 44, Title 35, Subchapter III, and Section 3542 of the U.S.C. defines "confidentiality" as "preserving authorized restrictions on information access and disclosure, including means for protecting personal privacy and proprietary information. [NIST SP 800-100]".[6]

Information security management systems – overview and vocabulary (ISO/IEC 27000:2014) defines "confidentiality" as "property that information is not made available or disclosed to unauthorized individuals, entities, or processes".[7]

Integrity

Information is useful and reliable only if it is accurate and not modified against the intentions wanted of the originator. "Integrity" needs to be protected appropriately by means such as appropriate authentication, routing protocols, appropriate configuration of systems, and application security. Consider the following scenarios to understand:

- You have received a letter purported to be from a customer company and they have sought some important information to be divulged to one of their suppliers. You find something fishy in the letter and upon investigation, you find that the letter was fake and originated by a supplier company and not by the customer company.

- You divulged critical, confidential information about the strategy of your competitor company, purported to be leaked by one of their employees, but you find that it was conveyed to you in a misleading way in order for you to make the wrong decision.

- You were given the correct information, but only a portion of it, whereas the other portion of the information which was crucial if you would have been told would have given you an entirely different perspective on the matter.

Chapter 44, Title 35, Subchapter III, and Section 3542 of the U.S.C. defines "integrity" as "guarding against improper information modification or destruction, and includes ensuring information non-repudiation and authenticity [NIST SP 800-100]".[6]

Information security management systems – overview and vocabulary (ISO/IEC 27000:2014) defines "integrity" as "property of protecting the accuracy and completeness of assets".[7]

Availability

Information today is stored in systems, databases, storage units, or, most recently, on the Cloud. In today's fast-paced world where opportunities can be lost fast and the speed of decision making is important, the availability of crucial information at all times has become necessary. Consider the following scenarios to understand this concept:

- You are required to send an important note to your customer and you find that your e-mail system or Internet is not responding.

- You are required to carry out certain work and your reference documents are in a particular database and the particular database is down for technical reasons.

- You are required to initiate an important request through one of your applications and you find that the application is not responding.

Chapter 44, Title 35, Subchapter III, of Section 3542 of the U.S.C. defines "availability" as "ensuring timely and reliable access to and the use of information. [NIST SP 800-100]".[6]

Information security management systems – overview and vocabulary (ISO/IEC 27000:2014) defines "availability" as "property of being accessible and usable upon demand by an authorized entity".[7]

For information security to be complete and the organizations or individuals to be protected, it is necessary that all three properties or aspects are to be ensured. Emphasizing only one at the cost of others may lead to the reduced efficiency and effectiveness of any organization.

Parkerian Hexad

Donn B. Parker, one of the information security specialists of repute, brought out some alternate perspectives of the properties of information security. In addition to the three properties specified through the CIA triad, he brought out three more descriptors or properties, namely, possession, authenticity, and utility, thus forming a hexad known as the Parkerian Hexad. The Parkerian Hexad also groups confidentiality and possession, integrity and authenticity, availability and utility, pairs together as these are related.[8]

The definitions provided by the Parkerian Hexad for the six properties or descriptors are as follows:[8]

- "Confidentiality" is defined as the "quality or state of being private or secret; known only to a limited few."

- "Possession or Control" is defined as "a state of having in or taking into one's control or holding at one's disposal; actual physical control of property by one who holds for himself, as distinguished from custody; something owned or controlled."

- "Integrity" is defined as "unimpaired or unmarred condition; soundness; entire correspondence with an original condition; the quality or state of being complete or undivided; material wholeness."

- "Authenticity" is defined as "authoritative, valid, true, real, genuine, or worthy of acceptance or belief by reason of conformity to fact and reality."

- "Availability" is defined as "capable of use for the accomplishment of a purpose, immediately usable, accessible, may be obtained."

- "Utility" is defined as "useful, fitness for some purpose."

The Parkerian Hexad describes "confidentiality" as a little different from the traditional definition of "confidentiality" that is provided by U.S.Code/NIST. This hexad considers "possession" as an important element which may impact confidentiality. The "possession" of confidential information can sometimes lead to such threats like blackmail, extortion, sabotage, or destruction. Similarly, proprietary and personal information considered by traditional definition to be confidential may in fact be confidential or not confidential, depending upon the nature of the information or timing of the information divulgence.[8]

The Parkerian Hexad describes "integrity" as a little different from the traditional definition of "integrity" that is provided by U.S.Code/NIST. This hexad doesn't consider "authenticity" as a part of "integrity" and as a different property, which has to do with the validity or genuineness of the information than the unimpaired condition of the information. Again here, "non-repudiation" is considered a different aspect than "integrity" and as related to "authenticity" as it refers to validity or genuineness of the information.[8]

Parkerian hexad considers "availability" along with "utility" as information even if available is of use only if it is usable or has utility. It differs from the traditional definition in that "availability" has nothing to do with "reliable access".[8]

As seen above, the Parkerian Hexad gives a different perspective of the characteristics or properties of information security.

A simple view of the above properties is represented in Figure 3-8.

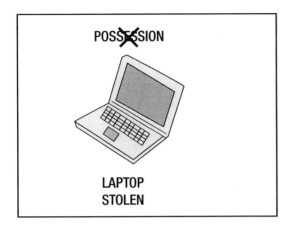

Figure 3-8. *Six properties of information security with simple examples*

Implementation of Information Security

It is not easy to implement information security. All the pillars of information security have to be given adequate thought. Proper scoping has to be done for the efforts and proper planning has to be done involving all the stakeholders. Planning has to be backed by strong execution of the same and overcoming the barriers as execution is carried out. Focus on ensuring the success of implementation is necessary with all the relevant people assigned and involved appropriately.

Figure 3-9 gives the typical information security implementation cycle. Depending upon the context of the organization there may be different models used for implementation.

Figure 3-9. *The implementation cycle of information security*

An effective approach to the implementation of information security is the key to its success. Organizations at different stages of their existence may approach the implementation in different ways. An organization already in existence usually drives its journey on the path to information security primarily through the initiation of risk assessment. Hence, various standards and frameworks highlight the risk assessment aspect as the important step in the overall context of implementation of information security. However, a new organization may initiate its journey on the path to information security through the determination of its business requirements, determination of infrastructural and technological requirements to facilitate/enable business, and through the determination of business requirements for information security like the one suggested by SABSA methodology.

Risk Assessment

There are various risk management methodologies available for ensuring effective risk assessment. Some of them are: Risk Management – Principles and guidelines (ISO/IEC 31000:2009); Operationally Critical Threat, Asset and Vulnerability Evaluation [SM] (OCTAVE®) from Software Engineering Institute, CMU, Pittsburgh;[9] risk assessment methodology specified by NIST (SP 30, 39 & 53); Risk IT framework by Information Systems Audit and Control Association, US;[10] and FMEA. An organization can use any methodology but the risk assessment as a process has to be carried out methodically and effectively to derive the required benefits. An understanding of the risks in the context of the entire organization, keeping in mind the vulnerabilities and threats to information assets even from the outside world, understanding the current controls that are in place and quantification of the risk to understand risk exposure normally drives the risk response including the risk mitigations to be carried out. Risk mitigations are determined based on the effective controls already implemented by other organizations, suggested by other agencies, by implementation of tools, through policies and processes, through other additional controls as required including awareness and training of the employees, contractors and suppliers, or through deterrents like legal agreements. Employees normally include temporary workers too.

Planning and Architecture

In an existing organization, planning may commence with the commencement of planning for effective risk assessment involving all the stakeholders as relevant. In a new organization, the planning may be carried out to effectively approach achievement of information security using relevant steps as suggested by appropriate frameworks or methodologies. Plans also identify the owners for various activities, roles, and responsibilities for the effective execution of these plans. The schedules used also clearly depicts the timelines, keeping in mind various dependencies and constraints. The steps planned depend upon the methodology or framework used. Planning needs to be carried out for an integrated, methodical, and well-coordinated approach, leading to effective information security infrastructure or architecture rather than an ad-hoc approach that can create side effects or make the implementation ineffective. Effective information security infrastructure or architecture provides ease of use and generates confidence to all the stakeholders including business users.

In an existing organization, risk assessment provides the input for the planning. The implementation of additional controls determined to mitigate are planned through the risk treatment plans. These actions are clearly assigned to the appropriate owners with clearly identified timelines. Well-implemented risk treatment plans ensure that the organization is well protected.

Gap Analysis

Things change: the business may change, the technology changes, the people change. Changes are the only constant in today's world. Also, the vulnerabilities until now unknown will have been exposed to the world or reported. Hence, we have to ensure that our protection systems continue to work even under these constant changes. In order to ensure this, a periodical gap analysis needs to be carried out which sometimes throw up significant surprises. This ensures a check on the implementation of the policies, procedures, and processes, as well as the effectiveness of the existing protective mechanisms or controls including the effectiveness of the information security architecture. This may be done through periodical risk re-assessments leading to additional controls to be implemented through new risk treatment plans.

Integration and Deployment

As discussed earlier, any implementation done in silos rather than organization-wide does not provide adequate protection. Instead, it can create an inconvenience in the usage and also expose us to more threats. Hence, an integrated view at all times in the totality of the business and the organization is required. Also, an effective deployment of all intended policies, procedures, and processes, along with the intended implementation of information security architecture and its various layers is required. All the efforts related to information security need to be thought of in an integrated manner by involving all the relevant stakeholders and need to be implemented based on their dependencies. Incomplete implementation or inadequate attention to any one of the layers may defeat the controls built in other layers. For example, there is no use in implementing a tool for the analysis of the alerts unless the persons who are required to analyze them are trained on the same. Similarly, implementation of new policies and procedures will be useless unless the persons who should understand them and follow them are not aware of them or are not trained on using them. The implementation of new tools is of no use unless the internal people know how to configure and use them effectively. Relevant people need to be trained, and tools, if any, need to be configured appropriately. The correct working of such tools should be confirmed by testing as required and defects, if any, have to be fixed or their impact understood and only then these tools have to be used. All these steps need to definitely be a part of the planning we talked about earlier in the chapter.

Operations

Information security should not be ignored in day-to-day operations. It should be an integral part of all the activities. Operations need to be carried out strictly according to the established policies, procedures, and processes. Any violation to speed up the activities or ignorance can lead to serious consequences. Similarly, not carrying out certain activities which are essential as per the policies and procedures, can defeat the very purpose of information security. Hence, operations should be tightly controlled for effective information security. For example, backups were not taken because the system administrators were busy on another activity. This defeats the protection provided through backups. The installation of a patch without taking sufficient precautions can bring down the system itself. Not carrying out the maintenance of UPS can bring down the UPS leading to an abrupt shutdown of the systems leading to system or data corruption. All operations should be guided by appropriate processes (standard operating procedures) and carried out as per the plans. A non-maintained earth pit can be a significant issue. Not checking the backup media through periodical restoration may lead to the tape being not readable or restorable when required.

Monitoring

Monitoring is an integral part of any activity whether it is business related or information security-related activity. Any organization needs to keep monitoring the threats to it so that it can react to the threats effectively and on time. This activity is time-consuming. For example, to find out about all the intruder activities manually through logs is a humungous activity. There are many tools available to monitor, filter, detect, and/or to correct and alert on such aspects. For example, firewalls and IDS/IPS. Even simple things like disk space monitoring and bandwidth usage monitoring, if not done on a timely basis, may lead to systems not being usable or available. In the field of information security, in order to understand the causes of the breaches and incidents, sometimes the forensic analysis (where the causes may not be obvious or straight forward) may have to be carried out. This will enable us to understand the causes clearly and put in place our defensive mechanisms so that such incidents can be avoided or reduced.

Legal Compliance and Audit

One of the biggest threats to an organization's existence is non-compliance to legal requirements. Organizations can be permanently shut down if the non-compliance is severe. Sometimes, organizations may be made to shell out huge penalties for non-compliance or negligence. Furthermore, there are a lot of laws enacted to prevent the misuse of information technology and those need to be adhered to. These may require special skills to understand the compliance in the context of information technology. Hence, periodic audits by knowledgeable independent or internal experts will help the organizations to understand the non-compliance issues and plug them out before they become severe.

Another thing to consider here is the compliance check on various policies, procedures, or processes implemented by the organizations. We all know that most of the time, these policies or processes are written wonderfully, but people who are trained on them over a period of time, these can be forgotten. Sometimes, the context changes, but these policies and processes are not modified. New employees join the organization but they are not trained on these policies and processes. Normally, in almost all of the organizations, most of the employees are always on either fighting one or other types of business fires, working on or solving one or another crucial burning issue. Consequently, the requisite attention and focus on effective implementation of these policies and processes takes a back seat or gets into a low priority mode. Hence, it is strongly suggested that every organization should have strong periodic internal audits coupled with external audits by independent experts occasionally. The non-conformances identified and the suggestions made in these audits should be placed before the management and necessary actions have to be determined and implemented across the organization. Management should provide necessary focus on these so that even if the organization wades off a little, it is again brought back to the right path.

Crisis Management

The Crisis Management Plan, Business Continuity Plan, or Disaster Recovery Plan are interchangeably used to denote a single entity, even though there are subtle differences between them. For the purpose of discussion here, let us consider them as a single entity. Organizations can face crisis because of natural disasters, mistakes of employees, senior management, or because of the external attacks like the attacks from the hackers. Organizations cannot sit idle. They need to respond effectively and also restore their business back to normalcy after such attacks. Towards this purpose, a well-planned business continuity and crisis management plan should be put in place by every organization. Disaster recovery and business continuity should become an integral part of the planning process of every organization. Ideally, every organization should carry out the business impact analysis to identify the critical businesses for which continuity is essential and also the tolerance time frame up to which the organization can wait before the business need to be commenced. A business continuity plan should be put in place clearly identifying the roles and responsibilities of all the concerned stakeholders. All the stakeholders need to be trained and the business continuity plan should be tested to check that it works as required when actually it has to be put into action. Crisis declaration is an important step. As every event or incident is not a crisis, a senior person should be empowered to identify a crisis when it arises, as he has the maturity and knowledge to declare a situation a crisis.

Principles of Information Security

If you look closely, you will find that there is going to be a close relationship between what we discussed so far in this chapter and what we are going to discuss here. The principles of information security were established as far back as 1996 by the National Institute of Standards and Technology of United States of America through Special Publication 800-14: "Generally Accepted Principles and Practices for Securing Information Technology Systems." We feel that these fundamental expectations are valid and relevant even in today's context.[12]

While there are many approaches that may be used to ensure information security, there are some minimum expectations which need to be met invariably by all the current systems, irrespective of their size. These eight fundamental principles of information security are the ones which we are going to discuss in brief in the following paragraphs.[12]

- Principle 1: Computer Security Supports the Mission of the Organization

    As we have seen, every organization has objectives to achieve, whether they are business goals or social goals. Any other system is rendered useless, whether it be information technology system or procedures or otherwise, if it does not enable the achievement of these primary objectives of the organization in conjunction with the goals of these systems too.

- Principle 2: Computer Security is an Integral Element of Sound Management

    This principle is straight forward and it cannot be more relevant than in today's world. In today's well connected world, where the attacks can happen on any system from any other part of the world and nobody can be absolutely sure of the protection put in place, information security can be ignored only at the peril of an organization.

- Principle 3: Computer Security Should Be Cost-Effective

    At the end of the day, every organization has to sustain, continue to sustain, and grow its business and profitability. Even organizations with social objectives have limited funding available to them and the expectation is that they use it judiciously. Hence, just because an excellent security system is available in the market, one should not go ahead with it unless the benefits accrued by its usage are far more than the costs of their purchase and implementation. This is one of the fundamental requirements for any organization of any size in any business.

- Principle 4: Systems Owners Have Security Responsibilities Outside Their Own Organization

  Today, in the era of the Internet and web applications, many of the systems are used by users, whether employees or customers, from outside the organizational physical boundaries. Every individual has the right to be assured that the system or applications that she/he is using is secure. It is the organization's responsibility to ensure that safety is built into these applications and their users are duly assured of the security in them. No organization can shirk its responsibility in this regard as the growth of business, in recent times, depends on new tools of doing business.

- Principle 5: Computer Security Responsibilities and Accountability Should Be Made Explicit

  Having clarity is what makes the difference when it comes to achievement. As we have seen, decisions are not made by the people who are normally working with the data because the authorities are not clearly defined and assigned. Such a state of confusion can lead to disasters in organizations today, as computer security incidents or breaches and disasters on account of them have to be dealt with using speed, precision, and clarity. In our discussions, earlier in this chapter, we have elaborated on the whys and hows of clear demarcation for information security, roles, responsibilities, and authorities will ensure successful compliance towards information security. Negligence cannot be excused in the field of information security as organizations can be severely affected with reputation loss, business loss, penalties, etc. Accountability is brought in clearly and effectively through clarity on roles, responsibilities, and authorities.

- Principle 6: Computer Security Requires a Comprehensive and Integrated Approach

  Most of the organizations operate in a highly competitive environment. For their efficiency and effectiveness, all aspects of business, business enablers and business protection systems have to work in perfect harmony and need to complement and supplement each other seamlessly into a comprehensive and integrated approach. This is what we emphasized throughout our discussions in this chapter, including in the context of information security frameworks / architecture.

- Principle 7: Computer Security Should Be Periodically Reassessed

  As we discussed earlier, changes are the only constant in this world. In the changing context, we need to navigate in the right direction. In order to check for our direction and do course corrections, we need to do periodical reassessment of the organizational computer security. We have already discussed the benefits of the periodical gap analysis through periodical risk assessment as a means of course correction.

- Principle 8: Computer Security is Constrained by Societal Factors

  It is true that there is a possibility of conflict between information security requirements and societal factors, e.g. logging activities and privacy requirements. While each of them has significance of their own, we need to ensure a balance between these. The balancing depends upon the context and expectations. It is possible that under certain circumstances, one can complement and support the other.

The aforementioned fundamental principles of information security are further substantiated through additional principles for engineering effective information security through NIST's special publication 800-27 Revision A: "Engineering Principles for Information Technology Security (A Baseline for Achieving Security)."

Chapter Summary

- In this chapter, we attempted to lay a strong foundation for the next few chapters. We explored four important layers of information security, namely Physical Security (which includes Hardware Security), Network Security (which includes Communications Security), Software Security (which includes Operating System Security, Applications Security and Security of Utilities/Tools), and Human Security (which is people) related. We saw how each of these layers contribute to overall information security at any organization. We also saw how the policies, procedures, and processes contribute to the overall scheme of information security. Through a context diagram, we also depicted various important controls of each of these layers.

- We explored various security threats and categorized them into external threats and internal threats based on the origin of these threats. Then we identified some of the important external and internal threats under each of the layers, including Physical Security, Network Security, Software Security, and Human Security.

- We also explored the generic multi-layered approach to information security architecture which can be used by any organization and we looked at important components of each of these layers. We also looked at additional aspects covered by "defense-of-depth" and how it can help an organization to respond to information security breaches or incidents. We touched upon some of the important frameworks/architectural models of information security like ISO/IEC 27001:2013 complemented by ISO/IEC 27002:2013, NIST SP-39 and SP-53 and SABSA. We then explored the above frameworks/architectural models in detail and how these lead to a secure information security architecture for any organization. We also looked at the advantages and disadvantages of each of these.

- We examined the three important pillars of security: People, Policies, Procedures and Processes, and Technology. We explored how the organization has to equip itself for effective implementation of information security, the importance of independence of information security personnel, and what the typical information security roles and responsibilities are. We also stressed the need for clearly specifying the authorities related to information security. We then detailed how policies, processes, and technology effectively contribute to and support people in implementing information security.

- We discussed the CIA triad (which was the traditionally accepted model of information security) and the Parkerian Hexad which extended upon the CIA triad. We explored some of the important definitions of confidentiality, integrity and availability from the U.S.Code/NIST and other standards/forums. We went through the fact that various definitions are in variant with each other. We also looked at the variances between the definitions from NIST and those from the Parkerian Hexad. We also looked at some of the examples of each properties of information security as per CIA and as per the Parkerian Hexad.

- We suggested one approach for effectively implementing information security in any organization, that is, both a new organization and an existing organization. We elaborated upon the need for risk assessment and the various frameworks for risk assessment, importance of appropriate planning, and the need for having robust information security architecture, periodical gap analysis, and the need for execution discipline in operations, the importance of regular monitoring, the importance of legal compliance and periodic audits, and crisis management.

CHAPTER 4

■ ■ ■

Access Controls

Introduction

In general terms, providing security means "freedom from risk and danger". In the context of information security, it is securing against:

- Access to information by unauthorized persons
- Modification to information by unauthorized persons
- Destruction of information by unauthorized persons

This means basically, any type of access to information needs to be protected. Whether the access is physical such as accessing CPUs, hard disks, or logical, as in accessing the system directly or remotely, access needs to be restricted and thus, information needs to be protected.

Access control is considered the most important aspect of information security and is an important pillar of information security. Access control can be implemented in various ways depending on the environment. This may entail locking your computer room, your system, restricting access to the system using login and passwords, protecting your data using file protection or encryption, encrypting network communications, or checking a digital signature before accessing the data.

Access control has two components – authentication and authorization. Authentication is verifying the identity of a user or a host that is accessing the system or network resource. The goal of authentication is also determining from where and how the resource is being accessed – whether the system is being accessed from a private computer or public computer (internet café) or if it is being accessed during normal working hours or after working hours. Authorization is permitting or restricting access to the information based on the type of users and their roles – employee, contractor, administrator, or manager.

Examples of access control:

- Entering into a server room or data center using physical key or finger print authentication or by keying in the access code
- User prompted to provide username and password when accessing computing resources
- Remote user prompted to provide user name and password when accessing network from outside of the organization
- User denied access while accessing confidential documents related to the company or a client
- User denied access while accessing personnel related details

Confidentiality and Data Integrity

Different information or data in the organization has different sensitivities as far as confidentiality is concerned. Some data may be accessed by everyone as there is no security risk, even if it is known to the entire world. Other information may be highly confidential and may have to be shared only with a few individuals or be restricted to only a few individuals. Various levels of data sensitivity can be ensured only by controlling appropriate access through proper authentication and authorization.

Similarly, the integrity of the information/data is another important property that is protected through access controls. The importance of data integrity can be illustrated by a simple example. Imagine that you have made an online purchase of $100. By accident or deliberate intervention, your data has been modified and you receive a bill for $1000 – who will take the loss? In another example, your prescription drug dosage of 10 milligrams (mg) has been modified to 100 mg – imagine the consequences. Hence, one of the most important aspects of information security is the integrity of data – whether your data can be modified by all users or not, and any data should be possible to be modified by only authorized users.

Unauthorized modification or destruction of information leads to loss of integrity. Integrity concerns the origin of the source of information, and the correctness and completeness of information. Data Integrity protection can be provided by having preventive mechanisms as to who can access the system, appropriate access controls, and detective mechanisms in regards to who is trying to modify/destroy the data, preventive controls such as locking the systems down after a pre-specified number of unauthorized attempts. This leads to an important element of the overall guidance for information access at any organization – an Access Control Policy.

Who Can Access the Data?

Data is accessed by different types of users within an organization – the data owner, database administrator, data architect, and vendors. Each of them has a different role and function to perform on the data. For the database and its administrators, "data integrity" means to ensure that the data being entered in the database is accurate and consistent. The database designer/database administrator designs appropriate table structures, relations, and views and sets certain rules on them to ensure proper access to, and integrity of, data. For a data owner, "data integrity" means to ensure appropriate business rules that are defined on the data are intact and the data is being accessed as per the defined rules. For a vendor, "data integrity" means accuracy and consistency of the stored data. Between any two transactions and updates, data should not have been altered, and should have proper error checking and validation routines. There is no doubt that there are more definitions and meaning for "data integrity," but they all mean the same thing – how or who accesses the information/data, and how information/data access can be protected and monitored.

There are different methods for protecting data integrity, such as generating checksums, file integrity software, and encryption. Checksum computes the sum of total digital data. This checksum is verified at both ends of the transmission. If there is no data integrity loss, then the checksum should be the same at both ends – before and after the transmission. There are several algorithms available for calculating the checksum. Most sites today offer either MD5 or SHA-1 checksum to users. File integrity software checks on by whom, how, and when the files have been accessed. It monitors the access of individual documents/files. You can set alerts when an unauthorized user tries to access any file or data. Encryption ensures both the integrity and confidentiality of data.

What is an Access Control?

An access control is a security feature that controls access to systems and resources in the network. The goal of an access control is to protect information from being lost, stolen, deleted, or modified either intentionally or accidently by those who are not authorized to access it. There are three methods of access:

- Network Access – Users on a network can access all the resources on the network. Hence, network access also needs to be restricted, protected, and monitored. For example, users who can access the HR and finance department LAN can be restricted.

- System Access – Users accessing the systems on the network. It can be one of the servers, printers, or any other shared device on the network. The access to these devices should be restricted, protected, and monitored continuously.

- Data Access – Users constantly accessing data on the network resource. Users accessing and modifying files, documents, and databases. Any data that is being accessed should be restricted, protected, and monitored.

The challenge of security programs is to ensure that data is not modified or deleted by unauthorized users. Although security programs cannot improve the quality of the data, they definitely can help in protecting data by applying access controls to ensure that any changes to data are intended and applied correctly. Access controls are a very critical requirement for both commercial and government organizations to prevent fraud and errors. It is imperative that no user can modify data in a way that renders the data corrupt or causes loss of financial integrity or make it unreliable for appropriate decision making. Examples of government systems include the Air Traffic Control system, Social Security, welfare system, IRS tax information, the birth and death registry, housing, and passport and military records. Examples of commercial systems include medical records, employee personal information, credit/financial reporting, the payroll system, income tax information, and customer details.

Data integrity can be protected by granting access to the resources on a need-to-know and need-to-do basis. Various types of users need different levels of access. For example, internal users may need full access whereas external users and contractors may need read-only access. Users should be granted access based on the roles, responsibilities, and job functions that they perform. Resources should also have different classification levels. For example, documents should be classified as confidential, private, public, or internal use only. A detailed log should be maintained so that in case of any fraud or data loss, logs can be reviewed to find out the root cause and the culprit. Access privileges should be judiciously granted on a need-to-know and need-to-do basis to ensure data is protected.

Authentication and Authorization

Authentication is the first step in granting access to a user for the resources. It is the process of identifying a user and verifying whether he/she is authorized to enter into the organizational network and access the resources. This is very similar to having a photo identification card check at the main entrance of the building. The user name and password are the most commonly used method to authenticate a user. The user name and password provides a relatively weak security as they can be stolen or guessed. Because of increasing threats to security, there are other methods introduced to complement the user name and passwords. Depending on the nature of business, one can consider implementing the appropriate authentication and authorization technique.

Authentication and authorization technologies involve:

- Proving who you are (identity card, smartcard)

- Verifying who you are (password, finger prints, etc.)

Authentication and Access Control Layers

Access control provides limits on who can access which resources and what he or she can do with it. The user needs to be identified before he can be given access to the organizational information. Access must first be granted by administrative policies, then the technical controls, and finally, physical access. There are various authentication techniques that organizations can implement and are broadly classified under three layers – administrative, technical, and physical, as shown in Figure 4-1.

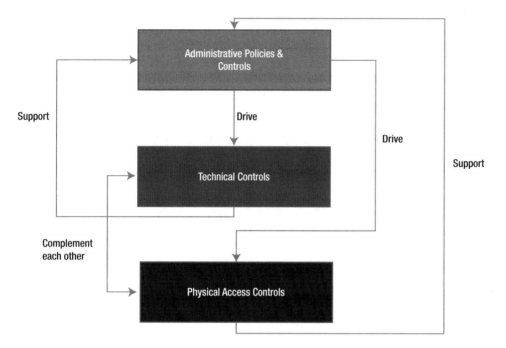

Figure 4-1. *Access control layers*

Administrative Access Controls (Layer)

These controls are administrative in nature and are required to prevent the risk of improper or inappropriate access control or detect such improper or inappropriate access controls. These are ensured through policies and processes; appropriate description of roles and responsibilities; and proper segregation of duties.

Access Control Policy

Each organization has to clearly specify its philosophy of access control which becomes the basis for all access control activities. The policy provides absolute clarity as to the access control models the organization believes in, such as "discretionary," "mandatory," "non-discretionary," or "hybrid". Some of the attributes of such a policy are the clarity as to whether authorization provided can be further delegated or not. The policy may specify the ground rules for classification of information which becomes the base for the access control. Even though the content and depth of the access control policy may differ from one organization to another, broadly speaking, all access control policies set the tone of the organization's intent and approach to access controls.

Personnel related – jobs, responsibilities, and authorities

Ideally, each job in the organization may require access to information for different purposes. Certain information must be only "read" by people so that they are aware of the information and/or for executing the information. Some others may require not only to "read" the information, but also to further "update" or "modify" it. Some others may require creation of new information, that is, "writing" the information to organizational repositories. Some may require all of these permissions. Again, there can be "individual" or "group" accesses defined based on the jobs and responsibilities. Authorities may rely on certain persons to further delegate their access or may clearly specify the contours of further delegation of access controls. Data owners are the ones who ideally decide on who, what, and when the data can be accessed, depending upon business requirements and enabling jobs, responsibilities, and authorities.

Segregation of duties

One of the important organizational requirements is to avoid fraud, such as that with financial connotation or frauds due to the violation of the organizational policies. For example, purchase value of an item increased by $1,000 may be a fraud from the perspective of financial implication, whereas the recruitment of a person by changing his qualification and experience or by editing a background verification report may be a violation of organization policy. Hence, it is necessary for there to be appropriate segregation of the duties where the policies have to be enforced and financial integrity has to be ensured. These responsibilities should lie with different individuals. Segregation of duties is traditionally one of the controls deployed by organizations and is important to be considered even while access authorization is provided.

Supporting policies and procedure

The organization also needs to ensure complementary controls through other supporting policies like the following: a) Hiring Policies, b) Disciplinary Policies, c) Employee Termination Policy, and d) User registration for computer access. These policies provide clear direction to the organizational personnel. For example, organizational hiring policies may clearly specify whom not to recruit, like those with criminal backgrounds and so on. Hiring policies may also specify the need for background clearance, such as address, criminal records, education, and earlier employment verification. Disciplinary policies may clearly specify which behaviors or acts of employees are not acceptable in the organization and what are the possible consequences of such violations. Similarly, an employee termination policy may specify when and for what reasons an employee's services may be terminated. The policy on user registration for computer access may clearly specify the reason for accessing the information, so that the access is provided only upon verification of that intent. Each such policy supports the organization to set the discipline required for providing access to and use of information.

Control Over Information Access to Trade Restricted Persons

If you consider U.S. export laws, a few of the employees or contractors of these organizations may be from trade restricted countries or working in trade restricted countries. Some of the high-end technology and related technical documentation/information may not be shared with such personnel unless a specific license to share such information is obtained from the competent authorities. Proper administrative controls need to be put in place to identify, determine, and control access to such persons to ensure compliance and confidentiality.

Technical (Logical) Controls

Technical controls are usually introduced through or on technological products, tools, or utilities. These again help the organization to either prevent or detect or contain inappropriate and improper access controls. Some of these are passwords, smart cards, encryption, network access controls, and system access controls.

Passwords

Traditionally, passwords were the only form of access control. However, passwords were also easily prone to being guessed or cracked either because of the ignorance of the users or because of the inappropriate implementation of these on the networks or operating systems or on the applications. Strong passwords are one of the absolute requirements in today's world which is technologically advanced and the technology can crack the passwords in a matter of seconds if they are found to be weak. The passwords can be "static," "dynamic," or a combination of both. A static password is one which is the same for each login. A dynamic password is one which is generated newly each time a user has to enter a password (normally generated using a soft token, a hard token, or by using SMS based interfaces). Some systems use a combination of both.

Smartcards

Smartcards normally complement password controls. These provide an additional layer of security by adding another layer to gain access. These may be implemented through various technologies like HID, RFID, or Chip-based smart cards.

Encryption

Data encryption protects information from the loss of confidentiality and integrity because it requires a key to decipher the encrypted information and this key is available only with the intended recipient. Encryption provides sufficient security to the information, either stored or transmitted, unless the encryption algorithm is weak, the encryption key is weak, or the encryption key is not well protected. Encryption, if well implemented, can provide access to only the authorized personnel.

Network Access

A network has many components like routers, switches, and cables. Network components are required to be hardened. Default passwords on them have to be changed. Strong authentication and handshake mechanisms have to be implemented in the network equipment like firewalls, intruder detection/prevention systems, and so on to ensure that only authorized users are allowed connections to be established, attempts by unauthorized users to penetrate are detected or declined. Network components have to ensure that they are establishing connections to only authentic or valid systems to which the connection is intended. Access to ports has to be provided for appropriately and all unwanted/unused ports have to be closed.

System Access

There are various levels of access possible to operating systems as well as to applications. These need to be set up appropriately on a need-to-know and a need-to-do basis. Giving administrative privilege to all users for operating systems can lead to serious infections or violations. Similarly, giving unlimited access to applications should be avoided or it will lead to serious integrity issues.

Physical Access Controls

Physical access controls are again one of the important layers of either preventive or detective controls which supplement or complement other forms of control in mitigating the risk of inappropriate or improper access and modifications to the information.

Network Segregation

For ease of understanding, let us assume that you are an IT service provider organization and you work for two competing banks. It is necessary that the information pertaining to one bank is not accidentally or intentionally accessed by the personnel who work for the other bank. Physical segregation of the two networks can help ensure high confidence to the customers.

Perimeter Security

Clearly identifying the organizational boundaries and ensuring that the perimeter is secured, restricts improper and inappropriate access to the organizational resources. Some of the important controls of use are electrical fences, microwave barriers, CCTV cameras, and sensor-based intrusion detection systems.

Security Guards

Security guards are the traditional sources of preventive and detective physical controls. Even today, these security guards provide the assurance of physical access controls by ensuring that the entry and exit controls are appropriately provided for and monitored. Activities such as the checking of identification cards/badges, ensuring that nobody tail gates employees, those without official badges are allowed access only after duly verifying their identity or visitors are allowed access only after due verification and where required only with an escort, monitoring the movement of employees and visitors in secure areas are some of the ways in which security guards are used. They can also ensure the securing and protecting of unlocked and unattended information assets like laptops. Other areas where they are used are for monitoring fire control panels and water leakages. However, for effective protection through security guards, proper background verification of these security guards needs to be ensured.

Badge Systems

Badges/identification cards are the traditional mechanisms used to control access and are still the popular means of providing access. Special/secure areas may require special types of badges or other complementary authentication mechanisms like smart cards, passwords, or biometric controls.

Biometric Access Controls

Biometric access controls use some physiological features/aspects of the human body to provide access to human beings. The features used to provide access differ from person to person such as finger print scans, iris scans, retina scans, palm scans, facial scans, and voice. Some of these, like finger prints and iris scans are widely used.

Access Control Strategies

Access control models are based on requirements, technology, and implementations. Different types of access control models exist. The most popular access control models are a Discretionary Access Control (DAC), Mandatory Access Control (MAC), Role Based Access Control (RBAC), and Attribute Based Access Control (ABAC).

Discretionary Access Control (DAC)

In this model, the access control is based on the owner's discretion. The owner of the resource can decide to whom he/she should grant permission to access, and exactly what they are allowed to access. This is the most common model used in most of the file sharing utilities both in the Microsoft operating system and in UNIX. The CHMOD command in UNIX allows the user to share the files in the network. In DAC, the permission is granted to those who need access and it is classified as a "need-to-know" access model. One of the examples of this type of implementation is Access Control Lists (ACLs).

Mandatory Access Control (MAC)

In the Mandatory Access Control (MAC) model, shown in Figure 4-2, usually a group or a set of people are provided access based on the clearance given to a specific level of access depending on the classification of information/data. For example, data that is "top secret" is available to a set of people based on their clearance level to access "top secret" documents. Such people also have clearance to access lower level classified information, but, lower level cleared employees will not have access to a higher level of classified information. This does not grant them access without any restriction. In such a system, they are required to access the documents or information only on a "need-to-know" or on a "need-to-use" basis to fulfil their job related responsibilities. We can often find this model implemented in government organizations where the access depends on the sensitivity of the documents (secret, top secret, etc.), and the responsibilities of the individuals who are working on the project are clearly defined.

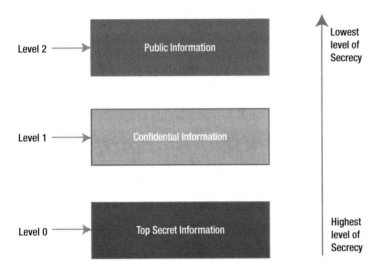

Figure 4-2. *Example of a Mandatory Access Control*

Role-Based Access Control (RBAC)

As the name suggests, access control is granted based on the roles and responsibilities of an individual working in the organization, that is, on a "need-to-do" or a "need-to-use" basis as shown in Figure 4-3. For example, an engineer's role would be restricted to accessing design documents and software. He can add, delete, or modify his own data or code but cannot access the project level or production data. Also, he will not have access to the HR database or financial database. To cite another example, a customer service representative might require access to payment status, shipping details, or previous order history, in order to assist customers and may have "read" only access to such data as he is not required to modify these. Similarly, a system administrator will have a more privileged access to the system than the rest of the employees. However, a system administrator may not have a "root" access and password, because it has been restricted by his manager. An RBAC is the best system for a company that has a high employee turnover.

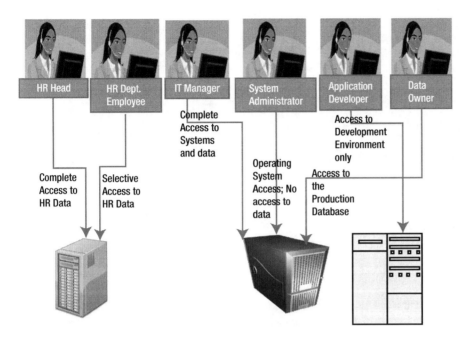

Figure 4-3. *A Role Based Access Control*

Attribute Based Access Control

Access can be granted using attributes – subject attributes like identity, roles; object attributes like device name, file, record, table, applications, programs, and network; environment conditions like location, time, and the like as shown in Figure 4-4. When the role assigned to a subject is used as the single attribute to control access, it is known as a Role Based Access Control (RBAC). An Attribute Based Access Control (ABAC) provides access on the basis of multiple attributes. NIST special publication 800-162:[1] "Guide to Attribute Based Access Control (ABAC) Definition and Considerations" defines RBAC as "an access control method where subject requests to perform operations on objects are granted or denied based on assigned attributes of the subject, assigned attributes of the object, environmental conditions, and a set of policies that are specified in terms of those attributes and conditions."

---

[1]NIST special publication 800-162.

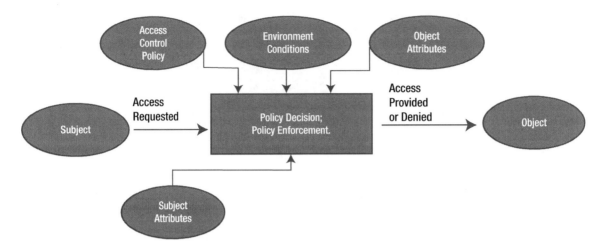

Figure 4-4. ABAC Access Control Mechanism

Unlike identity based ACLs and the role based RBAC, ABAC does not attach access to either subjects or to roles directly. ABAC can dynamically check for various rules based on the subjects, objects, and other attributes specified and decide on granting access depending on a set of rules or policies specified in terms of those attributes and conditions. Rules or policies decide what operations are allowed for which type of subject on which type of objects and under what conditions. Operations can be read, written, deleted, modified, edited, and executed. ABAC allows policies, subjects, or objects to be created and managed separately yet relating them dynamically during the granting of access. Access Control Mechanisms make the decisions whether or not to grant access based on the applicable policies and attributes. The current global corporate setup with diversities and complicated structures, where multiple organizations work together collaboratively, the subject based access control policies and role based access control policies are difficult to be implemented effectively with respect to the intent of access controls. Of course, ABAC is not as simple and straight forward to implement. It is complex but very useful in providing better access controls. Some of the examples of ABAC are: Extensible Access Control Markup Language (XACML) and the Next Generation Access Control standard.[1]

Implementing Access Controls

In the following section we have described different mechanisms used for implementing access controls effectively.

Access Control Lists (ACLs)

Access Control Lists are the primitive choice for implementing access to network resources. These are implemented in the devices that provide access to a network. A network device or a computer system is configured with the rights that need to be provided to each user to each item on the network. Each resource has two basic rules – deny and allow. When an ACL is configured, for example, user1 is allowed to access a specific server in the network whereas user2 is denied access to the same server. This may seem like a simplistic approach, but the implementation may have several complex rules. Two levels of ACLs are implemented – file system level ACLs and Network level ACLs.

File System ACLs

Files have three basic rights – read, write, and execute, respectively allowing a user to read the contents of a file, write to the file, and execute the file if it is a program application or a script capable of running on the system. Further, the file access can be given at the user level as well as the group level. If a user belongs to a particular group, he or she has certain access to files and vice versa. In the case of file systems, a file or a directory may also have multiple access rules attached to it. In UNIX (and many other operating systems), access permission for every file and directory is controlled by two identifications – the User Identification number (UID) and the Group Identification number (GID). Every user has a unique user name and is a member of at least one group. This information is stored in a password file. Only the administrator can create or modify a user name and its permissions.

An example of the output that is produced by the 'ls –l' command is shown in Figure 4-5.

```
root@machinename: /var

root@machinename var#ls -l
total 48
drwxr-xr-x  2 root root     4096 Apr 19 12:09 backups
drwxr-xr-x 19 root root     4096 Apr 15 20:06 cache
drwxrwsrwt  2 root whoopsie 4096 Jul 18 07:35 crash
drwxr-xr-x 70 root root     4096 Apr 16 12:44 lib
drwxrwsr-x  2 root staff    4096 Oct 14  2013 local
lrwxrwxrwx  1 root root        9 Jan  6  2014 lock -> /run/lock
drwxr-xr-x 17 root root     4096 Jul 24 07:52 log
drwxrwsr-x  2 root mail     4096 Oct 17  2013 mail
drwxrwsrwt  2 root whoopsie 4096 Oct 17  2013 metrics
drwxr-xr-x  2 root root     4096 Oct 17  2013 opt
lrwxrwxrwx  1 root root        4 Jan  6  2014 run -> /run
drwxr-xr-x  8 root root     4096 Jan 27 16:39 spool
drwxrwxrwt  2 root root     4096 Jul 23 22:26 tmp
drwxr-xr-x  2 root root     4096 Apr 16 13:15 www
root@machinename var#
```

Figure 4-5. *ls – l command*

Field 1: A set of permission flags
Field 2: Link count
Field 3: Owner of the file
Field 4: Associated group
Field 5: Size of a file in bytes
Field 6–8: Date and Time of the last modification
Field 9: Name of the file

Network ACLs

Network ACLs, shown in Figure 4-6, provide secured access to a network. It acts as a network filter to filter out unnecessary traffic. It is not as sophisticated as a firewall or other network security devices, however, it provides the basic access security to a network. ACL filter enables you to control traffic into and out of your network. This control is as simple as permitting or denying hosts inside the organizational network. ACLs are normally configured at the access device such as routers or switches. When a packet arrives at the router, the router extracts the ACL rules and based on the ACL rule, the packet is permitted or denied (dropped). ACL is implemented at the network layer of the TCP/IP and OSI model.

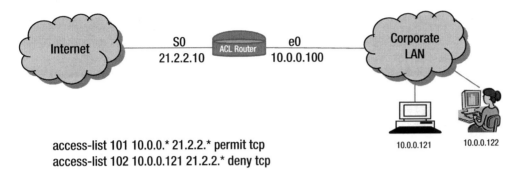

access-list 101 10.0.0.* 21.2.2.* permit tcp
access-list 102 10.0.0.121 21.2.2.* deny tcp

Figure 4-6. *Example of Network ACL*

ACLs consist of the permit/deny rule, source IP address, destination IP address, and the traffic type (IP or TCP). As soon as a packet enters the network, its source and destination addresses are checked against the ACL rule and based on the rule packet, it is either permitted or denied into the network. Advanced rules also check for the type of traffic. For example, the FTP uses TCP port 21 to transfer files and the Internet Message Access Protocol (IMAP) uses port 143, and secured e-mail port 22.

AAA Framework

Authentication, Authorization, and Accounting (AAA), shown in Figure 4-7, is a security framework to support secured access to a network through the security services – Authorization, Authentication, and Accounting.

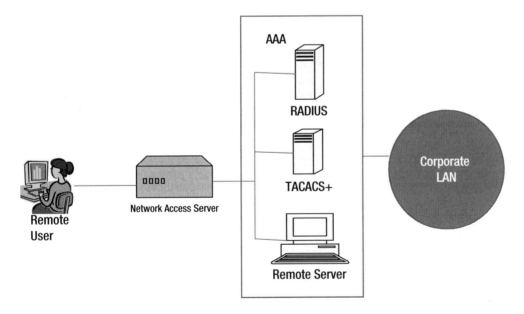

Figure 4-7. *AAA configuration*

Authentication refers to the process of identifying and verifying a particular user by his profile such as the user name, password, phone number, digital signature, and digital certificates. Authentication is the way a user is identified and verified prior to being allowed access to particular resources inside an organizational network and its resources. After the authentication, a user's authorized credentials are checked to provide the secured access.

Authorization determines whether a particular user is authorized to perform certain activities on the resources. Typically, this function is inherited from authentication when a user logs on to an application or a network. When a user logs on to the network, he is checked for his authorization credentials such as time restrictions, resource access restrictions, multiple access or single access, and same user logging from multiple locations at the same time.

Accounting provides resource utilization information related to users for the purpose of billing and cost allocation. By enabling the accounting feature, you can collect user identities, number of bytes transmitted and received, commands executed on the servers, and start and end times, for the purpose of a security audit.

AAA uses protocols such as RADIUS, TACACS+, or Kerberos to administer access controls. A typical configuration of AAA is as shown in Figure 4-7.

RADIUS and TACAS+

Remote Authentication Dial-in-User Service (RADIUS) is a protocol enabling centralized AAA for network access. RADIUS protocol supports authentication, authorization, and accounting for remote dial-in access, virtual private network (VPN) access, Digital Subscriber Line (DSL) access, and other network access. The RADIUS protocol is described in RFC 2865 and RFC 2866.

RADIUS is a client/server protocol. A central RADIUS server authenticates RADIUS clients which try to access the network and its resources. The RADIUS server maintains user profiles and server access information in a central database, thus providing better access control security. It also allows companies to setup and maintain policies that can be applied to each user and to track resource usage for billing and for recording network statistics.

TACACS (Terminal Access Control System) is an authentication protocol commonly used in UNIX networks to allow a remote user to access the network after authenticating his login credentials. RADIUS uses UDP whereas TACACS+ uses TCP. Hence, many system administrators recommend TACACS+ because TCP is a reliable protocol. RADIUS combines authentication and authorization in a user profile, whereas TACACS+ separates the two functions. For more details, you can refer to RFC 1492.

LDAP and Active Directory

The Lightweight Directory Access Protocol (LDAP) is an application level protocol that defines the method by which information across an organization can be accessed. LDAP is often used by organizations to store user information for authentication and authorization purpose. It is also used for storing "roles" for information for application users.

LDAP is based on a client/server model. Any client accessing the network resources or an application must first authenticate itself to the LDAP server. Once the LDAP server authenticates the client and checks its resource authorization, only then is access permitted to the client. LDAP implementation can be based on RFC 1777, RFC 4510, RFC 4511, and RFC 2251.

The main benefit of LDAP is that rather than managing user lists for different applications and login IDs to access networks, LDAP can be used as a central directory where any user can be authenticated and authorized from anywhere on the network.

Active Directory is an LDAP compliant database and services are developed by Microsoft. This provides authentication and authorization services. An Active Directory stores information of the user, system, resource, or group as an object and is managed centrally. The objects are organized into organizational units (OUs) and are linked by Group Policy (GP) settings. Active Directory is a trademark of Microsoft service and is an integral part of the Windows 2000 architecture.

IDAM

Identity and Access Management (IDAM), shown in Figure 4-8, refers to the processes, technologies and policies for managing digital identities and providing authentication and authorization controls to ensure data integrity. An IDAM solution enables a single identity across organizations as well as partner networks.

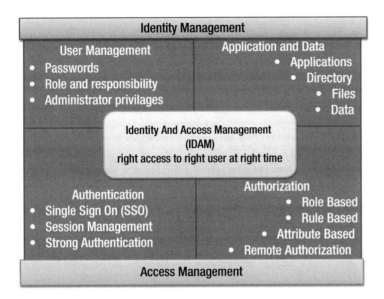

Figure 4-8. *The IDAM Framework*

An IDAM solution helps organizations to protect resources from unauthorized access, and to comply with security regulations. The goal of IDAM is to provide the right information to the right user at right time.

IDAM is comprised of people, processes, and policies to manage user identity and access in an enterprise network. IDAM can be classified into four major categories: authentication, authorization, user management, and data management as shown above. The ultimate goal of IDAM is to provide secured access to the right user, to the right information, at the right time.

Active Directory (AD), Single Sign-On (SSO), Password Manager, Security Token Services (STS), OAuth, and RBAC are technologies and are related to the implementation of IDAM solutions.

Single sign-on (SSO) is a user authentication process that permits a user to enter his credentials only once in order to access multiple applications. The SSO process authenticates the user for all the applications that he has the rights to and eliminates the process of entering the login id and password when they switch to a different application during a particular session.

Chapter Summary

We examined what authentication and authorization mean. We explored the importance of access controls and the need for an access control in the context of confidentiality and integrity requirements.

We described the different access control types like network access, system access, and data access. Furthermore, we specified the three layers of access controls: administrative layer, technical (logical) layer, and the physical layer. Each of these layers serve as important mechanisms to control access to valuable information. Then, important access control methods like Discretionary Access Control (DAC), Mandatory Access Control (MAC), Role Based Access Control (RBAC), and Attribute Based Access Control (ABAC) were explored. Where required, the pros and cons of these are explained.

We discussed how the effective access controls can be implemented technically. Access Control Lists, AAA Framework, RADIUS and TACAS+, LDAP and Active Directory, and the IDAM Framework were explained in detail with supporting diagrams. Single Sign-On (SSO) as an important component of IDAM Framework was also explained.

CHAPTER 5

■ ■ ■

Information Systems Management

Introduction

Today's world is complex. Organizational environment is becoming increasingly complicated with the integration of various technologies to provide better business delivery. While one's need of effective and efficient delivery is fulfilled through the means of new technologies, such as internet, video, audio, business presentations, and business meetings, interplaying with each other, the other need requires more focus and strengthening, that is, information security. Businesses have to protect the confidentiality, and the integrity of business information while making their systems available for continued business. A few minutes of down time of an e-commerce business site can lead to a significant amount of missed business or switching over of the business to a competitive supplier. A breach of confidentiality or integrity can lead to reputation loss, huge penalties, or significant revenue loss. To ensure information security, we need to act proactively.

When pro-activeness does not stop the breaches, we need to react effectively and efficiently and when breaches cannot be avoided we need to recover the businesses as fast as possible to provide continued services to the customers. Risk Management when applied in the right spirit, with the deployment of the right methodology, with the involvement of the right people, with the application of the right thinking, and with the execution of the actions effectively, can provide a reasonably good proactive approach to ensure that there is a high chance of avoiding information security breaches or incidents. In spite of being proactive, we cannot be assured that the security breaches cannot happen, as this evolving world provides a lot of opportunities and ways to breach the system. Incident response provides a reactive method to ensure that the breaches are handled, contained, and recovered from effectively. In spite of effective risk management and incident response systems in place, you cannot still be assured of continuity of business or speedy recovery when the organization is affected by severe security breaches or disasters. Hence the need for effective disaster recovery and business continuity systems to be put in place which is again a proactive as well as a reactive system to ensure that the business can still continue in spite of disasters or severe security incidents when there is high probability of speedy recovery. Most of the businesses may go out of business or may lose a significant number of customers if they are not able to recover within a reasonable time frame. Similarly, some of the businesses cannot sustain a short period of lack of availability of systems as some of their business is highly critical and needs to be continued at any cost even at a reduced level of activity / volume.

An effective risk management approach supported by an effective and efficient incident response, supported by an effective and efficient disaster recovery and business continuity system can ensure that the businesses are able to sustain and provide continued services to their clients in spite of serious security breaches or disasters.

Unfortunately, there are hundreds of theories proposed by the experts and varied practices employed by various organizations with respect to risk management, incident response, disaster recovery, and business continuity. The definition of each of these words, from incident to disaster to recovery to continuity varies from theory to theory. In order not to confuse our readers with too many theories and too many definitions we are providing here simple definitions in simple terms with respect to each of these as well as a simple and practical way of handling each of these, which in our view is suitable to most of the organizations in this world. Further, each of the aspects like Risk Management, Incident Response, and Business Continuity Planning can be strongly supported or advocated through a policy driving the same with clear commitment from top management. However, as we have seen, such policies are merely put in place either because of the requirement of a standard or because of some customer insistence without much thinking and most of the time not revisited for years and are not referred to by the organizational personnel and losing the requisite sanctity. Hence, we have not focused in this chapter much on the policies except with regard to Incident Response Policy which we have included here as guidance.

Risk

Risk is the chance of something adverse happening which has negative consequences on the organization and in the context of this book on information security.

Incident

Any event of consequence to the organization where the organization faces potential loss or is exposed to potential loss can be considered as an incident. Loss can be monetary, business, reputation or loss of customers.

Disaster

Any grave situation which brings down the business partially or fully and which is of serious consequence to the organization can be considered as a disaster. These often may be on account of natural disasters but sometimes these may be on account of manmade activities like terrorism or at other times, they can be on account of severe security incidents like a severe infection of malware crashing all the critical servers. In a way, disasters can be considered more severe than an incident.

Disaster Recovery

Businesses are ongoing and they are meant to be ongoing or continuous entities. Businesses have competitors who always want to take away others' customers or the market share. Businesses hence have to recover their businesses from each disaster speedily so that they are able to service their customers effectively before they plan to switch over to the competitor. Even though disaster recovery can mean any recovery from any disaster, many times it is referred to in the parlance of recovery of IT infrastructure and systems, which in today's context performs a lead role in any business.

Business Continuity

All businesses are ongoing entities. It may be acceptable for a business which is non-critical to its customers to be shut down for a few days but a critical business like banking, health care, telecommunications, e-commerce, and others cannot be shut down for more than a few minutes to more than a few days depending on the business. Hence, they need to continue to sustain the continuity of the critical business may be at a lower scale or volume than the normal scale or volume. Business continuity assures that the plans and systems are in place to continue the business in spite of incidents or disasters. Business continuity includes business recovery post any disaster and is one of the important components as the speed at which you recover from downtime or disruption or disaster and continue business is critical for the success of any organization.

Risk Management

Risk is the chance that something can go wrong or of an adverse event taking place. In the context of information security, risk is something which can impact the availability, confidentiality, or integrity of business or personnel information. Examples of some of the common risks include: laptops being stolen and the data on them being stolen, a person tail gating somebody stealing some critical files, or a person who got the credentials through social engineering means gaining access to the server and copying confidential data, or somebody tapping into the network and modifying the messages being sent, or somebody physically stoning or ransacking the building during a riot, or that of natural hazards like floods. Threats are the risks. Risks need to be proactively managed.

There are various methodologies to carry out risk assessments by the organization. Organizations are also free to come up with their own risk assessment methodologies depending upon their context and their experience. We are exploring one such methodology that is easy to use and practical and has been effectively used for some time.

First, risks need to be identified. Then they need to be analyzed for the probability of their occurrence and the impact if they do happen. Based on the probability of their occurrence and the impact if they happen, the risk exposure or risk level has to be decided. Depending upon the risk exposure of the organization to any particular risk, the risk has to be either avoided, transferred, mitigated, or accepted. Risk can be accepted only when the organization is exposed to minimal risk that it can sustain. Where the risks are decided to be mitigated, additional controls to mitigate them have to be determined. It is normally necessary at this point to determine the additional controls, but it is also extremely important to ensure that these controls are effectively deployed and their continued effectiveness is monitored and ensured. Organizational internal and external context may vary from time to time, maybe due to a competitor environment or due to legal changes or may be due to the way the business is done or else due to the technological changes.

The risks in the revised context need to be analyzed and additional controls need to be implemented as required to ensure that the organization continues to drive sufficient controls to protect information security. It is recommended that each organization has its own clearly defined risk assessment methodology which drives the risk assessment in the organization. This should cover the entire process of risk assessment including the acceptable risk exposure value and guidelines on various risk responses. Figure 5-1 illustrates the risk assessment life cycle.

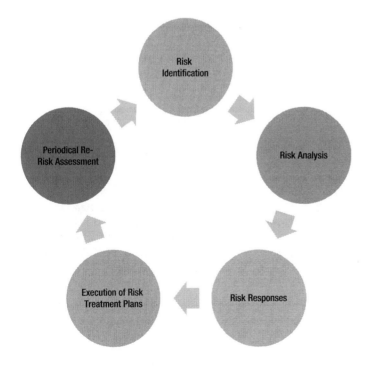

Figure 5-1. *Risk Assessment Life Cycle*

Again, we have seen some organizations using the asset value to calculate the total financial impact. We have seen this approach failing mostly because of lack of accurate asset value. Further, some organizations also try to assess the business impact of the risks in financial terms. Again, as we have seen, it turns out to be mostly guess work rather than based on uniform, good, prudent ways.

In view of the preceding information, we have provided a simple, practical way that works for most of the organizations, which at the same time uses best in class practices from various guidelines and standards including from ISO/IEC 27001:2013 – Information Security Management System – Requirements.

Identification of Risk

The first step to identify the risks in the context of information security is to identify all the information assets of the organization. Information assets include the infrastructure, facilities, hardware, software, applications, utilities and tools, data, employees, contractors, and suppliers which are needed to run any business.

Table 5-1 lists typical information assets that are found in organizations.

Table 5-1. *Typical Information Assets*

Function	Information Asset
Human Resources	Employee Personal Records (with PII); Other Employee Records (Offer Letters, CVs, Offer Letters, Certificates, Performance Appraisal, etc.); Human Resources Management System; Employees (may be further categorized based on type of employees); Suppliers/Third Party Vendors; Recruitment Test Papers and Answer Keys; etc.
Training	Training Material; Training Quiz/Test Papers; Training Feedback and Analysis; Online Tools used for the Training; etc.
Marketing & Sales	Proposals; Marketing Strategies, Marketing Plans; Communications with the Customers including on the scope of new projects, pricing, etc.; Visit Plans of the departmental personnel; etc.
Project Management & Project Teams (including Product Development Teams / Engineering Teams)	Proposals; Communications with the Customers; Customer Provided Property such as Hardware; Customer Provided Information/Data; Project Artifacts; Applications; Utilities; Open Source Software; Third Party Software; Software Code Developed; New Concepts/Innovations yet to be patented; New Processes Invented; Design Documents, Architecture Documents; etc.
Information Technology	Desktops/Workstations; Laptops; Servers; Printers; Communication Equipment; CD/DVD Writers/Tape Drive; Backup Tapes; Scanners; External Hard-disks/USB Pen Drives; Original Licenses/License Keys; Network Cabling; Firewall, Router & Log Analyzer; ISP/External Connectivity; Physical Keys; Specific Servers like Anti-Virus Servers, Application Servers, Database Servers, Patch Management Server, FTP Server etc.; Other utilities used like Remote Connectivity Tools, Monitoring Tools, etc.; Logs of various servers/applications, system administrator activity logs; Encryption Keys; Root and other Administrative logins and passwords; etc.

(continued)

Table 5-1. (*continued*)

Function	Information Asset
Finance & Legal	Vendor Agreements/Contracts; Financial/Banking Details/Records; Statutory Records including Notices received, Cases Pending, etc.; Financial Instruments; Payroll, Tax and such other details; Digital Signatures; Login Ids and Passwords of Authorized Persons authorized to carry out different types of tasks on tools like SAP, Oracle Financials, etc.; Compliance Filings; Various reports filed with various statutory and regulatory agencies, etc.
Quality	Process Documents; Quality Records including Audit Records, Management Review Records and other records; Testing Records; Defect Details; Best Known Methods; etc.

Note: a) The functions mentioned are only sample functions and the organizations may have more functions than the above or may be differently organized; b) Some of the above assets may be again bucketed into common, specific depending upon the differential risks e.g. management laptops have different risks compared to the clerical laptops; Customer-provided data like Patient Details, Credit Card details have different risks than the data without much sensitivity like generic data like details of the machines on the shop floor, etc., c) Again, the records / documents may be classified as hard copy records / documents or soft copy records / documents as they carry different risks; d) Tools / Utilities may have to be classified separately depending upon the purpose and their capability; etc.; e) Above list is not comprehensive. It is only illustrative. There may be hundreds of other documents / records / tools / utilities etc. which may be included which may also differ from organization to organization.

The second step is to identify the threats the organization is exposed to with respect to each function within the organization. This may be done based on the historical data with the organization; or data obtained from the local and / or regional and / or national and / or international agencies or institutes of relevance or other sources of learned and reliable information. Additionally, expertise of the organizational employees, contractors, and suppliers is used. Another way is to identify the vulnerabilities the organization is exposed to like tail gating, lack of effective policies, lack of awareness / knowledge, technical vulnerabilities like security flaws in the utilities or applications used, the organization location, and so on, and then identify the threats which may exploit these vulnerabilities. Another way is to identify the threats first and then identify the vulnerabilities which may lead to such threats. However, it is necessary to identify various pairs of threats and vulnerabilities an information asset is exposed to. Each information asset may be exposed to different vulnerabilities which may lead to different threats or each threat may be due to different vulnerabilities. Also, different vulnerabilities may sometimes lead to the same threat. For example, a fire threat may result from storing old paper records and inflammable material in the organization, the kitchen being allowed to use electric or gas stoves, or weak wiring.

A vulnerability of not having adequate awareness of policies may allow some non-employee to tail gate an employee which can lead the stranger to steal confidential files or papers, destroying the data center by planting a bomb, firing at the employees, or killing the employees. This makes clear the need for identifying different sets of vulnerabilities and threats.

Some of the typical pairs of threats and vulnerabilities are listed in Table 5-2.

Table 5-2. *Threats and Vulnerabilities*

Threat	Vulnerability
Malicious Destruction	Lack of Physical Security
Theft and Fraud	Lack of Physical Security
Fire	Lack of Environmental Protection
Flood	Lack of Environmental Protection
Misplace / Loss of Documents	Inadequate Document / File Handling Procedures
Malicious Destruction	Incorrect Access Rights
Theft and Fraud	Incorrect Access Rights
Data Corruption & Loss of Data	Lack of Backups
Theft and Fraud	Access of Production Data to Application Maintenance Engineers
Theft and Fraud	Lack of effective software change management leading to unauthorized changes
Theft and Fraud	Lack of Segregation of Duties
Misuse of Equipment and Facilities	Inconsistent Compliance with Security Policies
Access of Facilities / Systems / Applications / Data by Ex-Employee or others and Possible Thefts and Frauds	Lack of Proper Exit Procedures
Technical Vulnerability	Inadequate Configuration
Undesirable Impact	Inadequate Patch Validation
Malicious Software Infection	Lack of Adequate Monitoring Mechanisms
Malicious Software Infection	Technical Incompatibility
Prey to Social Engineering Tricks	Inadequate Security Awareness & Training
Misuse of credentials	Infrequent change of passwords / Weak Passwords
Technical Failures	Improper / Inappropriate Maintenance
Intrusion / Unauthorized Data Access	Inadequate Firewall / Router Policies
Single Point of Failure	Lack of Redundancy
Service Deficiency	Choice of Wrong Service Provider

Note: a) Above list is only illustrative. It is impossible to cover all threats and vulnerabilities; b) The Threats and Vulnerability applicability depends upon the Information Asset.

The third step is to identify each information asset, the pair of threat and vulnerability, the impact on each of the aspects of information security, that is, confidentiality, integrity, and availability. This can be a rating provided to each information asset, for each pair of threat and vulnerability, in terms of the impact on each of the information security aspects (confidentiality, integrity and availability) that can be compromised or breached. Table 5-3 describes the potential impact on security objectives.[1]

Table 5-3. *Levels of Impact on Security Objectives*[1]

Security Objective	Low Impact	Medium Impact	High Impact
Confidentiality	The unauthorized disclosure of information could be expected to have a limited adverse effect on organizational operations, organizational assets, or individuals.	The unauthorized disclosure of information could be expected to have a serious adverse effect on organizational operations, organizational assets, or individuals.	The unauthorized disclosure of information could be expected to have a severe or catastrophic adverse effect on organizational operations, organizational assets, or individuals.
Integrity	The unauthorized modification or destruction of information could be expected to have a limited adverse effect on organizational operations, organizational assets, or individuals.	The unauthorized modification or destruction of information could be expected to have a serious adverse effect on organizational operations, organizational assets, or individuals.	The unauthorized modification or destruction of information could be expected to have a severe or catastrophic adverse effect on organizational operations, organizational assets, or individuals
Availability	The disruption of access to or use of information or an information system could be expected to have a limited adverse effect on organizational operations, organizational assets, or individuals.	The disruption of access to or use of information or an information system could be expected to have a serious adverse effect on organizational operations, organizational assets, or individuals.	The disruption of access to or use of information or an information system could be expected to have a severe or catastrophic adverse effect on organizational operations, organizational assets, or individuals.
Amplification	A limited adverse effect means that, for example, the loss of confidentiality, integrity, or availability might: (i) cause a degradation in organizational capability to an extent and duration that the organization is able to perform its primary functions, but the effectiveness of the functions is noticeably reduced; (ii) result in minor damage to organizational assets; (iii) result in minor financial loss; or (iv) result in minor harm to individuals.	A serious adverse effect means that, for example, the loss of confidentiality, integrity, or availability might: (i) cause a significant degradation in organizational capability to an extent and duration that the organization is able to perform its primary functions, but the effectiveness of the functions is significantly reduced; (ii) result in significant damage to organizational assets; (iii) result in significant financial loss; or (iv) result in significant harm to individuals that does not involve loss of life or serious life threatening injuries.	A severe or catastrophic adverse effect means that, for example, the loss of confidentiality, integrity, or availability might: (i) cause a severe degradation in or loss of organizational capability to an extent and duration that the organization is not able to perform one or more of its primary functions; (ii) result in major damage to organizational assets; (iii) result in major financial loss; or (iv) result in severe or catastrophic harm to individuals involving loss of life or serious life threatening injuries.

Low impact on any security objective is given a value of 1, medium impact on any security objective is given a value of 2 and high impact on any security objective is given a value of 3. If any security objective is not applicable to the information asset under consideration then it is given a value of 0. For each information asset, for each pair of threat and vulnerability, the impact value for confidentiality plus the impact value for the integrity plus the impact value for availability gives the total asset impact value. Asset impact is optionally categorized as C1, C2, C3 based on the following total asset impact values listed in Table 5-4.

Table 5-4. *Asset Category Classification Based on Asset Impact Value*

Asset Impact Category	Total Asset Impact Value
C1 – High impact asset	Total Asset Impact Value of 7 or 8 or 9
C2 – Medium impact asset	Total Asset Impact Value of 4 or 5 or 6
C3 – Low impact asset	Total Asset Impact Value of 1 or 2 or 3

The fourth step is to identify the controls already implemented by the organization to manage this risk. These controls may be physical security like security guards; awareness sessions wherein the employees are made aware of the do's and don'ts or specific steps to be taken to avoid, control, and mitigate the risks; or implementation of a tool in the organization like a firewall that eliminates such a risk.

Risk Analysis

Risk analysis is the next important step. At the end of the risk analysis we need to quantify the risk in terms of quantified risk exposure. This is different from the impact levels on confidentiality, integrity, and availability we discussed in the earlier paragraphs.

For a particular information asset, for each of the pair of threat and vulnerability, we identify the actual impact on the business. For example, a banking server compromised and misused may impact the entire business severely, including potential loss of customer confidence, reputation loss, loss of data integrity, or monetary loss. Then we determine the probability of this risk (also known as the likelihood of risk), as shown in Table 5-5. Probability of the rating is from 1% to 99%. A probability of 100% means that the risk is already true and has already occurred.

Table 5-5. *Risk Probability Ratings*

Probability	Description	Probability Value
Almost certain	Several times a week or day	5
Likely	More than once per month	4
Moderate	Up to several times a year	3
Unlikely	2–5 times every 5 years	2
Rare	Unlikely to occur	1

Then for each pair of threat and vulnerability we identify the possibility of detection and assign a rating in a scale of 1 to 5. However, here the lower the possibility of detection, the higher the rating and the higher the possibility of detection the lower the rating, as shown in Table 5-6.

Table 5-6. *Possible Detection Ratings*

Possibility of detection	Description	Probability Value
Extremely Low	Probability of detection is 0 to 20 %	5
Low	Probability of detection is 21 to 40 %	4
Medium	Probability of detection is 41 to 60 %	3
High	Probability of detection is 61 to 80 %	2
Extremely High	Probability of detection is 81 to 100 %	1

Once all three (total asset value, probability of occurrence and the rating for the possibility of detection) are determined for each of the threat and vulnerability pairs, then the risk exposure is quantified using the following formula:

```
Risk Exposure = Total Asset Impact Value x Probability of Occurrence x Possibility of Detection
```

The organization should have decided the risk exposure it considers as acceptable as a part of the risk assessment methodology adopted by it. It should not be too high that it leads to acceptance of every risk and it should not be too low that it leads to compulsory mitigation, avoidance, or transfer of every risk. Organizations are free to set their own acceptable risk xposure threshold depending upon their risk appetite.

Risk Responses

For each pair of threat and vulnerability, the calculated risk exposure is compared with the risk exposure considered acceptable to the organization (i.e., acceptable risk exposure). Where the risk exposure is less than the acceptable risk exposure, the risks are normally accepted by the organization and no further action is taken.

Acceptable risk exposure is decided by the organization as per its risk assessment methodology. Normally, this is the value of risk exposure below which the organization perceives the risks need not be focused on as the risks are very low and not worth pursuing.

There may be some other risks that the organizational management may want to consciously accept, such as the organization may allow mobile phones with cameras to be brought into the organization even though there is a risk that the cameras may be misused. The risk exposure in this case may be more than the acceptable risk exposure value. But, the organization may want to accept the risk because of its belief in the employees, considering other positive uses of mobile phones, not to demotivate the employees. Such practices of accepting the risk or not accepting the risk based on a specific context differ widely from organization to organization. As we have seen, some organizations may be very conservative in accepting the risks whereas other organizations may be relatively liberal in this regard when it particularly relates to inconveniencing the employees.

If the risk exposure is more than the acceptable risk exposure value then either the risk has to be avoided by mistake proofing (i.e., by implementing such measures that eliminate the possibility of such a risk occurring at all, such as if there is an unused entry or exit – mistake proofing is done by locking and sealing it permanently), the risk has to be transferred to others, or the risk has to be mitigated. Some of the possibilities of the transference of risk is to take up insurance for the risk of loss from fire or transference of risk of ineffectiveness or inefficiency through outsourcing of the work to the experts in that area. However, transference of risk is not possible in most of the cases.

Where the risks are not possible to be either avoided or to be transferred then they need to be mitigated. Mitigation is carried out by determining additional controls to be implemented. These controls may be awareness training, or may be implementation of a tool to monitor and provide alerts so that timely actions can be taken, or may be implementation of methods and techniques like encryption, or may be implementation of a security certificate for the URL, or may be introduction of additional validations and / or exception flows in the application software, or implementation of better processes. The additional controls implemented should be such that they have either the capability to reduce the probability of occurrence or reduce the impact or increase the probability of detection or a combination of these. These additional controls or actions implemented should have to be assigned in such a way that there is high probability that the risk exposure is reduced below the acceptable value of risk subsequent to the implementation of the additional controls. All the additional controls to be implemented including the risk avoidance and risk transfer actions have to be assigned to relevant owners for effective actions.

Perceived risk exposure post implementation of additional controls should be collated against the existing risk to understand whether the additional controls are likely to bring the risk below the acceptable risk exposure value. Where it is perceived that the additional controls are unlikely to reduce the risk exposure below the acceptable value, the risks are to be brought to the attention of senior management of the organization and approval has to be obtained for bearing the residual risk.

Execution of the Risk Treatment Plans

The risk treatment plans (actions on account of earlier steps) are assigned through an Excel sheet or organizational action tracking tool to the respective owners and are tracked through the same on a regular basis. It is essential that the requisite focus and attention is provided by the management to ensure that these actions are invariably taken. Otherwise, the entire risk management exercise will be futile. Risk owners not only execute the necessary actions, but also ensure that the necessary processes to implement them effectively are defined and everybody (as relevant and required) is trained on those processes. Awareness of the risks and the actions required to be taken by all (as relevant and required) are also made known to everybody. The assigned action owners, upon implementation of the actions, check for the revised probability of occurrence, revised impact rating, and revised rate of detection. Where the risk exposure upon effective implementation of controls has not led to lowering the risk exposure below the acceptable risk value, then additional controls have to be implemented. Management has to be kept informed of the necessity and implementation of such actions so that requisite resources are deployed and the support is accorded for their effective implementation.

The Importance of Conducting a Periodic Risk Assessment

The organizational risk scenario changes when the business changes, the infrastructure changes, the technology deployed changes, and the competence of the personnel changes. These changes cannot be ignored, as these have the potential to impact the effectiveness of the controls already implemented and change the earlier risk profile of the organization. Whenever such significant changes are carried out by the organization or on a periodical basis (ideally on a six month to maximum of annual basis), re-risk assessment has to be carried out across the organization, and additional controls as required have to be determined and implemented. Proactive approach in this regard ensures that the effectiveness of the controls is maintained.

Figure 5-2 shows detail from a template that may be used for a risk assessment.

Information Asset	Threat	Vulnerability	Current Controls	Impact Description	Impact on Confidentiality Rating	Impact on Integrity Rating	Impact on Availability Rating	Total Asset Impact Value	Probability of Occurrence	Possibility of Detection

Figure 5-2. *Risk Assessment Template (detail)*

Incident Response

Before we discuss incident response, we need to be able to differentiate between three aspects: information security weakness, information security event, and information security incident.

To cite an example, suppose an employee tailgates another employee without swiping in his access card. This is a security event but cannot be considered as a security incident as the employee would have otherwise also come inside by obtaining a temporary access card if he had forgotten his access card. Suppose the tailgating is done by an ex-employee or a stranger. Then it is a security incident as it has the potential of leading to loss or disruption etc. Information security weakness in this case may be that once the employee has swiped his access card and gets into the organization the door takes a lot of time to close and lock down. Information security weakness may be that a utility you are using in the organization has a security loophole. Information security weaknesses if left unattended may lead to information security incidents. All the information security events may not be information security incidents but need to be evaluated to check whether they point towards a possibility of an information security incident. For example, a log shows that somebody was trying to access one of our servers from outside the organization. On checking, you may find that it was one of the employees who had authorization to have access to that information. Hence, it was an information security event which you cannot ignore, but upon evaluation you found that it is not an information security incident.

Potential security incidents need to be proactively protected against but some of the security incidents cannot be protected against like the unknown vulnerabilities in an application or operating system or a new virus or worm attack. However, where it is not possible to proactively protect against these we need to have alerting or detective mechanisms which alert us to the possibility of a security incident. For example a newly downloaded program is behaving suspiciously as found by your anti-virus or anti-malware tool. You need to check for what kind of suspicious activities are carried out by it, where it was downloaded from, and whether it is performing as intended, before you decide to act on it. Firewalls, IDS/IPS, anti-virus, and anti-malware software are some of the tools / utilities which provide you detective controls.

Once a security incident is identified, it cannot be left alone without attending to it. If the security incident was the tailgating by an ex-employee / a stranger or an application functionality behaving erratically, then the security incident has to be investigated to find out the root cause(s) for the same, so that corrective actions can be determined and taken to either fix the root cause(s) or mistake proof the issue itself.

If the incident is a serious one like a worm attack or a virus attack with serious implications then the actions or response has to be quick to contain the issue from spreading and containing the consequential damage.

In view of such a serious situation, having an effective incident response is necessary for all organizations. In order to achieve this objective, all organizations need to follow a well ordered Incident Response Life Cycle and have a comprehensively detailed Incident Response Plan. Incident Response Life Cycle defines various phases through which an incident has to be managed for incident responses to be effective not only in containing and spreading the effects, but also avoid recurrence of same or similar incidents. Incident Response Plan is the output of the Incident Response Preparation Phase and provides a well thought-out and well-articulated Incident Response Plan which enables the organizations to deal with incidents effectively and efficiently.

Figure 5-3 illustrates the Incident Response Life Cycle.

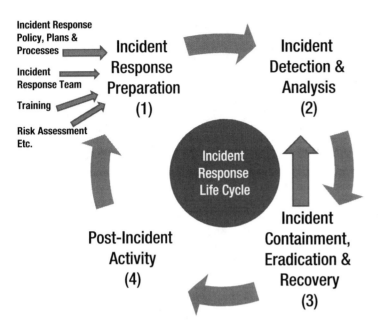

Figure 5-3. Incident Response Life Cycle[2]

Incident Response Policy, Plan, and Processes

Incident Response Policy should be put in place by management of the organization demonstrating its commitment to the Incident Response. This policy directs and provides guidance to the entire organization and provides the base for the Incident Response Plan and related processes.

Incident Response Policy

Incident Response Policy provides management direction towards Incident Response and also emphasizes the management's commitment to the same and highlights the "musts" as far as Incident Response is concerned. Incident Response Policy covers the following areas.

Purpose and Scope of the Policy

This should clearly define the purpose of incident response, namely, what the organization wants to achieve through incident response. This should also describe the scope of incident response in the organization. The scope can be the entire organization or a particular unit or a specific group of units and the type of incidents and circumstances.[2] It highlights management's commitment and addresses what the management feels as mandatory to be followed with regard to incident response.

Definition of Information Security Incidents and Related Terms[2]

From organization to organization, the definition of information security incidents can differ. It is necessary that the organization clearly defines what it means by an incident and related terms like incident response, incident recovery, and incident response team.

Organizational Structure, Roles, Responsibilities, and Authorities

Any policy cannot be implemented effectively and efficiently unless there is a proper structure to support it in the organization. The structure should be composed of clear roles with clear responsibilities. For an incident response, many times somebody needs to act expeditiously without any bureaucratic approval cycle in order to carry out immediate containment or control activities. Therefore it is necessary that some of the roles have to be provided with authorities which may be beyond their normal authorities. An organization's structure, roles, responsibilities, and designated authorities have to be clearly defined and described so that there is no ambiguity, and that no confusing actions are taken.

All the people in the organization have to be clearly informed of the organization structure, roles, and responsibilities as the incident response has to be quick and requires coordination between various functions and personnel of the organization and cannot happen without this clarity across the organization. Otherwise, egos and organizational bureaucratic setups can create hurdles during an incident response which can delay the response significantly leading to a higher level of disruption or damage or theft. The roles, responsibilities, and authorities should provide the authority to the incident response team even to confiscate the equipment or disconnect the equipment and to monitor and investigate suspicious activities.[2] This also should make it clear what and which types of communications to the outside world or to the related agencies are permitted and who is permitted to carry out the same.

Incident Response Teams constitute personnel with complementary skills, experience, and capabilities. Head of the Incident Response Team is normally vested with significant authority to make decisions at times of need to effectively contain and recover from incidents.

Ratings of Incidents

All incidents do not require the same level of attention. Some of the incidents may be localized incidents and may have a local impact. Some may be organization-wide incidents with organization-wide impact. Some incidents may impact critical business areas and others may impact non-critical business areas. Some incidents may be easy to be responded to while some others may be very complex which can be responded to only by experts. Some incidents may have high impacts and some incidents may have low impacts on the organization. In order that the organizational personnel and the incident response team do not get confused, clear guidelines have to be provided as to the severity of various types of incidents. Speed of action required to be taken and the priority depends upon the severity rating of the incident.

Measurements

Any critical activity in the organization has to be measured to understand either its effectiveness or efficiency or both of these. The measurements provide us with the clear view of where we stand with respect to performance and bring out the opportunities for improvement. But, measurements to be made should be appropriate and should be defined in clear terms so that the measurements actually provide us the information as per the intended objectives of these measurements.

Incident Response Plan

The Incident Response Plan should clearly define what is considered as an incident in the organization. Second it should clearly identify the potential types of incidents the organization is exposed to based on the infrastructure of the organization, IT architecture of the organization, types of operating systems, and tools and utilities used by the organization. Third, it has to clearly describe what needs to be done if a new and unanticipated incident is faced by the organization. This may include who needs to be notified, and who will make a final call as to what needs to be done. The Incident Response Plan also has to specify external agencies or forums if any need to be informed or consulted with.

The Incident Response Plan covers the following areas.

Purpose and Scope

Purpose of the Incident Response Plan and the scope as to which type of incidents, pertaining to which location and which functions is made clear in this section.

Strategies, Goals, and Approach to Incident Response

Incident response strategies, goals, and approaches including the incident monitoring strategies, incident response strategies, strategies related to organization to effectively handle incidents including the team composition, internal and external coordination, and total or partial outsourcing of the incident response need to be clearly planned for and appropriate responsibilities are to be assigned to named personnel with appropriate backups so that there is a guarantee that in case of any incidents, they are handled effectively.

Internal and External Communication Plan

The communication for identifying the incidents, declaring the incidents, and responding to the incidents needs to be clear and should come from the persons authorized to carry out such communications. The communications should be within the defined boundaries and the communications should be appropriately worded. The clarity as to how internal communications need to be handled and how the external communications need to be restricted are to be clearly planned for.

Plan for the Incident Response Capability[2]

An organization requires adequate, suitable incident response capability in order to be effective and efficient in incident response. Any organization has to assess its current incident response capability in terms of availability of techniques, tools, and utilities and the resource competence including the skills to handle incidents. If it does not have the internal capability either the option to outsource or to acquire the capability through new recruitments has to be looked into. Plans to have appropriate, adequate, and suitable incident response capability have to be clearly delineated with action responsibility and target dates clearly assigned.

Measurement of Incident Response Capability and its Effectiveness

It is necessary to measure the incident response capability of the organization including that of the outsourced portion of the incident response capability. Periodic assessment of the same will close up the gaps between the expectations and the current realities. Organizations are not static. People with expertise and assigned key responsibilities may leave the organization. The same holds true for outsourced organizations.

At the time of outsourcing, the particular organization may have excellent capabilities but over a period of time it is possible that it would have lost the capability or would have had its capability reduced because of the attrition of key people. Further, the new technologies being implemented or changes to the technologies being implemented can make the requisite incident response capability differ from what was originally planned. Further, we also need to measure the effectiveness of the implemented capability. These may be possible to be measured by the responses that have been provided to the incidents which have occurred. Similarly, it may be possible to test some of the incident response through mock scenarios and testing of the possible incidents.

It is important to consider the various types of incidents possible and how they have to be handled so that there is no ambiguity. At least processes have to be clearly defined in respect to high impact incidents. These may be based on the common attack vectors.

Integration with the Other Plans of the Organization

An organization may have other plans like Risk Management, Disaster Recovery, and Business Continuity Plans. It is necessary that all these plans are integrated in such a way that each plan complements the other plans and does not contradict the other plans.

Incident Response Processes

Incident response processes are the important elements for the success of the incident responses. Various possible incidents from virus infection to malware infection to server crashes to denial of service attacks to bomb threats to many such possible incidents have to be thoroughly planned. Where the possibility of these incidents is high, the incident responses have to be discussed and planned for by having appropriate incident response processes.

These processes have to be detailed enough with various possible scenarios and appropriate responses. These processes have to detail how these incidents are identified and analyzed. These need to be supported additionally by templates, forms, and checklists as relevant so that it is easy to implement the expectations of these incident response processes effectively.

Incident Response Teams

Incident Response Team(s) is/are an important component and highly influence the success or failure of the effectiveness and efficiency of the incident response. This team requires the knowledge, experience, and skills to ensure that the incident detection, incident containment, and incident eradication are carried out effectively and efficiently.

Incident Response Team(s) can be dedicated teams or may be "on call" teams depending upon the criticality of the business, exposure of the organization to the incidents, competence of the IT resources, and resilience of the information security infrastructure.

Incident Response Team structuring based on distribution of the Responsibilities

Incident Response Teams are normally structured based on best fit distribution of the responsibilities among various centers.

Centralized Incident Response Teams[2]

Centralized Incident Response Teams are usually suitable for smaller organizations with less geographical spread. In big organizations such a structure can lead to lack of effective coordination due to various reasons like cultural reasons, internal political reasons, and bureaucratic decision making.

Distributed Incident Response Teams[2]

Distributed Incident Response Teams are suitable for multi-business, multi-locational organizations with distributed IT infrastructure. Each of these centers or group of centers may have their own Incident Response Team. In today's world, where each center is connected to the other centers and where the same business is carried out in various geographies and where the IT infrastructure is distributed based on efficiency and competency, it is necessary to have a person or group coordinating the efforts of these various Incident Response Teams as the same incident may affect multiple locations or an incident at one center may impact the business carried out at other centers.

Hybrid Incident Response Teams

It is possible that the expertise to handle the incidents in not uniformly distributed across various locations of an organization. In such a case it is possible to constitute a Central Incident Response Team at the prime location of the organization or technological hub of the organization with Incident Response Teams at the other centers as required. Incident response for some of the smaller centers or the centers which may lack the requisite expertise may be directly taken care of by a Central Incident Response Team. In such a model, it is possible to authorize the individual Incident Response Teams at various centers to act independently in case of local incidents and keep such incidents reported to the Central Incident Response Team. But, in case of purely local incidents the Central Incident Response Team assumes the advisory role if any support is required by the local Incident Response Teams. All the incidents which have impact across the businesses or locations or of higher impact are handled by the Central Incident Response Team. Necessary actions are directly taken by the Central Incident Response Team or as per the directions of the Central Incident Response Team by the distributed Incident Response Teams.

Incident Response Team Structuring Based on who Constitutes the Teams

The teams have to be constituted with appropriate competent resources. This depends upon the business, technology infrastructure, tools, and utilities used. If the team is not composed of competent resources it is possible that incidents may not be recognized sufficiently early or incident response may be delayed or incident response may not be effective. All organizations may not have in-house competence for effective and efficient incident response. They may have to complement internal competence with external expertise to effectively deal with incident response. Again the Incident Response Team can be constituted with full-time members or part time "on call" members. This depends upon the business criticality as well as IT infrastructure robustness, probable incidents, and IT resilience. The pros and cons of each of these structures have to be evaluated in the context of the organization and then an appropriate decision has to be made based on the well-evaluated and well-considered trade-off [3].

Fully Employee Constituted Incident Response Teams

If the organization has adequate internal competence then the Incident Response Team can be constituted internally. But, if the Incident Response Team is required to be available 24x7 and required to be deployed as it is, it is better to constitute a separate Incident Response Team with the experts specifically recruited by the organization. However, if it is enough to constitute an "on call" Incident Response Team then it is more effective to constitute the team internally with the expertise already available in-house.

Fully Outsourced Incident Response Teams

Here, the organization arranges for the entire team to be constituted by outside experts. Usually this may be through a single outsourced entity. However, it may be a group of organizations to which the outsourcing is done with complementary expertise, even though such a scenario is seen less in practice. This type of team constitution is usually found in smaller organizations for which it is difficult to internally source the requisite expertise. It is possible that such teams may have a tough time providing for effective and efficient Incident Response sometimes because of bureaucratic responses or hindrances or because of lack of effective authority delegated to them.

Hybrid Teams: Partially Constituted by Employees and Partially Constituted by Outsourced Contractors

Here, the organization constitutes its Incident Response Team with chosen internal employees and chosen outsourced contractors. This model is likely to work the best because the internal expert resources are complemented through other rare / non-available skills from the outsourced contractors. As the internal employees constitute a good portion of the team bureaucratic hindrances or lack of authority impeding effectiveness and efficiency of the incident response may not be an issue in this case.

Ensuring Effectiveness of Incident Response

As discussed earlier, incident response is not always easy for the following reasons:

- The actual incident may be the one that was not anticipated

- Key members of the incident response team and their backups may not be available when the incident actually happens

- Incident response plan is beautifully drafted but the stakeholders are not trained effectively on the plan

- Incident response teams are not staffed suitably or adequately

- Incident response plan was not updated for a long time and has become non-useful because of the changes to the infrastructure and systems over a period of time

- Incident Response Processes are outdated and are not in sync with the currently deployed technology

For effective incident response execution the following steps have become essential:

Preparation[2]

Any battle is half won before it begins if the preparations are done well. Similarly, preparation is very important to ensure the effectiveness of the incident response. Following are the important aspects of the preparation:[2]

- Risk assessment and identification of the risk mitigation steps to overcome the non-acceptable risks including the threats likely to lead to incidents

- Training the resources on the possible incidents and providing them the awareness and knowledge to enable them to effectively prevent the incidents, such as virus prevention programs, strong password, or encryption training

- Effective formulation of the Incident Response Team constituting suitable and appropriate structure and members with the requisite capability

- Well thought out and preventive IT infrastructure and physical security infrastructure

- Effective Incident Response Policy, Incident Response Plan, and supporting Incident Response Processes

- Validation of the Incident Response Plans and Incident Response Processes to ensure that they work when required

- Training on the execution of the Incident Response Plans

- Regular update to the Incident Response Policy, Incident Response Plan, and Incident Response Processes in tune with the changes to or at the organization

- Configuring the setup including those of tools / utilities used by the organization appropriately

Important aspects to be considered during the preparation are:[2]

- Internal and external contact details including those of on-call members, Incident Response Team members, and external agencies.

- Incident Reporting Mechanisms including the e-mail ids, contact phone numbers, or tools / utilities through which incidents can be reported.

- Incident Response War Room: This is the place designated for the Incident Response Team to operate. Primarily the Incident Response Team Leader directs and guides the team from here and can be contacted here. This room is provided with multiple telephone lines and other accessories to ensure effective communication in and out of this War Room.

- Incident Tracking Tool/Utility: Incidents need to be tracked including the status of the incidents and various actions taken at various places to ensure that the actions are executed as proposed. This is the incident repository which needs to be kept updated and which provides the Incident Response Team Leader to provide accurate and correct information related to incident status to internal and external stakeholders, as relevant.

- Readily available or accessible Incident Response Plan and Processes

- Secure Storage Facility: This is provided to store and preserve the evidence obtained during incident investigation.

- Mobiles or Tablets: These enable effective communication during the incident among internal and external stakeholders.

- Incident Analysis Hardware and Software such as Forensic Workstations, Backup Devices, Laptops and/or desktops, Servers, Portable Printers, Forensic Software, Digital Cameras, Video / Audio Recorders, Blank Media and other tools / utilities as relevant which help out in effectively analyzing the incidents; analyzing, collecting, and preserving the evidence.[2]

- Incident Analysis Resources including List of Ports, Network Diagrams / Maps, Configuration Management Database, Operating System and Database and Application related documentation.[2]

- Incident Mitigation Software which enables restoration and recovery of Operating Systems, Applications enabling IRT to create clean OS and application images.

Incident Detection[2]

Incident detection[2] is the next important step. All the incidents are not possible to be anticipated. However, there are some common threads among certain groups of incidents and these are normally known as Common Attack Vectors. These Common Attack Vectors enable us to understand and use the possibility of providing more specific responses. Table 5-7 lists the Common Attack Vectors.[2]

***Table** 5-7. Common Attack Vectors[2]*

Common Attack Vector	Description
External / Removable Media	An attack executed from removable media or a peripheral device—for example, malicious code spreading onto a system from an infected USB flash drive
Attrition	An attack that employs brute force methods to compromise, degrade, or destroy systems, networks, or services (e.g., a DDoS intended to impair or deny access to a service or application; a brute force attack against an authentication mechanism, such as passwords, CAPTCHAS, or digital signatures)
Web	An attack executed from a website or web-based application—for example, a cross-site scripting attack used to steal credentials or a redirect to a site that exploits a browser vulnerability and installs malware

(continued)

Table 5-7. (*continued*)

Common Attack Vector	Description
Email	An attack executed via an email message or attachment—for example, exploit code disguised as an attached document or a link to a malicious website in the body of an email message
Impersonation	An attack involving replacement of something benign with something malicious—for example, spoofing, man in the middle attacks, rogue wireless access points, and SQL injection attacks all involve impersonation
Improper Usage	Any incident resulting from violation of an organization's acceptable usage policies by an authorized user, excluding the above categories; for example, a user installs file sharing software, leading to the loss of sensitive data; or a user performs illegal activities on a system
Loss or Theft of Equipment	The loss or theft of a computing device or media used by the organization, such as a laptop, smartphone, or authentication token
Other	An attack that does not fit into any of the other categories

Precursors and Indicators of Incidents[2]

It is most difficult to understand whether the incident is occurring or has already occurred and the type, extent, and / or magnitude of the incident. Precursors provide an indication that there is a possibility of an incident happening, such as if there is an email or telephonic threat to the organization, a terrorist attack, or there have been failed attempts made to break into a critical system.

Indicators provide the signals that the incident is either occurring at this point of time or has already occurred, such as file checksums do not match, some data is leaked and published on a public website, somebody has already defaced the website, an increased number of files are getting corrupted day by day, or higher than normal utilization of the traffic is observed. It is possible that some of these indicators may be false positives and would have happened because of an employee's unintended mistake which was not even observed by the employee concerned or because of a wrong restoration by oversight or a wrong update. We may not have either a precursor or an indicator in case of some of the incidents, such as a new exploit of a new vulnerability just uncovered by a hacker or a misconfiguration newly exploited by an internal knowledgeable employee.

However, these precursors and indicators, when available, provide us an opportunity to speed up our responses and many times provide us the opportunity to either stop an incident from happening or reduce the impact of the incident.

Sources of Precursors and Indicators

Some of the sources of the precursors and indicators are described in Table 5-8.[2]

Table 5-8. *Common Sources of Precursors and Indicators*[2]

Source	Description
Alerts	
IDPSs	IDPS products identify suspicious events and record pertinent data regarding them, including the date and time the attack was detected, the type of attack, the source and destination IP addresses, and the username (if applicable and known). Most IDPS products use attack signatures to identify malicious activity; the signatures must be kept up to date so that the newest attacks can be detected. IDPS software often produces false positives—alerts that indicate malicious activity is occurring, when in fact there has been none. Analysts should manually validate IDPS alerts either by closely reviewing the recorded supporting data or by getting related data from other sources.
SIEMs	Security Information and Event Management (SIEM) products are similar to IDPS products, but they generate alerts based on analysis of log data (see below).
Antivirus and antispam software	Antivirus software detects various forms of malware, generates alerts, and prevents the malware from infecting hosts. Current antivirus products are effective at stopping many instances of malware if their signatures are kept up to date. Antispam software is used to detect spam and prevent it from reaching users' mailboxes. Spam may contain malware, phishing attacks, and other malicious content, so alerts from antispam software may indicate attack attempts.
File integrity checking software	File integrity checking software can detect changes made to important files during incidents. It uses a hashing algorithm to obtain a cryptographic checksum for each designated file. If the file is altered and the checksum is recalculated, an extremely high probability exists that the new checksum will not match the old checksum. By regularly recalculating checksums and comparing them with previous values, changes to files can be detected.
Third-party monitoring services	Third parties offer a variety of subscription-based and free monitoring services. An example is fraud detection services that will notify an organization if its IP addresses, domain names, etc. are associated with current incident activity involving other organizations. There are also free real-time blacklists with similar information. Another example of a third-party monitoring service is a CSIRC notification list; these lists are often available only to other incident response teams.
Logs	
Operating system, service and application logs	Logs from operating systems, services, and applications (particularly audit-related data) are frequently of great value when an incident occurs, such as recording which accounts were accessed and what actions were performed. Organizations should require a baseline level of logging on all systems and a higher baseline level on critical systems. Logs can be used for analysis by correlating event information. Depending on the event information, an alert can be generated to indicate an incident.

(continued)

Table 5-8. (*continued*)

Source	Description
Network device logs	Logs from network devices such as firewalls and routers are not typically a primary source of precursors or indicators. Although these devices are usually configured to log blocked connection attempts, they provide little information about the nature of the activity. Still, they can be valuable in identifying network trends and in correlating events detected by other devices.
Network flows	A network flow is a particular communication session occurring between hosts. Routers and other networking devices can provide network flow information, which can be used to find anomalous network activity caused by malware, data exfiltration, and other malicious acts. There are many standards for flow data formats, including NetFlow, sFlow, and IPFIX.
Publicly Available Information	
Information on new vulnerabilities and exploits	Keeping up with new vulnerabilities and exploits can prevent some incidents from occurring and assist in detecting and analyzing new attacks. The National Vulnerability Database (NVD) contains information on vulnerabilities. Organizations such as US-CERT33 and CERT®/CC periodically provide threat update information through briefings, web postings, and mailing lists.
People	
People from within the organization	Users, system administrators, network administrators, security staff, and others from within the organization may report signs of incidents. It is important to validate all such reports. One approach is to ask people who provide such information how confident they are of the accuracy of the information. Recording this estimate along with the information provided can help considerably during incident analysis, particularly when conflicting data is discovered.
People from other organizations	Reports of incidents that originate externally should be taken seriously. For example, the organization might be contacted by a party claiming a system at the organization is attacking its systems. External users may also report other indicators, such as a defaced web page or an unavailable service. Other incident response teams also may report incidents. It is important to have mechanisms in place for external parties to report indicators and for trained staff to monitor those mechanisms carefully; this may be as simple as setting up a phone number and e-mail address, configured to forward messages to the help desk.

Analysis of the Incidents:[2]

As discussed earlier, all the indicators at all times may not provide accurate information and may lead to false positives. Hence, the mere presence of an indicator is not sufficient to presume that an incident has occurred or is occurring. A suspected incident has to be analyzed based on the indicators and other related information and then the analysis has to be confirmed. At the same time, it is necessary to understand the cause of the incident (may be an intentional attack, may be a misconfigured system, may be an employee mistake, may be unintentional violation of a policy impacting the system, etc.) to effectively deal with the incident. Many a time, experts may have to be involved in the analysis of the incidents to understand the correct causes and to arrive at effective solutions. Sometimes it may be too late to do anything as the confidential information is already released to the public. Sometimes only partial containment is possible. However, corrective action should be identified to either remove the possibility of such an incident happening or the possibility of root cause(s) from happening.

Table 5-9 details actions that may help in simplifying incident analysis, or making incident analysis relatively easy.[2]

Table 5-9. *Actions that may help in analyzing incidents effectively.*[2]

Action	Description
Profiling of Networks and Systems	Profiling is measuring the characteristics of expected activity so that changes to it can be more easily identified. Changes possibly indicate an incident even though sometimes these may be false positives.
Understanding Normal Behaviors	Study of networks, systems, and applications to understand their normal behavior will provide us sufficient clues to understand and identify abnormal behavior.
Creating a Log Retention Policy	Log information is critical information. This will provide leads into possible threads from earlier activities like reconnaissance activities. Having the logs for sufficient lengths of time ensures that there is a traceability to the thread of related activities as some of the incidents may be uncovered after substantial time of its occurrence.
Performing Event Correlation	Events can be correlated from different sources of information e.g. firewall logs to server logs to the application logs.
Clock Synchronization	Clock synchronization across all the physical and logical systems ensures that the incidents and evidences can be correlated easily. This provides adequate strength to the evidence collected from the legal stand point.
Maintaining and Using a Knowledge Base	This knowledge base acts as a quick reference source for the incident handlers. It should be easily searchable database. This knowledge base needs to be maintained updated with changes to the same in tune with the changes to the organizational scenario.
Using Internet Search Engines for Research	In today's world, Internet acts as a very important source of quick reference and useful information. We should be careful to ensure that the information is authentic, useful and relevant in the context of the incident faced by us.
Using tools / utilities as relevant	Use utilities like packet sniffers as relevant to collect more data to provide adequate information on the incident so that the action to be taken can be understood clearly.
Filtering the data	Various tools and utilities like SIEM, IDPSs etc. collect huge amount of data. It is not possible to go through each of these data. Data need to be filtered suitably and appropriately to identify possible patterns and possible indicators.
Seeking assistance from others	Various governmental and non-governmental sources can provide us information as to the current incident scenarios which may be applicable to us also. Keeping in touch with other Incident Response Teams from other companies or governmental and non-governmental agencies / forums can provide us crucial inputs on recognizing the incidents as well as analyzing the incidents effectively. However, caution should be exercised as to when we need to share the information.

Incident Impact Analysis and Prioritization of the Actions[2]

An incident may have impact on the functional aspects or on the CIA (Confidentiality, Integrity, and Availability) aspect of information security or both on the functional aspects as well as the CIA aspect of information security. Higher the impact, higher shall be the prioritization related to the actions to contain or to recover from them. Recoverability effort is also one of the important aspects which drive the prioritization of the actions. It is possible to recover from some of the incidents very easily with low effort, such as an isolated breach of one of the non-critical servers. It may be very difficult to recover from some of the other incidents and it may take weeks to recover e.g. a major security glitch in the application which is deployed across multiple systems in the organization. Further, in some cases if the information is already compromised, such as confidential information stolen already made public, there is no way you can recover from the situation for that particular instance.

Incident Documentation and Incident Notification[2]

Complete details of the incidents have to be captured including the analysis details, causes identified, containment actions identified and taken, and corrective actions identified and taken. These details can be tracked through an online system wherein the incident handlers need to update the details as they proceed with the analysis and take appropriate actions. It is important to document online or through paper based records various information related to the incidents. These not only come in handy later come in the evidence to be produced before legal authorities but also as future knowledge base as to what were the indicators, what were the analysis details, what were the causes, what actions were identified, which actions worked and which did not, whether the containment was effective, and if so to what extent, what was the magnitude or impact of the incident, whether the recovery actions worked or not, etc. These are crucial knowledge from the future perspective. Hence, the documentation cannot be ignored. Similarly, updating the status of the incident regularly on the online system should not be forgotten as the Incident Response Team Leaders as well as other key stakeholders like CIO, Chief Information Security Officer, or Owner of the data or system compromised, may be reviewing the status online or Incident Response Team Leaders may use the status for internal and external communication. Any wrong communication gives the wrong impression about the organization.

All the relevant and identified stakeholders (i.e., internal as well as external), depending upon the incident and corresponding incident response plans and processes, have to be communicated with regularly on the incident and its status. Typical stakeholders for the incident reporting are Chief Information Security Officer, Chief Information Officer, Business / Data / System Owner, Other internal and external Incident Response Teams, Human Resources (in case of breaches by employees), Public Affairs department (incidents of public concern where the status need to be informed to the public or where the incident attracts adverse publicity), Legal Department (where there are legal implications of the incident or where the incident has to be dealt with legally), and other governmental agencies / departments as relevant.

Incident Containment, Eradication, and Recovery[2]

Incident containment is very important to limit the impact on the business. The containment actions may be disconnecting or isolating the infected system from the network so that it does not infect other systems. Subsequent to the containment or in conjunction with the containment eradication of the cause(s) of the incident has to be done by identifying appropriate corrective actions. If mistake proofing of the systems is possible, like reconfiguring the system and thus avoiding recurrence of the same incidents in the future, the mistake proofing has to be attempted. However, you may have to weigh the costs of actions against the benefits from the actions and the residual risks. Further, recovery has to be attempted to ensure that the systems are restored effectively to their original positions at the time of the incident, such as if the data integrity is impacted because of the incident, then the data has to be restored to the accurate data by either nullifying the impact of the incident or to the last known state of data with the integrity intact and further transactions have to be re-applied. If the availability of the data is impacted the system has to be restored so that the legitimate users can access the same, such as after a DDoS the access to the server / system is restored to the legitimate users. In case of impact on confidentiality, possible eradication may be removal of the published data from those sites which had published the same (possibly nothing much could be done if somebody had already copied the data from there). All of the three aspects are important to ensure the effectiveness of the incident response.

Containment Strategy[2]

Early containment is important to the success of effective Incident Response. Containment reduces the actual damage or inhibits the resources from being exhausted, such as delinking an infected machine limits the spread of infection to other machines or diverting the attacking traffic to a sandbox, which avoids a denial of service attack. Containment strategy shall be spelt out clearly so that the incident handlers do not get confused but have absolute clarity on what prioritizes the containment. Sometimes it may be dangerous to carry out the containment if the containment action may make malicious software to act differently or severely. Hence, containment action should be well thought out by the experts. Some of the criteria for containment strategy are:

- Possible damage if the containment action is not carried out

- Whether the damage is likely to be increased if the containment is not carried out

- Services assured to the customers

- Time and resources needed to implement the containment strategy

- Type of the containment solution (temporary, permanent, etc.)

- Likely effectiveness of the containment strategy

- Evidence preservation requirement (NIST's SP 800-61 Rev 2)

The containment strategy should be kicked in as early as possible if the damage is likely to escalate because of further compromises possible or is likely to spread significantly impacting other business areas. However, the downsides of a containment action, if any, have to be understood before applying the containment actions.

Evidence Gathering and Handling[2]

Evidence needs to be gathered from two perspectives: first to understand how the attack is happening and where the attack is happening, second is to capture and preserve the evidence if legal ramifications are there or a legal battle has to be waged against the incident subsequently. If the evidence has to be used for legal purposes, then the evidence has to be collected as per the legal requirements, according to the prior consultation and understanding from the legal experts. It is also necessary to document how and when the evidence was collected and how it is preserved, how it is protected. A chain of custody for the evidence with clearly documented handover should be preserved. It is also necessary to take a snapshot of evidence as early as possible before application of any containment action so that the evidence is of value during the legal proceedings.

Eradication and Recovery[2]

Eradication is carried out as soon as possible. Eradication is getting rid of the vulnerabilities exploited or infection, such as a virus that infected being deleted, the misconfiguration of the system which was exploited is corrected, the defect in the application which was exploited is fixed, the operating system weakness which was exploited is appropriately patched, and changing the compromised passwords. Understanding the cause(s) of the incident is very important to do effectively.

Recovery is restoring the system back to normalcy, that is, undoing the adverse effects of the incident by restoring back the crashed operating system, correcting the integrity of the database, restoring back the correct data if the integrity of the data was impacted, or setting right the parameters altered by the incident.

Also, it may be useful to ensure from the learning of the incident that better logging, auditing, and monitoring are built into the systems so that the future detection of such incidents is easy. Effective eradication and recovery is often not easy and takes time. Some of them require infrastructural changes which may need budgeting, proper impact study, evaluation of alternative tools, and a plan for implementation of the selected tool.

Once the eradication and recovery is completed, the compromised system(s) need to be monitored to ensure that the eradication and recovery are effective. This gives the assurance that the incident is either possible to be detected easily in the future if it repeats or such incidents are possible to be prevented.

Post Incident Analysis and Activities[2]

Every incident and the way it was handled, provides significant learning which cannot be lost. The learnings from each incident need to be captured and analyzed so that the learning can be applied to future incidents as applicable. Also, in case legal actions are to be pursued then the evidence has to be organized and submitted to the appropriate authorities so that the legal actions can be initiated and pursued effectively.

Analysis of Learnings

Analysis of the learnings has to be carried out at least in the case of major or critical incidents. Periodic analysis meetings can be carried out in respect of collation of the learnings from other incidents. Ideally all the stakeholders who were involved in the incident detection, incident handling, and incident response should be involved in the meeting. The entire incident has to be deliberated upon and the results have to be collated:

- What had happened and when?
- Whether all the contacts could be contacted or were there issues in reaching the contacts like wrong e-mail ids or wrong / old contact numbers or the resources had already left the organization?
- Whether the incident response processes were effective or had to be modified on the fly to handle the incident effectively?
- Whether the incident handling led to any side-effects or adverse impacts and if so, what were they and how could they have been avoided?
- Was there a better way to respond to the incident than the way it was handled?
- Was there a better way to organize the response team?
- What information was needed but was not available on time?
- What learning from this incident can be applied to avoid probable similar incidents?
- What precursors and / or indicators were useful in identifying the incident and which of these will be helpful for future?
- Was the internal communication and external communication effective? Were they useful? Are there possibilities to improve upon these?
- What utilities / tools are required to better identify, prevent, analyze, or handle such incidents?
- Data related to the incident like duration of the incident, efforts spent on various phases of incident handling, types of incidents and their categorization based on various aspects like attack vectors used, external / internal attacks, etc.

Many more such questions can be asked to understand what went right, what went wrong, what could be done differently or better going ahead, and how these learnings will be useful for the future.

Use of Incident Data[2]

After analyzing these learnings, the improvement activities based on these learnings have to be initiated which may lead to the update of the Incident Response Plan and Incident Response Processes. Also, awareness and trainings may have to be improved based on these learnings.

Further, where legal actions have to be initiated, the details of the evidence collected have to be submitted to the legal department so that they can arrange for the legal recourse.

Data collected during the incident analysis has to be retained for a sufficiently long period for the following reasons [3]:

- Some of these may be useful at a later period of time, as some of the impacts of the incidents which are not identified now, may be identified later

- Some traces of future incidents may be found or some activities which are precursor activities for future incidents may be possible to be correlated to at a later date

Disaster Recovery and Business Continuity

As we discussed in the Introduction to this Chapter, Disaster Recovery normally applies to the IT infrastructure and IT systems even though it can be applied by some organizations in the context of all disasters. Business Continuity as mentioned here below provides for continuity of business in the context of disasters as well as business recovery post disasters. Normally, Incident Response Mechanisms handle disasters of smaller gravity, particularly security incidents and Disaster Recovery and Business Continuity Plans address higher order disasters. An organization may have a single plan covering all incidents and disasters or may have different plans for different aspects. However, where the organizations have multiple plans, it should be ensured that the scope of each plan is clearly defined and there is no conflict between these plans, instead these plans complement each other. In the following sections, we discuss all the three plans: Disaster Recovery Plan, Business Continuity Plan and Business Recovery Plan. All of these plans form a single composite plan that is known as Business Continuity Plan.

How to Approach Business Continuity Plan

A clear approach to the formulation of the Business Continuity Plan ensures that it considers all the important aspects and according to the scope of the business continuity that the organization wants to achieve.

Figure 5-4 illustrates the three important components of an effective Business Continuity Plan:

- Disaster Recovery Plan

- Business Continuity Plan

- Business Recovery Plan

Figure 5-4. *Components of Business Continuity Plan*

Assign Clear Roles and Responsibilities

For any project to be successful, it is necessary to define and assign clear roles and responsibilities. This is true even in the case of the formulation of Business Continuity Plans. The important roles and responsibilities in the context of the formulation of the Business Continuity Plans are described in the following sections.

Sponsor

Any plan will not be successful if there is no top management commitment. It is necessary from the perspective of provision of resources, allocation of sufficient budget, and getting the requisite infrastructure that Business Continuity Planning effort has the concrete backing of the top management. Ideal sponsor for the Business Continuity Plan is the Chief Executive Officer or the President or the Vice President of the organization. In case of specific unit level plans it can be the head of that particular unit. Such a person should demonstrate not only his / her commitment through funding and provision of resources, but also by intervening and resolving any barriers to the effective formulation of Business Continuity Plans. The sponsor should discuss with the Project Manager and formulate the scope of the Business Continuity Plans so that the Business Continuity Planning Team puts its efforts in the right direction and without any ambiguity. Budget for the entire business continuity planning also should be decided and conveyed by the Sponsor to the Project Manager.

Project Manager

Formulation of the Business Continuity Plan should be treated like a project. Hence, there should be a designated project manager. In the context of the Business Continuity Plan this person is normally known as Business Continuity Planning Coordinator. Some organizations may call such a coordinator as Contingency Planning Coordinator. Business Continuity Plan formulation project should have a planned start date and a planned end date. The activities or tasks to be carried over this period of time should be clearly planned in the schedule with the responsibility clearly assigned to relevant and appropriate personnel. Dependencies between various steps or tasks or activities of the plan have to be identified. A tool like Microsoft Project Plan or any other scheduling software or tool should be of help to carry this out effectively. The Project Manager or the Business Continuity Planning Coordinator can be an external consultant or an internal employee with prior experience in such a plan formulation or may be an internal management person supported by an identified external consultant. Communication Plan is an important component of planning for Business Continuity Plan formulation. It is the responsibility of the Project Manager or the Business Continuity Planning Coordinator to ensure an effective Communication Plan.

Business Continuity Planning Team

The Project Manager or Business Continuity Planning Coordinator in discussion with the sponsor or on his/her own should identify the team members who need to be part of the Business Continuity Planning Team. Ideally it should be a cross-functional team representing the members from the business, IT team, information security team, facility management and security team, human resources team, Sales and Marketing, Community Relations and Public Affairs, and Supply Chain / Purchasing, Finance. Experts or external consultants may also be included as part of the team.

Life Cycle of Business Continuity Planning

For Business Continuity Plans to be effective in addressing all the components of the plan including disaster recovery, business continuity and business recovery, organizations need to follow a well-defined Life Cycle of Business Continuity Planning. The success of the organization and its ability to withstand a disaster or serious business disruption depends upon the adequate thinking provided to each aspect of the life cycle, detailing of the same so that it is understood by everybody as relevant, tested for the assurance that it will work as expected in case of need and will enable the organization to bounce back effectively and efficiently on to the path of business continuity and business recovery. The Life Cycle of Business Continuity Planning is illustrated in Figure 5-5.

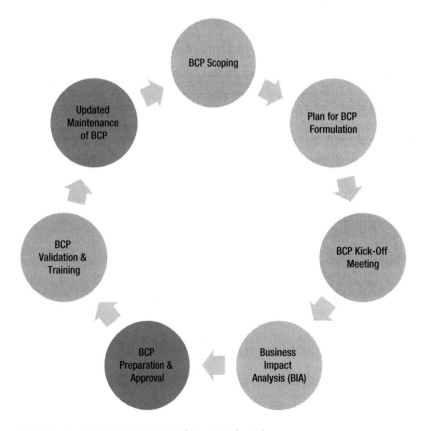

Figure 5-5. *Business Continuity Planning Life Cycle*

Scoping

Appropriate scoping is very important and the starting point of a good Business Continuity Planning exercise. Whether the scope is the entire organization, for specific location, for specific business, or for specific department should be clearly set by the Sponsor of the Business Continuity Plan in his / her discussion with the Business Continuity Planning Coordinator. The scope should be written down and signed off by the Sponsor to ensure that there is no disconnect between what was expected by the Sponsor and what was understood by the Business Continuity Planning Coordinator.

Plan for Formulation of Business Continuity Plan

A draft Project Schedule has to be prepared with a clear planned start date and planned end date. Various activities or tasks to be planned to formulate the Business Continuity Plan are identified. Assignments of the planned activities to various team members are also carried out. Dependencies between various tasks are also identified. Pre-requisites for important activities and success criteria for important activities are also identified. This draft schedule is discussed with the Business Continuity Team during the Business Continuity Plan Kick-Off Meeting and is finalized.

Communication Plan is an important component of planning for Business Continuity Plan formulation. This plan very clearly delineates how the status of the formulation of Business Continuity Plan is communicated to various stakeholders including the Sponsor and when and how the issues related to the plan are communicated. This plan also delineates channels of communication and various meetings that are part of overall communication strategy. This also includes the communication of any changes including changes to the scope, changes to the cost, and changes to the project plans. This draft communication plan is discussed with Sponsor to check that the plan is as per the expectations of the Sponsor. This plan is then discussed broadly during the Business Continuity Plan Kick-Off Meeting and agreed to.

Business Continuity Plan Kick-Off Meeting

This is an important meeting of the Business Continuity Planning Team wherein the scope of the Business Continuity Planning is discussed so that everybody on the team is clearly aware of the scope. The broad plan prepared by the Business Continuity Planning Coordinator will be discussed with the team and depending upon the team's views necessary additional tasks / activities are incorporated, timelines are revised, dependencies are added / modified, and the responsibilities for various tasks are reassigned where required.

This meeting also discusses the risks to the schedule, risks to the achievement of the objective of the plans, and risk of the resources planned to be employed (non-availability, over engagement in other critical activities etc.).

Any issues expressed by the team members are considered, discussed, and necessary actions to be taken are planned for / determined.

Business Impact Analysis (BIA)

Business Impact Analysis is at the heart of Business Continuity Planning. Data from various local agencies, regional agencies, national agencies, and international agencies, as relevant, are collected related to applicable disasters and taken into consideration during the Business Impact Analysis.

The first activity as a part of the Business Impact Analysis is to list out various Business Lines of the organization and to understand their relative contribution to the organization and their relative criticality in terms of revenue and profitability. This also has to take into account impact on the customers of those business and possibility of the customers moving to other organizations if they are not supported. Business Impact Analysis will allow an organization to determine as to how much time each of these business lines can be down without significantly impacting the customers, and also how much a reduced level of service can sustain the business for some time. Table 5-10 provides an example of how different lines of business determine the criticality of business continuity and recovery.

Table 5-10. *Criticality Analysis of Different Lines of Business*

Business Line	Business Share (% of total business of the organization)	Profitability %	Criticality of Business Continuity and Recovery
Business Line A	54%	12%	Critical
Business Line B	17%	18%	Critical
Business Line C	15%	5%	Non-Critical
Business Line D	14%	-2%	Non-Critical

Assurance made to the customers of various service levels, impact on the customers due to the business downtime / service downtime are taken into account and minimum time within which business needs to be continued even at the reduced levels of scale or reduced service levels have to be identified. This step is very crucial for the success of effective business continuity.

Then we look at the risks to the systems enabling and supporting each of these business lines including IT infrastructure, software, applications, tools, and utilities from various applicable threats or scenarios including from natural disasters, infrastructural breakdowns, riots and strikes, system downtime because of issues like virus infection, and server crashes. We identify the top risks based on their probability of occurrence and their likely impact on each of the business lines. We use the data available while arriving at these. The focus here is on availability as this is the risk we want to cover primarily as part of BIA. However here, we go beyond the normal risk assessment and assume that the disaster is likely to happen and think of what steps the organization needs to take to recover from disasters and continue the business if the disaster comes true in spite of controls put in place.

On the basis of the criticality of various Business Lines and the corresponding applicable risks or scenarios, relative ranking is used for prioritization of recovery and focus on business continuity. This step is very crucial for the success of effective business recovery. Additionally, it is good to understand, at this point in time, the implication of downtime or disruption on the confidentiality, integrity, and primarily availability (as BCP addresses primarily the issue of availability). The same guidelines from NIST's FIPS PUB 199 as used in the Risk Management Section may be referred to understand the impact. The rating may be 1 or Low; 2 or Moderate; 3 or High i.e. one in a numerical scale and the other at risk level.

From the above the following three important aspects of Business Continuity and Recovery are decided:

Maximum Tolerable Downtime (MTD): This is the downtime or outage or disruption considered as tolerable by the stakeholders particularly business users in the context of a specific business line. Beyond this period of downtime, it will be perceived that the downtime will have severe impact on the business. This provides the inputs for the recovery method and processes to be used.[4]

Recovery Time Objective (RTO): This is the maximum time by which the recoveries of the affected systems have to be accomplished. This provides the input for the technologies to be used for effective recovery. This has to be less than the MTD as the recoveries of the systems well before the MTD are necessary to ensure that the business can be carried out effectively after MTD. Further, testing of the integrity of the system and data restored shall also be checked and ensured before MTD. This provides for time to get a new server (rented or redeployed within the organization or leased etc.), install the operating system, install the application, configure the system appropriately, restore the backup from the backup media, check the system for effective restoration and roll it out for production, etc. Where the RTO is more than the MTD, then the Top Management has to be consulted as to the risks to the business and necessary steps as required have to be planned for as per the guidance of the Top Management.[4]

Recovery Point Objective (RPO): This is the point of time before the disaster or disruption or outage that the system can be brought back to. This applies to the data and usually depends upon the number of hours of data we can afford to lose. This decides the required backup frequency and type of backup. If the data is critical and can't be lost at all, then online real-time mirroring of the data may have to be looked into. However, whenever strategizing such things the cost vs. benefits have to be considered.[4]

The analysis that we've discussed is better known as the Business Impact Analysis (see Figure 5-6). Typically, the organization determines five business areas and five relevant disasters (as per the thumb rule), which need to be addressed for business continuity as well as recovery. This number may vary from organization to organization; however, looking to continue all the business lines, and always at the same level of performance, is possible to achieve only at high redundancy. It requires a high investment to support business continuity, and may not be a prudent business decision. As mentioned earlier, based on the relative criticality of the selected business lines, the recovery and continuity efforts are prioritized. Consequently, critical systems supporting those business lines and the priorities for their recovery also are identified.

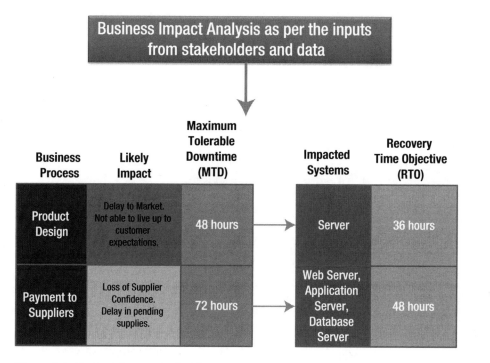

Figure 5-6. *Business Impact Analysis*[3]

For some customers or some businesses, it may cost significantly if the business doesn't continue at the time of disaster or as early as possible after the disaster. For example, e-commerce business with high competition and huge volumes of business may lead to huge losses or potential business losses even if the systems are out for part of the day. Hence, we need to identify the need for continuity of business while recovery efforts are underway.

Adequate and appropriate resource deployment is the next important step in the process of effective recovery. Facilities, staff, hardware, operating system and other software, application software, data, tools and utilities, and relevant records are the important resources required to ensure effective recovery. These should be identified well ahead of time in appropriate quantity with appropriate capability to ensure effective and efficient recovery.

Again, while most focus is on recovery, as discussed earlier, not all business lines may require continuity of business immediately after the disaster as this can be enabled in case of most disasters only at a high cost like hot sites setup and maintenance.

Whether the business can be continued at a lower scale from the same site or from another alternate site depends upon the type of disaster impacting the current site. Heavy floods or huge fires or earthquake, or damages on account of terrorist strikes through bombs etc. may lead to total or high devastation at the current site and hence it may not be possible to recover the services mostly within the MTD from the same site. Hence, in case such disasters are perceived strongly (i.e., with relatively high probability), then business continuity or business recovery from other alternative sites may have to be planned for. If the immediate continuity of the business from another site is required, then alternative hot sites may have to be setup. If the business can wait for some time, then there is a possibility to recover and continue the business from other alternative sites by having alternative warm sites. If there is substantial time available as MTD, then it may be enough to have a cold alternative site or a reciprocal arrangement with some other organization. These alternative sites may be the ones owned already by the organization or may be the sites leased out for the specific purposes of business continuity or may be the sites of other organizations with which we have reciprocal arrangements.

In most of the cases, the disasters may have localized impact in which case business may be possible to be routed temporarily through some other sites where possibly only the personnel have to be shifted temporarily along with the requisite equipment like laptops etc. Some of the cases can be handled effectively by having reciprocal arrangements with other organizations in a neighboring town or city which can be easily reached within a reasonable time-frame.

Business Continuity Plan Preparation

Once the business lines to be supported along with the applicable disasters and the corresponding systems to be recovered and / or business operations to be continued from alternative sites are decided along with the priorities attached to them, the detailed Business Continuity Plan is drawn up.

The Business Continuity Plan lists out the Business Lines determined to be supported (as per BIA) as part of BCP as per their priorities. For each of the business lines the top few identified and applicable disasters impacting them as determined during the BIA are listed out. Based on each disaster scenario, the systems to be brought up and the resources required for the recovery process are listed as determined during the BIA.

The next step is to identify the Preventive Controls. Preventive Controls are such controls which make it possible to reduce the impact or the possibility of some of these disasters, such as fire through mechanisms like smoke / fire detectors, fire alarm systems, and fire suppression systems. Many of these would have been considered as a part of organizational information security risk management activities. If not, possible preventive controls are now identified and assigned to appropriate personnel for effective execution.

For each of these listed disasters, what should be done during the first 24 hours, first 48 hours, first 72 hours of disaster are identified. These may be arranging for alternative servers, alternative routing of the network traffic, operating out of alternative sites (including where applicable other locations of the organization itself), restoration of the system files and data on to the alternative servers set up etc. The MTD and RTO are taken into consideration while planning these. The objective is to ensure that the business and supporting systems are brought back before the MTD. These have to be supported by effective and well-planned recovery processes.

Effective recovery depends upon the contingency strategies planned for. Some of the contingency strategies are backup and recovery methods, offsite storage strategies, provisioning of alternative cold, warm, or hot sites. Reciprocal arrangements for alternative sites, provision for receipt of backup equipment from the hardware vendor, inventory of internally deployable alternative systems necessary equipment to be stocked internally etc. are also required to be planned as part of these strategies. Service Level Agreements or timelines have to be agreed with suppliers, where appropriate, to ensure timely and effective support. All these should be in tune with the determined recovery strategies / plans and should support the RTO and RPO. These should be appropriately captured as part of the BCP. Cost vs. benefit analysis should be carried out while deciding these and appropriate strategies have to be selected keeping in mind RTO and RPO.

Outage assessment procedures like assessing the cause of an outage, potential impacts of the outage, damages possible to the infrastructure and systems, time required to bring back the situation to normalcy, and so on have also to be planned as part of the BCP.

Various recovery procedures and their sequence of execution have to be planned for in detail as part of the BCP or as addendum to the BCP or as a separate companion plan. Procedures to check the effectiveness of the recovery activities during the reconstitution phase also have to be planned for as part of BCP.

Various roles and responsibilities to effectively execute the Business Continuity Plan are determined and documented as part of the BCP. While BCP Coordinator plays an important role in the entire planning and execution of the BCP, there are other roles and responsibilities which are important to ensure effective execution of the BCP. One of these is the Crisis Management Lead who is the senior person from the organization who is empowered to declare the situation as a crisis upon evaluating the scenario and the possible damages or impacts. Other roles may be the Travel Coordinator for arranging for travel during the disaster, Purchase Coordinator who initiates necessary purchases as per the plan, Facility Coordinator who sets up the alternative site / facility, Server Recovery Team, Network Recovery Team, Database Recovery Team, Legal Affairs Team, Public Affairs Team, etc. while the BCP Coordinator takes overall lead and provides overall guidance for the effective execution of the BCP. Also, backups for each of the critical roles is also decided and assigned as part of the BCP.

Crisis Communication and other communication plans are also part of the Business Continuity Plan. These very clearly describe who is empowered to communicate with the internal and external world on the crisis and what kinds of communications are normally allowed in case of the relevant disasters. Even the forms and templates as necessary to support the same may be provided. The line of communication chart is also provided as needed, if the communication at various centers has to be percolated down / to others through various personnel of the organization. Activation criteria for important communications like crisis announcement and various notifications to be provided prior to the disaster, during the disaster, or after the disaster are also documented clearly as part of the BCP.

The primary and secondary contact details like landline numbers, mobile numbers, e-mail ids, and addresses of personnel assigned with various roles are captured as part of the BCP. The contact names and details of various critical suppliers like offsite backup custodial service providers, critical suppliers to whom critical work has been outsourced, etc. are also captured as part of the BCP.

Designation of the war rooms and the facilities to be available in the war rooms, the type of documentation to be carried out during the entire BCP life cycle; who is responsible for the documentation as scribe, and so on are planned for clearly as part of the BCP.

The plan is concluded with all the necessary contents as above and reviewed with the sponsor for completeness, consistency and correctness.

Business Continuity Plan Validation & Training

The Business Continuity Plan has to be tested and validated to get the requisite assurance that it works effectively when required. Testing and exercises are part of this validation. This is an important step of the Business Continuity Plan and cannot be missed out.

Testing enables plan deficiencies to be identified and addressed by validating one or more of the system components and the operability of the plan. Testing should be performed as far as possible in an environment akin to the current operating environment of the organization. Each of the recovery processes mentioned in the plan should be tested to get the assurance that they work when executed. Some of the things tested as part of BCP validation are:[3]

- Notification procedures;

- System recovery on an alternate platform from backup media;

- Internal and external connectivity;

- System performance using alternate equipment;

- Restoration of normal operations.[4]

This testing has to be carried out methodically using the test plans with clearly defined test scenarios (ideally worst case scenarios) and success criteria based on the defined test objectives. Test Plans should also test for the time-frames for each of the critical processes. This enables us to understand whether recovery is possible as per RTO or not.

Based on the outcome of the tests, necessary modifications or improvements may have to be made to the BCP.

Training on the BCP has to be provided to various roles mentioned in the BCP. The primary focus should be on the objective of the plan, communications to be carried out by and among various roles including reporting processes, coordination between various roles, do's and don'ts, team specific processes, responsibilities attached to individual roles, and security requirements. All the stakeholders have to be involved in the training mandatorily and clarify their doubts so that they are effective when it comes to the execution of the plan in case of eventuality.

Various exercises are conducted to ensure that the plan is appropriate and works when needed. Some of the popular exercises used are:

- Table Top Exercise[4]: This is normally done as a class room discussion based exercise. Here, no equipment is used. Various stakeholders meet and discuss their responsibilities in the case of an emergency and how will they respond in the context of a specific scenario provided by the facilitator.

- Functional Exercise[4]: Simulated environment is used and emergency processes are implemented by various teams. The teams carry out their emergency responsibilities in the simulated environment. It provides them hands on experience as well as tests the validity of the plans and processes. These may be exercising specific responsibilities of specific team members or exercising specific processes etc. These may be limited to specific aspects of the plans or may be a full scale exercise of the plan.

Table Top exercises may be enough for low impact systems. Limited functional exercises may be required for medium impact systems. Full functional exercises may be required in case of high-impact systems.

Up-to-date Maintenance of the BCP

With significant changes to businesses or infrastructure or systems, the BCP need to be reviewed and the need for its continued currency or the need for update to the same has to be ascertained. In case, the changes have impact on the BCP, it needs to be updated. Where the changes to the BCP are significant, then re-training of the resources and re-validation of the BCP are important. Even in case the BCP is static in terms of its technical contents, the BCP may require periodical updates and trainings on account of changes to the personnel and their responsibilities, and contact details. Like the original BCP, modified BCP also has to be reviewed and approved by the Sponsor of BCP.

Chapter Summary

- We discussed security breaches on confidentiality, integrity, and availability aspects of information security. We also made it clear that the risk management, incident response, disaster recovery, and business continuity planning are critical to ensure that the impacts on or compromises to confidentiality, integrity and availability are reduced significantly. We also stressed upon numerous theories around these concepts and found that they are diverse and many a time confusing. We also defined some of the key terminologies used in the chapter in our simple and practical ways to avoid confusion to the readers.

- We explored Risk Management and looked at each of the components of the risk management life cycle including risk identification, risk analysis, risk response, execution of risk treatment plans, and periodical risk assessments. Each of these were explained and elaborated in detail. Detailed guidelines are provided so that the users can effectively carry out the risk assessment. A useful template for risk assessment is also provided as reference.

- We also explored upon the Incident Response Policy, Plan, Processes, and the Incident Response Life Cycle. We looked at the importance of the preparation activities. We elaborated in detail upon incident detection including incident analysis, incident containment including containment strategies, incident eradication, and incident recovery. We also explained how the post incident analysis like learning, use of data collected are important, and useful steps leading to the improvement to the incident response mechanisms.

- We examined the Business Continuity Plan (including the Disaster Recovery, Business Continuity, and Business Recovery). We elaborated upon the important roles and responsibilities related to the formulation of the BCP. We also elaborated upon the planning required to arrive at the BCP. We also examined, as part of the BCP Life Cycle, the importance of Business Impact Analysis, and how it becomes the base for the formulation of the BCP. We also looked at the broad contents of the BCP. We also highlighted the need for validation of the BCP through Testing and Exercises. We also explored how training helps in the effective implementation of BCP. Then we highlighted the need for keeping the BCP updated with the changes.

PART III

■ ■ ■

Application Security

This section addresses primarily information security issues that are related to application and web security, and discusses malicious software infection and how to avoid such infection through mechanisms like anti-virus software. We also explain how cryptography has provided fillip to information security and how it can assure confidentiality and authenticity.

In Chapter 6, "Application and Web Security," we look into the fact that ensuring security of the software (including operating system, applications, tools, and utilities) and networks are most difficult because various things can go wrong. Some of the typical vulnerabilities they are exposed to are: misconfiguration, not validated inputs, defects/errors in the coding, man in the middle attacks, man in the browser attacks, session hijacking, weak encryption keys, weak/default passwords, weak authentication mechanisms, SQL Injection, and Buffer Overflows. We mention that increased use of software and web-based applications over the Internet has increased the exposure of these to various kinds of attacks. We also mention that we are yet to catch up with best practices on application development and infrastructure set up so that we have a fairly good chance of winning the race with the attackers. We then highlight what can go wrong with the software applications like medical software and aviation-related software and discuss some fundamental aspects of any application security from completeness of inputs to maintenance of integrity of data in transmission.

We look into the impact of each of these aspects in detail. We then explore the importance of effective application development life cycle in ensuring strong and secure software applications. In this context we explain the need for considering security requirements during the initial phases of application design and development life cycle and the need for effective design of the security requirements. Need for strong risk assessment as to what can go wrong and secure coding standards are highlighted. We then highlight important design and development guidelines which include understanding security requirements to architecting and designing for security to secure coding to strong reviews and testing to strong configuration management to strong release management. We look at the reasons for issues on the web and important attacks on the web like SQL or command injection, buffer overflows, session hijacking, cookie poisoning, password cracking, and cross-site scripting. We then discuss the vulnerabilities of web browsers, web servers, and web applications. We also discuss how to overcome the web browser, web server, and web application related vulnerabilities. Finally, we discuss the role of SSL and Digital Certificate in securing the web application communications.

Chapter 7, "Malicious Software and Anti-Virus Software," as the title suggests, identifies the purpose of such software is to create harm or damage to systems or to people or to both. Further, in this commercially oriented world, it seems that the companies are in a hurry to push across their technology and tools without strictly ensuring that the users of their technology and tools are protected. One strong example of this is that even though these companies are aware that "non-validated inputs" are the most exploited, still they do not take care to ensure proper validations.

Unfortunately, all these new technologies and tools provide opportunities for the people with bad intentions to find, understand, and exploit the loopholes or flaws in them. The advanced technologies while being beneficial to people and organizations in many ways, at the same time provide potential for knowledgeable users to connect to other systems from their mobiles and tablets and exploit them. Even though people who use the Internet are generally aware that there are some security threats of using the internet, most of them are not aware of the specifics of these threats and what can go wrong with their systems or to their financial assets or to their well-guarded secrets or information. Most of them are not even aware of why their identity credentials should not be made known to others and what can go wrong because of it. There are many more risks which the applications and systems are exposed to.

Fortunately, anti-virus software came to the rescue of individuals and organizations. Malicious software is generally known as malware. Spyware, adware, trojans, backdoors, viruses, worms, and botnets are all considered malware and are described. We also look into the types of viruses and how virus infection happens. We then look into the history of malware and the measures that can be taken to counter each of these types of malware. We also look into some of the recent malware attacks and explore the current scenario of malware with statistical perspective. Then we explore the need for anti-virus software and the expectations from anti-virus software and their vendors. We then list some of the key anti-virus software and explain their features. We offer a few general words of caution to users of anti-virus software.

Chapter 8, "Cryptography," examines the increasing use of the Internet as a commerce tool, and how most of the businesses are using the Internet today to carry out transactions, commerce, and transfer of money. It is important for the users, banks, and commercial institutions, to make sure that the information is secured and no one is able to read the data or change the data during the transmission. If computer systems can code the plain text and the receiver understands this coded message, and is able to interpret it, then users feel more secure to transmit data over the Internet or any other media. This method of coding plain text messages to a secret coded message is called cryptography. The method of disguising the plain text to hide the actual data is called encryption. The new encrypted text is called ciphertext. The encrypted data is not readable by others and hence it is secured. Once it reaches the destination, the receiver can reverse the process to read the ciphertext and this process is called decryption.

Encryption and decryption is done using a key or code. Sometimes, only one key is used to perform both encryption and decryption or sometimes two separate keys are used, one for encryption and other key for decryption. It is used for ensuring integrity and authentication as well. Cryptography is widely used everywhere from Internet to telephones to televisions. While application of Internet is increasingly demanding and growing, hackers are cracking cryptographic algorithms and researchers are working on providing better algorithms and keys so that user's data and authentication is protected. Cryptography, encryption, and decryption are performed using a mathematical function, often known as cryptographic algorithm. The cryptographic algorithm makes use of one or more of the keys to encrypt the data. Strength of the encryption depends on the keys and cryptographic algorithm which makes use of these keys to encrypt.

There are three types of mechanisms used in cryptology: symmetric encryption (which uses the same key for encryption and decryption), asymmetric encryption (which uses different keys for encryption and decryption known as public key and private key) and hashing functions/algorithms which are used to code information like passwords and ensure the authenticity of the documents. Asymmetric encryption which is also known as public key cryptography is enabled through Registration Agencies and Certificate Agencies. Public Key Infrastructure is built by Certificate Agencies to handle the PKC mechanisms effectively. The Certificate Agencies issue the Digital Certificate to the organizations identifying them effectively in the digital world. To ensure the confidentiality of the document, the document is encrypted using the receiver's public key by the sender and decrypted by receiver using his own private key.

For authenticity of the document, the encryption is carried out by the sender using his own private key and the receiver uses the sender's public key to decrypt the same. For ensuring both confidentiality and authenticity of the document both private key of the sender and public key of the receiver are used for encryption while for decrypting both public key of the sender and private key of the receiver are used. We also looked into Hash Function Cryptography and their uses. We also looked at the applications of the cryptography and the security issues related to cryptography and the disk encryption mechanisms.

CHAPTER 6

■ ■ ■

Application and Web Security

Introduction

As we have explored in earlier chapters, security applies to all the components of the systems including physical infrastructure like building, electricity, cables, and so on; hardware; network; software; tools / utilities; human beings including resources internal to the organization and contractors / suppliers who may be working from within the organization or outside the organization. Any part of the entire chain of components can be ignored from security perspective only at the peril of an organization.

Infrastructure is protected through physical security including fences. Hardware is protected through logical access control systems which are smart card based or biometric based or similar mechanisms or by physically securing the system, such as laptops locked to the desk through a locking cable. Physical infrastructure and hardware are relatively easy to secure (even though they have their own challenges like securing laptops during travel etc.). However, ensuring security of the software (including operating system, applications, tools / utilities) and networks are most difficult because of various possibilities as to what can go wrong. Some of the typical vulnerabilities they are exposed to are: misconfiguration, not validated inputs, defects / errors in coding, man in the middle attacks, man in the browser attacks, session hijacking, weak encryption keys, weak / default passwords, weak authentication mechanisms, SQL Injection, and Buffer Overflows.

Increased usage of software and web based applications over the internet has increased the exposure of these various kinds of attacks. Hence, securing them effectively should be the focus of all the designers and developers of such systems. People may believe in "If something has to go wrong it will go wrong." It may be so. But because something can go wrong - not acting on the possible issues is akin to a king inviting the enemy with a red carpet without even fighting the battle, which can only cost the king dearly. However, if we look at the history and data from the history, it is very clear that we are far behind in the race of attacks on software applications and web applications. We are yet to wake up and catch up with the best practices on application development and infrastructure set up, so that we have a fairly good chance of winning the race or at least giving the best possible fight.

Software Applications

More and more work, which was being done earlier by hardware components, is being carried out currently by software or software applications. For e.g. look at the functions carried out by the embedded systems in any automobile. It has substantially increased and many of the functions of a car or an airplane are now directed or controlled by software or software applications. Hardware can fail because of mechanical faults or component aging or component manufacturing defects or weaknesses of the material etc. However, in case of well thought out and well-designed hardware, such chances are less and also may be possible to be detected relatively easily.

Think of medical devices. More and more medical devices are moving to software based from mostly hardware based platforms. Think of an embedded device which is implanted in the human body. Imagine that there is a defect in the software or firmware on it. You need to patch the device to overcome this defect. You have to communicate wirelessly with the device to patch the device. Imagine you update a wrong patch and the problem gets aggravated rather than resolved. For all practical purposes, we will include firmware here as part of software. Think of somebody else tampering with the implanted device wirelessly[1].

Recently there was an incident of Air India Dreamliner flying from Melbourne to Delhi which was required to make an emergency landing at Kuala Lumpur (software malfunction in the cockpit). Earlier in the day, it was reported that the cockpit computers stopped working and the aircraft landed without any navigation aid (which was later denied)[2, 3]. Luckily the pilots were experienced and could navigate the flight effectively and ensure an emergency safe landing. Think of a situation a few years from now if pilots become so tuned to the helpful cockpit and navigation systems that they may become handicapped without these systems. They may not be able to navigate the flight even for a few minutes without these systems and the passengers' life may be at high risk. It may be possible for a passenger to wirelessly impact the cockpit system or for a maintenance engineer to be part of the terrorist team and adversely program the cockpit systems.

Further, the software can get corrupted, can get hacked, data can be manipulated, data can be overwritten, algorithms may be wrong or wrongly implemented, exceptions may not be handled effectively, and errors may not be handled effectively.

A software application is as good as what it does. It should not do more than what it is expected to do. At the same time, it should not fail to perform what it is expected to do. The following eight characteristics are fundamental from the perspective of an application's security (see Figure 6-1):

1. Completeness of the Inputs

2. Correctness of the Inputs

3. Completeness of Processing

4. Correctness of Processing

5. Completeness of the Updates

6. Correctness of the Updates

7. Maintenance of the Integrity of the Data in Storage

8. Maintenance of the Integrity of the Data in Transmission

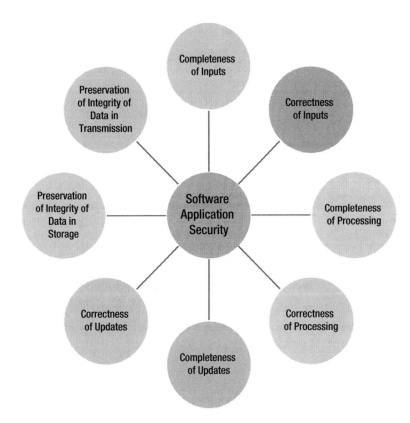

Figure 6-1. *Aspects of Software Application Security*

Completeness of the Inputs

Let us take an example from the field of banking to illustrate this characteristic. Every application has both master data as well as transaction data. Master data is almost fixed and may change only periodically depending upon the changes to the policies or changes to the rules, including Types of Deposits, and Rates of Interest for various tenures of deposits. Types of deposits can be Current Account, Savings Bank Account, Fixed Deposit, Cumulative Deposit, and Recurring Deposit. The rates of interest can be different for various types of eligible institutions and individuals and for various periods of deposit. Transaction data is related to a particular transaction, such as opening of a fixed deposit, application of interest to a deposit, and closing of a deposit.

It is necessary that the inputs taken are complete in all respects so that there is no issue later on to carry out the necessary transactions. Let us take a banking application. For example, when opening a fixed deposit, we did not obtain the type of the depositor and hence we are not able to decide on the appropriate rate of interest; when opening the account we did not obtain the details as to which account the periodic interest should be credited to, because of which, during the interest run we are not able to credit the amount to the corresponding account. Not taking the complete inputs (at least the mandatory ones) can hold back the completion of a transaction and such mistakes should be avoided as it impacts the business adversely and puts the customers at great inconvenience. Hence, it is necessary that the completion of the inputs should be checked by the application and ensured.

Let us take an example of a hospital application. For example, while admitting a patient, the details of the allergies that the patient is susceptible to are not obtained. Consequently, the doctors will be in dilemma as to the application of any medicine which may have side effects. Think of a situation if the patient is unconscious and no close relative is around and because of this lack of information, the doctors do not know how to act.

Completeness of the inputs, particularly of all the critical master and transaction related data in case of banking applications, has to be ensured by the application. Similarly, completeness of all the critical inputs which have bearing on the integrity of the data also has to be ensured. The relevant checks have to be built in the applications to ensure this.

Ineffective database design or inadequate input validation can lead to errors related to completeness of inputs.

Correctness of the Inputs

Another important characteristic every application has to ensure and every software developer has to ensure is that the inputs are correct (i.e., accurate). Integrity of any database or data set depends upon the correctness of the inputs. The inputs have to be validated for accuracy. Some of the inputs can only vary between certain values. In applications like banking, medical devices, and aviation, accuracy of master data is critical.

Think of a situation where the cockpit navigation system of an airplane is guided by a map with wrong coordinates for an airport - imagine what can go wrong!! Think of a ventilator medical device which senses the flow of oxygen wrongly (e.g., when the oxygen is being supplied slowly, the gauge is showing the oxygen as being pumped fast) and subsequent to this observation, the oxygen input is further reduced, imagine what can happen to a patient whose breathing is already impaired!! Think of a medical device which takes the unit of medication as grams instead of milligrams - imagine what can go wrong if a patient is administered a drug which is required to be administered in milligrams instead of in grams! All these can lead to serious implications endangering lives.

All critical data needs to be validated to ensure that they are accurate. One of the ways to ensure the same is to have bound checks on the tolerance for accuracy, another way may be to re-verify or checking of the data through somebody else before the data is accepted. Exceptions have to be handled effectively. Tallying with the control totals is one of the mechanisms to ensure the accuracy. However, in this method there are possibilities of compensatory mistakes.

Inadequate input validation or bounds checking or checks with respect to acceptable values lead to errors related to accuracy or correctness of the inputs.

Completeness of Processing

Another important characteristic every application has to ensure and every software developer has to ensure is that the processing of the information is complete. Integrity of the database or data set also depends upon this. The processing has to be checked to ensure that it was complete. In applications like banking, medical devices, aviation and such other critical applications, this aspect can be well appreciated.

Take a banking example. You have initiated a transaction of transferring USD 2 million from one of your accounts in one bank to your other account in another bank. What if the processing ensures that USD 2 million is debited from your account from where you are transferring the amount and USD 2 million is not credited to your other account? If the situation was the other way round, that is, my other account got credited with USD 2 million but my account which was to be debited did not get debited, I may be happy but what would happen to the bank? What if an X-ray taken does not show the portion of the bone which is cancerous? What if a brain scan shows the cancerous tissue with a displacement of only half an inch? Possibly, good tissue may be removed instead of the malicious tissue. Again, implications of such errors can be many.

Completeness of processing has to be checked by every critical application and confirmed. If the processing is partially complete, then the partially completed portion has to be reversed and the entire transaction has to be redone or the other portion has to be completed to ensure the integrity of the data. Comparison of earlier data, like the total interest paid for the last quarter when compared with this quarter, would indicate the possible mistake if for example the deposits have reduced and the rate of interests have reduced but the total interest paid for the quarter has increased!! Some of the issues related to completeness of issues can happen if you were in the middle of the processing and the system crashed or because electricity went off, the processing abruptly stopped as we did not have UPS backup.

In a transaction oriented system, the check on the completion of all parts of the transactions is critical to ensure the completeness of the processing.

Correctness of Processing

Another important characteristic every application has to ensure and every software developer has to ensure is that the processing of the information is accurate. If this is not taken care of by the applications, again integrity of the data becomes questionable and data may become useless or not reliable.

What if your airplane calculates the distance to the next mountain wrongly? Imagine if it calculates the distance as 100 miles instead of the actual distance of 50 miles? What if you are travelling on such an airplane? What if the medical device pumping a medicine into the patient's body calculates the quantum of medicine wrongly? What if the banking application calculates the interest on your loan account wrongly at 109% whereas it was supposed to calculate the same at 9%?

The above type of mistakes in processing may happen because of the mistake in logic employed or may be on account of mistakes in an algorithm used or may be on account of wrong master data used, wrong application component used, or wrong menu used.

Correctness (i.e., accuracy) of processing has to be checked by every critical application for every critical processing and confirmed. If the processing is wrong, then the defects in the application have to be fixed appropriately.

Application weaknesses like SQL injection, Command Injection, Buffer Overflows, and Cross Site Scripting Attacks can severely impact the application data integrity if these are not taken care of while designing and developing the applications.

Completeness of the Updates

Like the completeness of the inputs, the completeness of the updates also has to be ensured by the applications. Updates are typically to the master data. Suppose the rates of interest on the fixed deposits have been reduced w.e.f. 1st of January 2014 but the same is not updated on the master data, the interest to the depositors will be paid at a higher rate of interest and consequently the bank will lose a substantial amount of money. Imagine that a patient was operated upon yesterday but his record was not updated with the fact of this operation, think of a possibility of his being taken again to the operation theatre for another operation. Of course, the operation may not happen as the wound and sutures are already there but think of the time and effort spent on scheduling, prepping, and so on.

Verification of all critical updates has to be provided through the application to ensure that no critical update is left out and the critical updates are complete in all respects and not partially.

Correctness of the Updates

Like the completeness of the updates, the correctness of the updates is also important. If a patient has to be operated upon the left knee and the update in the medical record of the patient has been made that the procedure is required for the right knee (e.g., knee replacement operation) by oversight or mistake, it is possible that the patient, very much under general anesthesia, may realize the blunder only after the operation is over. He may have to suffer doubly because he already has a problem on his left knee and now he is additionally operated on the right knee!!

Verification of all critical updates for correctness has to be provided through the application to ensure that no critical update is wrong and that the critical updates are accurate in all respects and not partially.

Preservation of the Integrity of the Data in Storage

This refers to the integrity of the data in the underlying database of any application or data under the custody of any application. It should not be possible for anybody to modify this data directly without the authorized provisions of the application. If anybody can modify the underlying data of any application, then the application and data loses its sanctity. For example, the deposit in the banking account of a particular person is USD 1,000,000. The same is modified, without authorization, directly through back end, by running an unauthorized script, to USD 10,000,000. These types of possibilities seriously impact the credibility of the applications.

There are various mechanisms used by the application developers to avoid such issues. Some of these are record checksums, database checksums, or the system is configured in such a way that data can only be modified through the normal application interfaces and not through backend or through any other script directly, regular integrity check runs throwing up the mistakes, strong logging mechanism which ensures that critical data is checked regularly with the corresponding audit logs / pre-image.

Preservation of the Integrity of the Data while in Transmission

We are now in the highly networked era. Applications may be distributed or databases may be distributed. Data may have to be transmitted from one system to another, may be across the oceans and across the continents, such as ecommerce transactions, and credit card transactions. Such data are prone for Man in the Middle Attacks or Man in the Browser Attacks, and similar attacks which can lead to unauthorized modification of the data being transmitted.

Hence, application security should consider the security of the data while in transmission and ensure secure transmission of critical data through mechanisms like encryption.

Importance of an Effective Application Design and Development Life Cycle

A strong, well-defined Software Application Design and Development Life Cycle is essential in any organization that develops critical applications like medical applications, nuclear plant control applications, missile control applications, gas / oil pipeline control applications, electricity control applications, banking applications, and rail network control applications.

Effective time has to be spent during the initial phases of the development life cycle: Requirements Gathering and Analysis and Architecture & Design to understand thoroughly the expectations or requirements of the application. These should also focus on non-functional requirements like processing time, response time, integrity requirements, availability requirements, scalability requirements, flexibility requirements, usability requirements, reliability requirements, and security requirements. Integrity of the data and security of the data are very crucial to be considered at each phase of the design and development life cycle. Sufficient consideration for all the applicable functional and non-functional requirements should be provided for at the design stage by according adequate thinking.

At each phase, strong risk assessment focus should be provided which should bring out what can go wrong. Based on the risk assessment results, necessary risk mitigation or risk control steps have to be built into the applications or into the procedures governing those applications like segregation of duties among the employees, and multiple checks. Some of these controls are possible to be built through the application itself, such as a transaction that is routed for second check before it is debited to the account.

Programming languages and the code itself may bring out security issues. Secure coding standards are emerging. Application architects, designers and developers are learning from various issues they have encountered, technical / technological loop holes or deficiencies they have observed, or those which were reported in the media, and so on. Deficiencies of the third party tools used, deficiencies of the underlying platforms including those of the operating system, and the database systems have to be considered.

Strong testing at various phases of development right from Unit Testing to System Testing to Integrated Testing has to be ensured. When changes are carried out to the existing products, Regression Testing has to be ensured. These tests complement each other and have to be done without fail. The test cases and the corresponding test data have to be well thought out and included as part of the Test Case Design. Similarly, testing should not only focus on what is expected to be done by the application but also what it should not do.

Unfortunately, "thinking" consumes (as per my knowledge of our brain's working) lots of energy. Hence, as human beings, we hesitate to carry out adequate thinking. In order to ensure that the applications are effective i.e. they do only what is expected and not do what is not expected of them, adequate and sufficient thinking has to be carefully provided during each and every phase of the Application Design and Development life cycle. This pro-activeness on our part can lead to effective, strong, and robust applications which are capable of protecting the users / end-users and their interests.

Important Guidelines for Secure Design and Development

Any software design and development team typically adheres to the following generic guidelines, which are illustrated in Figure 6-2:

- Understand the Security Requirements of the application (functionality and data related) and document them as part of the Requirements Specifications Document.

- Ensure that the Security Requirements are considered during Architecture and Design

- Follow Secure Coding Standards

- Validate all the inputs including the boundary checks, check against allowed values, and format.

- Ensure strong login mechanisms (including the need for strong passwords)

- Ensure encrypted transmission of data (where the confidentiality of the data has to be maintained and integrity is of prime importance) – like in case of banking applications, medical software involving patient health and safety, aviation, nuclear safety, military systems and weaponry, satellite systems, and such other critical domains / systems

- Ensure periodic mandatory change of passwords

- Appropriate privileges / access rights to various processes of the applications and various roles – work on Least Privilege Principle

- Appropriate handling of errors (including customized error messages which do not give out unnecessary information)

- Appropriate exception handling mechanisms built into the application

- Appropriate configuration – All settings have to be appropriately made

- Use of vetted algorithms

- Counter checks to ensure complete and accurate processing of critical processing

- Eliminate all unwanted / unused functions and routines

- Ensure proper log out mechanisms

- Use secure protocols

- Ensure proper logging and auditing mechanisms

- Have strong configuration management during development

- Have strong testing

- Have strong control over software releases

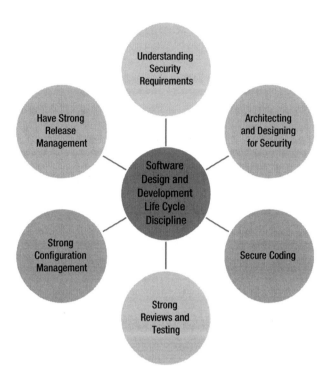

Figure 6-2. *Software Design & Development Life Cycle Discipline*

Some of the important secure coding practices that an application design and development team are required to follow are illustrated n Figure 6-3.

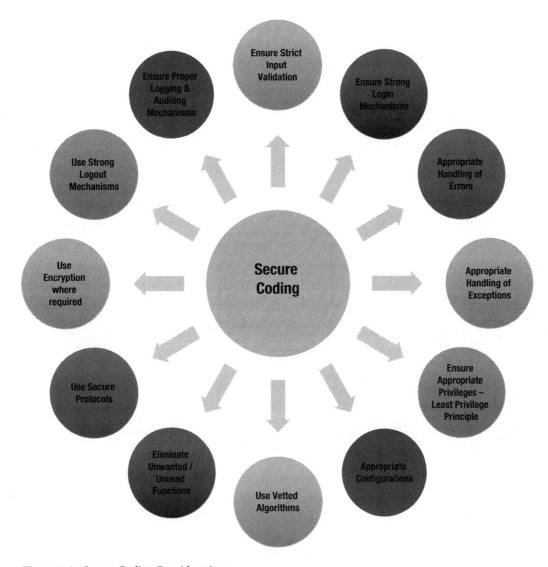

Figure 6-3. *Secure Coding Considerations*

Web Browsers, Web Servers, and Web Applications

Web Applications have become very popular because of their ease of operation and availability to a high number of users over the popular platform of World Wide Web or Internet.

Web Servers enable or facilitate the Web Applications by providing the requisite environment. Like any other three-tier-architecture application, Web Applications normally have a client tier (which is rendered through a Web Browser), a Business Layer which is facilitated through an Application Server, a Data Layer or the Backend which is facilitated through the database systems / servers. Web servers can be separate or a part of the Application server. Web Servers host websites or serve clients with requested web-pages. These web-pages may be static ones or dynamic ones created on the basis of a client's request. HTTP or HTTPS are the protocols typically used for communication between clients and Web Servers. A Web Server is typically a computer program running on a physical server.

Web Servers serve Web Applications. A Web Server, an Application Server and a Database Server should ideally be on separate hardware / physical servers for security reasons but may be on a single hardware / physical server in smaller organizations. Web Applications are software components which provide requisite functionality to the end users. Web Applications facilitate the clients to access the functionalities required by them and also facilitate access to the data lying in the database or data store. They provide for various functionalities like ecommerce, creating / updating of the blogs, providing feedback, carrying out banking transactions, ticketing etc.

The way a typical web-application works is illustrated in Figure 6-4.

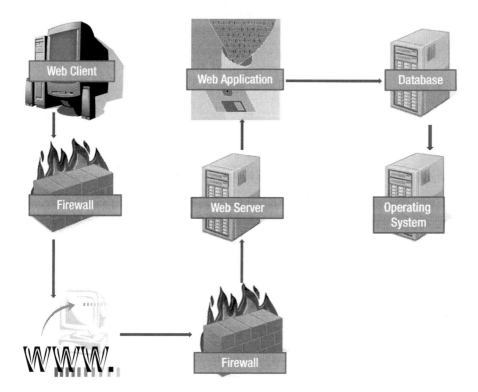

Figure 6-4. *How a Web Application Works*

Each of the three components: Web Browsers, Web Servers, and Web Applications, has its own vulnerabilities. Together, they also combine to create other vulnerabilities. The reasons for this are illustrated in Figure 6-5.

Figure 6-5. *Important Reasons for Issues on the Web*

Vulnerabilities in Web Browsers

Web Browsers are well known and the most used in today's Internet based world. Some of the most used browsers are Microsoft's Internet Explorer, Google's Chrome, and Mozilla Firefox. However, these different web browsers are designed and coded differently, and thus have different vulnerabilities. Some are less used and some are extensively used. Less used ones may be found to have less vulnerabilities may be because the hackers have not found much value in making lots of effort in finding their vulnerabilities in order to exploit them.

Some of the typical vulnerabilities a Web Browser (may vary from one browser to another) is prone to are:

- Inappropriate Configuration
- Unnecessary or Untrusted Add-ons
- Malware (like scripts and executables) run on the Web Browser
- Not patching up or carrying out the security updates

Inappropriate Configuration

It is observed that in many cases, the configuration of the web browsers would have been carried out inappropriately. Pop-up may not have been set to be blocked, allowing the possibility of download of malware / spyware. All types of cookies, by default, would have been allowed whereas it may be risky to allow third party cookies by default, without validating them. Also, all types of scripts would have been allowed to be downloaded / run without any validation.

This is very risky as this may lead to the download of malware (without the user being even aware of it) which can impact the leakage of data held on the computer, crash of the applications, crash of the computer, or leakage of data being transmitted through the browser. Configurations of interest are security settings, privacy settings, and protocols allowed.

Unnecessary or Untrusted Add-ons

Usually, as seen, most of the users of the internet have a habit of downloading the add-ons without really verifying whether they are trustworthy. These add-ons may not be the trusted ones and may lead to malware infection of the web browser unless they are downloaded and enabled cautiously after verifying their usefulness and trusted status. The best way is to keep the unwanted add-ons disabled when you do not want them. This will also increase the performance of the web browser, which would have been reduced because of enabling too many add-ons.

Malware or Executables run on the Web Browser

Malware and other executables can be executed on the Web Browser. These can lead to theft of the data from the system on which the Browser runs (transfer of data from the system to the attacker), execute programs that can infect the system or crash the system or modify the integrity of the data on the system or lead to many such similar adverse impacts on the system.

No Patching up or Carrying out the Security Updates

From time to time, defects or security flaws have been observed in the web browsers. Some of these may be minor but some of these could also be major ones. It is necessary to protect ourselves from such security flaws. Everybody needs to ensure that updates to the browser, particularly security updates, are applied invariably. It is best to enable automatic updates in case of individuals as otherwise we may forget to update them manually. In case of organizations, they can analyze / test the possible impact of such updates on their infrastructure / various applications before carrying out such updates. However, evaluations, patches, and updates should be applied as early as possible if they are applicable to the organization and do not have any adverse impacts. Ideally such updates have to be ensured centrally in big organizations.

How to Overcome the Vulnerabilities of Web Browsers

The following precautions are some of the ways to overcome Web Browser vulnerabilities:

- Configure the Web Browser with appropriate settings – Consult experts if required
- Keep the Web Browser regularly updated with Updates and Security Patches
- Disable or Uninstall unnecessary or untrusted add-ons
- Understand the errors thrown up by the browser like Expired Certificate alerts and then act on them appropriately – If not understood, do not simply act on the same – Consult the experts
- Configure your Operating System properly – Change the default settings to appropriate settings
- Have a well known and reputed Anti-Virus installed on your Operating System

Vulnerabilities of Web Servers

The following web servers are typically used: Internet Information Services (IIS) Windows Server from Microsoft Corporation, Apache Web Server, Nginx Web Server, and Tomcat Web Server.

Some of the typical vulnerabilities of web servers include:

- Default Users and default permissions not changed

- Sample files / scripts not removed

- Default configuration not changed

- Directory permissions not set up properly

- Security loop-holes or defects in the web server software or underlying operating system not fixed / patched up

Other typical attacks possible on the web servers and web sites are:

- DNS attack which redirects users to another web server

- URL Poisoning which redirects users to another URL

- Man in the Middle Attacks

- Password Cracking

- Cookie Poisoning

- Compromise of underlying servers like Email Server and FTP Server

- Buffer Overflow attacks

- SQL Injection attacks

Some of these are self-explanatory and some others like Buffer Overflow attacks and SQL Injection attacks are explained in more detail in the context of Web Application Security.

Default Users and Default Permissions are not changed

Usually, Web Servers like Internet Information Services come with default users with default or no passwords and default permissions. It is necessary to look at the need of actual users and appropriate user IDs and strong passwords have to be set. Default permissions have to be modified according to the need.

Sample files and scripts are not removed

In order to enable the users to set up the Web Server effectively and enable requisite functionalities, Web Servers like IIS come with some sample files / scripts. These need to be removed as they may not be used by the experienced system administrators. If not cleaned up and allowed to lie on the Web Server they may be misused by hackers to attack the Web Server. Hence, all such unwanted sample files / scripts should be cleaned up by removing them from the Web Server.

Default Configuration is Not Changed

Configuration of the Web Server has to be done effectively. Default configurations have to be evaluated and based on the need of the organization and related web applications, these configurations have to be set appropriately. Some of the configurations to be set appropriately are: setting up of SSL Certificates, setting up of administrative functions, setting up of encryption functions, and setting up of debug functions. Unnecessary and unwanted configurations have to be modified appropriately.

File and Directory Permissions are not Set Properly

It is possible that the system administrators have not set the permissions to various files and / or directories on the Web Server effectively. Using such improper / inappropriate permissions, will enable hackers to traverse various directories on the Web Server, which they are normally not authorized to access. This type of attack is known as Directory Traversal Attack and this is mostly observed in old, unpatched Windows IIS Web Servers.

Security Loop-Holes or Defects in the Web Server Software or Underlying Operating System

Various loop holes or defects related to a web server and the underlying operating systems come to the fore and get published by those who find it or the vendors-commissioned organizations which track vulnerabilities. The vendors then come up with solutions or patches / updates to address the same. Up-to-date patching up of the web server and the underlying operating system assures us that the web server is secured to a reasonable extent.

How to Overcome the Web Server Vulnerabilities

The following precautions are some of the ways to overcome Web Server vulnerabilities:

- Change / Disable Default Users and Default Settings and Configure the Web Server appropriately – Disable serving malicious file types which are not required from the perspective of the Web Application

- Regularly patch the Web Server

- Unnecessary and unwanted sample files / scripts to be removed

- Patch up the security loop holes on the underlying Operating System

- Set up file / directory permissions appropriately – Use Least Privilege Method – Set up only the privileges as absolutely required – Evaluate privileges before providing them – Apply the Least Privilege Method even to the database side and to the processes

- Analyze the impact of the changes from a security perspective and carry them out appropriately – Do not jump in and perform the changes without impact analysis

- Ensure strong passwords for both the user accounts and for administrator accounts – Implement periodic mandatory change of password policy

- Ensure that only the need-based ports are open and only the need-based services are active – Disable services like FTP, SMTP, and so on if not needed

- Encrypt the traffic as necessary

- Ensure data files are kept out of the Web Server

- Monitor the Logs regularly

- Delete unnecessary file shares

- Disable Tracing and Debugging

- Check for the validity of the Certificates

- As much as possible, use a dedicated machine for Web Server, other servers like database services should be installed on separate physical servers

- No local logins on the Web Server machine should be allowed

- Server side session ID validation

- Scan the Web Server periodically through Vulnerability Scanners to identify and fix the vulnerabilities

- Perform boundary checking / validations on the inputs

Web Applications

As discussed earlier, web applications provide the requisite interface to the clients to carry out the necessary interactions with the concerned servers and access relevant data.

Some of the important vulnerabilities in web applications include (see Figure 6-6):

- SQL Injection Attacks

- Command Injection Attacks

- Buffer Overflow Attacks

- Cross-Site Scripting

- Cookie Poisoning

- Session Hijacking

Figure 6-6. *Important Attacks on the Web Applications*

Most of these, like SQL Injection Attacks, Command Injection Attacks, Buffer Overflow Attacks, and Cross-Site Scripting happen because of non validated inputs. Inputs are processed by the application as they are fed, without further validation by the web application or the underlying database server.

SQL Injection Attacks

Any web application wherein the inputs are not validated before being processed further and where the database elements are not protected effectively by means of appropriate permissions, are likely to be targets of SQL injection attacks. These are possible when the user provided inputs on the web forms are used to create the SQL query (Select, Insert, etc.) and these inputs are not validated for the appropriateness before they are processed. This may happen through a login page or other input pages from the web forms. Inputs through a login page may allow the authentication to be bypassed and direct access to even the user-ids and passwords of others.

Many of the web applications use default error messages, which may make the users aware of the vulnerabilities possible in the concerned web form. All the error messages have to be customized so that they do not give out more information than necessary to the users or expose the internal vulnerabilities.

Most of the SQL injection methods fool the internal processing mechanism by defaulting the validation of input to be "true" so that the underlying SQL Query is fired even when the actual input is not the right one. Typically ".......' or 1=1- -" is the input used. Two hyphens (- -) stand for comments and makes the SQL statement beyond this point to be treated as a comment. Such SQL injections can throw up as a response, multiple rows from a table or an entire table.

Some examples of the uses of SQL commands are:

```
Blah';exec master..xp_cmdshell "dir c:\*.*  / s > c:\directorylist.txt"--

Blah';exec master..xp_cmdshell "ping 192.168.1.2"--
```

SQL Injection attacks allow the attacker to delete, alter database information, and to create / add new information to the database. This leads to the loss of integrity of the data within the database.

SQL Injection attacks are typically used to understand the database structure and database contents, getting data from the database, adding / modifying / dropping data from the table, and bypassing authentication, for executing commands remotely.

SQL Injection attacks can also be carried out using dynamic strings which are built and executed at a point in time.

Command Injection Attacks

Command Injection Attacks are carried out by the attackers by creating an input string which enables gaining shell access to the underlying web server. Some of the operators that are used to carry out this attack appear in Table 6-1[4].

Table 6-1. Operators Used for Command Injection Attacks along with Purpose of Attack

Operator	Purpose for which it is used by the Attacker
;	This is used to add execution of the additional unintended commands
<, >, >>	These are used to modify files or create new files
|	This pipe symbol is used to chain multiple commands
$, &&, ||	These symbols allow logical operations to be performed like 'AND' or 'OR' on the data before and after them

This type of vulnerability can also be used to inject code with malicious intent into the system files and also to execute scripts like HTML scripts.

Buffer Overflow Attacks

Again this attack becomes possible because of non-validated inputs. These happen, primarily, because of a lack of bound checks or a lack of validation in total. Buffer Overflow attack happens when a Web Application writes more data to a memory location than what it can hold, thus overwriting the adjacent memory space, leading to a buffer overflow. Here, the Web Application does not check the size or format of the input data before storing it in a memory variable.

Buffer Overflow Attacks allow the attacker to alter the sequence of process / program execution, control the process / program execution, and modify the internal variables leading to the execution of malicious code planted in the memory at a particular address. This overflow which overwrites the neighboring buffer area can lead to abrupt termination of the program being executed, incorrect outputs, and abrupt shutdown of the system. However, these types of attacks are normally intentionally crafted exploits where the return pointer is overwritten through buffer overflows to point to the malicious code inserted by the attacker and the execution of the same. The extent of the attack possible is dependent on the context in which the program attacked is running or the privileges under which the program is running.

Two types of Buffer Overflow Attacks can occur:

- Stack Based Buffer Overflows

- Heap Based Buffer Overflows

Both of these buffer overflows act like the holders of the variables until the corresponding program function needs them. Stack is a Last-In-First-Out method to refer to a memory address space which is used to hold the variables and to pass the arguments to the functions. Stack is a static location. Heap is again a memory address space, but is allocated dynamically by the program at runtime. Both are prone to Buffer Overflow Attacks.

In Stack Based Buffer Overflows, the buffer is overwritten by the overflow, which enables the attacker to overwrite the return pointer to point to the malicious code so that the malicious code is executed instead of the originally intended function / code.

The popular Stack Based Buffer Overflow Attack method is the "Smashing the Stack" attack. In this type of attack any input overflow will overwrite the other variables, base pointer, and return address. In the process the malicious code is also inserted by the attacker next to the return address. The attacker intelligently crafts this exploit in such a way that the overwritten return address points to the malicious code injected and leads to the execution of the same. For this attack to be successful it is necessary for the attacker to be able to predict the return address location on the stack as well as the correct return address. In order to enable this, the attacker normally uses multiple NOP (No Operation) instructions along with multiple times the predicted start address. Figure 6-7 illustrates the Stack Based Buffer Overflow Attack.

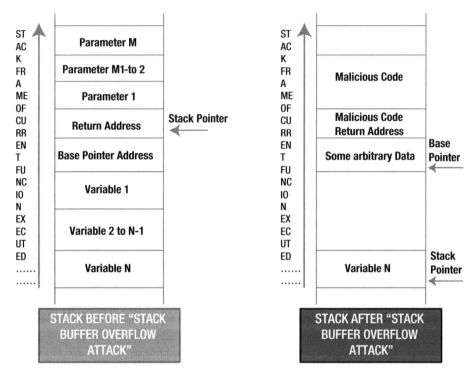

Figure 6-7. *Stack Based Buffer Overflow Attack*

Usage of the non-executable stacks or usage of "canary value" are some of the mechanisms used to avoid Stack Based Buffer Overflow Attacks.

Normally, Heap Based Buffer Overflows, take large inputs which will overwrite the heap management information. They may also overwrite other dynamic variables. The Heap Based Overflows can lead to unknown side effects. In these types of attacks, the program can typically open a command prompt or stop execution of the program.

Heap Based Buffer Overflows are common in C and C++ programming languages. These are possible because the objects are loaded onto heap and such objects hold both data as well as the pointers. The data can be made to overflow the pointers, thus overwriting the address of the program statement being executed to the malicious code. Also, the input data can overwrite the neighboring memory locations on buffer overflow. Figure 6-8 illustrates the Heap Based Buffer Overflow Attack.

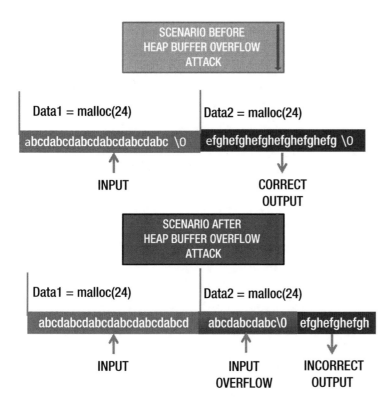

Figure 6-8. *Heap Based Buffer Overflow Attack*

Both the Stack Based Buffer Overflow Attack as well as the Heap Based Overflow Attacks are not easy and require elaborate study or proper prediction on the part of the attacker. The success for the attacker depends upon the right prediction.

Some of the C programming language functions like strcpy(), bcopy(), gets(), scanf(), sprint(), strcat() etc. do not validate the target buffer size and hence can lead to buffer overflows. No Operations (typically known as NOPs) are used in the Buffer Overflow Attacks to alter the sequence of execution of the program steps.

Cross-Site Scripting

Cross-Site Scripting again occurs mostly when the inputs are not validated. Attackers will embed the client side script in a Web Form in a field (e.g., "Comments" field) which is stored by the server and is provided to another unsuspecting user, in whose browser, the script embedded by the earlier user gets executed. This allows for easy embedding of malicious scripts by an attacker with the intention of getting it executed in the browser of other users who request such data and leads to the malicious results intended by the attacker. These types of attacks target the dynamically generated web pages. These attacks can also do other things like redirecting the users to other malicious servers, exploit the other user's privileges, and session hijacking.

These may also be initiated by the attacker through a well-crafted malicious link in an e-mail, which initiates a request to the malicious server, which in turn, returns a page with malicious content which gets executed on the user's web browser. These types of attacks can provide the user's cookies to the attacker, who can use the same to transact on a genuine and trusted site.

Similarly, Cross-Site Request Forgery Attacks can execute malicious code on a genuine server (e.g., trusted server of a bank) by exploiting the weakness on the web page of the bank. This requires the user to visit the malicious site which downloads the malicious code when he is in session with the genuine site so that the malicious code is executed on the genuine server.

Scripting languages like VBScripts, JavaScripts, HTML, and ActiveX are used by the attackers to craft these types of attacks.

Cookie Poisoning

This type of attack is normally carried out through Cross-Site Scripting. However, this type of attack also can be carried out through other means. Another popular method is where the attacker initiates a phishing attack, where a genuine looking link is sent to the user while he is in transaction with a genuine site and is convinced to click on the link which will steal the cookie and transfer the same to the attacker. The attacker can then modify the contents of the cookie as required to fool the genuine site or to carry out unauthorized transactions on the genuine site.

Session Hijacking Attacks

Session Hijacking happens in the following ways:

- **Session Sidejacking**: A user is connected to a genuine server like that of a bank. There is a session established. The session is tracked by the server through the session IDs. Usually, the attacker sniffs the traffic and then cuts off the traffic between the user and the genuine server and takes over the session by predicting the next sequence number of the communication between the genuine user and the genuine server. This typically uses the weaknesses of the Transport Control Protocol where most of the authentication is carried out at the beginning of the establishment of the session.

- **Session Prediction**: In this case the attacker sniffs any victim's traffic to the site like a bank and collects various session IDs. He can monitor the traffic pertaining to multiple users also. He then studies these session IDs to understand how they are generated. If the simple techniques like user ID, date, and time of the day is used it is very easy for the attacker to predict the session ID for any user, date, and time and then use the predicted session id to access the site.

  In case the session ids are generated using complicated algorithms, then he can use the brute force mechanism to crack the session ID logic and once he has cracked the same use the same to generate a valid session ID and use it to attack the site.

- **Session Fixation**: In this case the attacker has a legitimate account with the server, such as the server of a particular bank the account holders of whom he want to dupe. Once he initiates the login process, he will get the session ID. This session ID is then issued to the browser of the victim's machine. The attacker ensures that this session ID is maintained valid by him. Once the genuine user connects to the server the browser of the user uses this fixed session ID. Once the user is authenticated to the server concerned using his login credentials, the attacker uses the session ID so fixed to connect to the server concerned and carry out fraudulent transactions.

  The session can be fixed also through an e-mail purported to be from the bank but actually sent by the attacker with the session ID known to him. This can be done by terminating the connection in between a valid session user and the bank and then by sending an e-mail to the user that restores the connection, the link given in the email ID can be used. The email through which normally the link is sent is designed in such a way as to make the victim believe that it is from the valid source, such as the bank itself. Session Fixation Attack is illustrated in Figure 6-9.

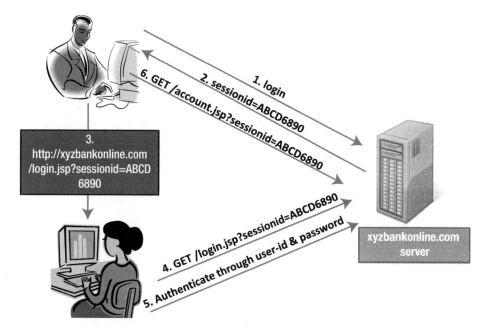

Figure 6-9. *Session Fixation Attack*

- **System Access**: In this case the attacker steals the cookie and thus steals the session key also. This happens when he has access to the victim's machine either directly or through the network. This can also be done by scanning the memory contents of the victim's machine. Once he steals the cookie he uses it to connect to the legitimate server.

- **Cross Site Scripting**: Here the user is conned to run malicious code on his computer which when executed steals the session key and sends it to the attacker. This attack can be done through an intelligently created link which the user believes in.

How to Overcome Web Application Vulnerabilities

The following precautions are some of the ways to prevent Web Application vulnerabilities:

- Invariably validate all the inputs including format checking, bounds checking, and acceptable values.

- Invariably configure Web Applications appropriately

- Regularly patch up all the servers including Web Server, Application Server, Database Server (as relevant and applicable)

- Do not save your Login credentials including passwords on the Web Browser

- Do not save unnecessary information on your Web Browser

- Log off immediately after the work on a Web Application is over – Do not keep the session open unnecessarily for long

- Use strong encryption keys and strong encryption where required - Do not store the encryption keys on the Web Server - Use Secure Socket Layer (SSL) and Digital Certificate for strong authentication

- Define appropriate access rights

- Ensure appropriate Log Out mechanisms in the Web Applications

- Ensure that the Certificate is Valid and has not expired

- Implement effective Cookie Management including Cookie time-out, do not store passwords in a Cookie, authenticate Cookies

- Carry out regular Vulnerability Scans and Penetration Testing to understand and fix the underlying vulnerabilities

Secure Socket Layer (SSL) Security and Digital Certificate

Secure Socket Layer (SSL) protocol and the Digital Certificate ensure that the information exchanged between the Web Server and Client Browser is secure.

Secure Socket Layer (SSL) protocol is used to secure the communications between the Web Server and the Client Browser and uses public key encryption to exchange symmetric encryption keys between the Web Server and the Client Browser. These exchanged symmetric encryption keys are used for encrypting the messages between the Web Server and the Client Browser. Digital Certificate is used for the authentication of Web Server to the Client Browser. Authentication here means that the Web Server confirms that it is legitimate / genuine to the Client Browser. These Digital Certificates are issued by the certificate authority to any organization only after validating the entity to which they are issuing the Digital Certificate. Certificate authorities are the trusted agencies. Hence, it is not possible for a bogus / non-existent company to get the Digital Certificate from a recognized certificate authority. The Digital Certificate clearly shows to which organization it is issued and the validity of the digital certificate.

The SSL protocol ensures the confidentiality of the data being exchanged as the encryption cannot be so easily cracked. This protocol ensures that the integrity of the data being exchanged is genuine, as decryption fails if any piece of the encrypted information is changed / modified. The Digital Certificate provided by the Web Server to the Client Browser and validated by the Client Browser assures that it is handshaking with the legitimate / genuine Web Server.

SSL is used to encrypt transactions carried out through protocols like HTTP and FTP. SSL is also implemented on all the important commercially available browsers. The SSL process is illustrated in Figure 6-10.

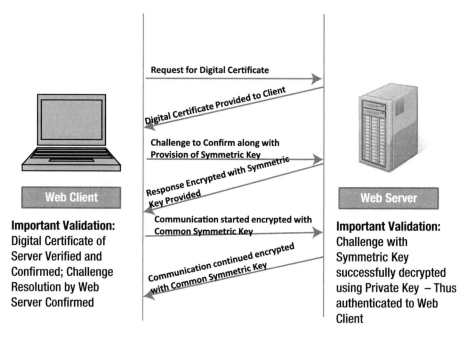

Figure 6-10. *Secure Socket Layer Process*

The six steps in the process are:

Step 1: The Client Browser requests the Digital Certificate from the Web Server with which it has to communicate.

Step 2: The Web Server provides its certificate to the Client Browser.

Step 3: The Client Browser checks the certificate to ensure that it is from a trusted certificate authority and contains the Web Server's "public key". The Client Browser then sends a challenge to the Web Server to check that the Web Server has the "private key" corresponding to the "public key" contained in the certificate. The challenge includes the symmetric key which will be used to encrypt the SSL traffic. This challenge cannot be responded to by others because only the genuine Web Server has the "private key".

Step 4: The Web Server decrypts the challenge using its "private key". Then it encrypts its response using the symmetric key it has received. Owing to this exercise, the Client Browser gets assured that it is communicating with a genuine / legitimate Web Server. Now, both the Client Browser as well as the Web Server have the same symmetric key which they can use for further communications between them.

Step 5: The Client Browser sends its request to the Web Server encrypting the request with the common symmetric key.

Step 6: The Web Server responds to the Client request by encrypting the response with the common symmetric key.

The Web Browser, if configured properly, will provide warnings on the certificate in the following cases:

- Certificate is invalid or expired

- Certificate not signed by recognized certificate authority

- Name on the certificate does not match domain name of the server

Ideally, in such a case, the user should not accept the certificate. If the certificate is accepted, the user is susceptible to attack.

TLS (Transport Layer Security) protocol is an improvement of SSL.

Chapter Summary

- We introduced the relative fact that infrastructure related security and hardware security are easy to handle compared to the security aspects related to software (which includes the operating system, software, software applications, utilities / tools, etc.) which are more complex and difficult to handle.

- We examined software security, namely, primarily software application security and how the integrity of software application is very important and what are the essentials to ensure this integrity. In this context, we explored in detail the eight fundamental aspects, Completeness of Inputs, Correctness of Inputs, Completeness of Processing, Correctness of Processing, Completeness of Updates, Correctness of Updates, Preservation of the Integrity of Data in Storage, and Preservation of the Integrity of Data in Transmission. We discussed all of these with relevant examples from critical domains / fields like banking, aviation, and medical devices.

- We explored how adequate and appropriate attention to security requirements and potential risks during the Software Design and Development Life Cycle can substantially reduce the vulnerabilities in the software application developed. We also explored how secure design and coding contribute to this regard. We then looked into some of the important aspects which have to be considered as part of Secure Coding.

- We reviewed the basics of Web Browser, Web Server, and Web Applications and how they work with each other and the uses of each of these.

- We explored the vulnerabilities of Web Browsers, and looked into some of the practices which will reduce the Web Browser vulnerabilities or possibilities of attack on / through Web Browsers. In this context, we looked into the importance of appropriately and securely configuring the Web Browsers, importance of not having unnecessary add-ons, and how the regular patching up / updating of the Web Browser software will help.

- We elaborated on the vulnerabilities of Web Servers and looked into some of the practices which will reduce the Web Server vulnerabilities or possibilities of attack on Web Servers. In this context, we looked into the importance of modifying / removing default users / passwords, ensuring the removal of sample files / scripts, modification of the default configuration into appropriate configuration, fixing of the defects / loop holes in the Web Server software as well as the underlying Operating System.

- We discussed the vulnerabilities of Web Applications, and looked into some of the practices which will reduce Web Application vulnerabilities or possibilities of attack on Web Applications. In this context, we looked in detail into some of the important attacks like SQL Injection Attacks, Command Injection Attacks, Buffer Overflow Attacks, Cross-Site Scripting Attacks, Cookie Poisoning Attacks, and Session Hijacking Attacks. We also explored some of the important steps / actions we need to take to avoid becoming prey to Web Application attacks. We then explored the role of SSL and Digital Certificate in securing the communication between the Web Client and the Web Servers. We also provided a passing remark that Transport Layer Security (TLS) protocol has expanded upon the SSL concepts further, so that the persons interested can further study the same.

■ ■ ■

CHAPTER 7

Malicious Software and Anti-Virus Software

Introduction

The intent of "Malicious Software," as the name suggests, is to create harm or damage to systems or to people or to both. As science can be used for both good and bad purposes, software can also be used for both good and bad purposes. Some people or groups use software or exploit software loopholes inappropriately, for fun or to highlight their technical skills. Many others do it for financial gains, for taking revenge, or to create fear in others. Of late, these are misused for political or religious gains or for terrorism. Many countries are spying on each other and many militaries have a Cyber Warfare division.

The general belief in today's world is that, technologically we are getting more advanced, which is, of course, very true. Additionally, they believe that these new technologies protect us or are designed to protect us. But, in this commercially oriented world, it seems that the companies are in a hurry to push across their technology and tools without strictly ensuring that the users of their technology and tools are protected. One strong example is that, even though these companies are aware that "non-validated inputs" are the most exploited, they still do not care to ensure proper validations. Unfortunately, all these new technologies and tools provide opportunities for people with bad intentions to find, understand, and exploit the loopholes or flaws in them.

Unlike in the prior century, we are now in the era of a well-connected world which can be reached from one end to the other in a matter of seconds. Improved connectivity coupled with improved internetworking infrastructure has increased the speed at which we can connect when disasters occur, the ease with which we can do business across the globe, the ease with which we can share information with our peers, and the ease with which we can access knowledge. However, at the same time, these have also exposed us to unwanted downsides. The technologies allow knowledgeable hackers and crackers to connect to your system or your mobile or your tablet, sometimes without your even being aware of this. Recent incidents with Apple's "Find My iPhone" and "Find My Mac" services exploited by the hackers locked out users from their own devices!![1]

Even though people who use the Internet are generally aware that it can present certain security threats, most do not realize the extent of these threats—and how they can harm their systems, financial assets, or privacy. They do not know that once their personal data has been acquired by others, it can be used to steal their identity, in turn allowing these thieves to access their bank or social media accounts. Most of the general users of the internet may not even know what scripts are and how a cross site scripting attack can bring miseries to them or lead them to financial losses. This vast gap in the awareness of these specifics is being misused by hackers and others with bad intention. A simple example is the certificate error thrown up by the browser. We have seen people simply and automatically ignoring these and going ahead with their work. They do not even recognize this as a potential threat!! They do not even know that, at that point of time, they may be getting connected to a malicious server rather than the legitimate and intended server.

Most of the people are not aware that pirated software can create lots of issues for them or to their systems, as well as create malicious infection. Most people believe that any off-the-shelf software is good. They generally believe that all the apps (applications) for iPhone or Android that are available, either on the official sites or anywhere else on the internet are good. Most of them are not aware that many of these apps on legitimate shopping sites can have intentional or unintentional security issues. Similar is the case with free software. People believe that free software is good. The general public is not aware that many of this free software has been maliciously created with intentions of stealing your data, stealing your personal or financial information, tracking your activities, or misusing your accounts or credit cards.

Most of the hacker tools, with information of how to hack systems, are easily available on the internet for even a child to experiment with. Some people may experiment with these for fun, find something interesting enough to exploit, and may go on exploiting the loopholes they have found. Others may intentionally learn the loopholes and use them for devious purposes.

We have seen earlier how, in the world of the internet, web browsers, web servers, and web applications are prone to exploits. We also saw how the software applications in general, including critical software like banking applications and medical applications can be misused by bad people. Of course, most of us are already aware that even the operating systems have their part to contribute by not being secure and new flaws are being found day in and day out!! We are also aware that the protocols used on the networks can also be compromised and the network used for bad purposes.

Of course, the only ray of hope is the real anti-virus software. Thanks to this community, some of these are available for free. The good thing is that most of them are commercially available for cheap rates. Another good aspect of these is that most of them are able to protect the user community to a large extent even though they are not fool-proof. Unfortunately, in spite of the easy availability of anti-virus software, their usage is still not up-to-the-mark. Even where people use them, most of the time, they overlook the alerts, they fail to update the virus signatures, or they fail to regularly do the scanning which tends to largely defeat the very purpose of these preventive or detective mechanisms.

Again, this race seems to always be won by the hackers, as they are the ones who are actually testing the software for loopholes, whereas in actuality, the security testing done by the application software developers is really meager. On the flip side, neither national agencies nor other forums in most of the countries are able to bring the required awareness among the people who use the internet and other latest technologies like mobiles and tablets. Now that we do most of the work through the internet and much of it on mobile, which, in most of the cases, are not protected even with basic anti-virus software, we are definitely at higher risk.

Malware Software

Malicious software is generally known as "Malware." So-called "spyware," "adware," "Trojans," "backdoors," "viruses," "worms," and "botnets" are all part of malware.

Introduction to Malware

Most of us would have experienced, ranging from a small scale to a larger scale, the impact of malware on our systems. Some would have experienced corruption of files, corruption of data, deletion of data, crash of hard disk, and corruption of operating system. Others would have experienced that their credit cards were misused; their bank accounts were fraudulently misused, the information pertaining to them was misused, or the confidential information pertaining to them was leaked. Some others would have experienced that their entire system was compromised and used to attack others. The experience can vary from one person to another person, but we believe that each one of us would have some part of this experience if we were conscious of what is going on with our systems. Of course, the caveat here is that all abnormal behavior in our systems need not always be because of malware, but at the same time, the probability of abnormal behavior on account of malware is high.

Covert channels

These are the channels of communication which are only meant for authorized usage or only meant for usage in a certain way or for certain purposes, but are available to all because of the technologies or protocols or applications or utilities we use. These are misused by the hackers or others. For example, a message or a file or figure may be hidden within another figure and sent to the attacker by an insider using the techniques of steganography as officially the figures are allowed to be transmitted within and outside the organization. The figure which is obvious to the eyes, it may be a greeting card or other legitimate figure.

Most of the reasons for this suffering is simple and can be traced back to the behavior of those affected. They would have either used pirated software to save money, downloaded a free software without verifying its authenticity or its vulnerabilities, downloaded so-called helpful utilities which will solve their day-to-day problems or would increase their productivity, would have installed an operating system or a software application in a hurry without enough attention to the appropriate configuration, would not even have configured their internet browser appropriately, they may be using bad practices like keeping their internet connections or connections to their applications on for long periods of time without switching off or logging off, sharing the user ids and passwords / PIN with others, not changing the passwords for years together, using weak passwords, and using the same passwords for all applications. Hence, awareness of do's and don'ts in this world of information technology is the one thing which needs the utmost stress. Anybody interested in furthering the good aspects of technology should strive for awareness, in whichever way they can, in the interest of information security.

Types of Malware in Detail

We listed some of the typical malware in the earlier section. We will look into the definitions of these in layman terms in the following paragraphs. A note of caution here is that these definitions may not be exclusive. There may be overlaps between these definitions, e.g. an adware or a Trojan can both be spyware.

Spyware

As the name suggests, their intention is to spy. They spy for information, pertaining to either persons or organizations, which can be used later for malicious purposes. They track or monitor the activities of others. The information collected is either misused or passed on to other interested parties. There are even official spyware which are used by Governments and national agencies. These work secretly or in stealth mode. Examples include Tracking Cookies, which track what you did on the web pages, and Keyloggers (e.g., ComputerSpy), which can log everything you've typed including user IDs and passwords.

Adware

These are typically software applications. The purpose of these is to generate revenue for the owner of the site, which compensates for the amount spent by him in creating the software application. These may be part of many websites. These advertisements may be in the form of popups, streaming messages, through sections on the web page, or through a bar on the screen. These may be interesting and eye-catching advertisements or unwanted advertisements. However, the underlying code within these advertisements may track a user's personal behavior and pass on the information to the interested third parties. Many of these advertisements also publish free ware like games and tools. Again these may be planted there with a malicious intention and being clicked on to explore further, may download malicious software which may carry out the intended functionality, but at the same time, they may also carry out many unintended activities without the user being even aware of them, unless he/she is protected by a strong anti-virus software.

Trojans

This is the short form used for "Trojan Horses." These are programs with malicious code embedded within a presumably well intended application or utility or tool or game. These do the intended function for the user in the foreground, but also do unintended functions like compromising the system and providing access to the system and its files to an attacker, in the background. These get downloaded along with other programs in which the users are interested. Some examples of the popular Trojans are: Flame, Zero Access, DNSChanger, Banker, Downloader, Back Orifice, Zeus, and Beast.

Viruses

These are basically malicious software that attach themselves to other files in the form of executables. These require carriers. They are self-replicating and get activated and infect other files when the carrier is executed. These carriers are usually genuine files like system files. Some of the popular viruses are: Michelangelo, Brain, Klez, Wullick-B, SQL Slammer, Sasser, and Blaster.

Worms

These are self-replicating malicious software which can propagate or proliferate on their own. They are like self-propelling rockets. They do not require a separate carrier. They can multiply themselves and can propagate out of the networks, infecting other networks and other systems, thus creating huge havoc or damages. Some of the popular worms are: Melissa, Explorer.zip, Love Bug, ILOVEYOU, Code Red, The Sober, W32.Nimda, and W32.Stuxnet.

Backdoors

Backdoors are the malicious software which are installed on a system with the intention of having access to the system at a later date. A backdoor may be installed through a Trojan. These are usually in stealth mode and get activated by the attackers based on their intentions. Examples are: Remote Access Trojans, Backdoor.Trojan, Trini, and Donald Dick.

Botnets

These are a network of zombies or a zombie army which are already compromised / infected by attackers and which are used for attacking other systems. These are used to initiate attacks like the denial of service or distributed denial of service, etc. on other systems. These attacks are carried out by pooling the infected systems as a botnet so that the impact can match the scale required. These networks of zombies have zombies from across the world. These are infected with a "bot" which connect them to "bot controllers" and other bots. Hence, these are known as "Botnets."

Most of these malware work silently or in stealth mode without announcing their arrival or presence, particularly spyware, Trojans, and Backdoors.

A Closer Look at Spyware

As discussed earlier in the chapter, Spyware is primarily used to record a user's activities, including the interaction with the computer, external world including the internet, and to send this data back to the attacker. These are carried out without the user's knowledge that is in a stealthy mode. These spyware hide their activities and the files related to them.

Data recorded and sent to the attackers may be user IDs, passwords, bank account numbers, other PINs, personal information, etc. These data are then used by the attacker to initiate new attacks. Some of this software, like adware, may be used to create inconvenience to users through unwanted pop-ups, redirecting to advertising sites. In addition, these may carry out dangerous activities like changing the settings of the browsers, firewalls / IDS; redirecting the user to malicious sites; reduce the performance of the system and reduce system security; install short cuts to malicious sites; add unwanted sites to favorite websites; and other unwanted changes to the system settings.

Some of these may entice the users as free anti-spyware utilities themselves. The most popular means through which these get installed are through cookies when you surf the websites, web browser add-ons which sound interesting and useful, or as a part of maliciously modified genuine software available for download through popular sites.

Desktop activity monitoring spywares, e-mail monitoring spyware, internet monitoring spyware, screen capturing software, audio and video recording software, USB-based spyware, mobile phone monitoring spyware are some of the popular categories of spyware. In addition, key loggers are another set of spyware which log your activities, mostly what you typed.

Some of the measures that users may take to counter such spywares are:

- Download software only from trusted sites

- Download only authenticated software – Verify the authenticity through all possible means before downloading

- Do not click on unwanted / non-trusted links in e-mails or websites

- Use virtual key boards for entering user IDs and passwords

- Use key-stroke interference software or Windows On-screen Keyboard Accessibility program

- Scan files before copying them

- Use different user IDs and passwords for different applications

- Use strong passwords and change them regularly

- Delete history, cookies, cache, other information immediately on logging out

- Do not store passwords on the systems

- Set security levels on your web browser appropriately

- Do not use untrusted third party systems for important transactions like banking transactions

Needless to say, use strong Anti-Virus software and keep it updated.

Trojans and Backdoors

As discussed previously, the Trojans are usually wrapped along with a useful program like a game, a useful utility, etc. which entices the victims to download them either through the links sent to them or through websites. These are either genuine looking or genuine programs or data which carry malicious code.

Backdoors are Trojans which are readily available at the command of the attacker and can be used any time by the attacker or can be instantiated based on user events or based on a timeline reached. Incidentally, some of the genuine programs which are installed for remote debugging purposes by applications may be used by the attackers as backdoors for malicious purposes. Backdoors are created normally by experts who have in-depth system knowledge and are normally carried out by adding a new service on the Windows OS.

The Trojans have the potential of wiping out everything on your hard disk including the FAT (File Allocation Table) to steal passwords to access the files on your system and read or delete or destroy or transfer them to the attacker. These can take over your entire system and use any commands or files on the system. These can virtually make your machine a slave to the attacker and allow him / her to use your system as he / she wants, including using your system to launch an attack on other systems. These can be active or time bombs embedded within your system.

Oftentimes, these get downloaded when you download a file which is very useful to you. These Trojans attach themselves to useful files using a wrapper and get downloaded along with these useful files and become active as per the intentions of the attacker. The triggers for their activation may be activity based or event based or time based. They may trigger whenever you are visiting a banking site, at a particular time of the day or when the commands are ready to be executed from a remote client controlled by the attacker, depending upon the intentions of the attacker.

Some of the purposes or impacts of Trojans are:

- Disablement of firewalls, IDS/IPS, Antivirus or similar highly useful defensive mechanisms

- Delete or replace files including those of the Operating System files, such as commands and drivers

- Proxy the system so that they can be used for attacks on others

- Include the system as part of Botnet which can then be used for attacks on others

- Create backdoors on the system which can be used for malicious purposes at a later date by the attacker

- Download other malicious programs

- Record the activities of the users so that the information can be used for malicious purposes

- Defraud you during your banking / financial transactions

Usually, these Trojans look for stealing credit card data, financial information of the system users, identity related information pertaining to the users, confidential information of value to the attacker or other interested parties, obtain user credentials, obtain user details, and use the compromised system for attacks on others.

Trojan attacks usually become evident by abnormal activities on the compromised system. Some of these may be, the web browser getting redirected to unknown and unanticipated pages, strange entries in your bank accounts or credit card statements, your passwords are changed without your knowledge, unusual activities on your hard disk and other hardware including modems or mouse, unexpected chat boxes being opened and closed, sudden reboot of the system, sudden shut down of the system, mouse pointer disappearing, screen saver changes or color setting changes, monitor toggling between on and off, unanticipated programs suddenly getting executed, and windows START button becoming invisible. As discussed earlier, some of the Trojans, like backdoors, may not throw up any abnormal activities and may carry out their work stealthily.

There are many types of Trojans. Some of these are Command Shell Trojans, E-mail Trojans, Proxy Server Trojans, SPAM Trojans, VNC Trojans, Document Trojans, ICMP Trojans, HTTP Trojans, FTP Trojans, E-banking Trojans, Root Access Trojans, and Reverse Connecting Trojans.

Proxy Trojan infection is illustrated in Figure 7-1.

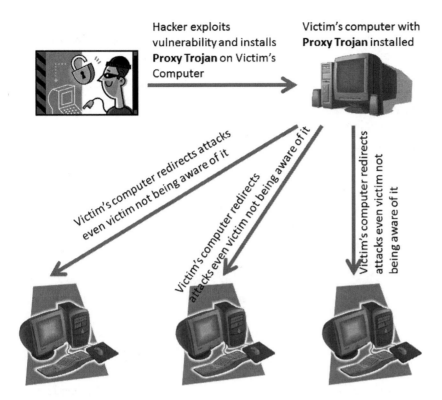

Figure 7-1. *Proxy Trojan Infection*

Root Access Trojans are an important set of Backdoor Trojans. These make your system slaves to the remote attacker. The server portion of these Trojans is installed on the system to be compromised. The client portion is used by the attacker. They open a network port on the compromised system thus allowing the attacker to use the compromised system the way he / she likes it and whenever he / she chooses to do it.

Reverse Connecting Trojans use a similar method as that of Root Access Trojans. They install a server, that is, Reverse World Wide Web Shell Server on the internal system. This system, on a periodic basis, connects to the external master system of the attacker and executes the commands of the master on the system. It is not easy to detect these types of attacks as they use the normal HTTP channel and hence are considered usual traffic between the browser and the web application.

Table 7-1 describes several Trojans.

Table 7-1. *Trojans and the Problems They Cause*

Trojan	Problems it Causes
Flame	This Trojan impacts the Windows operating system – Records screen shots, keyboard strokes, network traffic, other conversations.
Donald Dick	This Trojan impacts the Windows operating system – It allows complete access to the attacker on the compromised system.
Tini	This Trojan provides the attacker remote access to the command prompt on the compromised system.
SpyEye	This Trojan impacts the Windows operating system – It hides its own registry keys, its directory and configuration file. It injects malicious code in the running processes. It can capture network traffic, information from the browsers, initiate network packets, etc.
Zero Access	This Trojan impacts the Windows operating system – Impacts services.exe file - It is used to hijack user searches, initiate pay-per-click frauds, initiate malicious payloads – Modifies the registry keys to enable this.
DNSChanger	This Trojan is well known to target the Mac operating system – DNS settings of the compromised system are changed to those of the attacker which enable the attackers to have full access to the compromised system.
LetMeRule	This Trojan listens on any of the ports of the compromised system for which it is configured. The attacker can control the compromised system remotely.

Users can carry out regular scanning of the following to detect the Trojans which can act as complements to Anti-virus software:

- Suspect start up programs

- Suspect files including the directories

- Suspect entries in the registry

- Running programs which look suspect or possibly not initiated by the users

- Suspect modifications to the system files

- Suspect device drivers

- Suspect network activities

Some of these may easily be done using simple Windows commands like:

- sigverif: Most of the drivers in Windows are digitally signed by Microsoft. sigverif.exe or File Signature Verification Tool of Windows Vista, Windows 7, and Windows 8 allows you to check for unsigned drivers.

- sfc /scannow: System File Checker utility allows you to check for the integrity of the Windows System files.

- services.msc: Understand various services enabled on the system and the services running on the system at the point of time. Only knowledgeable users can understand the results.

Similarly, tools such as sysinternals and PC Tools Registry Mechanic may be used to understand the integrity of the system files and other files. However, you need to understand how these tools work before you use them. The genuineness of the tool itself should be verified before running it. Hashing techniques like MD5 and SHA2 may be used to understand the genuineness and / or uninfected position of the tool itself or files, as described in Chapter 8. One of the best ways to reduce the possibility of malware attacks, including Trojans, is to install a best in class Anti-virus software and always keep it updated.

How the Trojans get into your system is common for most of the malicious software. Some of these are:

- Download of interesting free programs, files, screen savers, and data from the web
- Download of interesting programs or utilities sent through internet messengers or tools
- Enticing attachments to e-mails
- Infected attachments received through e-mails from a genuine source
- Defects in software applications or web servers
- Fake programs on malicious sites or legitimate sites
- Genuine programs embedded with Trojans and reloaded on legitimate sites
- File sharing through peer-to-peer networks or through remote access
- Visit to untrusted sites leading to automatic download of malicious software
- Scripts maliciously introduced through cross-site scripting enabling download of malicious software

Some of the measures which can be taken up by most of the users to reduce the propensity for attacks by Trojans are:

- Do not open attachments of e-mails from strangers
- Do not open attachments, seemingly from known persons, but with strange and unexpected or non-contextual content
- Do not accept programs sent over instant messaging by strangers however enticing or useful they may sound to be
- Update your operating system, web browsers, applications you use with the latest patches / updates including security updates
- Always maintain the configuration settings of the operating system, web browsers, applications with the most appropriate settings – Do not leave them with default settings
- Ensure strong passwords
- Disable / Block all unnecessary ports at your system as well as on the tools like firewall
- Avoid downloading free software from unknown sites – Check for the authenticity of such sites and software
- Restrict permissions to the users on the system – Avoid providing unnecessary administrative privileges to user accounts
- Scan all CDs/DVDs/USBs with Anti-Virus software before downloading any content from them
- Avoid executing utilities / programs blindly
- Manage the integrity of system files and other files through hashes / checksums, etc.
- Use a strong Anti-Virus software with Firewall, IDS and other malware detection capabilities
- If you are a system administrator, do not allow users to download software directly from the websites – ensure they obtain appropriate permissions from you or get them downloaded through you – Have supporting security policies in this regard

Rootkits

Rootkits are malicious software installed without the user's awareness. These are installed with the following intentions:

- Hide rootkit's own activities and their presence

- Hide the activities performed by other malicious utilities / software installed on the compromised system

- Gather data of interest to the attacker and provide this data to the attackers silently

- Act as a repository of malicious programs serving other systems like zombies or bots

These rootkits contain various backdoor programs and other malicious utilities like network sniffers, and the tools which wipe off the logs. These replace some of the operating system functions and calls with their own malicious versions thus compromising the security of the targeted system. Once they are installed, they provide complete access to the attacker on the compromised system.

Rootkits are installed the same way as other malicious software. The types of rootkits include[14]:

- Firmware Rootkits: These hide in firmware.

- Kernel-Level Rootkits: Kernel is the core of the operating system which manages memory, processes, tasks and devices like disks. Kernel is the one which is loaded in the memory and resides in the memory till the computer is shutdown. These replace a portion of the original kernel code or add malicious code to the kernel or replace device drivers.

- Hypervisor-Level Rootkits: Hypervisor is the Virtual Machine Monitor (VMM) which controls different Virtual Machines running on a host. This allows a host to be shared by multiple operating systems. Hypervisor controls all the host resources and allocates them as necessary to the constituent operating systems. These modify the boot sequence and get executed themselves first, instead of the operating system or the virtual machine, as the case may be.

- Boot Loader-Level Rootkits: These replace the original boot loader with a malicious one.

- Library-Level Rootkits: These replace the original system calls with fake calls thus hiding the attacker's activities.

- Application-Level Rootkits: These replace application binaries with fake ones or modify the application behavior by various means.

Rootkits are not easy to detect as they are primarily meant to be working in stealth mode, hiding themselves and their activities. However, integrity checks, popular rootkit signature checks, runtime execution path profiling, and cross view based detection can help in identifying the rootkit infection.

You can take the following measures to counter the rootkits:

- Reinstall the rootkit infected operating system with a clean copy

- Reinstall the rootkit infected applications with clean binaries after backing up the data

- Restrict administrative permissions to the users so that they are not able to install malicious programs on their systems

- Have strong administrative credentials so that they are not easily compromised

- Always carry out restoration through trusted media / sources

- Install firewalls

- Keep your systems and servers always hardened

- Ensure that the systems, applications and utilities are updated / patched regularly

- Have strong awareness created within the organization against malware infection

- Do not install unnecessary software / applications

- Keep your system protected with strong anti-virus software with rootkit protection as a part of it and this software needs to be kept updated

- Verify the integrity of the system on a regular basis through different mechanisms through usage of hashing techniques or through file checksum verification techniques. The details have been provided in Chapter 8.

Some of the popular rootkits are:

- Windows NT/2000 Rootkit

- Fu

- KBeast

Some of the popular anti-rootkits available are:

- UnHackMe

- Stinger

- TDSSKiller

- Rootkit Razor

Viruses and Worms

As discussed earlier, a virus infects a file, for example - an executable file, and uses that file as a carrier. A virus requires a carrier file to hold it. A virus code is injected into a carrier program which is a genuine executable. Viruses can carry a Trojan code and ensure that the Trojans spread from system to system. Viruses spread when the carrier program, with the virus injected into it, gets executed. Viruses self-replicate upon the execution of the carrier program and infect other programs, documents or boot sectors of the computer, etc. Viruses use the same mechanism of spread, that is, through e-mail attachments; games; scripts; macros; through already infected genuine programs; installing of pirated software; carrying out downloads without checking the authenticity or genuineness of such programs and files; and compromised legitimate websites.

There is not much difference between Viruses and Worms. Viruses require a carrier program whereas Worms can stand on their own. Worms can self-replicate and spread on their own. Impact-wise, both can create havoc. Similar to the viruses, the worms can also carry Trojan code and spread the Trojans from system to system. Worms can traverse through the network, on their own. Worms do not attach themselves to other programs.

Viruses transmit through infected disks and files. Viruses can have different characteristics based on the type of virus. While most of them are meant to infect other programs, some can disguise themselves into other forms, some can encrypt themselves, and others can alter data or corrupt programs and files. They can easily infect other files and proliferate easily.

Viruses are normally designed by those who have good programming skills. Viruses replicate themselves and attach to the executable files before spreading further. When viruses attach themselves to the executable files, they alter the instruction pointer of the executable programs in such a way that the virus code gets executed first before the actual executable code. Figure 7-2 illustrates the infection process. While most of the viruses infect each time they are executed, some of the viruses, such as Friday the 13th, get executed only when the intended day or time or a particular dependent event occurs.

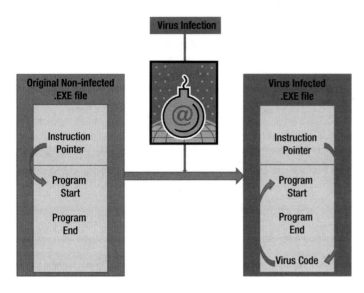

Figure 7-2. *How a Virus Executes*

The intention of viruses is primarily to damage others' systems. The target may be competitors, enemies – political, religious, or otherwise, or for financial gains. Some of the indications of a virus infected system are:

- Use of more CPU and memory resources

- Not able to load Operating System files

- Missing folders or files

- Lot of hard disk read / write activity

- System freezes up

- Many different errors thrown up

- System gives continuous beeps

- Display not working

However, as the above indications can also be on account of other reasons, these cannot be assumed as the conclusive proof of virus infection. However, having a strong Anti-Virus can alert you of the possible virus attack and help you remove / quarantine the same. How the Anti-Virus software identifies viruses will be discussed in the later portion of this chapter.

Table 7-2 describes some of the types of viruses and their characteristics.

Table 7-2. *Types of Viruses*

Virus Type	Important Characteristics
System or Boot Sector Virus	These typically move the Master Boot Record (MBR) to some other location on the disk and copy their own code to the MBR and thus get executed first when the system boots. These are basically shell viruses which form a shell around the executable to which it is attached and gets executed first before the control is passed on to the executable.
Macro Virus	These are usually written in Visual Basic Applications (VBA) and infect the files created by MS Office programs like Microsoft Word, Microsoft Excel.
File Virus	These infect files which are executed or interpreted, e.g., *.EXE, *.SYS, *.COM, *.PRG, *.BAT etc.
Encryption Virus	These viruses encrypt themselves and use a different key each time they infect a new file. Encryption leads to difficulty in its being recognized as a virus.
Multipartite Virus	These viruses infect multiple parts of the system at the same time. Example: Boot Sector as well as *.EXE files.
Stealth Virus	These escape anti-virus software by intercepting the anti-virus software calls to the Operating System and pointing it to the actual virus which provides a clean copy of the requested program to the anti-virus software.
Cluster Virus	These modify directory entries and point system processes to virus code, then the actual program, leading to the execution of the virus code. As usual, the virus executes itself first and then hands over the control to the file, the execution of which was requested.
Polymorphic Virus	These are viruses which transform themselves while keeping the original intention intact. These have mutation engines which enable them to mutate to various forms.
Metamorphic Virus	These are viruses which rewrite themselves before each infection.
Sparse Infecting Virus	These infect less. They infect occasionally. Example: Some viruses infect when they are executed for the 100th time or the file length is between two values or conditions like Friday the 13th.

The viruses infect the executables in two ways, Transient and TSR, that is, Terminate & Stay Resident. In the case of Transient infection, the virus transfers all the controls to itself. It usually corrupts or modifies its carrier program. In the case of TSR, the virus permanently remains in the memory even after the original program got executed and terminated.

Usually, unusual and abnormal activities can alert you to the possibility of a virus attack as specified earlier. Integrity checking of the files by regular hashing can also enable you to understand a potential virus attack.

The following measures can be taken by all (users / organizations) to reduce the propensity of attacks by viruses and worms:

- Have a strong Anti-Virus software installed on your system and keep it updated

- Have a strong Anti-Virus Policy and train all resources on the do's and don'ts

- Push the Anti-Virus software to all the connected systems from the Anti-Virus server. Do not leave it to the users.

- Have strong policies against unauthorized downloads

- Do not open attachments received from unknown persons

- Do not open strange attachments from even known persons

- While downloading the programs, check the error messages and carefully review the instructions. When in doubt, do not proceed with the installation.

- Regularly scan for the integrity of the system and other important files

- Scan the disks or USBs before downloading the files from them

- Take regular backups of all critical files and programs so that they can be restored back if they are corrupted

- Give attention to unusual activities on your system, investigate them and resolve if they are on account of virus infection

- Do not use pirated software

- Do not download free, music, video files from the internet from untrusted sites

- Run regular system scans using the deployed Anti-Virus software

- Understand the latest virus threats and take counter measures as suggested by competent authorities, like the operating system provider or the utility provider or Anti-Virus Tool vendors.

- Do not boot through the infected USB or disks

Botnets

Botnets are the powerful exploitation of the internet. These are controlled by the hackers who run the Command & Control (C & C) Servers. These C & C Servers take orders from the hackers who control them. Through these C & C Servers, botnet clients understand the commands to them and they carry out various attacks including attacks like distributed denial of service (DDoS). Figure 7-3 illustrates how a typical botnet works.

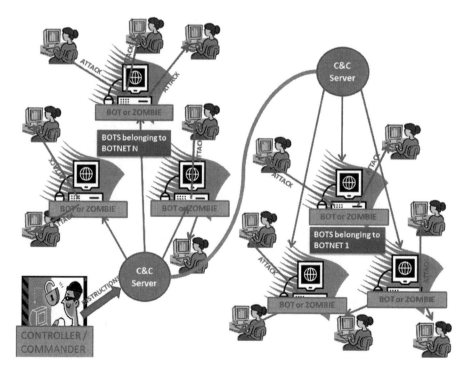

Figure 7-3. *IRC-based botnet DDoS Attack*

They have a built-in communication channel between the bot and the C&C and other bots. Each of these botnets may have tens of thousands to millions of compromised systems. These botnets are highly modular, flexible, and adaptive and can infect different systems in different ways based on their individual vulnerabilities. These botnets have the capabilities to infect the compromised systems gradually, over a period of time, so that even if one of the compromises was fixed by the owner organization concerned, it may be compromised again with a different infection for a different vulnerability. Once they compromise a system, they establish control over the system by rendering both the anti-virus and defense system of the compromised system useless, thus enslaving the systems to do the bidding of the master. Different botnets may be used for different purposes. These botnets collectively have the significant power of attacking even nations!! They cannot be easily disrupted / dismantled. They are used for attacking as the attack is pointed to these systems and not to the real hackers and also because of the power of a pool of computers to carry out a concerted attack. They have the capability to make anti-virus software and firewalls useless on the systems infected by them.

These are used by hackers who control them to fulfill the requirements of their customers which are malicious in nature. These may be to collect confidential information, to adversely impact the infrastructure of a particular organization, or for siphoning off the funds of high net worth individuals. Encrypting critical files or generating a DDoS attack against a particular organization and seeking a huge ransom to release the files or stop the attack are some of the interesting but malicious activities carried out by the botnets.

History of bots can be traced back to 1988 when their use was started for good purposes. The first malicious instance of bots was observed in 1999 with "Pretty Park". This bot had significant capabilities including user ID and password retrieval, uploading and downloading of files, capture of e-mail IDs, and inclusion of its own IRC Client.[2] Over the years, bots have multiplied their capabilities, including attack and communication capabilities. The infection process has become more automated.[2] They have become more flexible and adaptive i.e. they can act differently based on different contexts. They can possibly compromise any vulnerability and have become a menace in the well-connected world of internet. They can also specifically target a group of identified systems. There are currently millions of systems across the globe which are part of these malicious botnets and are at the command of their masters i.e. master hackers. These are actively used for almost all kinds of malicious activities including the chase of big money. Of late, Peer-to-Peer botnets are also increasing in numbers.

Internet of Things (IoT) is a plan to connect all devices, including house hold appliances, to the internet. These household appliances can be hacked and used as botnets, which are difficult to monitor and control.[3] Conscious and collective effort by the industry has led to the closure of some of the bots, such as Grum (Tedroo) and Mariposa. Botnet malware has now started targeting mobile devices, too.

Initially, it was thought that this race of hackers over others could not be won by the good part of the internet community. Of course, of late there are efforts to get the botnets dismantled by organizations like Microsoft and significant success has been achieved in this regard.

The important thing for everybody, right from individuals to organizations, is to protect their systems in such a way that the vulnerabilities are minimized to a large extent and constant vigil is maintained to ensure that they do not unknowingly become part of the botnets.

Brief History of Viruses, Worms, and Trojans

The word "computer Virus" was coined by Fred Cohen, a student from University of Southern California. The history of computer viruses started in the year 1982, with the virus 'Elk Cloner'. 'Elk Cloner' (1982) infected the Apple II Operating System, whereas the next virus, 'Brain' (1986), which had its root in Pakistan, impacted the boot sector.[4]

In 1987, IBM Christmas Worm originated. In 1988, Robert Morris released an Internet Worm which impacted a significant number of computers. In 1998, the spamming of AOL Trojans affected the users of AOL e-mail facility. Melissa hit in 1999 and was the first mass-mailing e-mail virus. Subsequently, ILOVEYOU Worm infected systems around the world, in the year 2000. The Melissa and ILOVEYOU viruses overwrote and deleted files on a huge number of PC's around the world, and used contact lists of users to enable their replication and spread.[4]

From 2000 onwards, we have seen many Trojans, viruses, and worms released, impacting various systems. The state of affairs is continuing even today with many new viruses and Trojans being released by people with malicious intentions. Luckily, to a significant extent, we are protected because of the emergence of strong Anti-Virus software.

However, we are still playing catch up with zero day attacks being reported and new viruses, Trojans infecting, and hackers becoming more aggressive and more precise.

The Current Situation

The following statistics illustrate the impact of recent attacks by Trojans and Viruses since 2010:

- Symantec Corporation's Symantec Threat Report 2013[5] - Volume 18 reports the trending up of zero-day vulnerabilities and that there were 14 zero-day vulnerabilities reported in 2012. According to this report, Stuxnet was responsible for 4 out of 14 zero-day vulnerabilities discovered in 2010 and the Elderwood Gang was responsible for 4 out of 14 zero-day vulnerabilities discovered in 2012. It also reports the following important details:[5]

    - 42% increase in targeted attacks in 2012.

    - 604,826 is the average number of identities breached per attack in 2012.

    - Mobile malware families increase by 58% in 2011-2012.

    - New and unique malicious web-domains increased from 55,000 in 2011 to 74,000 in 2012.

- McAfee Labs Threats Report[6] – Fourth Quarter of 2013 saw that McAfee Labs records more than 300 threats per minute. It reports some of the important details:[6]

    - 2.3 million unique malicious signed binaries were discovered. This number for the entire year was 5.7 million. This begs the question as to how confidently the user can believe that the certificate was signed by an authentic Certificate Authority

    - Mobile malware samples collected by McAfee Labs during the year 2013 totaled to about 3.73 million, an increase of 197% over the year 2012.

    - Increase of 40% in 2013 in the number of suspect URLs

An interesting outlook for 2014 has been predicted by McAfee Labs in its 2014 Threat Predictions report. Some of the highlights are:[7]

- Mobile malware growth to be on an increasing trend – New types of attacks likely to target Android phones

- Virtual currencies will fuel increasingly malicious ransomware attacks around the world

- In the spy versus spy world of cybercrime and cyberwarfare, criminal gangs and state actors will deploy new stealth attacks that will be harder than ever to identify and stop

- Social attacks will be ubiquitous by the end of 2014

- New PC and Server attacks will target vulnerabilities above and below the Operating System

- Deployment of cloud based corporate applications will create new attack surfaces that will be exploited by cybercriminals

Anti-Virus Software

Anti-Virus Software in today's context have become a must to protect us from various attacks, primarily emanating from the internet and from hackers / attackers with malicious intent. We are constantly connected to the external world now through WIFI, LAN/WAN, and Bluetooth.

Need for Anti-Virus Software

The need for Anti-Virus Software has amplified because more and more banking / financial, purchase transactions are carried out by users through the internet. The need for Anti-Virus Software has increased further, because most of the general users of the system are unaware of the specific risks of transacting over the internet, even though they are generally aware that there are some risks. Also, nobody in today's world has the time to be very cautious while carrying out the transactions on their systems or through systems on the internet. We can see the effect of not having an Anti-Virus Software by purchasing a new desktop / laptop and being connected to the internet for some days and carrying out all kinds of transactions. Possibly, we could unauthorized entries in our banking account, we could see our credit cards being misused to make unauthorized purchases, and we may receive complaints lodged against us that our system is initiating attacks on others. This happens because our system would have been heavily infected with malware.

Some of the important attacks from which an Anti-Virus Software has to **protect** the users (other than protecting and cleaning malware infection including Trojan, virus, worm, bots, rootkit, and backdoor infection) are:

- Session Hijacking

- Man-In-The-Middle attacks

- Phishing

- Malware downloads

- Theft of credentials and identity theft

- Execution of malicious links

- Visit to unsafe sites

- Cross-Site-Scripting attacks

- Identify and fix / warn on security vulnerabilities

- Recording of user's key strokes and activities

- Expectations from Anti-Virus Software and their Vendors

Every one of us requires an Anti-Virus Software, which is all inclusive and protects us fully. We do not expect an Anti-Virus Software which only deals with, for example, Viruses but not with Trojans or not with rootkits; we do not want an Anti-Virus Software which can identify malicious web-sites but cannot keep my transactions on the web secure. We want an all-encompassing Anti-Virus Software.

Effective Anti-Virus Software is expected to provide the following features:

- Anti-Virus Features

- Anti-Worm Features

- Anti-Trojan Features

- Anti-Rootkit Features

- Anti-Spyware Features

- Anti-Phishing Features

- Anti-all other type of malware features

- Scan even compressed files

- Scan e-mails

- Automatically detect USB

- Automatically clean infected files

- Quarantine infected files

- Registry Protection

- Instant Messaging Protection

Furthermore, users want a strong support for any issues observed, like a virus attack, which the Anti-Virus Software is not able to clean or an anomalous behavior, which cannot be explained or understood by the users, whereas, the Anti-Virus Software does not raise any alerts, instead keeps confirming that there are no issues with the system. They want live chat or telephonic support immediately and also e-mail support for not so urgent issues. This is quite obvious as they are worried about something happening to their system and the possible consequences of the same.

An Anti-Virus Software which can keep track of ongoing malicious activities and keep updating not only to address the known malicious issues but also to predict and pre-empt the issues whenever they happen, are the ones most desired by the users. However, in this dynamic world which is still evolving with too many technologies and varied systems, this may possibly be too much to ask for in an Anti-Virus Software. Nonetheless, the Anti-Virus Software needs to make substantial efforts in this direction and should be able to reasonably predict the probable attacks and stop the attacks based on the intelligence collected by it.

Increasingly, the general community also has high expectations of Anti-Virus vendor companies. The community expects them to set up labs and test various technologies and applications proactively, so that the vulnerabilities are understood and fixed even before they are exploited by the malicious hackers / attackers. You may observe, from the foregoing discussion on the current scenario, that a significant number of zero-day vulnerabilities were discovered by the malicious attackers and not by the vendor companies or by the Anti-Virus vendor companies. There is significant effort being used by these Anti-Virus vendor companies in this regard. However, the scenarios and the target space are so large, it may be practically impossible for them to imagine, anticipate and proactively check for all those vulnerabilities. Hence, we are always at the risk of an attack!!

A good aspect of these companies is that they provide various reports of the threats which occurred during the quarters and during the year. They also publish the current scenario on their websites. These should give a good understanding of the current threat scenario to most of the users. Unfortunately most of the users are not aware of the availability of such reports and may not explore them. There is hardly much push to bring in awareness among the user community by the national agencies in most of the countries except in countries like the US, where organizations like NIST, supported by other Federal Agencies, are doing significantly good work on this front. It is good to see that McAfee Lab has gone ahead and also published potential threat scenario or predicted threat scenario for the year 2014. However, more awareness has to be brought in to the users, which is a very difficult, uphill task unless various corporations and governments take this responsibility consciously and execute them.

Top 5 Commercially Available Anti-Virus Software

The following five, according to us, are the top notch commercially available Anti-Virus Software (not in the order of ranking – we consider them almost equally good based on our personal usage experience and our interaction with the users of these during our consulting assignments over the years):

- Symantec Norton Anti-Virus

- McAfee Anti-Virus

- Kaspersky Anti-Virus

- Bitdefender Anti-Virus Plus

- AVG Anti-Virus

There are many Anti-Virus Software which we have not used and are not aware of. Hence, we will not be commenting on them and as such it does not mean that others which are not mentioned here are not good.

All the products provide reasonably strong, online, real time protection and continuously monitor and warn you / block you from threats. Normal scans and updates happen automatically. They also have various products which provide different levels of protection. There are again products for the general users and for the Enterprise. Here, we are looking mainly from the perspective of general users. The list of features provided may not be complete. We do not guarantee the features or their performance but have collated here the features of interest to the general users. This is not a recommendation to the user to buy this software. The users have to do their own due diligence, before they purchase any of the products, by evaluating the value, usefulness of these products in the context of the activities they carry out on their systems.

Symantec Norton Anti-Virus Software

Symantec offers many Norton Anti-Virus products. Norton 360 and Norton Internet Security are both good products for general users. Symantec uses exclusive, patented layers of protection which provides excellent protection against viruses, worms, rootkits, Trojans, bots, malicious web sites, malicious downloads, identity theft, spam, and social media scams. Some of the important features of interest are Insight to identify safety of files, Norton Community Watch to track files and global threats, proactive protection through SONAR Behavioral Protection, Scam Insight, Safe Web, anti-phishing, network mapping and monitoring[8].

This product supports all three major web browsers, that is, Internet Explorer, Google Chrome, and Mozilla Firefox. This product also supports all major versions of the Windows from Windows XP to Windows 8.

Norton Power Eraser is an interesting tool which will check and remove deep rooted infections, if any.

It is very easy to install and easy to use. Excellent support is available from Symantec. Over the years, the product has matured significantly and has become user friendly and performance friendly.

McAfee Anti-Virus

This is another Anti-Virus Software of interest. Like other products, this also cleans up most of the malware from Trojans to viruses to worms to rootkits to other malware. It has many products in its suite. McAfee All Access or McAfee Total Protection is a good one for general users. Some of the interesting features of the same are keeping zero-day threats and botnets away, folder and file encryption, social network protection, wireless network protection, advanced web protection with color coded indication of the safety of the website, privacy and pc optimization tools, anti-phishing, two way firewall, and good parental controls.[9]

Kaspersky Anti-Virus

This is another Anti-Virus product of interest. In the suite of products available, Pure 3.0 Total Security provides the highest security features. It provides protection against viruses, from worms to rootkits to Trojans to bots and other malware to a significant extent. Some of the interesting features are proactive detection of unknown malware and rollback of harmful activity, automatic exploit prevention, hybrid protection by using the power of the cloud and PC of the user, safe money to protect banking/financial transactions, two-way firewall, application control, anti-phishing, and easy to use encryption.[10]

Installation of this product does not require a restart. You can set your preferences and then the software will do the rest of the monitoring. It prevents hackers from locking the user's system.[11] It detects new threats and prevents them from infiltrating the system.

Bitdefender Anti-Virus

This is another Anti-Virus Software of interest. Like other products, this also cleans up most of the malware from Trojans to viruses to worms to rootkits to other malware. Bitdefender Total Security may be a product of interest for general users. Some of its interesting features are new wallet to store credentials, 24x7 credit monitoring service, social network protection, immunization of USB, opening of e-banking and e-shopping pages in a separate and secure browser, making security-related decisions for you, and chat encryption.[12]

Installation is easy and quick. It does not require reboot after installation and carries out a pre-installation scanning.[11]

AVG Anti-Virus Software

This is another useful Anti-Virus Software product. Its interesting features include online shield, protection during instant messaging, safe web surfing and searching, two way protection from malicious links, data safe to encrypt and protect passwords.[13]

A Few Words of Caution

There are many other free Anti-Virus tools and free versions of some of the commercially available tools. The users are advised to check the features in the context of their usage, either directly or through the help of others with knowledge, before selecting and relying upon free Anti-Virus software. Some of the so called free Anti-Virus Software may be spyware themselves!

Similarly there are many different products in the suite of any anti-virus software vendor. You need to check for the features and suitability and appropriateness of the product chosen in the context of your operating system, the activities you carry on the system before selecting the product. Please do not go by the general opinion of others.

Once you have an Anti-Virus Software installed successfully on your system (after your cautious evaluation and selection), you need to regularly ensure the following:

- Carry out regular scans including full scans – Do not skip them

- Whenever in doubt or see abnormal activities, ensure that you scan the system to find out any malicious infection. After scanning you may find that no issues were highlighted by anti-virus software. In case you still feel that your system may be infected either contact your anti-virus vendor and obtain additional support from them or use other tools recommended by them in such situations, some of which may be freely available on their web-site, example Norton Power Eraser, McAfee Virtual Technician.

- Keep your Anti-Virus Software updated with patches / updates – Do not stop these updates

- Ensure that you evaluate any errors thrown up by your Anti-Virus and make a considered decision after going through the error and understanding it – Do not simply say "OK" or "Ignore"

- Always ensure that your Operating System and other applications you use are patched

- Be very cautious while accessing unfamiliar links or visiting unfamiliar websites or using third-party applications from the web

- Be aware of any abnormal behavior of your system and investigate it to ensure that it is not because of any malware infection

- Keep yourself aware of malware and related information, currently ongoing threats, by going through the Anti-Virus Vendor companies websites.

- Be cautious, be vigilant, always.

Chapter Summary

We discussed how people with bad intentions create malicious software. We looked at the general expectation that, as technology improves the information security should also increase. But generally, it is not so. We then looked at how information security can be compromised speedily in today's well-connected, internet driven world, while at the same time the speed of the internet and infrastructure expansion helps us in lots of useful ways. We discussed the vast gap in the awareness of the general public with respect to the specifics of different possible information security issues. They have a generic, broad understanding that something can go wrong on the internet. We also discussed how Anti-Virus Software has come to our rescue against the battle on malicious software.

- We discussed briefly the impacts of malware and how our own practices adversely impact us by way of malicious infection.

- We defined in brief, each of the malicious software like Spyware, Adware, Trojans, Viruses, Worms, Backdoors, and Botnets. We also mentioned that these definitions are not exclusive and there is a significant overlap between these definitions and the same malicious software, in one context known as Trojan, may be a Backdoor in another context.

- We looked at what spyware are and what they do. We looked at how they help the attackers to record the activities of the users and capture the details of the users. We also looked at some of the examples of spyware like keyloggers. We identified types of spyware and also the measures we need to take to avoid the infection of spyware.

- We looked at what Trojans and backdoors are. We looked at what these are meant to do. We discussed how they work. We then explored various types of Trojans and what they do. We looked at different backdoor software and explored rootkits. We then looked at what measures should be taken by us to reduce the infection of Trojans and backdoors.

- We also looked at viruses and worms. We briefly differentiated between them. We looked at the way viruses and worms spread. We also discussed how the viruses carry out their work. We then explored various types of viruses and what they do. We then looked at what measures should be taken by us to avoid the infection of viruses and worms.

- We explored in detail what bots are, and how they significantly impact today's world through armies known as botnets. We looked at what these are capable of and how these work. We then identified some of the measures which should be taken by us to avoid the infection of bots. We also looked at a brief history of botnets.

- We discussed in brief the history of malware. Then, we discussed some of the recent instances of attacks of Trojans and Viruses and the current scenario of malware infection.

- We also discussed about the need for Anti-Virus Software and went on to explore expectations from Anti-Virus Software and their vendors. We listed and discussed these in significant detail.

- We explored in brief the important features of five of the commercially available good Anti-Virus Software.

- We cautioned users of Anti-Virus Software, and suggested steps they might take to ensure their Anti-Virus Software is effective in combating the malice of malicious software.

CHAPTER 8

■ ■ ■

Cryptography

Introduction

It is easy for someone to read data if it is in plain text, and confidential and sensitive messages in plain text can be easily compromised. Information meant for a specific set of eyes must be carefully guarded. Spies use secret codes to communicate with their secret agents. Julius Caesar never trusted his messengers carrying message to his generals. He encrypted his messages by replacing every A with a D, every B with E, and so on, so only the intended recipient could decipher the message.

Information security is the protection of organizational/personal data from unauthorized users. The basic components of Information security are: Confidentiality, Integrity and Authenticity, and Availability. Confidentiality is secrecy. No one else should read the data apart from the one who is sending the data and the authorized receiver. With the increasing use of the Internet as an e-commerce tool, it is important for users, banks, and commercial institutions to make sure that their information is secured and no one is able to read change the data during its transmission.

When computer systems can code plain text and the recipient understands and interprets this coded message, users feel more secure transmitting data over the Internet, or any other media. This method of coding a plain text message into a secret coded message is called cryptography. The method of disguising plain text to hide the actual data is called **encryption**. The new encrypted text is called ciphertext. The encrypted data is not readable by others and hence it is secur. Once it reaches its destination, the receiver can reverse the process to read the ciphertext. This process is called *decryption*. The typical process of encryption and decryption is illustrated in Figure 8-1.

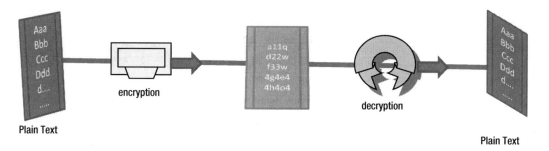

Figure 8-1. Encryption and Decryption

Cryptography is the process of converting simple plain text into secret text called ciphertext, and converting ciphertext back to its original simple text, as shown in the Figure 8-1. The process uses algorithms known as crypto-algorithms to perform the encryption and decryption process.

Encryption and decryption are done using a "key" or "code." Sometimes, only one key is used to perform both encryption and decryption; sometimes two separate keys are used, one for encryption and the other key for decryption.

In today's Internet world, cryptography applications are used to enable digital signatures, money transfers, online shopping, online booking, and credit card payments, where authentication and privacy are crucial. Cryptography makes transactions on the web more secure through digital certificates, 3-D secure, and other encryption technology.

With the rise in government surveillance of Internet data, which is making headlines every day, people are even more concerned about their privacy and personal data. E-mails sent in plain text can become a serious problem, as someone could tap the network and read your personal e-mail–something that has become quite common. Hence, companies prefer to use encrypted e-mail for employees–certainly, for senior executives at the very least. Though encrypting e-mail may or may not protect an individual or business completely from government surveillance, it can certainly keep your data safe from intruders who are looking to find useful information from your e-mail.

Cryptography is mainly used to protect confidentiality of the data. However, it is not restricted to the confidentiality. It is used for checking integrity and authentication processes as well. For example, in many governance processes, a signature is an essential part of the process for authentication and maintaining integrity. If we make this process computerized, where approval, and other governance is done via network or Internet, then we need a mechanism to authenticate the user's signature digitally (digital signatures), and provide a digital timestamp. Cryptography provides such a mechanism.

Cryptography is also used to regulate access to your cable or satellite television. It is controlled centrally and only the channels you are subscribed to can be accessed and all other signals are "scrambled" using cryptographic technology. For example, pay-per-view, annual, or monthly subscriptions are all controlled centrally by scrambling and unscrambling signals based on the payment. Setup boxes installed at houses, hotels, and other places will have the ability to decode the channels only upon receipt of payments.

Although cryptography is widely used, its application on the Internet is increasingly demanding and growing as hackers are cracking cryptographic algorithms. Researchers are working on providing better algorithms and keys so that users data and authentication is protected. Cryptography is still fundamentally based on problems that are difficult to solve because of the complexity of the keys for decrypting and encrypting messages or signing documents digitally.

Cryptography, cryptanalysis, and cryptology are interrelated. In general cryptography refers to the technique of encrypting and decrypting plain text. Cryptanalysis refers to analyzing and breaking the keys used for encryption and decryption (generally used by hackers). Cryptology refers to both: study of cryptography and cryptanalysis.

In this chapter, we will focus on the basics of cryptography and its application. We will not be covering in-depth analysis of cryptography itself. There are several textbooks and papers that exclusively discuss different cryptographic algorithms and techniques. Bruce Schneier is known as an authority on cryptography. He has contributed to the community with more than 10 useful books related to the concept of cryptography and has several blogs on the topic.

Cryptographic Algorithms

In cryptography, encryption and decryption are performed using a mathematical function, often known as cryptographic algorithm. The mathematical function consists of keys: a word, number, or phrase. The cryptographic algorithm makes use of one or more of these keys to encrypt the data. The same plaintext can be encrypted using different keys to get different ciphertext. The strength of the encryption depends on the keys and cryptographic algorithm which makes use of these keys to encrypt.

There are three types of cryptoalgorithms (based on key), which are discussed in detail in this chapter:

- **Symmetric Key (Secret Key Cryptography)**: Uses a single key to encrypt and decrypt the messages

- **Asymmetric Key (Public Key Cryptography)**: Uses one key to encrypt and another key to decrypt the messages

- **Hash Functions**: Uses a mathematical transformation that transforms the message into a fixed length data that is unique to the corresponding source. These transformations are carried out using hashing functions/algorithms and are not normally reversible or are one way hashes.

Figure 8-2 illustrates the above three types of cryptography.

Symmetric Cryptography (One Key for both encryption and decryption)

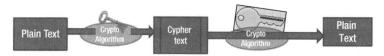

Asymmetric Cryptography (One Key for encryption and one key for decryption

Hash Function (one way cryptography): Only encryption of Plaintext.

Figure 8-2. *Three types of Cryptography*

For any encryption approach, there are two major challenges: key distribution and key management. Key distribution is a mechanism to convey the keys to those who need them to establish secure communication. Key management is to manage large number of keys and provide the right key to the right user as needed.

Symmetric Key Cryptography

In this technique a single key is used to encrypt and decrypt the data. Both, the sender and receiver must share the same key in order to share confidential information. Because a single key is used for both encryption and decryption, this method is called symmetric cryptography. In this method, a single key, which is secret, must be known to both the sender and receiver.

Symmetric key cryptography operates in two modes, stream or block. In stream mode, each bit is considered for encryption whereas in block mode, blocks of data are considered for encryption. In case of block mode, one block of data is encrypted using the same key but in case of stream mode, the same block will have multiple key to encrypt the data. Since the messages are normally more than one block, block mode method needs a mechanism to arrange different blocks together.

Figure 8-3 illustrates how the symmetric key cryptography is used to ensure confidentiality of the message that is sent.

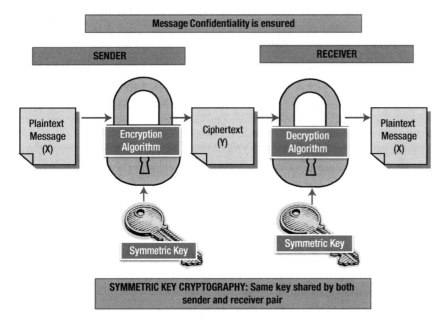

Figure 8-3. *Symmetric Key Cryptography*

There are several algorithms developed for both the modes. The Data Encryption Standard (DES) and the Advanced Encryption Standard (AES) are two block cipher algorithms recognized by US government. DES was developed by IBM as a standard for applications in 1977 and since then it has been used in many applications. DES was the most popular algorithm used across a wide range of applications from ATM encryption to e-mail privacy. [1] However, the known and exploitable weaknesses of DES have caused the community to discourage its use.

In stream mode, encryption is performed one byte at a time. Instead of blocks of data, each byte is encrypted using a stream of keys. RC4 is a variable-key-size stream cipher developed in 1987 by Rivest. RC4 is a stream cipher licensed by RSA which is a widely used stream cypher method.

Some of the most popular cryptoalgorithms are:

- Data Encryption Standard (DES)

- Advanced Encryption Standard (AES)

- Rivest Cipher (RC)

- International Data Encryption Algorithm (IDEA)

- Blowfish

DES is one of the first widely used algorithms but it has been cracked and no longer considered secured. AES is used by the US government and IDEA is used by European nations. Blowfish is an open-source symmetric algorithm created in 1993.

Key Distribution

Distribution of the key and managing the key between different set of users is the most challenging task. Symmetric key cryptography is more useful for encryption of files or file systems in the local machines and less useful for communication between the two systems in the network because of "key distribution" challenges.

There are two ways of solving key distribution problems. One approach is to physically exchange the keys in advance. The secret keys are personally handed over to the parties, which is manual. The second approach is to use a "Trusted Key Distribution Center" to distribute the keys, a trusted network entity with whom one has shared the secret key. This process can be automated.

Suppose Anna and Barry want to communicate using a symmetric key. But, they have never met before and thus they do not have the shared keys to exchange information. Now, there are two problems, one is sharing the key but more important is sharing the key with a person who is a stranger but still wants to communicate. A solution that is often adopted is to use a trusted party known as Key Distribution Center (KDC).

The KDC is a server that manages different symmetric keys with each of the registered user. Each user who wants to communicate with the other user must register with KDC. KDC will check the credentials of each user to ascertain the authenticity. A user who wishes to communicate with the other user, let's say, Anna wants to communicate with Barry, Anna and Barry both have to first register with KDC. Anna takes the first step to send a request for a key as well as the user it wants to communicate. Once the request is processed with proper authentication, KDC sends shared key to both Anna and Barry. Henceforth, both can communicate with each other with the secret key that was given to them by KDC. KDC can also set expiration and other parameters of the key.

Figure 8-4 illustrates the entire process of symmetric key distribution through the KDC.

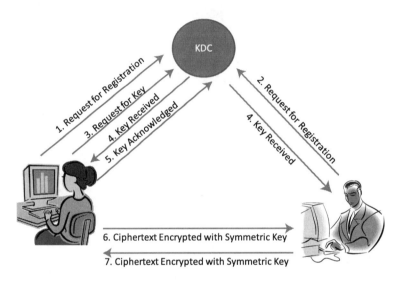

Figure 8-4. *Symmetric Key Distribution Center*

Asymmetric Key Cryptography

There are two problems with symmetric key cryptography:

- Distribution of key – Secret key sharing among senders and receivers. If there are n parties involved in the communication then n(n-1) keys to be distributed. Managing this many keys is another problem.

- Authenticity – Trust and Authenticity of two parties.

In 1976, Diffie and Hellman at Stanford University came up with a new method to solve both the problems of symmetric cryptography that changed the world of cryptography and digital communication radically. This new method is called **Public Key Cryptography** also known as **Asymmetric Key Cryptography**.

Public Key Cryptography

Public key cryptography uses a pair of keys for encryption and decryption. A ***public key*** is used to encrypt the data and a ***private key*** is used to decrypt the data. Using the public key, anyone can encrypt the data, but they cannot decrypt the data. In this approach, both sender and receiver have the ability to generate both keys (using a computer system) together. However, only the public key is made known to the other party, who can download this key even from a web server; the private key is not known to anyone. It is not sent to the other party, hence the problem of distribution of the key never arises. In case of intrusion or any other problems, the system can generate a private key, and a corresponding public key that can be published again. The algorithms that generate keys are related to each other mathematically in such a way that knowledge of one key does not permit anyone to determine the other key easily.

Figure 8-5 illustrates how the confidentiality of a message is ensured through asymmetric key cryptography (alternatively known as public key cryptography).

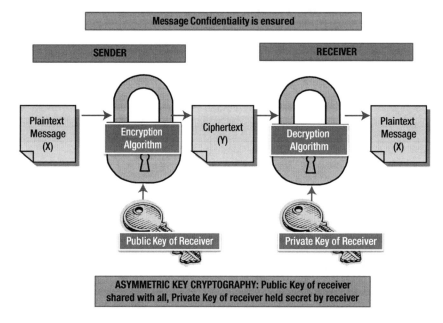

Figure 8-5. *Public Key Cryptography – How Confidentiality is ensured*

Figure 8-6 illustrates how the authenticity of the message is ensured through asymmetric key cryptography (i.e., public key cryptography).

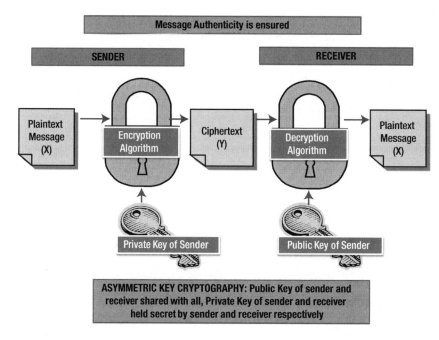

Figure 8-6. *Public Key Cryptography – How Authenticity is ensured*

Figure 8-7 illustrates how both the message confidentiality and authenticity are ensured through asymmetric key cryptography (i.e., public key cryptography).

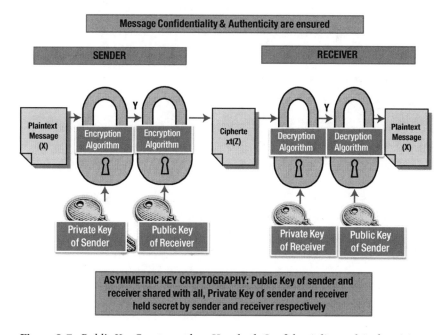

Figure 8-7. *Public Key Cryptography – How both Confidentiality and Authenticity are ensured*

The Public Key Cryptography (PKC) concept was invented by Whitefield Diffie and Martin Hellman in 1976 paper. The primary benefit of the PKC is that only the public key is shared, the need to share private key via some secure channel is eliminated, and private keys are not transmitted or shared. A public key system is constructed using a mathematically infeasible solution where one key cannot be generated using the other key and both the keys are required for a secured communication. The historian David Kahn[2] described public key cryptography as "the most revolutionary new concept in the field since polyalphabetic substitution emerged in the Renaissance."

There are many algorithms based on PKC, but the most popular ones are:

- Diffie Hellman

- RSA (Rivest, Shamir, Adleman)

- Digital Signature Algorithm (David Kravitz)

RSA Algorithm

RSA is an encryption and authentication algorithm developed by Ron **R**ivest, Adi **S**hamir, and Leonard **A**dleman. It is used in many applications including browsers. The algorithm is owned and licensed by RSA Security which is part of EMC[2]. It uses one key for encryption and another key for decryption. The mathematical function for generating keys itself can be found in specifications and standards as well as in the RSA web page. Using the mathematical functions, two sets of numbers (keys) are generated: public key and private key. Both the public key and private keys are required for encryption and decryption but private keys are kept private by the owner and are never sent across the Internet. The public key is used to encrypt the data and private key is used to decrypt when the message confidentiality has to be maintained.

Authentication can be provided by using the PKC system and RSA algorithm (RFC 3447). The message is encrypted using the private key of the sender to authenticate the sender. As the sender's private key is only held by the sender, encryption by using the private key by the sender authenticates that the message was in fact originated by the sender himself. During the authentication process, a private key is used by the sender and the receiver decrypts using the public key. This does not guarantee confidentiality, but does assure the authenticity of the message. When the original message is transformed using the message digest function and encrypted by the private key, it is known as a digital signature. It is also possible to encrypt a portion of the message being sent using the private key of the sender to demonstrate the authenticity rather than encrypting the entire message. Such a system should have the capability that the unencrypted portion is not possible to be modified without the modification of the encrypted portion.

Table 8-1 summarizes the entire authentication process.

Table 8-1. *Steps in the Authentication Process*

Process	Key	Owner
Send encrypted message digest (i.e., digital signature)	Private Key of sender	Sender
Decrypt signature	Public Key of sender	Receiver
Send encrypted message	Public Key of receiver	Sender
Decrypt message	Private Key of receiver	Receiver

The RSA keys are derived from a variable size encryption block and a variable size key. The key-pair (public and private) is derived from a very large prime number, chosen according to special rules. The strength of RSA depends on the key length but choosing a long key can slow down the system. For bulk data encryption, it is recommended to use DES for better performance.

If you want both the confidentiality and the authenticity of the message, the following encryption mechanism has to be used:

- The message has to be first encrypted using the private key of the sender.
- The encrypted message is then encrypted using the public key of the receiver.
- The encrypted message is sent to the receiver.
- The receiver on receiving the encrypted message decrypts it using his (receiver's) private key.
- The semi-decrypted message is then decrypted using the public key of the sender.
- The receiver obtains the plain text message.

Advantages of Public Key Cryptography

The advantages of public key cryptography are:

- No need to exchange the keys
- Another key cannot be derived from one key
- The confidentiality of the message can be ensured by using the public key cryptography
- It is possible to establish authentication of the sender by using public key cryptography (digital signature)
- It is possible to ensure the confidentiality and authentication of the message at the same time
- It is possible to use public key cryptography for session key exchange

Applications of PKC

Public Key Cryptography is used in a number of applications and systems software. Some examples of application of cryptography are:

- Digitally signed document
- E-mail encryption software such as PGP and MIME
- RFC 3161 authenticated timestamps
- Digital signatures in the Operating System software such as Ubuntu, Red Hat Linux packages distribution
- SSL protocol
- SSH protocol

Public Key Infrastructure (PKI)

A Public Key Infrastructure (PKI) enables users to securely transact through the use of public key cryptography. Key pairs are obtained from a third-party trusted authority called Certificate Authority (CA). The PKI provides an infrastructure to issue a "digital certificate" that identifies an individual or organization. Based on the identity of the digital certificate, transactions are made securely over public networks such as the Internet. The PKI is based on the use of public key cryptography, which is commonly used.

A public key infrastructure consists of:

- A Certificate Authority (CA) that issues and verifies digital certificates. A certificate includes the public key or information about public key

- A registration Authority (RA) which verifies the user's authenticity for CA before CA issues a digital certificate

- A secured storage place to hold the certificates and public keys

- A certificate management system

- Hardware, software, policies, procedures, and people used to create, manage, and revoke digital certificates along with the distribution and storage of the digital certificates

A certificate contains information referring to a public key, issued by a Certification Authority (CA). The information in the certificate should conform to the ITU (IETF) standard X.509 v3. Certificates conforming to that standard include information about the published identity of the owner of the corresponding public key, the key length, the algorithm used, associated hashing algorithm, dates of validity of the certificate, and the actions the key can be used for.

Certificate Authority (CA)

A CA is responsible for issuing certificates. CA issues the digital certificate based on the recommendation of RA. This digital certificate is signed by the CA using its own private key. The CA issues the certificate which contains the public key of the party who owns the certificate. Certificates have to be purchased from the CA. CA can issue a certificate only after it confirms all the credentials to prove your identity. Once identity is proved, it stamps the certificate to prevent modifications of the details contained in the certificate. CA is analogous to a passport agency. An individual or organization may have any number of certificates issued by different CAs. Different web applications may insist to use a particular certificate. For example, a particular bank may insist to use a certificate issued by that bank for a secured transaction, whereas some other web site may accept any certificate issued by any CA.

Registration Authority (RA) is a third-party verification agency for a Certificate Authority (CA), to perform the verification of the organization or individuals who have applied for the certificate. Final component of the PKI is the Certificate Management System (CMS) through which certificates are published, renewed, or revoked. Examples of Certificate Authority (CA) include Verisign, Thawte, SSL.com, RapidSSL, Network Solutions, GlobalSign, Digicert, Enutrust.net, PinkRoccade, and PKI.CAcert. [24]

Digital Certificate

Digital Certificate provides an electronic identity to conduct secure transactions by providing your identity (authentication). It is similar to a passport or driver's license. With a digital certificate, an organization or an individual can provide authentication for all the transactions with friends, business partners, and other online services. Digital certificate assures identity among all the parties involved in the transactions. The most widely used format of a digital certificate is as defined by the CCITT X.509 standards. [25] Digital certificate uses public key cryptography to verify the integrity of the certificate itself.

Hash Function Cryptography

Hash functions, also called message digests, use a fixed length hash value to transform the data that makes it difficult for someone to decrypt or change the data without affecting the hash value, thus securing the data from intruders. Hashing functions are one-way mathematical functions that are easy to compute but hard to reverse. A hash function

H( ), applied on input (x), and returns a fixed string, h_s. Mathematically it is written as $h_s = H(x)$. A cryptographic hash function in general should have the following properties:

- Flexible input length (x)

- H(x) should be relatively easy to compute

- H(x) is one way function and cannot be reversible

- The output is of fixed length and does not depend on input length

Hashing is generally used in the following situations:

- Password management in case of PPP, CHAP, and Microsoft EAP. This method of cryptography is normally used in operating systems to protect passwords.

- Digital signatures and file integrity checkers to check the integrity of data.

Hashing functions are used to vouch for the integrity of the message by appending the message with the hash value. If the message is changed, the hash value when recomputed will not match the precomputed hash value. In order to avoid man-in-the middle attacks, it is ideal to send the hash value in a secure way to the intended party. Such secure transfer is possible using public key cryptography.

Further, hash value is used to store passwords of the operating systems like Microsoft Windows. Here, the original passwords are not stored; instead the SAM corresponding hash values are stored. These provide high security to the passwords, as hash value is not reversible to find out the original password. Only when the passwords are entered in the system will it compute the hash value and check with the hash value stored in the SAM.

"Salting" the password before hashing by either suffixing or prefixing it with a random string decreases the possibility of cracking the password.

Hashing is also used in some of the implementation of digital signatures which vouches for the integrity of the message sent. Hashing functions are also used in virus detection as well as intrusion detection.

Figure 10-8 illustrates how hashing ensures the integrity of the message that is sent.

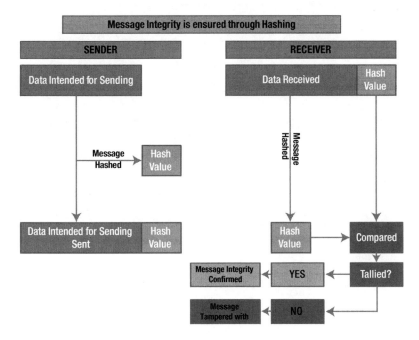

Figure 8-8. *Message Integrity Check through Hashing*

Popular Hashes

MD5 (Message Digest Function 5), SHA1 (Secure Hash Algorithm 1), SHA2 (Secure Hash Algorithm 2), and SHA3 (Secure Hash Algorithm 3) are the popular hashing functions /algorithms. MD5 outputs are of 128 bits and are popularly used for storing of the passwords as well as to ensure file integrity. MD5 is prone for collision.

SHA algorithms again provide for one way hash. SHA1 provides for 160 bit output. SHA-224, SHA-256, SHA-384, and SHA-512 are known as SHA-2. SHA3 is the most advanced hashing function which was announced by NIST in 2012. SHA-3 has a unique structure known as sponge construction.

MAC (Message Authentication Code) is another popular hash function which is also known as a Keyed Hash Function.

Digital Signatures

A digital signature is like a handwritten signature but it is in the digital form for an electronic document. The document containing the digital signature is verified by the recipient using a hash function to check whether the message has been altered either intentionally or accidentally during the transmission. If the message is altered, the hash function returns a different result. Digital signature ensures authenticity and non-repudiation.

Here, usually the hash value is encrypted with the sender's private key. This provides for the authenticity. When the receiver decrypts the private key using the sender's public key, he gets the hash value. He can check this hash value with the hash value generated using the hash algorithm from the message received. Alternatively, both the message and the appended hash value both can be encrypted with the sender's private key in a similar way as above. If both the hash value received and the hash value generated from the message received tally that means the integrity of the message is maintained. Because it has been signed by the sender's private key, the message sender is also authenticated. Another alternative is to encrypt the message and the hash value using the symmetric key shared between both the parties.

Summary of Cryptography Standard Algorithms

Table 8-2 summarizes some of the **Symmetric cryptographic** algorithms that are used today.

Table 8-2. *Summary of Symmetric Cryptographic Algorithms*

Symmetric Key	Description
Data Encryption Standard (DES)	Developed by IBM in 1970 adopted by National Institute of Standards and technology (NIST)
Triple-DES	A variant of DES that employs up to three 56-bit keys and is recommended replacement of DES.
DESX	Devised by Ron Rivest with a 120-bit key length
Advanced Encryption Standard (AES)	Officially replaced DES in 2001. Uses a key length of 128, 192, or 256 bits and blocks of length 128, 192, or 256 bits. Federal Information Processing Standard (FIPS) PUB 197[3] describes a 128-bit block cipher employing 128, 196, or 256 bit key.
CAST-128/256	DES-like substitution permutation algorithm employing 128 bit key length of 64-bit block. It is defined in RFC 2144[4] and RFC2162[5]. CAST is named after its inventors, Carlisle Adams and Stafford Tavares.

(continued)

Table 8-2. (*continued*)

Symmetric Key	Description
Rivest Ciphers (Ron's Code) (named after Ron Rivest)	RC1 – not implemented RC2[6] – 64-bit cipher RC4 – variable length key RC5[7] – A block cipher supporting 32, 64,or 128 bit key length RC6 – 128 bit key improvement over RC5
Blowfish[8]	A symmetric 64-bit block cipher invented by Bruce Schneier. It is a substitute for DES and is in use by large number of commercial products.
Twofish[9]	Designed by Bruce Schneier and team. A 128 bit block cipher with 128,192, or 256 key length. Used in hardware encryption.
Camellia[10]	Developed in 2000 by Nippon Telegraph and Telephone (NTT) Corp and Mitsubishi Electric Corporation (MEC). Suitable for both hardware and software implementation. Is a 128-bit block size, supports 128,192, or 256 key length. RFC 4312 describes the application of Camellia in IPSec. RFC 5581 describes the application in OpenPGP.
MISTY1[11]	A block cipher using a 128-bit key length and 64-bit blocks. It is used in both hardware and software applications. Described in RFC 2994
SEED[12]	128-bit key length and 128-bit blocks. Developed by Korean Information Security Agency (KISA) and adopted as a national standard encryption algorithm in South Korea. Described in RFC 4269
ARIA[13]	A 128-bit block cipher employing 128,192, or 256-bit key length. Described in RFC 5794
CLEFIA[14]	128-bit block cipher with a key length of 192, 256 bits developed in 2007 by SONY corporation. Is one of the latest algorithms to support high performance software and hardware applications. Described in RFC 6114
KCipher-2[15]	K-Cipher-2 has been used for industrial applications especially for mobile health monitoring and diagnostic services in Japan. Described in RFC 7008
GSM (Global System for Mobile) Encryption	All mobile communications are over the air and vulnerable to security threats as it is open to eavesdroppers with an appropriate receivers. Several security functions are built into the GSM to safeguard subscribers privacy[16]: Authentication of the registered subscribers Secure data transfer Subscriber identity protection For authentication process, A3 authentication algorithms are used. For encryption and decryption of data A8 algorithms are used.
GPRS Encryption	The A5/4, A5/3, and GEA4, GEA3 algorithms are based on the 3GPP ciphering algorithm (F8). Mitsubishi Electric Corporation holds essential patents on the Algorithms[17] ETSI is Custodian of the 3GPP™ confidentiality and integrity algorithms UEA2 & UIA2, UEA1 & UIA1, and EEA3 & EIA3 which have been developed through the collaborative efforts of the European Telecommunications Standards Institute (ETSI), the Association of Radio Industries and Businesses (ARIB), the Telecommunications Technology Association (TTA) and ATIS

Table 8-3 summarizes the Public-Key Cryptography Algorithms that are commonly used today.

Table 8-3. *Summary of Public-Key Cryptography Algorithms*

Public Key Cryptography Algorithms	Description
RSA[18]	RSA is an encryption and authentication algorithm developed by Ron **R**ivest, Adi **S**hamir, and Leonard **A**dleman. It is used in many applications including browsers. The algorithm is owned and licensed by RSA Security which is part of EMC[2]
	NIST currently supports three different RSA algorithm implementations. ANSI X9.31-1998 and is called RSA. The other algorithms are specified in the PKCS #1 v2.1: RSA Cryptography Standard dated June 2002. They are defined as signature schemes with appendix and are called RSASSA-PSS and RSASSA-PKCS1-v1_5. FIPS 186-4 imposes additional constraints on these RSA algorithm implementations[19]
Diffie-Hellman	Diffie and Hellman came up with their own algorithm but does not support authentication. Details are described in RFC 2631
Digital Signature Algorithm (DSA)	Specified by NIST's Digital Signature Standard for digital signature authentication process
Elliptical Curve Cryptography (ECC)[20]	A PKC algorithm based on elliptic curves with small keys.
Public Key Cryptography Standards (PKCS)	A set of interoperable standards and guidelines developed by RSA Security (now EMC[2]):
	RFC 3447: RSA Cryptography Standard RFC 2898: Password based Cryptography Standards RFC 2986: Certification Request Syntax Standard version 1.7 RFC 2315: Cryptographic Message Syntax Version 1.5 RFC 2985: Selected Object Classes and Attribute Types version 2.0 RFC 5208: Public-Key Cryptography Standards (PKCS) #8: Private Key Information Syntax Specification Version 2

Table 8-4 summarizes some of the Hash function algorithms that are commonly used.

Table 8-4. *Summary of Hash Function Algorithms*

Hash function Algorithm	Description
MD2	Produces an output of 128-bit "message digest".[21] It is conjured that it is computationally infeasible to produce two similar message digest. An algorithm intended for digital signature application where a file must be compressed. Designed for systems with limited memory, such as smart cards. Described in RFC 1319[21] and RFC 6149
MD4	Designed specifically for fast processing software applications. Described in RFC 1320 and RFC 6150
MD5	Improvement of MD4 algorithm. Described in RFC 1321
Secure Hash Algorithm (SHA) 1	NIST's Secure Hash Standard algorithm. Produces 160 bit hash value. Published in NIS's FIPS PUB 180-1 and RFC 3174
Secure Hash Algorithm (SHA) 2	The United States has adopted a suite of Secure Hash Algorithms (SHAs), including four beyond SHA-1, as part of a Federal Information Processing Standard (FIPS), specifically SHA-224 (RFC 3874), SHA-256, SHA-384, and SHA-512.[22]. This can produce hash values that are 224, 256, 384, or 512 bits in length
SHA-3	SHA-3 is a new algorithm as an alternative to SHA-2. In 2007, **SHA-3 competition**[23] was a launched and it received 64 submissions. NIST announced Keccak as the wined of the SHA-3 cryptography hash algorithm competition and the new SHA-3 algorithm is in press release. Keccak was designed by a team of cryptographers from Belgium and Italy. They are: Guido Bertoni Joan Daemon Michael Peeters Gilles Van Assche
Others	**RIPEMD** – optimized for 32-bit processors to replace 128-bit hash function **HAVAL** (HAsh of VAriable Length – can create hash values of 128, 160, 192, 224, or 256 bits length **Tiger:** Replacement for SHA and MD5. Run efficiently on 64-bit processor.

Each of the algorithms in Table 8-4 is used in different applications and for different purposes. For example, Hash function algorithms are well suited for data integrity. Any change made to the content during the transmission will result in a hash value different from the original value sent by the sender. Since it is highly unlikely that the same hash value is generated for two different messages, data integrity is ensured.

Symmetric key cryptography is suited for encrypting and decrypting messages, thus providing privacy and confidentiality. The sender can generate a key for each data session to encrypt the message and the receiver can decrypt the message but needs to have the same key for the same session. Symmetric key cryptography also may be used for file encryptions.

Public Key cryptography technique uses a pair of keys called private and public. This is used for not only confidentiality of message but also for non-repudiation and user authentication.

Table 8-4 provided an overview of different algorithms used for different types of cryptography techniques. Table 8-5 provides an overview of some of the common cryptographic algorithms that are used in various applications, particularly in e-commerce applications.

Table 8-5. *Overview of common cryptographic algorithms used in various applications*

Algorithm	Description
Capstone[26]	CAPSTONE is an NSA developed, hardware oriented, cryptographic Device. It implements cryptographic algorithm that is implemented in CLIPPER chip. In addition, the CAPSTONE chip includes the following functions: 1. The Digital Signature Algorithm (DSA) proposed by NIST as a Federal Information Processing Standard (FIPS); 2. The Secure Hashing Algorithm (SHA) recently approved as FIPS 180; 3. A Key Exchange Algorithm based on a public key exchange; 4. A general purpose, random number generator which uses a pure noise source.
Clipper[27]	CLIPPER is an NSA developed, hardware oriented, cryptographic device that implements a symmetric encryption/decryption algorithm. The cryptographic algorithm (SKIPJACK) is completely specified (and classified SECRET). The cryptographic algorithm (called CA) has the following characteristics: 1. Symmetric, 80-bit key encryption/decryption algorithm; 2. Similar in function to DES (i.e., basically a 64-bit code book transformation that can be used in the same four modes of operation as specified for DES in FIPS 81); 3. 32 rounds of processing per single encrypt/decrypt operation;
Federal Information Processing Standards (FIPS) [28]	Federal Information Processing Standards Publications (FIPS PUBS) are issued by NIST after approval by the Secretary of Commerce pursuant to the Federal Information Security Management Act (FISMA) of 2002. The computer security and crypto-algorithms used by U.S Government
GOST	GOST is a family of algorithms used by Russian Federal Standards used by Russian Government. RFC 4357: Additional Cryptographic Algorithms for Use with GOST 28147-89, GOST R 34.10-94, GOST R 34.10-2001, and GOST R 34.11-94 Algorithms RFC 5830: GOST 28147-89: Encryption, Decryption, and Message Authentication Code (MAC) Algorithms RFC 6986: GOST R 34.11-2012: Hash Function Algorithm RFC 7091: GOST R 34.10-2012: Digital Signature Algorithm (Updates RFC 5832: GOST R 34.10-2001)
Identity-Based Cryptography Standard (IBCS) (described in RFC 5091)	IBE is a public-key technology, but one which varies from other public-key technologies in a slight, yet significant way. In particular, IBE keys are calculated instead of being generated randomly, which leads to a different architecture for a system using IBE than for a system using other public-key technologies.

(*continued*)

Table 8-5. (*continued*)

Algorithm	Description
IP Security Protocol (IP sec)	The IPSec is a set of protocol suites which provide confidentiality and authentication services at the IP layer. RFC 2411 describes the overview of IPSec protocol. IPSec protocol suites include:
	RFC 4301: IP security architecture. RFC 4302: IP Authentication Header (AH), RFC 4303: IP Encapsulating Security Payload (ESP) RFC 4304: Extended Sequence Number (ESN) Addendum, RFC 4305: Cryptographic algorithm implementation requirements for ESP and AH. RFC 4307: Cryptographic algorithms used with IKEv2. RFC 4308: Crypto suites for IPsec, IKE, and IKEv2. RFC 4309: The use of AES in CBC-MAC mode with IPsec ESP. RFC 4312: The use of the Camellia cipher algorithm in IPsec. RFC 4359: The Use of RSA/SHA-1 Signatures within Encapsulating Security Payload (ESP) and Authentication Header (AH). RFC 4434: Describes AES-XCBC-PRF-128, a pseudo-random function derived from the AES for use with IKE. RFC 5996: The Internet Key Exchange (IKE) protocol, version 2 RFC 2403: Describes use of the HMAC with MD5 algorithm RFC 2405: Describes use of DES-CBC RFC 2407 (application of ISAKMP to IPsec), RFC 2408 (ISAKMP, a framework for key management and security associations), and RFC 2409 RFC 2412: Describes OAKLEY, a key determination and distribution protocol. RFC 2451: Describes use of Cipher Block Chaining (CBC) mode cipher algorithms with ESP. RFCs 2522 and 2523: Description of Photuris, a session-key management protocol for IPsec.
Internet Security Association and Key Management Protocol (ISAKMP) (Described in RFC 2408)	The Internet Security Association and Key Management Protocol (ISAKMP) defines the procedures for authenticating a communicating peer, creation and management of Security Associations, key generation techniques, and threat mitigation (e.g., denial of service and replay attacks).
Message Digest Cipher (MDC)	Invented by Peter Gutman, new Zealand. More details can be found in `https://www.cs.auckland.ac.nz/~pgut001/`
HMAC: Keyed-Hashing for Message Authentication (RFC 2104)	HMAC is a mechanism used for message authentication using cryptographic hash functions such as MD5, SHA-1, etc.
The Keyed-Hash Message Authentication Code (HMAC) Described in FIPS-198[29]	HMAC is used with any iterative approved cryptographic hash function, in combination with a shared secret key. The cryptographic strength of HMAC depends on the properties of the underlying hash function.

(*continued*)

Table 8-5. (*continued*)

Algorithm	Description
NSA - Advanced Encryption Standard (AES)	Advanced Encryption Standard (AES) with key sizes of 128 and 256 bits, per FIPS PUB 197 for encryption
Elliptic Curve Digital Signature Algorithm (ECDSA) Described in FIPS 186-3	Using the curves with 256 and 384-bit prime moduli
Secure Hash Algorithm (SHA)	Using 256 and 384 bits. Described in FIPS180-3
Cryptographic Suites for Secure Shell (SSH).	Described in RFC 6239. Secure Shell Transport Layer Protocol
Pretty Good Privacy (PGP)	Philip Zimmermann developed this algorithm for email and file storage applications. It uses RSA for key management and digital signatures, IDEA for message encryption, and MD5 for computing hash value. More information can be found in RFC 1991.
Secure Hypertext Transfer Protocol (S-HTTP)	An extension to HTTP to provide secure exchange of documents over the World Wide Web. Supported algorithms include RSA and Kerberos for key exchange, DES, IDEA, RC2, and Triple-DES for encryption.
Secure Sockets Layer (SSL) Described in RFC 6101	SSL is a security protocol that provides communications privacy over the Internet. This is mainly designed for secure HTTP and FTP connections. This protocol allows applications to communicate securely to prevent any attack on confidentiality and data integrity. SSL also uses MD5 for message digests and X.509 public-key certificates. For more details, refer to RFC 6101.
Transport Layer Security (TLS)	TLS uses 3DES, SHA, DSS and Diffie-Hellman. TLS also provides data privacy and data integrity. TLS was developed to replace SSH. For more information, please refer to RFC 5246.
TrueScript[30]	Open source, multi-platform cryptography software that can be used to encrypt a file, partition, or entire disk.
X.509	ITU-T recommendation for the PKI infrastructure is mainly used in the Telecommunication industry.

Disk / Drive Encryption

With the increased use of the mobile devices like laptops and the storage of confidential data on their hard disk and data carried on USB and other drives, we need to protect the data from theft and misuse. Hence, the disk encryption utilities have emerged. The entire hard disk, USB drive, and other drives can be encrypted so that the data on them cannot be read and misused by unauthorized persons. Now, we have the possibility to burn the data on to portable disks but encrypt them so that unauthorized persons will not be able to misuse them.

The utilities and tools such as TrueCrypt and Gilisoft are widely used for disk encryption, and are found to be very effective in disk encryption. There are many other tools available such as DriveCrypt, DiskCryptor, Rohos Disk Encryption, and Symantec Drive Encryption.

Attacks on Cryptography

There are various attacks possible on cryptography. Some of the common attacks are:

- Rubber Hose Attack: Obtaining by force the secret key like password to the file from those who have them

- Ciphertext-only Attack: Here the attacker has the ciphertext and tries to get the encryption key using the ciphertext

- Known-plaintext Attack: Here the attacker has some plaintext. Using this he tries to get the encryption key

- Chosen-plaintext Attack: Here the attacker uses his own plaintext. He then encrypts them and analyses the resulting output, i.e., ciphertext.

- Adaptive Chosen-plaintext Attack: Here the attacker uses various plaintexts. The subsequent plaintext will be used by him based on the result of earlier output.

Brute force and Frequency Analysis methods are popularly used by the attackers to break the encryption key.

Chapter Summary

- We discussed encoding of messages to ensure the secrecy of the message being sent. We also explored encryption, decryption, cryptography, cryptanalysis, and cryptology. We discussed how cryptography helps in maintaining the confidentiality of the message as well as assures the authentication of the message.

- We explored various cryptographic algorithms such as symmetric key cryptography and asymmetric key cryptography. We also explored the problem of key distribution in the case of symmetric key cryptography and how this can be resolved using the third party. We then explored the asymmetric key cryptography and under that looked into the public key cryptography and how it resolves the issue of key distribution. We looked into the concepts of private key and public key. We also elaborated further as to how this helps out in ensuring the confidentiality of the messages being sent as well as the authentication of the messages. We briefly touched upon the RSA algorithm. We then briefly touched upon the applications and advantages of the public key cryptography. We also briefly touched upon Public Key Infrastructure, the role of Certificate Authority, and Digital Certificates.

- We briefly discussed hashing algorithms, some of the popular hashing functions/algorithms, and the uses of hashing functions/algorithms. We also briefly described how Digital Signatures are implemented using hashing algorithms.

- We listed various symmetric, asymmetric, and hashing algorithms along with further references to them.

- We looked into the disk encryption mechanism to protect the drives / disks from misuse and then concluded the section with the possible attacks on cryptography.

PART IV

■ ■ ■

Network Security

This section explores networking fundamentals and various network-related vulnerabilities and mechanisms provided for securing networks like firewalls, IDS/IPS, and Virtual Private Networks.

Chapter 9, "Understanding Networks and Network Security," introduces networking fundamentals, including the components of basic communication and computer communication. A network connects two or more computers to communicate with each other or for the exchange of information among the systems. Networking is the sharing of resources within the network. Data communication and computer networking go hand in hand. Data communication is the exchange of information across a medium, and networking is the connecting of two devices to facilitate the exchange of information from one system to another. When computer devices are connected in a network for communication, it consists of the following components: Message, Host, Receiver, Medium, and Protocol.

Then we discuss various network topologies, such as bus topology, ring topology, star or Y topology. We also discuss local area networks, wide area networks, metropolitan area networks, and the concept of internetworking. We then elaborate upon the OSI Seven Layer Model in detail, including the functions and working of various layers viz. Layer 7: Application Layer, Layer 6: Presentation Layer, Layer 5: Session Layer, Layer 4: Transport Layer, Layer 3: Network Layer, Layer 2: Data Link Layer, Layer 1: Physical Layer and the protocols used/supported by each layer. We then explore the TCP/IP Model with the functions and protocols of each layer (i.e., Application Layer, Transmission Control Protocol (TCP) Layer, Internet Protocol (IP) Layer, and Network Access Layer). We then discuss the differences between the OSI and TCP/IP Models. We then explore the network vulnerabilities and threats under three categories: Security Policy Weaknesses, Technology Weaknesses, and Configuration Weaknesses. We then describe each network-related attack, including Denial of Service (DoS) and Distributed Denial of Service (DDoS) and under that Ping of Death, TCP SYN Flood Attack, e-mail Bombs, Tear Drop, and Smurf Attacks. Then we look into other network attacks like Masquerade/Spoofing Attacks, HTTP Tunneling, SSH Tunneling, Session Hijacking, and Attacks on Network Equipment. Then we discuss the ways in which we can counter the network attacks.

Chapter 10, "Firewalls," first defines firewall in the real world as a means to build protection from fire with the intention to slow the spread of the fire through a structure. Next, we apply the same concept to a network. A network firewall is intended to stop unauthorized users from accessing the network and services from other outside networks. The most common deployment of firewalls is between an organization's trusted network and an untrusted network, typically the Internet. The Internet Service Provider (ISP) connection usually terminates at a border router and then connects to a firewall.

We describe basic firewall functions like packet filtering and application level proxy. We then explain that packet filters usually permit or deny network traffic based on the following criteria: source and destination IP addresses; protocol, such as TCP, UDP, or ICMP; source and destination TCP or UDP port addresses; flags in the TCP header – ACK, CLOSE, and SYNC; IP fragmentation flag; direction of the packet – inbound or outbound; and physical interface. We then explain the packet filtering firewalls. A packet filter firewall is configured with a set of rules which define when to accept or deny a packet. When the firewall receives a packet, the filter checks the rules defined against IP address, port number, protocol, and so on. If the rule matches, then the packet is accepted or rejected in the network, depending on the rule.

We then discuss the advantages and disadvantages of packet filtering firewalls and Stateful Packet Filtering. We then explain how Application Level Gateways (ALG) inspect packets all the way up to the application layer and determine whether a packet is allowed or denied. It gives higher security than packet filtering, as the inspection is done all the way up to the application. However, this takes more CPU processing time and requires knowledge of application protocol. An Application Level Gateway runs independently, copies and forwards information across the gateway, and functions as proxy server. It prevents a direct connection between a trusted server or client and an untrusted host. The proxies are application specific. Any new application that comes to the market needs to be informed to the application proxy; otherwise rules may not get executed on this application. It sits between a network firewall and trusted host. It can filter packets at the application layer. We then describe best practices for firewalls and how firewalls can be audited to understand their effectiveness.

Chapter 11, "Intrusion Detection and Prevention Systems," defines Intrusion in layman's language as, "Unwanted or unauthorized interference." As it is unwanted or unauthorized, it is normally carried out with bad intentions. The intention of such intrusions is to collect information related to the organization, such as the structure of the internal networks, operating systems, tools/utilities, and software applications used by the organization, and initiate connections to the internal network to carry out the attacks. Intrusions are normally perpetrated by outsiders, but intrusions by internal authorized persons carrying out attacks by the misuse of their authorization, or by internal authorized persons by going beyond the official parameters of their authorizations, are also possible and need to be protected against.

An Intrusion Detection System (IDS) is a hardware/software combination that detects intrusions into a system or network. An Intrusion Detection System (IDS) complements firewalls by providing thorough inspection of packets' headers and their contents, thus protecting against attacks that a firewall might otherwise perceive as benign network traffic. An Intrusion Detection System (IDS) inspects each and every packet's content traversing the network to detect any malicious activity. Every packet is peeled all the way to the "data content" component, and its data content is inspected for malicious activity; if it is found to be harmless, it is reassembled and sent. This makes IDS very process intensive when compared to firewall. We then describe the four important aspects of the results of IDS monitoring: false positives, false negatives, true positives, and true negatives.

We then cover the two types of IDS–host-based and network-based–and the pros and cons of both. Intrusion Detection and Prevention Systems detect intrusions through the following mechanisms: signature-based detection, anomaly-based detection, or stateful protocol analysis. We then explain how each of these mechanisms works and discuss the architecture of IDS/IPS and describe each of its components: a hardware appliance, management console, a database, and connectivity to network management consoles, including signature update server. We then discuss the types of attacks IDPS are able to detect and prevent. We then explore the typical responses by IDPS, like Block or Deny the packet, Reset connection, Dropping the packet, and Reconfigure firewall. We then describe various modes, like passive mode and active mode, in which the IDPS can be deployed.

Chapter 12, "Virtual Private Networks," starts with a discussion of the business case for using Virtual Private Networks (VPNs). A VPN is a private network (similar to a leased line), but uses the public network (Internet) to connect to remote sites. VPN creates a "virtual" tunnel connection routed through the Internet from the company's trusted network to the remote office or to a mobile work force. With VPN, you can send data via a public network that emulates a private link between two parties or two networks. Then we discuss the advantages of VPN like cost savings, smooth and seamless integration, secure remote access, extranet connections, and low maintenance. We then describe types of VPNs based on the types of communications supported, namely, Remote Access (Host to site) and Site to site. Within site to site VPNs, we again explore two more types: intranet based VPNs and extranet based VPNs.

We also explain Host to Host VPNs. We then explore the characteristics VPN protocol architecture should support including viz. tunneling, data authentication and data integrity, anti-replay services, and data encryption. We then list various protocols which support VPNs. We then explain in detail each of the following protocols: PPTP, L2TPv3, GRE, and IPSec.

Chapter 13, "Data Backups and Cloud Computing," introduces the idea "availability" as one of the important aspects of information security. Data Backups are the first line of defense against system crashes, corruption of data, exploits leading to data integrity issues, accidental loss of data, or loss of data due to mistakes. Data Backups stem from the fact that the disks on which the data is stored are prone to failures and can lead to a single point of failure. Data Backups provide for continued operation by effective restoration of data and assured continued availability of the systems. Cloud computing has brought in new avenues of hope for low cost usage of applications, to low cost application development and deployment possibilities, to low cost infrastructure acquisition. The cloud computing phenomenon has also elevated issues related to security and privacy. We then explore the need for Data Backups by citing some of the examples which show how data backups protect us from availability and integrity issues. We then explore types of backups, such as online backups, near-line backups, offline backups, full backups, incremental backups, differential backups, onsite-backups, offsite backups, highly automated backups, scheduled and automated backups, and manual backups. Then we looked into various RAID levels.

We then explore other fault tolerance mechanisms like Server Clustering, Electronic Vaulting, Remote Journaling, and Server Mirroring. We then describe the role of storage area networks in providing backups and disaster recovery. Then we discuss how cloud infrastructure helps in backup strategy and database backups. We then explore various backup and restoration strategies. We then list some of the security considerations related to backups and then explore some inherent issues related to backups and restoration, as well as best practices related to backups and restoration.

Cloud computing allows the use of third party applications, platforms, and infrastructure under a pay as you use model. This affords the flexibility to increase or decrease usage depending on organizational necessities. Outright benefits are that you need not make a huge upfront investment to build infrastructure or purchase development applications or tools. The beauty of cloud computing is that the users can access services from the cloud using their web browsers or thin clients or even equipment like smartphones and tablets.

Most corporations who fight their competition for better market share, who have lots of confidential proprietary or intellectual property rights information or are highly innovative, for whom the integrity of data is of prime importance cannot accept cloud computing in its current form. The risks related to security and privacy issues–including confidentiality, integrity, authenticity, authorization, privacy, and availability–need to be weighed against the benefits cautiously. Exposure of cloud infrastructure, platforms, and applications to different current and potential threats has to be analyzed and weighed against the benefits. Then we explain three service models: Software as a Service (SaaS), Platform as a Service (PaaS), and Infrastructure as a Service (IaaS).

We then explain the four deployment models: Private Cloud, Public Cloud, Community Cloud, and Hybrid Cloud. Then we explore the benefits of cloud computing like Upfront Capital Expenditure (CAPEX) versus Pay as you use Operational Expenditure (OPEX); Elasticity or Flexibility, Reduced need for specialized resources and maintenance services; On Demand Self-Service Mode versus Well Planned Time Consuming Ramp Up; Redundancy and Resilience versus Single Points of Failure; Cost of traditional DRP & BCP versus the DRP & BCP through the Cloud Environment; Ease of use on the Cloud Environment. Then we look into the important enablers of cloud computing like the Internet, Network Bandwidth and Reliability, Server Virtualization, cheaper and more reliable equipment, Standardization, and Advancement in Technology.

We then explore the main security and privacy concerns in the cloud computing, namely Compliance, Lack of Segregation of Duties, Complexity of Cloud Computing Environment, Shared Multi-tenant Environment, Internet and Internet Facing Applications, Control of the Cloud Consumer on the Cloud

Environment, Types of Agreements related to Service Levels, Privacy etc. with the Cloud Provider, Data Management and Data Protection, Insider Threats, Security Issues on account of multiple levels, Physical security issues related to Cloud Computing environment, Cloud Applications Security, Threats on account of Virtual Environment, and Encryption and Key Management. We then describe some of the mechanisms that can address security and privacy concerns in a cloud computing environment, like Understand the Cloud Computing environment and protect yourself, Understand the Technical Competence and segregation of duties of the Cloud Provider, Protection against Technical Vulnerabilities and Malicious Attacks, Regular Hardening and Appropriate Configurations of the Cloud Computing Environment, Data Protection, Encryption, Good Governance Mechanisms, Compliance, Logging and Auditing, Patching/Updating, Application Design & Development, Physical Security, Strong Access Controls, Backups, and Third Party Certifications/Auditing.

CHAPTER 9

■ ■ ■

Understanding Networks and Network Security

Introduction

Before we discuss network vulnerabilities and threats, we should understand why such threats exist. In order to understand this, we need to know the basics of computer communication and networking. In this chapter, we will be discussing the basics of computer networking, Open System Interconnection (OSI), and Transmission Control Protocol/Internet Protocol (TCP/IP) models, and types of networking vulnerabilities that exist and then explore the relevant vulnerabilities and threats.

Networking Fundamentals

A network connects two or more computers to communicate with each other or for the exchange of information among the systems. Networking is sharing of the resources within a network.

In basic communication, there are three components involved: the sender, the receiver, and the media. In the case of two people communicating with each other face to face, within a short distance, the media could be just air. As shown in Figure 9-1, communication is completed only when the sender and receiver understand each other and are able to comprehend the information. In order to comprehend the information that is being exchanged between the sender and the receiver, the communication "protocol" could be common "language." **Protocol** is a set of rules defined by the communication channel in order to comprehend the information that is being exchanged and in normal human communication, it is a common language understood by both the parties.

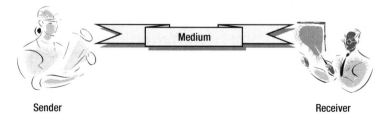

Sender　　　　　　　　　　　　　　　　Receiver

Figure 9-1. *Basic communication*

Let's say that the sender understands a different language and the receiver understands a different language. For discussion's sake, let's say the sender understands French and the receiver understands German. Assume that both have to exchange information, the media is Facsimile (FAX) in France and Telegraph in Germany. This communication has increased the complexity as both sender and receiver do not have a common language and there is no common media. The communication needs translators who understand both the languages or two translators – one who understands the sender's language (e.g., French) and another common language (e.g., English), another who understands a common language (e.g., English) and the receiver's language (e.g., German). These translators translate to the senders and receivers. A media translator transfers facsimile information on to the telegraphic information and vice versa.

As shown in the Figure 9-2, this type of communication is called layered communication. Through the different layer, communication is achieved, each layer has a specific task, and tasks are broken down into simple and specific tasks. Though both sender and receiver do not have a common language, they are still able to interoperate with the help of layered communication.

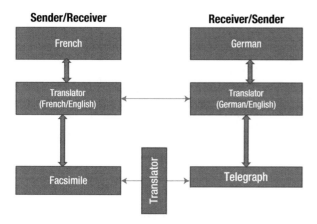

Figure 9-2. *Layered Communication*

Computer Communication

In the case of data communication, computer devices are connected logically to each other and data is transmitted from one computer system to another or from one device to another device as shown in Figure 9-3. A **network** connects two or more computers to communicate with each other or for the exchange of information among the systems. **Networking** is sharing of resources within the network. Data communication and computer networking go hand in hand. Data communication is the exchange of information across a medium and networking is connecting two devices to facilitate the exchange of information from one system to another in a connected network. When computer devices are connected in a network for communication, it consists of the following components: Message, Host, Receiver, Medium, and Protocol. When these network components (the host, receiver, medium, protocol, and other devices) are connected with each other, physically or logically, the primary consideration is whether the systems are able to communicate effectively with each other. Use of appropriate systems or network components with deployment of appropriate protocols ensures effective communication among the systems.

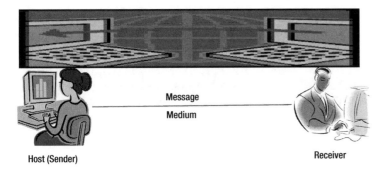

Figure 9-3. *Computer communication*

The network components are:

- **Message** is the information one computer system is sending to another.

- **Host** is the sender of message.

- **Receiver** is one who is receiving the information.

- **Medium** is the channel of communication. It can be copper wire, optical fiber, or wireless.

- **Protocol** is the set of rules in order for two systems to communicate.

Network and its Components

Network "topology" refers to the layout of the network. Topology defines the method of placing different nodes in a network and how the data is getting transferred between these nodes. It can be physical topology or logical topology. In physical topology, there is emphasis on the physical layout of the network whereas logical topology focuses on the transfer of data among the devices.

The common physical topologies that are used are:

- **Bus Topology:** In BUS topology, devices are connected in a series as shown in Figure 9-4. In this topology, all the devices are connected sequentially to the same line (as shown in the figure). This is a simple and low-cost solution but the failure of any single device or damage to the medium can bring down the entire network.

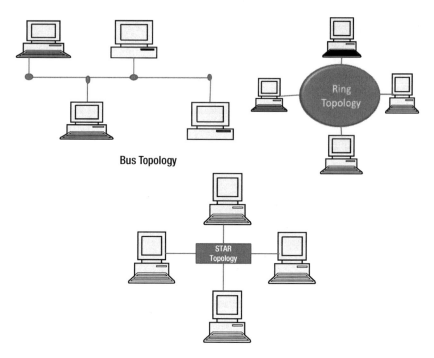

Figure 9-4. *Network Topologies*

- **Ring Topology:** All the devices are connected sequentially in the form of a ring (as shown in Figure 9-4). This topology is similar to the linear bus except that the ring ends at the start of the node. The disadvantage of the ring topology is, if any one of the devices breaks, the entire ring breaks.

- **Star or Y Topology:** All the devices are connected through a central hub (as shown in Figure 9-4). Unlike in the previous topologies, failure of a single device does not necessarily bring down the entire network unless the central hub device is down. This is the most popular topology currently deployed by many organizations because it is simple to build, connect, and it is simple to add and remove devices to/from the network.

Networks can be broadly categorized into:

- **Local Area Network (LAN):** A Local Area Network is a network that is confined to a relatively small geographical area such as a school or an office building and occasionally a group of nearby buildings. LAN connects a relatively small number of systems within the same organization. The most common LAN protocol is Ethernet.

- **Wide Area Network (WAN):** Wide Area Network (WAN) connects two or more LANs which are geographically apart. For example, an organization may have two different offices in two different places or countries and they are connected together to form a WAN. WAN connections comprises of several devices including multiplexers, bridges, and routers. WAN link can be a private dedicated link or a public link.

- **Metropolitan Area Network (MAN):** Metropolitan Area Networks (MAN) is a network of connected systems within the same metropolitan city. A MAN is larger than a LAN but smaller than a WAN. For practical reasons, a MAN is optimized for a large geographical area, and can connect two types of networks – LAN and WAN.

- **Internetworking:** As your organization grows, the networking requirement also changes. What started as one network (LAN) can connect to multiple LANs which are spread across the same geographical area or across different geographical areas. This is called as an internetwork – collection of individual networks. **Internetworking** refers to the connecting of networks of different protocols and procedures, and devices (as shown in Figure 9-5) so that they still can share information.

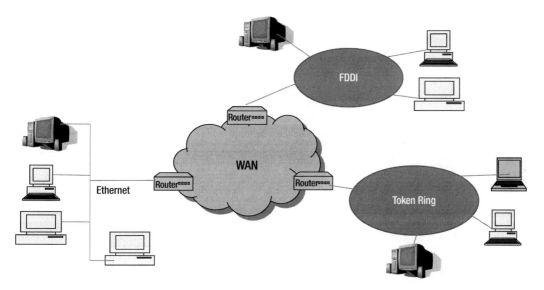

Figure 9-5. *Internetworking*

Network Protocols

A protocol, in computer communications terms, is a set of rules that governs the communication between two or more computers connected on a network. It is a common language for different vendor devices to talk to each other on a network.

In order to meet the challenges of multi-vendor devices on a network and to break the complexity of computer communications, there are two types of networking models that are developed based on the layered protocol approach. These models are the OSI and the TCP/IP. OSI is a seven-layer model whereas TCP/IP is a four-layer model which overlaps several layers of OSI functionality.

OSI (Open Systems Interconnection) Reference Model

ISO, the International Organization for Standardization,[1] is a global body of representatives from over 150 countries. The ISO is a nongovernmental organization that bridges the gap between the government, public, and private organizations. In 1982, the ISO and the International Telecommunication Union Standardization Sector (ITU-T)[2] developed a vendor-neutral, Open Systems Interconnection (OSI) protocol for devices communicating in a multi-vendor network environment. The OSI reference model divides the complex computer communication into seven distinct layers, with each layer having its own specific functions and protocols.

You may be wondering why the acronyms and name are not matching. Here is the explanation as described by ISO – "Because 'International Organization for Standardization' would have different acronyms in different languages (IOS in English, OIN in French for *Organisation internationale de normalisation*), our founders decided to give it the short form ISO. ISO is derived from the Greek isos, meaning equal. Whatever the country, whatever the language, the short form of our name is always ISO."[4]

Each of the seven layers is responsible for a particular function of data communication. For example, one layer may be responsible for routing the data between devices, while another layer may be responsible for establishing connection between the devices. The upper layers focus on presenting information to the user at the application level whereas the lower layers focus on transporting the information across the network without any data loss. Each layer is functionally independent of the other layers. In the OSI reference model, each of the layers extends services to the layer directly above it and is given services from the layer directly below it. Hence all the seven layers together bring about the communication between the devices in a network. Figure 9-6 describes the seven layers, and the functions that are performed by each layer.

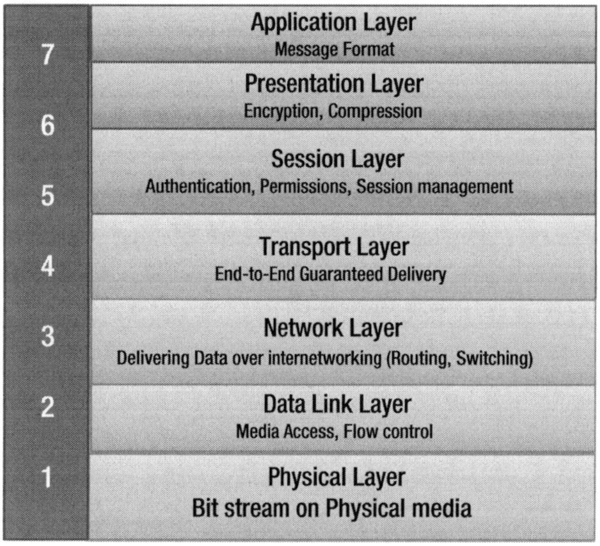

Figure 9-6. *OSI Seven Layer Reference Model*

The layers are described in the following section[2]:

- **Layer 7: Application Layer:** The Application layer has the responsibility of providing application services to the network applications such as e-mail, web, remote connection, file transfers, and database access. Some of the other functions that are performed at this layer include user authentication and data encryption. Application examples include *WWW browsers, Hypertext Transfer Protocol (HTTP), Simple Network Management Protocol (SNMP), Telnet, File Transfer Protocol (FTP), Domain Name System (DNS), Internet Message Access Control (ICMP),* and *Dynamic Host Configuration Protocol (DHCP).*

- **Layer 6: Presentation Layer:** This layer is responsible for presenting the data to the upper layers. This layer transforms the data into a required format that can be accepted by the applications in the application layer. For example, some Web browsers accept jpeg, some accept gif, some accept ASCII, and so on. This layer also manages techniques such as data compression and data encryption. Examples include *ASCII, EBCDIC, TIFF, GIF, PICT, JPEG, MPEG,* and *MIDI.*

- **Layer 5: Session Layer:** This layer manages the establishment, the usage, and the ending of the connections/sessions between the devices. This layer performs the function of establishing sessions between the devices, how long the sessions should be, which side will transmit, when to transmit and how long to transmit. Examples include RPC, SQL, and NetBios.

- **Layer 4: Transport Layer:** This layer's responsibility is to ensure that the delivery of data from one end point to another indeed gets completed without any errors. This layer implements error checking, recovery of lost packets to ensure the completeness of data transfer and flow control. Some examples include Transmission Control Protocol (TCP), User Datagram Protocol (UDP), and Sequenced Packet Exchange (SPX).

- **Layer 3: Network Layer:** This layer is responsible for routing of the data within the network. It is responsible for finding the shortest path from source to destination and route the packet through the intermediate devices such as router(s) or switch(es). Examples include Internet Protocol (IP), Internetwork Packet Exchange (IPX), and AppleTalk.

- **Layer 2: Data Link Layer:** This layer consists of two layers: Media Access Control (MAC) and Logical Link Layer (LLC). The Media Access Control Layer is responsible for taking the packets from the above layers and putting them onto the media in the form of bits. The media can be copper (wired), optical fiber, or wireless. LLC connects to the upper network layer. The function of the LLC layer is to control the frame synchronization, flow control of data, and error checking of the frames (Cyclic Redundancy Check). Examples include *IEEE 802.5/ 802.2, IEEE 802.3/802.2, Frame Relay, Asynchronous Transfer Mode (ATM),* and *Integrated Services Digital Network (ISDN).*

- **Layer 1: Physical Layer:** This layer is responsible for transmitting bits (0s and 1s) from one device to another device over a physical media. The media could be wire, wireless, or optical fiber. Both the Data Link layer and the Physical Layer functions are implemented at the hardware level attached to the computer as a peripheral device known as the Network Interface Card (NIC).

TCP/IP Model

The Department of Defense (DOD), as a part of research project, developed the ARPAnet protocol to connect devices in a network of networks (the "Internet"). Modification of this protocol for the public is what we know today as TCP/IP – Transmission Control Protocol (TCP) and Internet Protocol (IP). TCP/IP is made up of the following four layers:

- **Application Layer:** This layer combines the Application, Presentation, and Session layer functionalities of the OSI reference model. The function of this layer is to hand over the data received from the bottom layer to the application and to make sure the application is able to interpret the data that it has received from the other network device.

- **Transmission Control Protocol (TCP) Layer:** The function of this layer is to deliver data from the client to the server without errors or loss. Data can be lost during the transmission but TCP ensures that the data is not lost and triggers retransmission process until the data is correctly and completely received by the destination device. This layer overlaps the functionality of Transport Layer of OSI reference model. In this layer, the data received from the application is broken down into smaller "chunks" called segments.

- **Internet Protocol (IP) Layer:** This layer is responsible for moving the data from one node to another node. IP forwards the segments received from the TCP, referred to as packets, to the destination based on the IP address. This layer's function is very similar to the Network Layer function of the OSI reference model and implements various routing protocols such as Remote Imaging Protocol (RIP), Open Shortest Path First (OSPF), and Border Gateway Protocol (BGP).

- **Network Access Layer:** It combines the functions of the Data Link and the Physical Layers of the OSI reference model. The Network Access layer is responsible for creating data 'frames' for transmitting and receiving data from the physical layer. This function is implemented by a hardware and software Network Interface Card (NIC), an adapter connected to the computer through physical wires or optical fiber cables. There are several protocols implemented in this layer: Ethernet, Gigabit Ethernet, ATM, ISDN, and frame relay. It can support copper or optical interface.

Figure 9-7 illustrates the relationship between the OSI seven layers and TCP/IP.

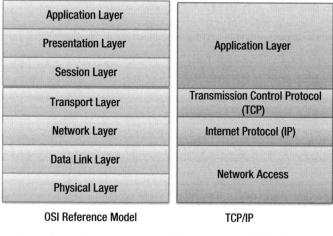

OSI Reference Model   TCP/IP

Comparison between seven layer OSI and four layer TCP/IP Models

Figure 9-7. *OSI and TCP/IP models compared*

Each layer provides a distinct function and works with its upper layer and lower layer. Each layer "encapsulates" its function and passes on to the next layer while transmitting the data. When the data is received from lower layers, each layer peels off its encapsulation to perform its function. For the complete data transfer, functions of all the layers are equally important and all the layers have to work together. Layered architecture breaks the network communication into simpler components thus aiding easy design, development, and troubleshooting. With the layered architecture, each layer's functions can be developed by a different vendor who needs to adhere to the standards specified by the OSI reference model. The OSI model ensures different types of network devices built by different manufacturers such as routers, switches, hubs, and adapters, are able to interoperate within the network.

The (Internet Engineering Task Force) IETF is an international community consisting of network designers, equipment manufacturers, internet operators, and researchers who maintain the Internet protocol and the smooth operation of the Internet. *RFC 1122*[3] explains the details of host-to-host communication. *RFC 791*[4] describes IP and *RFC 793*[5] describes TCP architecture.

Figure 9-8 shows the TCP/IP protocol architecture and shows the major applications in each layer. This is by no means an exhaustive or a complete list.

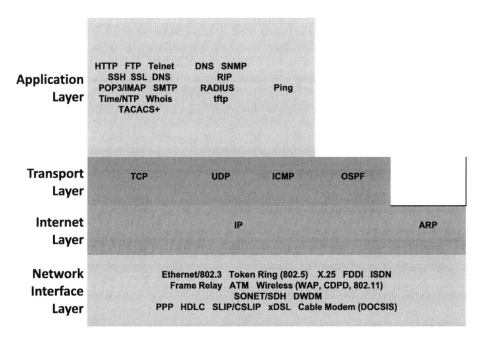

Figure 9-8. *TCP/IP and its functions*[6]

Network Vulnerabilities and Threats

With the advancement in computing, networking, and technology, the world is becoming more and more connected. Internet connects millions of computers and most of the geographies of this world. The Internet is a network of networks and consists of billions of users across private, public, university, and government networks sharing information across the networks. The Internet uses TCP/IP protocol and the underlying physical media can be wire, optical, or wireless technologies. The Internet serves an extensive range of applications, starting with e-mail, the World Wide Web (www), and social networks. Each application may use one or more protocols. There is a large amount of personal, commercial, business, government, and military information being shared on the Internet. There are billions of users, both good and bad, accessing the Internet. The bad guys, known as hackers and such other persons with malicious intent are a concern.

With so many computers, networking devices, protocols, and applications on the network, it has become a serious threat to information security. Any application, network device, or protocol can be vulnerable. The internet is crawling with people from all over the world who are continuously trying to test the security of various systems and networks. Some are simply testing for fun and others are fuelled by treacherous motives of stealing or revenge. A threat is an event that can occur by taking advantage of any vulnerabilities that exist in the network.

Any discussion on network security will include these three common terms:

- **Vulnerability:** An inherent weakness in the network, and network device. It could be hardware or software or both. Possible vulnerabilities could include routers, switches, servers, and security devices themselves.

- **Threat:** A threat is what can go wrong because of the exploit of the vulnerabilities or attack on the assets, such as data theft or unauthorized modification of the data.

- **Attack:** An attack is an unauthorized action with the intent to cause damage, or hinder or breach security of a network. An attack is launched by intruders to damage the network and network resources such as end-point devices, servers, or desktops which are vulnerable.

Vulnerabilities

One of the following three types of vulnerabilities or weaknesses can exist in the network:

- Security policy weakness
- Technology weakness
- Configuration weakness

Security Policy Weaknesses

Every organization should have security policies defined. However, the network can pose a security threat if the users do not follow the organizational security policy. Table 9-1 summarizes some of the common security policy weaknesses.

Table 9-1. *Common Security Policy Weaknesses*

Weakness	What can go wrong?
No written security policy	No enforcement of security policy across the organization leading to security incidents.
	Because of ignorance, mistakes may happen which can compromise the security.
	Intentional malicious acts also can be disguised as acts of ignorance.
No policy for hardware and software installations or updates	Unauthorized installations leading to theft of information; unauthorized modifications to the information.
	Unapproved modifications leading to unstable, attack prone network; ultimately leading to network crash.
	Unauthorized installations leading to malware infection. Intentional misuse of the network for personal gain.
Lack of Disaster recovery and Business continuity Plans	Confusion during disaster.
	Disasters may not be effectively and efficiently handled leading to reputation loss, business loss, or customer loss.
No Incident Response Team	Not able to handle security incidents / crisis, sometimes further complicating the situation rather than solving the problem.
No policy on usage of official assets	Misuse of official assets. Reputation Loss. Productivity loss. Can lead to malware infection.
No policy on Teleworking or Working from Home	Use of personal machines to connect to the network leading to the theft of data or infection of the office network.

Technology Weaknesses

Protocols are standards created to specify how an application should communicate. All connection oriented protocols have a state. Each state triggers certain events at certain time. Each state can be part of the connection, for example, a server waiting for response from a client or the transition between the close of connections. Specifications are not always complete, they are a good starting point and they could have limitations. Not all the applications are created by taking care of all the points mentioned in the specification. Such weaknesses in the protocol can be exploited.

All data traffic on the network is not malicious. However, traffic is allowed or denied by the security policies defined. By exploiting the weakness of the policy, attackers can bypass the security rules that can lead to policy violations. For example, TCP packets with SYN and RST flags enabled or an IP packet length can exceed the actual length specified in the standards. Although this packet can bypass security rules, if the remote device is not able to handle this erroneous packet, it leads to a possible attack. Table 9-2 summarizes the technology weaknesses that include protocol weaknesses, operating system weaknesses, and network equipment weaknesses.

Table 9-2. *Technology Weaknesses That Affect Networks*

Weakness	Description
TCP/IP Applications and protocols	HTTP, FTP, SNMP, SMTP, TCP, IP, and DNS are implemented as per the standards and specifications which have inherent limitations that can be exploited
Operating system	Microsoft Windows, Apple Macintosh, IBM OS/2, UNIX, and other operating systems have several security issues
Network device	Password weaknesses like default passwords not changed or lack of strong passwords requirement, authentication weaknesses, firewall holes, and user interface weaknesses

Configuration Weaknesses

Network administrators need to have adequate skills to configure networks and network devices to prevent security threats. Table 9-3 describes some of the possible configuration weaknesses.

Table 9-3. *Configuration Weaknesses That Affect Networks*

Weakness	Description
User Accounts	User accounts stored on devices must be secured. Exposing usernames and passwords can be a security threat.
Passwords	Password policy should be enforced at the user level. Passwords of major devices such as servers, routers, databases, should follow password policy set by the IT policy of the organization. Default passwords should not be allowed to be continued. The password secrecy should be preserved. These passwords have to be changed when an administrator leaves the organization. Passwords have to be periodically changed.
Configuration of TCP ports and Internet services	Should have a policy to define what application services should be allowed and for what purposes. A common problem is the lack of clarity in this regard and enabling some of the attack-prone ones like Java Script and VB Script or enabling the remote services or such other services without understanding the risks.
Default settings	If the network administrators do not change the default policy of the devices, it can cause serious security threats, such as default passwords are known to public, default permissions may be continued giving scope for attacks.
Misconfiguration of security and network devices	Misconfiguration of firewall and other network devices can cause serious security problems. For example, misconfiguration of access lists, routing protocol can cause serious security threats.

Threats

Internal threats and external threats are the two primary classes of threats to network security. They are illustrated in Figure 9-9. These threats are caused by attackers.

- **Internal Threats:** Internal threats are threats from someone within the organization, who has proper access to the network and network resources, who understands the network infrastructure well, who understands the security applications and the security loop holes. Someone within the organization can create and send out attacks by hiding his identity as he already knows enough inside information. According to the FBI, 80 percent of the reported security incidents are due to internal access and misuse of information by an insider of the company.

- **External Threats:** External threats are threats from outside the organization. They do not possess authorized access to the network resources. They work by gaining unauthorized access to the network and network resources with the intention of damaging the resources or for profit. These can be structured or unstructured:

  - **Structured:** Structured attacks come from technically competent hackers who belong to a class of highly motivated individuals. They understand vulnerabilities and develop sophisticated tools and techniques to penetrate without anyone knowing. These groups (also called hackers or crackers) may often be found to be involved in major crimes such as credit card theft or identity theft.

  - **Unstructured:** These threats are from inexperienced individuals testing their skills using some of the tools available in the public domain. Sometimes, these can do serious damage to company assets.

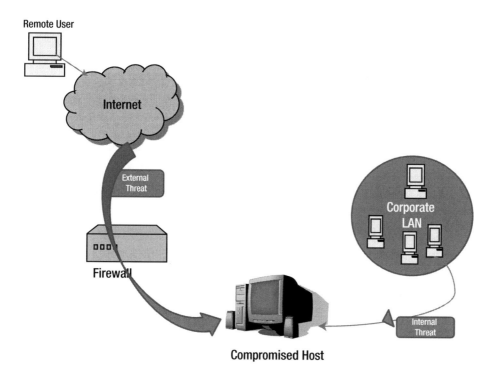

Figure 9-9. *Types of Threats*

Attacks

Attackers generally abuse the network "rules" established by security policies. The rules are broken in such a way that attackers send their traffic that appears to be normal traffic. Attacks can be classified into the following categories:

- Reconnaissance

- Denial of Service (DOS)/Distributed Denial of Service (DDoS)

- Other network attacks

Reconnaissance

To effectively launch an attack, the attacker should have the knowledge of the network, hardware used, software deployed, and its topology. Before an attack is launched, the attacker tries to gain this knowledge by scanning the network, which is called ***reconnaissance***. Reconnaissance is not an attack by itself; however, this could cause a serious security threat by allowing the weaknesses of the network or network resources to be made known to the attacker. This is more an information-gathering mission.

Quite often, reconnaissance is not detected for a considerable amount of time because they have no impact on the network.

Sniffing is one of the important reconnaissance methods used by the attackers to collect the information, such as user IDs and passwords, other information like session id, transactions being carried out, other confidential details, and business discussions carried out. Other popular methods used are pinging, banner grabbing, and port scanning.

Denial-of-Service (DoS) and Distributed Denial-of-Service (DDoS)

The purpose of the DoS attack, as shown in Figure 9-10, is to make the network resources inaccessible to the user and bring down the network itself by generating a huge amount of network traffic that overwhelms or crashes the server, exceeding the capacity of the routers and switches, overwhelming the CPU and memory utilization. In some cases, DoS attacks can target a specific device and cause the system to hang.

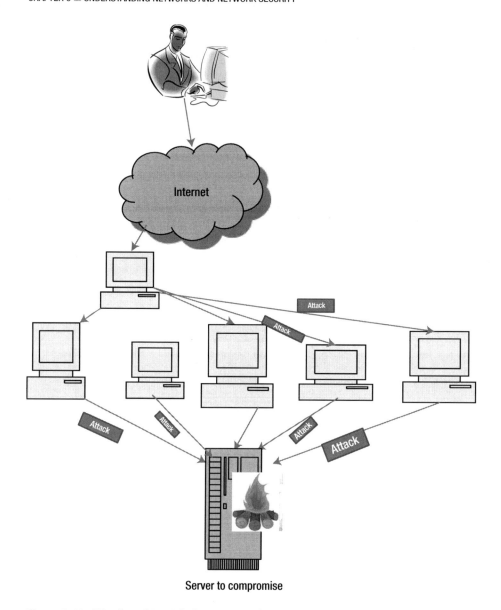

Figure 9-10. *Distributed Denial of Service Attack*

Sometimes, the attacker gets into one device in the network remotely and triggers simultaneous exploitation of systems on the network or uses multiple compromised machines to initiate simultaneous attacks, causing interruptions of network and network resources. The sudden increase in the network traffic can cause the server or router to go down quickly and become inaccessible to the legitimate users. This kind of an attack is called a Distributed Denial-of-Service (DDOS) attack which hides the true origin of the attack.

A DoS (DDoS) attack is an explicit attack to prevent legitimate users from accessing network and network services. Examples include:

- Flood the network, thereby preventing legitimate network traffic

- Target single device with too many requests thus bringing down the device

- Disrupt the connections between two legitimate devices thereby preventing access to a genuine service request

- Destruction or alteration of network configurations

- Consume the network bandwidth

The list of DDoS attack victims includes some major players including Microsoft, Amazon, HSBC, and YAHOO. In November 2011, the international bank HSBC was under an attack which targeted their servers that resulted in numerous customers being unable to withdraw money from the cash machines, as well as affecting its HSBC and First Direct websites.[7]

In 2004, the Microsoft Corp. was assailed by a DDoS attack induced by a Windows-based Mydoom-B worm.[8] The following are some of the common (D)DoS attacks (by name):

- **Ping of Death** – This is an exploit of TCP/IP protocol implementation. As per the RFC specification, the maximum size of an IP packet is 65536. The attacker uses the "ping" application to make up an IP packet whose size exceeds the maximum size specified. The remote system may crash or reboot if it does not know how to handle the oversized packets.

- **TCP SYN Flood Attack:** This attack is an exploit of TCP implementation of connection establishment process. TCP connection establishment requires three handshakes, as shown in Figure 9-11, before the actual data starts being transmitted. Each time a client application, such as a web browser, attempts to open a connection with the server, it sends a request (SYN flag), to the server and waits for the acknowledgement from the server. If the server accepts the connection, then it sends back an (SYN-ACK) acknowledgement and waits for the acknowledgement.

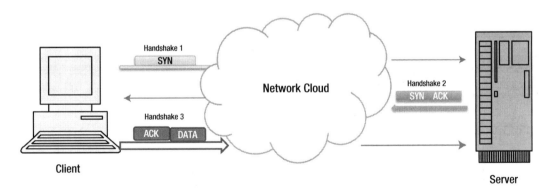

Figure 9-11. *TCP 3 Way Connection Handshake*

Once the client receives the acknowledgement from the server, it sends one more segment (ACK) acknowledging the receipt of the server's information. Once both the server and client handshake completes, the actual data transmission starts. This is sometimes referred to as TCP 3-way handshake. Since each connection information takes up memory and CPU resources, only a limited number of in-progress connections are possible. When the server establishes connection with the client, the server considers the connection as open and frees up the queued resources for accepting new connections. During a SYN flood attack, the server never sends back the ACK packet to the hostile client. Instead, the hostile client application keeps sending repeated SYN requests causing DoS. The attacking application generates spoofed packets that appear to be valid new connections and enter into the queue, but connections are never completed (RFC 4987)[9].

- E-mail bombs – An Application program that can send bulk e-mails to individuals, organizations, lists, or domains to vandalize an e-mail server

- Teardrop – An IP protocol exploit where the IP packet is fragmented in such a way that reassembling the packet can cause the system to crash

- **Smurf Attack:** Internet Control Message Protocol (ICMP) is used to test the availability of a network device by pinging the concerned node to determine its operational status. When the remote host sends a PING, the end device responds by sending a "reply" message. A smurf is a type of DoS attack in which a system is flooded with spoofed ping (ICMP) messages. This creates high network traffic and high consumption of network bandwidth and leads ultimately to the crashing of the remote system.

Other Attacks on Networks

Apart from the attacks that we have described previously, there are other attacks that can cause serious damage to the network security. Some common ones include spoofing attacks, HTTP Tunneling, and session hijacking:

- **Masquerade/Spoofing Attacks:** The network intruder masquerades the TCP/IP packet by an illegal IP address, falsifying the source address. The intruder fools the remote machine by an illegitimate source address but with valid user access privileges. In an IP spoofing attack, a malicious hacker from outside the network hacks into the network pretending to be an insider, a trusted user, of the organization, and spoofs the source address of a legitimate inside user thus gaining access to the network resources. This attack can also cause a broadcast in the network causing high network traffic. If the attacker manages to alter the routing tables, then response from the network resource can go to the spoofed destination address.

- **ARP Spoofing & DNS Spoofing:** The Address Resolution Protocol (ARP) spoofing is used to confuse the system to map incorrect MAC address to a particular IP address in the ARP table. Similarly DNS (Domain Name Service protocol) spoofing is to change the mapping of DNS entries in the DNS cache. Mac Flooding attacks are also similar to this.

- **HTTP Tunneling:** This method may be used by the insiders to overcome the firewall controls and send confidential information to the outside world without anyone inside being aware of the same.

- **SSH Tunneling:** These may be used to directly connect to a network stealthily and initiate attacks. This is an illegitimate use of a legitimate tool.

- **Session Hijacking:** A session between the user and the server can be hijacked by the attacker. Some of the methods used in this regard are session fixing and session prediction. Here, usually a valid session between the user and server is taken over by the attacker.

- **Attacks on Network Equipment including Routers:** The network equipment is traditionally prone to default password vulnerabilities because the network administrators not taking sufficient care in resetting these passwords. The weakness of the network configurations of a router is a new point of vulnerability. In addition to the administrator passwords, some vendors have a so-called "back-door" to their system for debugging purposes and to support the client in case an admin password is forgotten or lost. This back-door could also be exploited, if it is known to the attackers.

How to counter the Network Attacks

The following measures can be taken to counter the network attacks:

- Hardening of all network equipment with appropriate configurations and appropriate patching including firmware updates

- All default passwords to be substituted with strong passwords

- Defense in depth is implemented to avoid attacks like session hijacking

- Use safe session ID handling

- Session time-out to be set as appropriate to the application and its risks

- Set complicated session ID creation logic

- Use encrypted handshakes like SSL with Digital certificate or TLS, techniques like VPN

- Do not store passwords or critical information in the cookies

- Ensure that all the software used including utilities / tools are patched / updated

- Set easy-to-understand and clear security policies

- Create awareness among the employees on what can go wrong and what is expected from them – do's and don'ts

- Do not have the same user name and passwords for all the systems – use different ones

- Logout promptly after the work is over

- Ensure cookies, history, and offline content are removed after sensitive transaction sessions

- Do not click on the links in the suspect e-mails

Chapter Summary

- We looked into basic communication, computer communication, and the parties to and components of the communication. We also looked into the context of computer communication, and defined a network and networking. We equated the language of the oral or written communication to that of the protocol in the networked world.

- We explored the networks in particular and looked in to various network topologies like BUS, Ring, Star, or Y. We also identified the differences and weaknesses of each of these. We also looked into what is meant by LAN, MAN, and WAN and the differences among these.

- We elaborated upon the two models of networking: Open Systems Interconnection (OSI) and Transmission Control Protocol/Internet Protocol (TCP/IP). We looked into how the OSI model divides the entire structure of computer communication into seven layers and how the TCP/IP model divides the entire structure into four corresponding layers. We also looked at the method of communication between various layers like the upper layer being serviced by the lower layer while concurrently servicing its upper layer and that is how the communication happens between various equipment / components of network. We also looked at the details of the functions carried out by various layers and the different protocols used by various layers. We also explored and understood how the layers, protocols, and the specifications help vendors to create the equipment which interoperates with each other.

- We defined vulnerabilities, threats, and attacks to make the further discussions clear to the readers.

- We categorized the weaknesses or vulnerabilities into three groups: security policy implementation related, technology related, and configuration related. We also looked at various examples from each of these categories.

- We differentiated between internal and external threats; and between structured and unstructured threats.

- Then we detailed the issue of "reconnaissance," which is usually carried out by the attackers to gather information and how sniffing is an important part of this activity.

- We explored DoS/DDoS attacks and the various ways in which these attacks can be executed. In this context, we elaborated upon Ping-of-Death, TCP SYN flooding, e-mail bombing, teardrop, and smurf attacks. We also went through some of the real-world DoS/DDoS attacks.

- We explored other network threats like spoofing, session hijacking, HTTP tunneling, SSH Tunneling, and backdoors.

- We looked briefly at the measures we can take individually or at the organization level to counter the network attacks.

CHAPTER 10

■ ■ ■

Firewalls

Introduction

The Internet plays an important role in our daily life. Today, everyone is "connected" to everyone else almost at any given instant as we are connected to the Internet most of the time and interacting with others through e-mails or instant messengers like Skype or are using some applications on the web. With the innovation of high-speed computing devices, large-scale deployment of wireless networks, Web 3.0, Cloud computing, and social networks, "always connected" is a reality. The Internet continues to grow exponentially. Most of the businesses are connected on and through the Internet. E-commerce, e-business, and other Internet-related businesses are growing at a faster rate than ever before. According to an estimate by one of the leaders in network systems and services, the number of globally connected devices, which was around 8 billion in 2013, is expected to reach 25 billion by 2015, outnumbering the people by twice as much. And the number of devices that are going to be connected to the Internet is estimated to go as high as 50 billion by the year 2020.[1] According to the latest statistics, more than 75% of the world's population will be connected to the Internet by 2020. The Internet is bringing together people, processes, and data to make network connections more relevant to today's world. Demand for network-based applications and services is exponentially growing.

Though these applications have an immediate benefit to the end user, they can pose security risks to the individual user and the information resources of a company and government. Any information on the network is an asset and must be protected. Without adequate network security, many individuals, businesses, and governments are at risk of losing those assets. The goal of network security is to:

- Protect Confidentiality

- Maintain Integrity

- Ensure Availability

In the previous chapter, we discussed network security threats. Network attacks can be broadly classified into three categories:

- Network Access attacks: An intruder attempts to gain unauthorized access to a system to retrieve data. The attacker gains access by either cracking the network or system passwords or he already has access to the network but not to the resources. The attacker will use exploits to gain access. Improper configuration can often expose a service to substantial risk.

- Denial of Service (DoS) attacks: The purpose of the attacker is to bring the network and network resources down. The intent is to deny the authorized users access to the resources. He is attacking the availability of the network and resources. In Distributed DoS (DDoS) attack, the source consists of multiple systems that are spread across geographical boundaries.

- Reconnaissance attacks: The purpose is to identify the weakness of the system so that they can attack it at a later time. A typical reconnaissance attack consists of scanning the network devices for the open TCP port to see which application is running as well as to try to determine the operating system on which it is running.

The greatest threat arises from within the network, namely from insider attacks. Since an insider already has enough information about the network, network resources, and access to these resources, he/she can easily hack into the network. An outsider's skills combined with an insider's access could cause significant damage to an organization. Hence, the network has to be guarded from both insider and outsider attacks.

How Do You Protect a Network?

Information security has one purpose: to protect assets. How do you protect a network and be protected yourself? You build strong walls and fences to stop the enemy from entering your compound but provide a small, guarded door to friends. For a long time this was the strategy that was used for a "closed network," as illustrated in Figure 10-1.

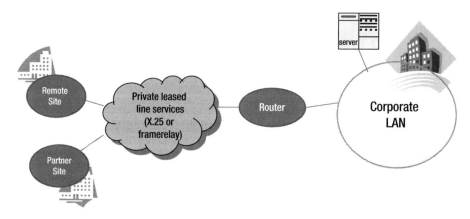

Figure 10-1. *Closed Network*

The original corporate network usually implemented a "closed network," which typically allowed secure access only to known parties and employees. In the early days, there was no outside connectivity and no World Wide Web. This worked well until the advent of World Wide Web and e-business.

As e-business, World Wide Web, and related applications continue to grow, a "closed network" was no longer closed and "private" networks started getting connected to the outside public Internet as well. Extranet connected internal and external business processes. Companies soon realized the value of supply chain management and Enterprise Resource Planning (ERP) systems to their business. Enterprises also realized the benefit of e-commerce applications to business partners and consumers, and connecting sales-force automation systems to mobile sales force. Today, an enterprise network demands an "Open Network" with the flexibility to connect to the Internet and web applications, and to support telecommuters and mobile sales force, accessing through mobile devices and much more as Figure 10-2 illustrates.

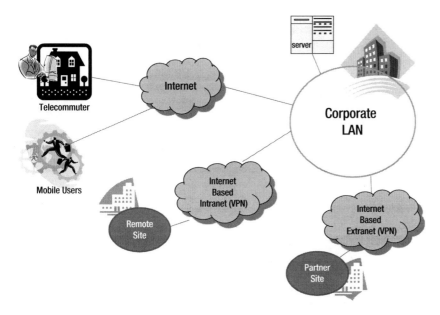

Figure 10-2. *Open Network*

Typical network architecture has three layers:

- Access Layer
- Distribution Layer
- Core Layer[2]

Network security can be translated to providing security at each of these layers – access or perimeter layer, distribution layer, and core layer. Different devices are deployed at each layer to protect the network and its assets.

In any fast-growing industry, changes are expected. As you keep adding more devices to the network, the risk also increases. Hackers are becoming smarter every day and many hacking tools are publically available on the World Wide Web. Attacking networks and associated resources has become relatively easy because of various tools and techniques available on the Internet. This is a cause for concern to organizations and enterprises. If the security of the network is compromised, there could be serious consequences, such as loss of privacy, breach of confidentiality, theft of identities, and legal liabilities. Figure 10-3 illustrates threats and their consequences.

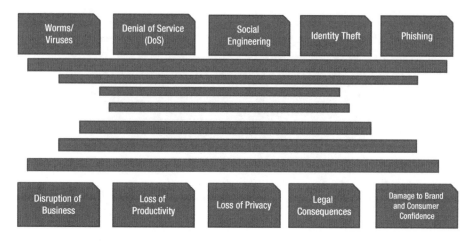

Figure 10-3. *Threats and consequences*

Various security devices such as Firewalls, Intrusion Detection Systems, Authentication and Access Control devices, and Virtual Private Networks (VPNs) are implemented at different layers. To understand these things better Table 10-1 provides an analogy.

Table 10-1. *Generic analogy of security devices*

Sl. No.	Description	Security Devices
1	Doorman, Lock and Key	Firewall
2	Passport and VISA	Access Cards, Biometric
3	Surveillance	Intrusion Detection System/Intrusion Prevention Systems
4	Escorting guests to your lab	Virtual Private Network (VPN)
5	Guards, Guard dogs	Intrusion Detection System/Intrusion Prevention Systems

In this chapter, we discuss firewalls. The chapters that follow cover Intrusion Detection System (IDS), Intrusion Prevention System (IPS), and Virtual Private Network (VPN), respectively.

Firewall

The term firewall, in the real world, means a wall built to protect from fire and intended to slow the spread of fire through a structure. The same concept is used in networks too. A network firewall is intended to stop unauthorized users from accessing the network and its services from other external networks. The most common deployment of firewalls is between a trusted network of an organization to an untrusted network, typically the Internet, as Figure 10-4 illustrates. Typically, the Internet Service Provider (ISP) connection terminates at a border router and then connects to a firewall.

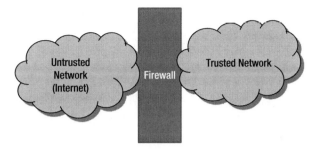

Figure 10-4. *Firewall Deployment*

Basic Functions of Firewall

A firewall in the networking world should examine the traffic that is entering into the network and pass the "Wall" based on some rules defined by the network and its resources. It acts as a security guard, who normally sits at the main gate, and checks your identity and access privileges and lets you in. Depending on the type of organization, the guards may screen people who are exiting the gate too. Many of the Internet and Information security concepts can be described using some of these practical examples.

If you talk to various vendors about a firewall and its function you will get several different answers or definitions. In its simplest form, a firewall is a combination of hardware and software devices, which bifurcates the internal network from the outside networks (Internet) and blocks certain traffic and allows some specific traffic. However, it has three basic functions (depending upon its type):

- Packet filtering: A firewall filters the IP packets. The IP headers of all the packets that enter or exit the network firewall are inspected. Firewall makes an explicit decision on each packet that enters as to whether to allow the packet or deny the packet.

- Stateful Packet Filtering: Here the packet filtering goes beyond basic packet filtering. This keeps track of state of connection flows for all the packets, in both directions. It also keeps track of all the IP addresses currently connected at any point of time.

- Application Level Gateways (Proxy): A firewall is also capable of inspecting application level protocols. This requires the firewall to understand certain specific application protocols.

Packet Filtering

As the name suggests, a packet filter filters the packets that are entering and leaving the network. The firewall inspects each IP packet and a decision is made. Each packet is compared with a set of filter rules and based on any match, the packet is either allowed, denied, or dropped. Packet filtering works on the network layer and transport layer of the OSI reference or TCP and IP layer of TCP/IP, as Figure 10-5 illustrates. It does not remember the state and hence it is called as *stateless firewall*.

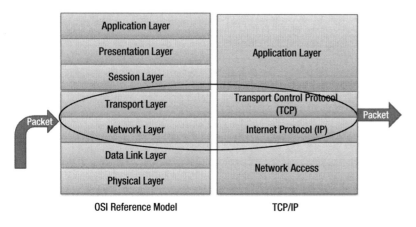

Packet Filter Data Flow

Figure 10-5. *Packet Filtering related Layers*

Packet filters usually permit or deny network traffic based on the following:

- Source and destination IP addresses
- Protocol such as TCP, UDP, or ICMP
- Source and destination TCP or UDP port addresses
- Flags in the TCP header – ACK, CLOSE, and SYNC
- IP fragmentation flag
- Direction of the packet – inbound or outbound
- Physical interface

How a packet filtering firewall works

Figure 10-6 illustrates how a packet filtering firewall works.

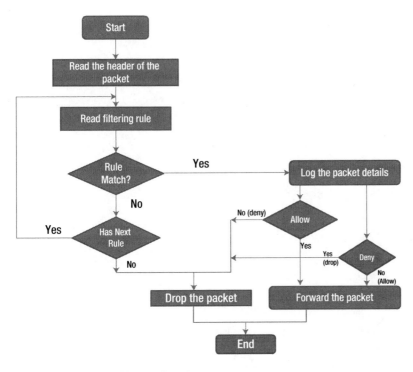

Figure 10-6. *Packet filtering flow diagram*

A packet filter firewall is configured with a set of rules that define when to accept a packet or deny. When the firewall receives a packet, the filter checks the rules defined against IP address, port number, protocol, and so on. If the rule matches "accept," then the packet is accepted in the network, otherwise it is dropped.

To understand configuring packet filtering rules, you need to first understand TCP/IP protocol, what an IP packet is and how they are handled at each layer. RFC 791[3] and RFC 793[4] provide the details of IP protocol and TCP protocol. From a packet filtering point of view, the IP header contains three important pieces of information:

- The IP source address – four bytes long, and typically written as 192.168.2.34

- The IP destination address – four bytes long, Just like source address

- The IP protocol – specifies whether it is a TCP packet or UDP packet, an Internet Control Message Protocol (ICMP) packet

If the network bandwidth is smaller than the source, IP may divide a packet into a series of smaller packets called *fragments*. Fragmenting does not change the structure of the IP packet, as shown in Figure 10-7, but it may set a flag inside the IP packet, stating that the body contains only a part of a packet.

Bits
0
4
8
12
16
20
24
28
31
Words
1
2
3
4
5
6
Version
IHL
Type of Service
Total Length
Identification
Flags
Fragmentation Offset
Time to Live
Protocol
Header Checksum
Source Address
Destination Address
Options
Padding
data begins here ...
Header

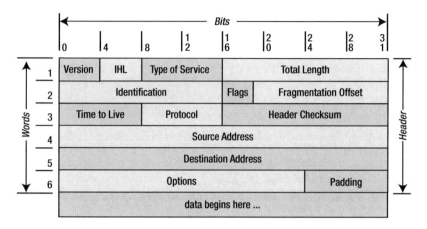

Figure 10-7. *IP Packet (source: RFC 791[3])*

TCP Layer

As Figure 10-8 shows, the TCP packet header contains the following information:

- The TCP source port – a two byte number, which specifies the application process that this packet belongs to
- The TCP destination port – a two byte number, which specifies the application process that this packet has to reach
- The TCP flags field – contains TCP protocol information such as connection establishment, closing connection, and size of packet

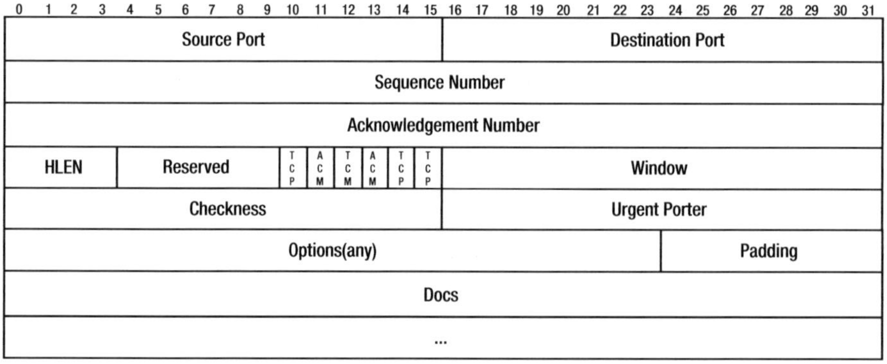

0 1 2 3 4 5 6 7 8 9 10 11 12 13 14 15 16 17 18 19 20 21 22 23 24 25 26 27 28 29 30 31
Source Port
Destination Port
Sequence Number
Acknowledgement Number
HLEN
Reserved
TCP
ACM
TCM
ACM
TCP
TCP
Window
Checkness
Urgent Porter
Options(any)
Padding
Docs
...

Figure 10-8. *TCP Header (source: RFP 793[4])*

An Example of Packet Filtering Rules

Let's say that you want to allow all the IP traffic between the external host (say 162.22.34.56) and the host on your internal network (class A 10.1.1.2). Table 10-2 lists the packet filtering rules.

Table 10-2. *Packet filtering rules*

Rule	Direction	Source Address	Destination Address	Application (TCP port)	Filter Set	Action
1	Inbound	Trusted external host (162.22.34.56)	Internal (10*.*)	Http	Any	Permit
2	Outbound	Internal	Trusted External host (162*.*)	SMTP	Any	Permit
3	Inbound or Outbound	Any	Any	TFTP	Any	Deny

Some examples of packet filtering rules are:

- Allow e-mail and HTTP (web) services, but block services such as TFTP and Telnet

- Block all incoming connections from outside systems except for SMTP connections (so that you can receive e-mails)

- Allow port 443 for all service destination addresses

- Allow port 80 for all service destination addresses

Advantages and Disadvantages of Packet filtering

The main advantage of the packet filter firewall is its simple rules: allow or deny:

- A strategically placed packet filtering firewall can protect the entire network. Most of the routers support packet filtering. If you have a border router placed just after Internet ISP, with the packet filtering enabled, you can protect an entire network regardless of the network size.

- Packet filtering is widely available in routers. Leading networking vendors like Cisco, Juniper, and HP, provide packet filtering on their core and edge routers known as Access Control Lists (ACL), which is configured in all the border routers.

There are several disadvantages:

- The packet filtering rules tend to be hard to configure. You need a lot of expertise and proper strategy to configure it right

- Once it is configured, it is difficult to comprehensively test and verify whether it is working correctly or not

- It is a stateless machine. It does not remember the state of the previous packet. Stateless packet filters are vulnerable to attacks. Hence, some of the attacks, such as spoofing attacks, can easily bypass firewall rules

Stateful Packet Filtering

The main disadvantage of basic packet filtering is that it is stateless. It does not remember the state of a telnet connection or an FTP connection flow already established or source port number of the client. In any application service, the TCP destination port is typically identified. For example, destination port for HTTP is 80 or FTP is 21. However, an FTP client can use any port and typically, this is dynamically chosen at run time. In basic packet filtering, since the firewall does not remember the previous state, and relies only on filtering rules, there is an amount of risk introduced, as some of the packets may bypass the firewall.

This type of risk is unavoidable for a basic packet filtering firewall. Therefore, all modern firewalls go beyond basic packet filtering, and are **stateful**. This means, the firewall keeps track of the **state** of connection flows for all the packets, in both directions – entering and exiting the firewall. The stateful firewall also keeps track of all the IP addresses currently being connected to the firewall.

A stateful firewall allows only those packets belonging to an allowed session. For example, instead of permitting any host to send data to the TCP port 8080, the firewall allows only those packets which already have the full TCP connection. Furthermore, it can check whether the packets are really of 8080 protocol traffic and it can enforce constraints at the application layer.

The main advantage of a stateful firewall is that the administrator no longer needs to write broad filtering rules, mentioning all the TCP services to allow or deny. The administrator needs to list the attributes of the flow's first packet in the rule base and the rest is taken care of by the firewall cache mechanism. An additional benefit is that the rules can be shorter. A single rule can describe the flow. Maintaining firewall rules becomes easy and prevents errors from creeping in. Finally, the stateful firewall provides better performance. With better structure of the table, a cache lookup can be made more efficient.

Network Address Translation (NAT)

An IP address is 32 bits long, and with the current schema, the maximum number of hosts you can have is about 4 billion different IP addresses. This puts a limit on the number of hosts that you can connect to the Internet. Since many companies have many hosts that need to communicate with the Internet, these 4 billion addresses are not enough and very quickly, these addresses get depleted. In 1994, RFC 1631[5] suggested a short term solution to this problem known as NAT (Network Address Translation). As it turned out, NAT not only solved the addressing problem, it became one of the ways to protect our internal network identity. RFC 791[3], defines a set of IP addresses in each class as private addresses, used only within the private network and the rest of the addresses can be used as public addresses. The reserved ranges for private network are:

- 10.0.0.0 – 10.255.255.255 (10/8 prefix)

- 172.16.0.0 – 172.31.255.255 (172.16/12 prefix)

- 192.168.0.0 – 192.168.255.255 (192.168/16 prefix)

The primary reason for this is to ensure that the IP addresses are allocated efficiently. A private range of IP address, for example, 10.0.0.0/8, which is not in use on the Internet, when tries to connect to the outside world, has to be replaced by a public address. This is done using NAT. For example, a host is listed as 10.62.1.3, which is the source IP address. After NATing, the source address is replaced by a public address of 23.2.32.3. The destination computer sees just this IP address; the internal network address is never known to the outside world. Therefore, NAT provides protection to the inside network resources. This process is shown in Figure 10-9.

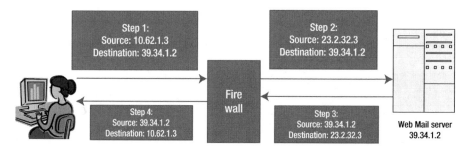

Figure 10-9. *NAT protecting internal network resources*

With NATing, companies can have only one public IP address. Any internal host that connects to the Internet or an outside network is NATed at the firewall. Internal hosts will never know that NATing has taken place. The destination host is also not aware of the NATing that has taken place. Thus NAT saves IP addresses. If more than one internal computer system is communicating with the Internet, as per the RFC 1631[5], all NAT firewall has to do is to change the source IP address, while it also needs to change the source port number with an unused port number above 1023 and keep track of this list temporarily during the connection.

NATing serves as a *basic security* measure that can make it a bit more difficult for an external attacker to map to the internal network IP addresses. When NATing is performed, the firewall rewrites the source IP address and stores both the altered source and destination IP addresses in the IP header. Internally, the firewall keeps track of the interface that is connected inside the network and interfaces connected to the outside network (global network). Global addresses are registered and assigned by an Internet Service Provider (ISP). The firewall internally identifies the packets as inbound or outbound, that is, in which direction the traffic is actually moving, and accordingly does the translations (NATing).

Static Translation

The NAT can use either a static or a dynamic mapping. In static NAT, configuration mapping is always fixed in a specific way. In a static NAT, a pool of inbound IP addresses are mapped to a pool of outbound IP addresses on a one-to-one basis. Once it is configured, it is fixed. This is particularly useful for a web server which has a consistent address that is accessible from the Internet. Figure 10-10 shows an example of a static NAT. Each inside address (172.16.1.1, 172.16.1.2, and 172.16.1.3) is mapped one-to-one with a global address (11.1.2.1, 11.1.2.2, and 11.1.3.3).

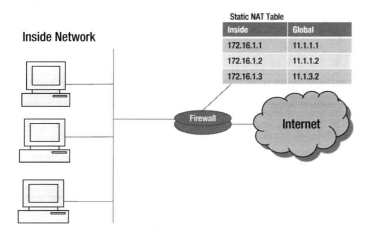

Figure 10-10. *Static NAT*

Dynamic Translation

In dynamic NATing, the mapping is not static. Mapping is based on the available IP address from a pool of public addresses. When a host inside the network requests access to the Internet, dynamic NAT picks up an IP address from a pool of addresses that has not been assigned and is not in use by any other host and assigns it to the host. Dynamic NATing is useful when fewer addresses are available and a larger number of hosts are to be connected to the Internet.

Port Address Translation (PAT)

When there is only one global IP address and multiple hosts inside the LAN trying to access the Internet, then we use what is called Port Address Translation (PAT). This situation is called overloading. The NAT/PAT box needs a way to keep track of the local addresses trying to connect to the Internet. This mapping is done using TCP/UDP ports. TCP/UDP uses 16 bits port numbers, which allows 65536 different services or source ports to be identified. When performing translation, PAT tries to use the original port number, if it is not used. If it is already in use, then the next available port number from the appropriate group is used.

The advantage of PAT is that multiple internal hosts can share a single global IP address. Global IP addresses are provided by ISP and they are expensive. Having one global IP address and with the help of PAT, organizations can save money. The second advantage is security. Internal networks are never exposed to the outside public network, making attacks from the outside more difficult and less frequent.

One disadvantage of PAT is the limitation on the number of hardware connections it supports. If too many internal hosts are trying to connect at the same time, then the hardware may run out of unused ports.

Application Level Gateways (Application Proxy)

As the name implies, an Application Level Gateway (ALG) inspects packets all the way up to the application layer and determines whether a packet is allowed or denied. It gives higher security than the packet filtering as the inspection is done all the way up to the application, as illustrated in Figure 10-11. However, this takes more CPU processing time and the necessity of having the knowledge of application protocol.

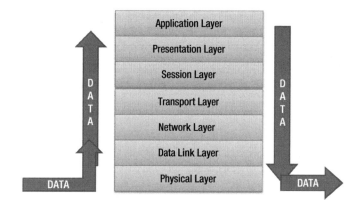

Application Level Gateway Data Flow

Figure 10-11. *How the Application Level Gateway Works*

An Application Level Gateway runs independently, copies and forwards information across the gateway and functions as a proxy server. It prevents a direct connection between a trusted server or client and an untrusted host. The proxies are application specific. Any new application that comes into the network needs to be informed to the application proxy, so that the rules may be set up and get executed for this application. It sits between a network firewall and a trusted host as shown in Figure 10-12. It can filter packets at the application layer.

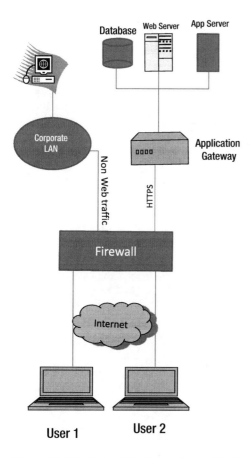

Figure 10-12. *Packet Filtering at the application layer using the Application Level Gateway*

An Application Layer Gateway maintains a complete TCP connection state and sequencing. ALG typically evaluates packets that are applied to the interface after security policies are applied. ALGs operate behind the NAT or a firewall. Some of the advantages of ALG include:

- Direct connection between internal and external hosts are not allowed
- User-level authentication is supported
- Packet is inspected right up to application data payload

However, there are limitations. The disadvantages of ALG include:

- More processing power required
- Slower than packet filtering
- Not every application protocol is supported. Whenever there is a new application, corresponding proxies must also be implemented.

Firewall Deployment Architecture

Firewall is the first layer of protection to your internal network. Depending on the security strategy of the organization, firewalls can be deployed at different layers in the network. The following deployment scenarios are the most common.

Option 1: Bastion Host

This is the basic option where the firewall is placed in between the internal and external network as shown in Figure 10-13. This topology is well suited for simple networks. This has a single boundary, hence, once someone penetrates the firewall, they have gained unrestricted access to the protected network.

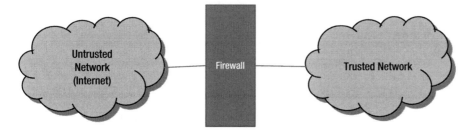

Figure 10-13. *Bastion Host*

Option 2: Staging Area or Demilitarized Zone (DMZ)

This topology allows organizations to host servers which face the internet directly, and separates the trusted network and the Internet (see Figure 10-14), thus allowing the users to access the internet securely. If a malicious user manages to compromise the firewall, he or she will not have access to the intranet services (provided the firewall is properly configured). This is the most commonly deployed architecture. The DMZ hosts all the servers offering public services, which face the Internet. The private zone contains all internal network resources such as the file server, the application server, the database servers, user workstations, and printers, which do not have any business connecting to the Internet. The DMZ zone hosts your public Web server, mail server, DNS servers, and other similar systems.

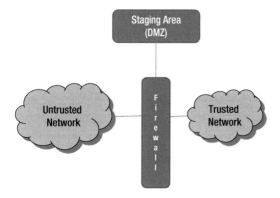

Figure 10-14. *Multiple Firewall Deployment - DMZ*

As more and more of the networks grow, the need to create a zone to protect internal assets has become imminent. Hence, many deployments now have a separate zone called Demilitarized Zone (DMZ) to separate the internal assets and the assets connecting to the Internet.

Multiple Firewall

In this scenario, you will deploy two or more firewalls to create two or more zones, as shown in Figure 10-15. Since you have more zones, the network is more secured and you can plan your organization security policy better. One division is to place your sensitive resources in a separate zone, for example, all accounting and finance servers in one zone, public facing servers such as the Web server, the Mail server, and the DNS server in a more secured DMZ zone. Systems that provide services to the general public (web server) may be placed in a different zone than systems which offer authenticated users services such as intranet applications.

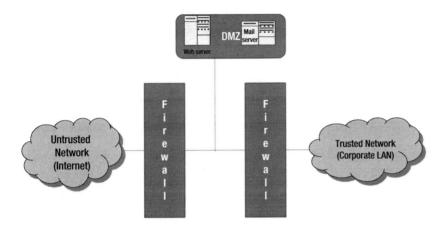

Figure 10-15. *Multiple Firewall Architecture*

Personal Firewall

A personal firewall, sometimes referred to as the desktop firewall, is a software-based firewall to protect a single system from intruders. Personal firewall protection is useful for those users who are always connected to the Internet using a Digital Subscriber Line (DSL) or a cable modem. Such connections use a static IP address, which makes the system more vulnerable. Personal firewall is better than anti-virus software as personal firewalls control the traffic on the Internet by filtering inbound and outbound traffic, and strengthening the user's preferences.

A personal firewall monitors the traffic that is going in and out of your system and grants access only to those who have passed the firewall policy set on the system. It identifies and blocks malicious software including viruses and worms. It also alerts when an unauthorized program attempts to hijack your system.

Antivirus software detects worms, viruses, and Trojans, but a personal firewall protects from intruders who attempt to hijack your system. Antivirus software along with a personal firewall can thwart many attacks on your system by blocking undesirable traffic.

Firewall Best Practices

Conceptually, firewall technology divides the enterprise network into a multiple segmentation of networks. Each segment represents a different level of trust and protection. Firewall rules allow for better control over the traffic on the network. If a hardware-based firewall is deployed, one should understand the security features supported by that particular hardware and configure the rules to provide maximum protection to your network. For the best protection of your network and firewall, the first thing is to change the default administration passwords and configure recommended firewall rules (never use the default configuration of the firewall).

The following types of traffic are always recommended to be blocked by the firewall rules (firewall configuration):

- Inbound traffic from a non-authenticated source system, for example, if you have branch offices in four different locations, your firewall rules should allow inbound traffic accessing your headquarters' network from these four locations and block others.

- Inbound traffic containing ICMP (Internet Control Message Protocol) traffic. For example, someone from outside can simply send continuous ping packets to the access router and overload the router thus denying genuine traffic.

- Inbound or outbound traffic from a host using source address which is the private address range as defined in RFC 1918[6] to avoid any spoofing attacks:

    - 10.0.0.0 to 10.255.255.255 (Class A)

    - 172.16.0.0 to 172.31.255.255 (class B)

    - 192.168.0.0. to 192.168.255.255 (class C)

- In addition, the following addresses also should be blocked:

    - 169.254.0.0

    - 192.0.2.0

    - 255.0.0.0

- Block any inbound with SNMP traffic

- Deny all traffic by default, and only enable those services as required

- Limit the number of applications that run on the firewall (VPN, DHCP, content filtering, etc.)

- Enable firewall logging and monitoring. It is also recommended to use Log monitoring solution to monitor security alerts

- Update firewall operating system patches regularly

- It is also recommended to run penetration tests on the firewall to check how secure your network is from attacks

- Schedule regular firewall audits

- Consider firewall in conjunction with other security devices such as:

    - Network based Intrusion Detection System (IDS)

    - Anti-virus software

    - Web content filtering software/hardware

    - URL filtering software/hardware

    - Separate authentication system such as LDAP or RADIUS

The following best practices can be applied to Firewalls:

- Understand firewall features while implementing them, including their capabilities and limitations. Firewall configuration requires understanding of information security and what you are trying to secure; understanding of TCP/IP protocol, applications that are running on your network, the type of users (contractors, staff, students etc.); knowledge of the type of firewall you are deploying and how you are deploying. Planning and architecture of network deployment is essential before configuring firewall rules. Also firewall features can vary from product to product. Available features need to be understood before configuring the firewall.

- Configure the firewall appropriately and carefully. Before configuring, you should answer the following questions: Do you need to configure DMZ (Demilitarized Zone)? How many network segments? Is it the entry or exit point firewall?

- Document the firewall build and configurations. The latest version of an operating system and firewall rules have to be documented. It is also recommended to regularly upgrade any patches available by the firewall vendor. Before making any changes to the firewall, rules need to be evaluated.

- Determine what you want to filter through the firewall and why. Once a decision is made then set the rules clearly on the firewall. Firewall rules are defined based on the security requirements and the type of applications you are running on your network. For example, do you need FTP? Do you want to allow your employees to access Facebook or Twitter? What are your security and IT policies related to pornographic sites? Do you want to allow remote access? Based on your applications and security policy your firewall rules are set.

- If there are multiple firewalls, then ensure that the rules set on each of these are complementary to each other and not conflicting with each other. For example, finance is on a separate segment and traffic control is more granular in nature. Only outbound traffic is allowed and limited inbound traffic is allowed.

- Ensure that the multiple entry points to the organization are appropriately protected with suitable equipment like firewalls

- All changes on the firewall have to go through a detailed impact analysis and have to be implemented only after approval from competent authorities or Change Control Board (as applicable to the organization). Before making the changes, business impact should be analyzed. How it is impacting the business should be assessed by all the business units and consensus should be taken for the changes.

- Change Control Board should approve the changes on the firewall. Changing firewall rules should have approval from all the stakeholders. Information security policy is defined based on the organization and business needs. Hence, any changes to firewall policy are changes to business policy and need proper process and approval. Without the proper approval process, firewall policies should not be altered. For example, a new partner network is allowed to access the internal network on a temporary basis, but it still needs to go through proper approval and business impact process.

- Relevant incident analysis should check on the working of the relevant firewall rules to discover any potential firewall weaknesses.

- Logging of firewall activities is essential. The logs have to be copied to a storage area and retained. Firewall logs have to be analyzed for any unwanted activities that would otherwise go unnoticed.

Auditing of Firewall

Periodic auditing of the firewall is a good practice at any organization. Some of the aspects to be considered during the audit are:

- Reasons for the firewall implementation – If rules were supposed to have been set, confirm that they are set appropriately

- Confirm that firewall configuration is appropriate and documented correctly

- Where multiple firewalls are deployed, are the rules defined complementary to each other and not conflicting with each other?

- Where there are multiple entry points to the network of the organization, are they all well protected appropriately?

- Confirm whether all changes to the firewall are carried out only after proper impact analysis and approval from competent authorities.

- Are the relaxations made to any of the rules of the firewall, including opening of specific ports for business purposes done only when justified and are carried out only for a limited period? Relaxations made are not left beyond the period for which such relaxations were permitted initially.

- Are firewall limitations, if any, considered during risk assessment and appropriate risk mitigations identified and applied?

- Are firewall logs held securely and analyzed regularly? Are the analysis results looked into and appropriate containment and corrective actions carried out?

- Are any issues identified through log analysis analyzed further and appropriate corrective actions taken?

- Are the firewall rules tested periodically? Are the test records maintained? Were there any issues observed during the testing? If so, are these issues resolved immediately by appropriate containment and corrective actions?

Chapter Summary

- We discussed how the Internet has transformed the way we carry out our business. While the Internet has substantial benefits we explored the fact that all these applications also expose the individuals and organizations to the information security risk. We then looked into the types of network attacks, including network access attacks, denial of service attacks, and reconnaissance attacks. We also looked at how insiders and outsiders potentially pose huge risks to organizations.

- We explored how we can protect the network and in turn get ourselves protected. We started the discussion of security of the network from the discussion on the "closed networks" implemented when there was no outside connectivity and no World Wide Web. We then looked into the fact as to how the development of World Wide Web and the applications thereon led to the necessity to allow connectivity from internal networks to the external network and vice versa. Hence, today, an enterprise network demands an "Open Network" with the flexibility to connect to the Internet and web applications, and to support telecommuters and mobile sales force, accessing mobile devices and much more. Then we looked into how this can lead to attacks on the networks by hackers using various tools available easily to them. We also mentioned that if the security of the network is compromised, there could be serious consequences, such as loss of privacy, breach of confidentiality, theft of identities, and legal liabilities. Then we mentioned that to protect the network, various devices like Firewalls, Intrusion Detection Systems, Authentication and Access Control devices, and Virtual Private Networks (VPN) are implemented at different layers.

- We discussed what a firewall is. A network firewall is intended to stop unauthorized users from accessing the network and its services from other external networks. The most common deployment of firewalls is between a trusted network of an organization to an untrusted network, typically the Internet. We then discussed the basic functions of firewall, including basic packet filtering, stateful packet filtering, and application level gateways (proxies). We then went on to discuss packet filtering and how packet filters allow or deny network traffic. Further, we elaborated as to how packet filtering firewalls work. We mentioned the filtering rules and how matching leads to the deny or allow rule to be triggered which in turn leads to dropping of the packet or forwarding of the packet. We also gave an example of packet filtering rules. We then went on to discuss the advantages and disadvantages of the packet filter firewalls.

- We also discussed the stateful packet filtering firewall, which keeps track of the state of connection flows for all the packets, in both directions and also keeps track of all the IP addresses currently connected to the firewall. A stateful firewall allows only those packets belonging to an allowed session. The main advantage of a stateful firewall is that the administrator no longer needs to write broad filtering rules, mentioning all the TCP services to allow or deny. The administrator needs to list the attributes of the flow's first packet in the rule base and the rest is taken care of by the firewall cache mechanism.

- We also discussed the Network Address Translation (NAT), both the static and dynamic translations pertaining to NAT and Port Address Translation (PAT) and how these features help in protecting the internal network details from the external parties.

- We examined an Application Level Gateway (ALG), how it inspects packets all the way up to the application layer, and determines whether a packet is allowed or denied. It gives higher security than the packet filtering as the inspection is done all the way up to the application. In this context we discussed that an Application Level Gateway runs independently, copies and forwards information across gateway, and functions as a proxy server. It prevents a direct connection between a trusted server or client and an untrusted host and that proxies are application specific. We then discussed some of the advantages and limitations of the ALG.

- We discussed firewall deployment architecture. In this context, we discussed bastion host, DMZ, and multiple firewalls. Then we went on to look at the personal firewall. A personal firewall, sometimes referred to as the desktop firewall, is a software-based firewall to protect a single system from intruders. We also looked at how this helps us.

- We explored some of the firewall-related best practices and then how firewall auditing can be carried out effectively.

■ ■ ■

CHAPTER 11

Intrusion Detection and Prevention Systems

Introduction

Intrusion in lay terms is unwanted or unauthorized interference and as it is unwanted or unauthorized, it is normally with bad intentions. The intention of the intrusion is to collect information related to the organization such as the structure of the internal networks or software systems like operating systems, tools/utilities, or software applications used by the organization and then initiate connections to the internal network and carry out attacks. Intrusions are normally carried out by people outside the organization. Sometimes, intrusions can be caused by internal authorized persons carrying out these attacks by misusing their authorization or by internal authorized persons who go beyond their area of authorization and such attacks also need to be protected against.

An Intrusion Detection System (IDS) is a hardware/software combination or a combination of both hardware and software that detects the intrusions into a system or network. IDS complements a firewall by providing a thorough inspection of both the packets' header and its contents thus protecting against attacks, which are otherwise perceived by a firewall as seemingly benign network traffic.

Firewalls look at the control rules; a packet is either allowed or denied. A rule specifies whether a host or a network, or an application should be allowed into the trusted network. To check the rules, a firewall has to just inspect the header of the TCP/IP protocol such as FTP, HTTP, or Telnet. However, it does not inspect the data contents of the network packet. Even if the data contains a malicious code, the firewall will allow this packet to pass through as the packet header has conformed to the rules configured in the firewall. Hence, you can still have a firewall but your trusted network can be compromised.

IDS inspect each and every packet's content traversing the network to detect any malicious activity. Every packet is peeled all the way down to the "data content" part and the data content is inspected for any malicious code and then the packet is reassembled back to its original form and then the packet is sent along. As you can see, every packet is dissected and then assembled back at layer 3, which makes the IDS very process intensive when compared to the firewall.

The firewall is a necessary component of an overall network security topology but is insufficient on its own. Most of the modern networks have IDS as an essential part of the security architecture.

Why Use IDS?

Why use IDS? The answer is very simple: We do not want somebody to enter our system with malicious intentions and carry out attacks on our systems, thereby endangering our whole network. We want to be alerted of any such activities so that we can act upon such incidents immediately and take actions to eliminate the root causes of such issues and eliminate any potential damages/disruptions caused by them.

Even if we have a good logging system of all the traffic entering into our internal network, it is tedious to go through these logs. It is manually impossible to differentiate between a malicious packet and a good network packet. Even with the help of computers, this is an intensive job which requires lots of processing power. We have seen that over the years, in this mostly connected world, connected through various means including tablets and mobile phones, bad people with bad intentions target various corporations as well as individuals. As it is impossible to detect such attacks manually to prevent or mitigate them, it has become imperative to have an automated tool to help us monitor the system for attacks. IDS has become a useful tool to provide this monitoring.

Before we begin our discussion, let's familiarize ourselves with some of the terms that are used in IDS/IPS technology:

- True Positives: These are alerts that something is not right when it is actually not right. Example: The IDS finds a packet as containing malicious code and it was actually true that the packet had malicious code, as confirmed by investigation.

- True Negatives: These are alerts that something is right when it is actually right. Example: The IDS finds a packet as containing no issues and it actually had no issues.

- False Positives: These are alerts indicating that something is not right with a packet when actually it is right. Example: The IDS finds a packet as having malicious code but it is actually a genuine code.

- False Negatives: These are alerts that something is right when actually it is wrong. Example: The IDS finds that a packet does not have any malicious code but it actually does contain a malicious code, as found through investigation.

Figure 11-1 provides explanations.

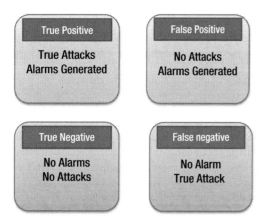

Figure 11-1. *Definitions of IDS/IPS Alerts*

Types of IDS

There are two types of IDS:

- Host-based IDS: Protects the end system or the network resources.

- Network-based IDS: Monitors network traffic for attacks. A Network IDS is deployed on the network near a firewall, on the DMZ or even inside the trusted internal network.

Host-Based IDS (HIDS)

Host-based Intrusion Detection System refers to the detection of intrusion on a single system. This is normally a software-based deployment where an agent, as shown in Figure 11-2, is installed on the local host that monitors and reports the application activity. HIDS monitors the access to the system and its application and sends alerts for any unusual activities. It constantly monitors event logs, system logs, application logs, user policy enforcement, rootkit detection, file integrity, and other intrusions to the system. It constantly monitors these logs and creates a baseline. If any new log entries appear, HIDS checks the data against the baseline and if any entries are found outside of this baseline, HIDS triggers an alert. If any unauthorized activity is detected, HIDS can alert the user or block the activity or perform any other decision based on the policy that is configured on the system.

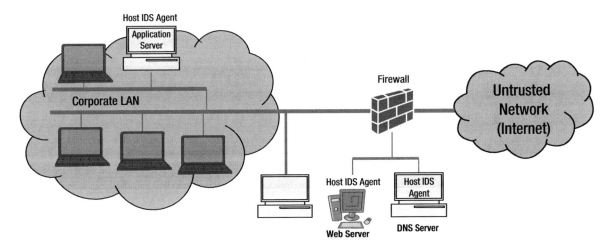

Figure 11-2. *Host-Based Intrusion Detection System*

Most of the HIDS products have the ability to prevent attacks also. However, it is initially deployed in the monitor mode and then once there is an understanding of the system activity, a baseline is created and then HIDS is deployed in prevention mode. The functionality of HIDS depends on the logs generated by the system and the fact that the intruders leave evidence of their activities. Generally, hackers get access to the system and install malicious tools so that future access becomes easier. If these tools change the operating system configurations, or entries of some windows registry, it is logged in the systems/event log, thus triggering an alert by the HIDS system.[1]

HIDS is generally installed on servers, or end point devices to protect the system from intrusion. The function of HIDS solely depends on the audit trails generated by the system. If hackers manage to turn off these logs, even if you have a HIDS agent running, it may not trigger any alerts. This is the biggest disadvantage of HIDS.

Advantages of HIDS are:

- System level protection. Protects from attacks directed to the system

- Any unauthorized activity on the system (configuration changes, file changes, registry changes, etc.) are detected and an alert is generated for further action

There are disadvantages also:

- HIDS functionality works only if the systems generate logs and match against the pre-defined policies. If for some reason, systems do not generate logs, HIDS may not function properly

- If hackers bring down the HIDS server, then HIDS is of no use. This is true for any vulnerability protection software

Network-Based Intrusion Detection System (IDS) / Intrusion Prevention System (IPS)

A Network-Based Intrusion Detection System (NIDS) [1] monitors (and detects) any suspicious activity on a network. It checks each and every packet that is entering the network to make sure it does not contain any malicious content which would harm the network or the end system. Network Intrusion Detection System sniffs the network traffic continuously. The traffic is matched against known signature profiles and if there are any abnormalities found in the traffic, then a NIDS triggers an alarm to the management console. A single sensor, as shown in Figure 11-3, deployed in promiscuous mode or inline mode can monitor/protect several hosts in the network.

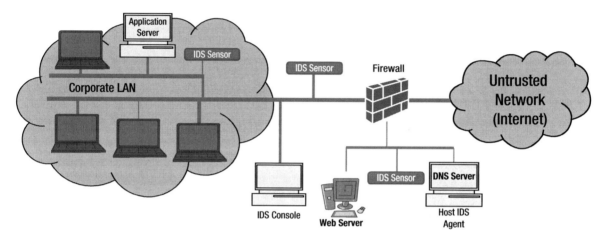

Figure 11-3. *Network-Based Intrusion Detection and Prevention System*

Network IDS protects the network and its resources from the network perspective. For example, network IDS can detect reconnaissance attacks, Denial of Service attacks right at the network level. NIDS generates alerts as soon as it discovers these attacks. NIDS is a hardware/software solution placed near the firewall as an independent device (sensor) and has network operating system (TCP/IP stack). Sensors have interfaces to monitor the network (monitoring interface) and a management interface which is used for controlling and receiving alerts and for sending these alerts to the central management controller.

An **Intrusion Prevention System (IPS)** is used to prevent the intrusion. It is an extension of IDS. IDS only detects whereas IPS protects the network from intrusion by dropping the packet, denying entry to the packet or blocking the connection. IPS and IDS together monitor the network traffic for malicious activities and IPS is considered as just an extension of IDS. The main difference is that the IPS are placed in-line to prevent intrusions and IPS can take decisions like dropping the packet, or resetting the connection along with sending alarms to the management console. An IPS can also detect/correct fragmented packets, Cyclic Redundancy Check (CRC) errors, or TCP sequencing issues.

Table 11-1 summarizes the key differences between the IDS and IPS. Today, most of the network-based intrusion systems combine both detection and prevention – Intrusion Detection and Prevention Systems (IDPS).

Table 11-1. *Key differences between IDS and IPS*

Intrusion Detection System (IDS)	Intrusion Prevention System (IPS)
Passively monitors network behavior and "detects" attacks	Actively analyzes network behavior and "prevents" attacks in real-time
Supports both Network and Host level detection	Supports both network and host level detection
Passive monitoring, does not sit in the data path	Active monitoring, deployed in-line mode
Key measure is detection accuracy	Key measure is lesser number of false positives
NIDS: ISS, Cisco, Enterasys, Symantec	NIPS: McAfee Intrushield, NetScreen, Tippingpoint.
HIDS: ISS, Symantec, Enterasys	HIPS: Cisco, McAfee (Entercept). Snort – an open source Network IDS/IPS developed by Sourcefire

Table 11-2 summarizes the pros and cons of Host-based IDS and Network-based IDS.

Table 11-2. *Pros and Cons of H-IDS and N-IDS*

	Pros	Cons
Host IDS	Protects from attacks at the host level No Bandwidth Impact	Impacts host resources – CPU, memory Operating System dependent One agent can protect one host only
Network IDS	Protects network and network resources Protects against DoS attacks	Sensor hardware is process intensive Prone to false positives.

How Does Detection Work?

The Intrusion Detection and Prevention Systems detect intrusions through the following mechanisms: signature-based detection, anomaly-based detection, or stateful protocol analysis. In this section we will look at each of the methods in detail.

Signature-Based Detection

This mechanism protects against known threats. A signature is a known pattern of a threat, such as:

- An e-mail with an attachment containing a known malware with an interesting subject (for example, an e-mail with the subject "I love you").

- A "remote login" by an admin user, which is a clear violation of an organization's policy.

Signature-based detection is the simplest form of detection because it just compares the traffic with the signature database. If a match is found then the alert is generated, if a match is not found then the traffic flows without any problem.

In signature-based detection, detection is based on comparing the traffic with the known signatures for possible attacks (see Figure 11-4). They can only detect known threats and hence, are not efficient in detecting unknown threats. To detect an attack, the signature matching has to be precise, otherwise, even if the attack has a small variation from the known threat signature, then the system will not be able to detect. For example, in the above example, instead of "I love you" if the subject is "love you", the system may not detect the threat. Hence, it is very easy for the attackers to compromise and breach into the trusted network.[2]

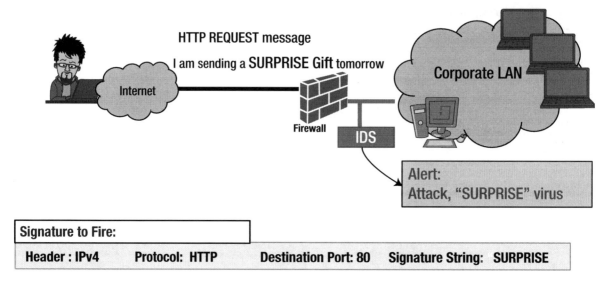

Figure 11-4. Signature-Based Detection (Flow diagram)

Signature database needs to be updated constantly, almost on a daily basis from the anti-virus labs such as McAfee, Symantec, TrendMicro, and other security providers. If the signature is not up to date, chances are that the IDS systems will fail to detect some of the intrusion attacks. The other disadvantage is that they have very little information about previous requests when processing the current ones.

Signature-based detection can offer very specific detection of known threats by comparing network traffic with the threat signature database. The detection can be enhanced if the network traffic inside the network can be made to learn specific patterns, thus reducing false positives. Signature detection engines tend to degrade in performance over a period of time as more and more signatures are added to the database. It takes more and more time for the engine to do a pattern search as the signature database is always growing as more and more definitions are added to it. Hence, a robust platform is needed for signature detection considering this growth. Table 11-3 summarizes the pros and cons of signature-based detection technique.

Table 11-3. Pros and Cons of Signature-based Detection Technique

Pros	Cons
Simple method to create	High false positives rate
Applicable across all protocols	High false negative rate
	Multiple signatures are required for a single vulnerability

Anomaly-Based Detection

Anomaly-based detection (see Figure 11-5) protects against unknown threats. An "anomaly" is anything that is abnormal. If any traffic is found to be abnormal from the baseline, then an alert is triggered by the IDS suspected of an intrusion. IDPS first creates a baseline profile that represents the normal behavior of the traffic. The baseline profile is created by allowing the IDS system to learn the traffic over a period of time so that IDPS can study the traffic behavior during peak hours, non-peak hours, night hours, early hours of business, and as per your organizational network behavior. After learning, the traffic collected over a period of time is statistically studied and a baseline profile is created. Once the IDS is changed from learning mode to detection/prevention mode, it starts comparing the regular traffic with the profile that was created, and if any abnormality or deviation from the baseline profile is found, then an alert is triggered cautioning the possible intrusion or the intrusion is prevented, if it is configured for prevention mode. Customized profiles can also be created for specific traffic behavior such as the number of e-mails sent by a user and user access attempts.

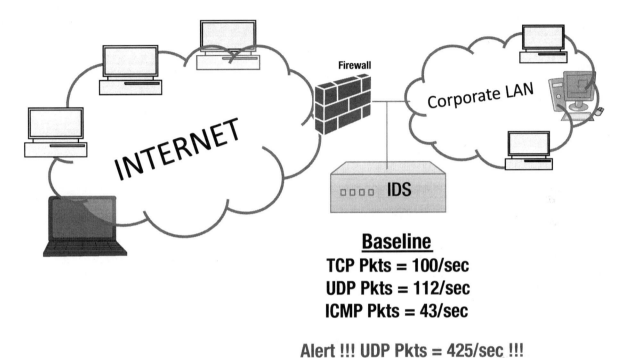

Baseline
TCP Pkts = 100/sec
UDP Pkts = 112/sec
ICMP Pkts = 43/sec

Alert !!! UDP Pkts = 425/sec !!!

Figure 11-5. *Anomaly Detection*

What is an anomaly? Here are some examples of anomalous behavior:

- Too many Telnet sessions on a single day
- HTTP traffic on a non-standard port
- Heavy SNMP traffic

For effective intrusion detection, IDS must have a robust baseline profile which covers the entire organization's network and its segments. It should cover normal traffic behavior of all the components which are aimed to be covered by the Intrusion Detection and Prevention System. Baseline profile can vary in complexity from a simple to a comprehensive content, depending on the characteristics of the network and its components. For example, a profile could include the following data:

- A web application logged in remotely by a specific set of users
- An application which has a specific acceptable password design
- Traffic during the peak hours and non-peak hours as defined by the organization
- Connectivity pattern from an external partner network
- Connecting from a set of mobile devices to the database server

The challenge of the anomaly-based detection method is creating an effective profile. The initial profile, sometimes referred to as the "training profile," is generated by studying the traffic pattern over a period of time. The time factor may vary from organization to organization. It could be a few hours to a few days. Once this profile is created, IDS is put into detection mode and every time there is a packet, a pattern is matched against the baseline profile. This baseline can be changed as and when required based on the traffic behavior. If any malicious activity already exists from the beginning, while building the baseline profile, this activity will also become part of the baseline profile and such kind of malicious activity will thereby go undetected. Hence, anomaly detection does not necessarily detect each and every unknown attack. The limitation is based on the baseline profile you create. However, a system administrator was alerted by IDS to Microsoft DCOM DOS vulnerability without having a specific signature.

Types of Anomaly

Anomaly-based Intrusion Detection and Prevention Systems (IDPS) protect anomaly caused due to violation of protocols, and application payload. It also protects against Denial of Service attacks and Buffer overflow attacks.

Protocol Anomaly

Protocol anomaly refers to the anomaly in the protocol format and protocol behavior with respect to the Internet standards and specifications. There are many aspects in TCP and IP protocol that needs to be monitored, for example, different flags, SYN, ACK, and FIN, and their combination in TCP header and the reserved flags of IP header. The way IP fragmentation and reassembly is implemented is as per the standards. If this anomaly is not detected by the IDS, the end host may not process these unconventional packets and this may lead to the crash of the system. At the application level, IDPS must be able to do deep protocol parsing to understand application level protocol anomaly. It also requires a deep understanding of the application semantics in order to detect application payload anomaly.

Some other examples include:

- Unusual TCP segmentation and TCP flags combination

- Corrupt checksum

- Incorrect IP fragmentation and reassembly flags

- Erroneous source and destination port numbers

- Illegal protocol commands and its usage

- Running protocol on non-standard port

- Presence of shellcode in unexpected application protocol fields

- Misuse of protocol and protocol services

Statistical Anomaly Detection – Statistical DDoS

Denial of Service (DoS) and Distributed Denial of Service (DDoS) results in a burst of traffic on the network which is not normal. In order to overcome this kind of attack, baseline profiles are created on the normal flow of traffic, as described earlier, based on statistical modeling, such as Naïve Bayes, to determine anomalous packets on the network. While learning the network traffic behavior, the function of statistical modeling is to compute the probability score for each of the data packets that is considered as normal traffic. The scores are computed based on the sampled data over a period of time and stored in a baseline profile. A threshold is set for each set of protocols and users. When the IDS is in monitoring mode, the data is checked against the baseline and the threshold. Whenever an anomalous packet is discovered and the scores are above threshold, then an alert is triggered. The reporting process will report only when the data is found to be anomalous for a sufficient period of time; otherwise, the IDPS will simply ignore the trace. Threshold can be set for different profiles, for different protocols, and for different users.[3,4]

When IDPS is in monitoring mode, if there is anything that is abnormal to the baseline, the system will generate an alert. But, it may turn out that the analysis results confirm that the alert found was a false positive. As a security administrator, one can expect a similar kind of traffic behavior appearing every other day and to minimize the spending of the same effort repeatedly, a threshold can be set so that anything within this threshold, the traffic is still considered normal and anything which exceeds this threshold is considered an intrusion. Thresholds can also be set for a set of users, or set of protocols.

Profiles based on the statistical measures can detect some of the DoS anomalies based on long- and short-term distributions or bursts of peak (i.e., high) traffic. The normal baseline profiles are continuously being learned while the system is in detection mode and the baseline is re-created to adjust the changing traffic pattern to avoid false positives.

By creating different profiles, DoS attacks can be prevented. For example, for each of the DoS attacks, a profile can be created. Knowing the pattern of SYN flood, a SYN flood DoS profile can be created. Whenever there is SYN flood traffic on the network, the IDS sensors can detect the SYN flood attack by comparing the network traffic with the SYN flood profile thus alerting a SYN flood attack. Similarly, UDP flood profile, TCP data segment profile, or ICMP flood profiles can be detected and alerted.

Though anomaly-based IDS has an advantage of detecting unknown attacks, defining rules for it is difficult. Each protocol must be analyzed, processed, and compared with a baseline. Any customized protocol makes it even more challenging.

Another major pitfall of anomaly detection is defining normal traffic while creating a baseline. Normal traffic has to be clean and should not have any malicious activity in the network. In case of any malicious activity during the learning process, then the baseline profile learns this and makes it harder to detect this intrusion or it may not even detect intrusion of such malicious traffic. For example, reconnaissance attacks such as fingerprint or directory traversal, which complies with network protocol, easily goes unnoticed since it complies with protocol and payload limitations. Some of the pros and cons of statistical anomaly detection are summarized in Table 11-4.

Table 11-4. *Pros and Cons of Statistical Anamoly Detection*

Pros	Cons
Detects Unknown Attacks	Prone to false positives
Prevents DoS attacks, Buffer Overflows	Longer detection time
	Analyzing Intrusion may be difficult with Anomaly
	Difficulty in creating baseline

Stateful Protocol Analysis Detection

This method is similar to the anomaly-based detection, except that the profiles are created by the vendors who supply the sensor equipment (IDPS). The profiles are predetermined and made up of the generally accepted benign network traffic activity as specified by the standards. "Stateful" means that the IDPS has the capability to keep track of the state of the protocol both in network layer and application layers. For example, in case of a TCP connection establishment state, the IDS should remember all the connection states. Similarly, in case of authentication, the initial connection session is in an unauthorized state and IDS should remember these states. After an exchange of some information between the two parties, the client and the server, the user is authenticated and allowed access to the network. During this period, the traffic is benign and the IDPS should remember the state or it will lead to false positives.

The stateful protocol anomaly detection method uses profiles that have been created based on standards and specifications specified by the vendor who generally complies with most of the protocols from the standard bodies (Internet Engineering Task Force). If any vendor has implemented protocols, with variation to the standards, it would cause difficulty for the IDPS in detecting and analyzing the states. In such cases, IDPS protocol models also need to be updated for the customized protocol changes.

The primary drawback of this method is that they are process- and memory-intensive like many protocols, and the IDPS has to keep track of their states simultaneously. Another problem is if an attack is within the generally acceptable protocol behavior, then it can pass through. If the protocol implementation varies from operating system to operating system then IDPS may not perform well in detecting the intrusions. The pros and cons of this method are summarized in Table 11-5.

Table 11-5. *Stateful Protocol Detection*

Pros	Cons
Stateful Inspection	Resource intensive
Reasonable checks on the standard protocol before an alert	Cannot detect variations to the generally acceptable protocol behavior policy
	Cannot detect any conflict between the standards and how they are implemented

IDS/IPS System Architecture and Framework

The architecture of a typical network-based IDS/IPS is as shown in Figure 11-6. It consists of a hardware device, management console, a database, and connectivity to network management consoles.

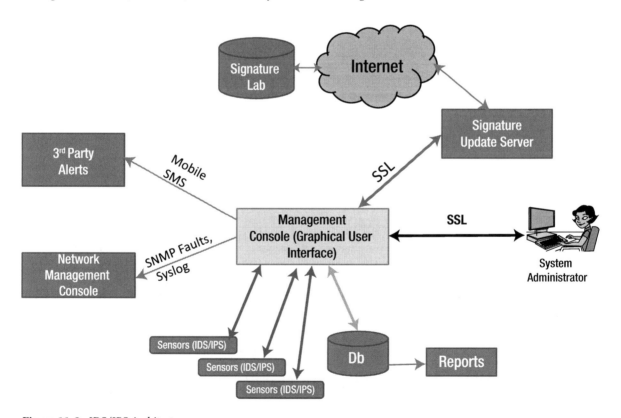

Figure 11-6. *IDS/IPS Architecture*

Appliance (Sensors)

The primary function of a sensor is to analyze traffic and respond when the attacks are detected. The sensor examines each and every packet's header and data content that enters the network. The sensor looks for a pattern and behavior in the network traffic that indicates malicious activity and sends alerts to the management console. The sensor examines the packets and checks against the user-defined policies or rule sets, which contains the priorities of the attacks to be monitored and the counter measures to be taken when an attack is detected.

If an attack is detected, the sensor sends an alert to the management console, logs the alert, and responds to the attack as per the defined policy. The policies for sensors can be configured to several types of responses - generating alerts, logging events, resetting TCP connections, blocking traffic at firewalls, scrubbing malicious packets, and even dropping the packets entirely before reaching the final destination.

DatabaseA database server is an important component of the overall IDS/IPS architecture. It is a repository of all the events triggered by the sensors, logs generated, user policies and profiles, and other functional information.

Management ConsoleA management console provides an interface to the users and administrators for configuring and managing sensor systems. The users connect to the management console through a client system over a web interface or any other client software. A Management Graphical Interface should provide the following:

- **Alert/Event Viewer:** Displays all the intrusions detected by the sensors, which have violated the defined set of policies. The alert viewers should be able to provide drill-down capabilities to view all the details of individual alerts such as host, destination, service, type of attack, and action taken.

- **Incident Generator:** This enables the creation of real-time correlative analysis of attacks on the network. This should provide the type of incident that has occurred and when it has occurred.

- **Report Generators:** To generate various security reports for the management and further analysis. It should have the capability of generating reports automatically as well e-mailing them to individuals.

- **System Configuration Tools:** Provides all the system configuration features. Setting polices, profiles, responses to attacks, sensor mode of operation, user created profiles, baseline scheduling, defining user roles and responsibilities, sending alerts to central network management console, and other sensor level configurations. It should also have the capabilities to send alerts to the central network management console and alerting administrators through triggering cell phone calls and SMS services.

Signature Update Server

For the IDS system to detect the latest vulnerabilities and threats, its threat signatures must be up to date. Sensors should be updated with the latest signatures regularly. Both the management console and the sensors should always be up to date with the threat signature set and software patches. A good system should have the capability to connect to the latest threat vulnerability lab(s) and download the signatures on a regular basis and update the sensor(s) that are detecting the intrusions.

In the architecture illustrated, the signature update server connects to the signature library to download the latest signature set and then the management console pushes the updated signature to the sensors. The polling interval of the update server, and the signature push to the sensors can be configured using the management user interface. Once the update server receives the new signature updates, the management interface determines what signatures need to be pushed onto the sensors based on the policies that are defined and applied. For example, a policy defined for a particular LAN segment will only update those signatures defined for that LAN segment (for example Windows security patches).

It is always advisable to configure the update server to get the latest signatures as soon as they are available to improve the overall level of protection, and having an automatic access to the signature lab reduces operational overheads.

Some of the other capabilities the architecture should support include[1]:

- **Logging capabilities:** Should support logging related to intrusion detection, incidents, and other system-related information and should be able to categorize the severity, the impact, and the priority of the intrusions and provide information regarding the prevention actions it has taken. The system architecture should have capabilities to store logs both locally and at a central repository and should have the capability to synchronize time with Network Time Protocol.

- **Detection Capabilities:** Should have broad and extensive detection capabilities; up-to-date threat signatures; the flexibility of customization and fine tuning of the baseline profiles and user-defined profiles to improve detection capabilities; the capabilities to set threshold limits to minimize false positives; and be able to block a connection after a set of failed connection time (retries).

- **Code viewing and editing capabilities:** Technologies should support viewing the virus code or threat code to understand the nature of the threat. This helps in writing a customized signature locally.

- **Prevention Capabilities:** It should have the flexibility to configure prevention capability for each type of attacks. It should support recommendation for prevention for certain unknown attacks and DoS attacks. This helps the administrator to fine tune the policy and reconfigure the sensors.

Attack types Detected by IDS

An Intrusion Detection and Prevention System (IDS/IPS) is a software/hardware combination that detects intrusions and if appropriately configured, also prevents the intrusion. An IDS inspects each and every packet entering the network by peeling off the packet header and its contents and doing a thorough inspection of the packet before allowing the packet into the network. It complements a firewall and the anti-virus software and protects against any attacks embedded within the packet data which goes unnoticed by a firewall.

The Intrusion and Detection System (IDS) should detect all the types of attacks, including Reconnaissance, Denial of Service (DoS)/Distributed Denial of Service (DDoS) and other network attacks, using techniques such as signature-based detection and anomaly-based detection. It should detect both known and unknown attacks. Table 11-6 summarizes the type of attacks that an IDS/IPS detects/prevents.

Table 11-6. *Attacks detected by IDS/IPS*

Attacks Detection by IDS/IPS	Attack Type
Shellcode in password Too many strange IP fragments Too much UDP than TCP Many HTTP requests than responses Buffer Overflow	Anomaly (Unknown attacks)
TCP SYN Flood attack ICMP Flood TCP or UDP Flood Ping of Death Smurf attacks Winuke Apache2 Back Teardrop SYN Flood UDPStorm IP Spoofing	Denial Of Service (DOS) and Distributed Denial Of Service (DDoS)
IP fragmentation overlap, options, etc. TCP segmentation overlap, options usage All checksum/length consistency	Protocol Anomaly Transport layer reconnaissance and attacks
DNS request – Illegal field value and combinations HTTP, SNMP, SMTP – Illegal use of commands Unusually short or long field lengths Unknown protocol port numbers – Gnutella on port 80, HTTP on port 89 URL encoding SQL Injection Attack Buffer Overflow Telnet/FTP escape sequence attacks	Application protocol anomaly
Nmap MScan Satan IPSweep Fingerprint Port scan/Network Scan	Reconnaissance

Responses by IDPS to the Intrusions

Intrusion Detection System (IDS) only detects intrusion. It sends alerts to the management console. It detects both known and unknown attacks by inspecting each and every packet that enters the network. However, IDS does not take any action by itself to protect the system or network. Whereas, Intrusion Prevention System (IPS), not only detects the intrusions, it also prevents the intrusions by taking one of the following proactive steps:

- **Block or Deny the packet:** When the next packet arrives from the same source, IDPS can simply block that particular user's data packets entering the network by automatically configuring the sensor to "block." The intended bad packet never reaches the destination and it is blocked at the entrance itself.

- **Reset connection:** Reset the session when the next packet arrives from the same source. Close the session of the intrusion source. The goal is to terminate the attack before it succeeds. When the attack is detected, RESET connection instructions should be sent to the host in the trusted network. Unfortunately, if the RESET packets are not received in time by the host in the trusted network, then the attacker may succeed. RESET is applicable only for TCP packets and cannot be used for UDP or ICMP packets.

- **Dropping the packet:** Completely drop the packet with intrusions. As soon as the intrusion is detected, identify the source and automatically configure the sensor to drop the packet from that source. The bad packets never reach the intended destination.

- **Reconfigure firewall:** Depending on the type of deployment and where the sensor is deployed, as soon as the intrusion is detected, IDPS can instruct the firewall next to it to change the "Access rules/policies" to deny the packet from the intrusion source, thus preventing any attackers from succeeding.

Deploying IDS/IPS

IDS/IPS is typically deployed either in detection mode or both detection and prevention mode. In detection mode, it is deployed to monitor the network. It sits in the network just like any other component and reads the data in silent mode without affecting the regular traffic. Whereas, the IDS/IPS prevention mode is deployed in such a way that the normal traffic passes via IDS/IPS. The detection mode is called the **Passive Mode** and the second mode is called the active mode or in-line mode.

Where and how you deploy the sensors depends on the organization security policy and its network topology. Requirement depends on the type of assets, configuration of the network, location of the aggregation points, type of traffic, and so on. Initially, it is always recommended to deploy in the detection mode. Once the IDS is able to understand the network and the baseline profile is stabilized, then it is better to move to the prevention mode.

Passive Mode

In passive mode, the traffic does not pass through the sensors. In this mode, the sensors monitor a copy of the actual network traffic. Each and every packet will be read by the sensor for any intrusion. In case of an intrusion, an alert is triggered and prevention measures are taken by the security administrators. In passive mode, the sensors are deployed in what is called as the **SPAN mode**.

Span Mode

Each switch comes with a SPAN port that can monitor all the network traffic going through the switch. A sensor is connected to this SPAN port, as shown in Figure 11-7, so that all the traffic flowing through the network, including the host's, the server's, and the client's can be monitored. If the switch is not configured properly or reconfigured, then the traffic may not be adequately monitored by the sensors. In case of heavy traffic, if the SPAN port is disabled by the switch, this again becomes a problem as the sensor will not be able to monitor the intrusions properly.

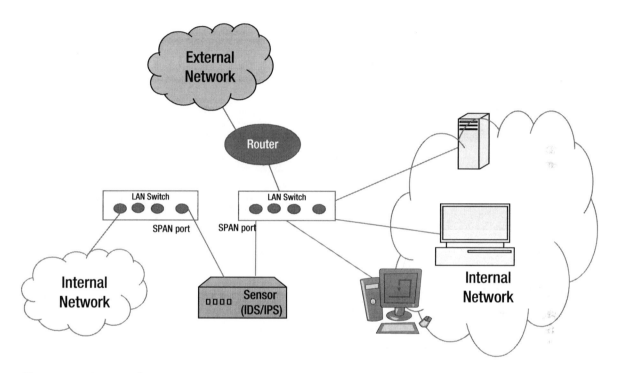

Figure 11-7. *SPAN mode*

Tap Mode

In this mode, network taps are placed on a single wire for a particular segment of the entire network. The sensors monitor the traffic on the tapped wire by copying every network packet that comes through the tap. Whenever there is an intrusion, alarms are triggered. Preventive measures are taken by the security administrators. Network taps are a special device connected to the media as shown in the Figure 11-8.

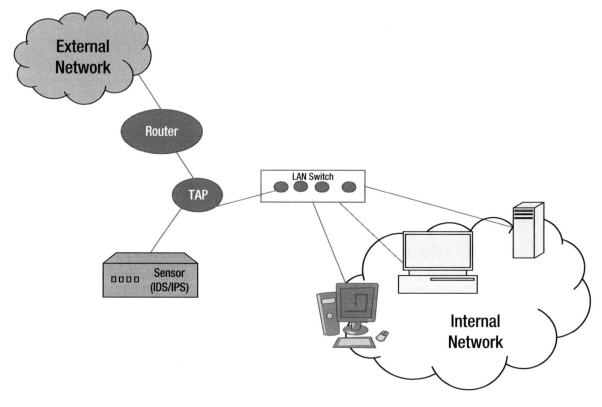

Figure 11-8. *Network Tap mode*

In-Line Mode

Sensors are placed directly in-line with network traffic as shown in Figure 11-9. Network traffic will pass through the sensor in real-time thus preventing intrusions into the trusted network. In-line sensors are placed next to the firewall and other network/security devices. It is placed with a clear distinction between internal network and external network. It is often deployed near the DMZ area where it is more secured from the internal network and has less traffic to process. Sensors can also be deployed inside the network to monitor the traffic that is going around inside the network and the traffic that is going out of the organization's systems. The deployment architecture solely depends on the organizational need and security architecture.

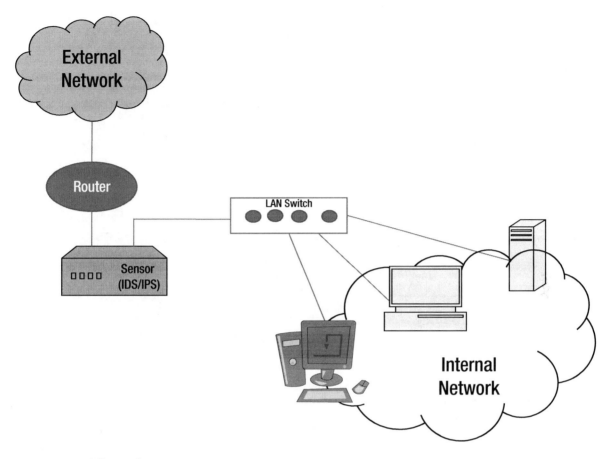

Figure 11-9. *In-line mode*

The benefits of using sensors in in-line mode are as follows:

- **Intrusion Prevention:** During in-line mode, the sensors are in prevention mode either by blocking the traffic or dropping the packets in case of intrusion, thus preventing malicious packets reaching their intended destination. The sensors can be configured for countermeasures such as reset connection, reconfigure firewall, or block the traffic as soon as they detect any intrusions by mediating the traffic flow.

    However, the risk of in-line mode is the granularity of identifying the malicious packets. The sensors should be designed to take preventive measures only against those packets that are malicious. Reconfiguring a firewall with false positives can prevent genuine traffic from entering or leaving the trusted network.

- **Processing at wire speed:** Sensors deployed in in-line mode should process packets at wire-speed, otherwise the traffic passing through the sensors can become a bottleneck and hinder the network performance.

- **Traffic Normalization (Packet Scrubbing):** Though the baseline profiles have been created with what is perceived to be normal traffic, sometimes ambiguities such as IP fragmentation can cause false positives. The sensors can reassemble IP fragments, TCP segments, at the sensor level, normalize the traffic, re-evaluate the profiles, and improve upon false positives.

It is important to deploy in-line mode sensors in a high-availability state. In in-line mode, there are high chances of the sensors becoming single points of failure which will result in a complete breakdown of the network. If a network is running in in-line mode, it is recommended to have two sensors in a high-availability mode as shown in the Figure 11-10.

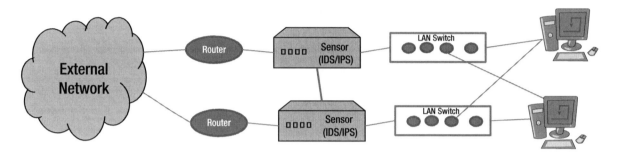

Figure 11-10. *In-line mode - High Availability*

IDS/IPS in Context

IDS/IPS complements both the firewall and the anti-virus software. IDSs provide protection to known attacks, unknown attacks, and DoS attacks. IDS peels off each network packet that enters the network, and inspects the data for any abnormalities, which a firewall is unable to do. However, a firewall acts as a basic security guard, who checks your identity and legitimacy before allowing you to enter the network, whether you are internal or external to the organization. Intrusion Detection and Prevention System (IDPS) is ideally deployed in monitoring/detection mode. If an IDPS lacks proper rules and the threat signatures are not up to date, then IDPS neither detects the intrusions nor prevents them. It is extremely important to have the threat signatures updated on a regular basis and connected to the signature labs directly.

Strategic placement of IDS/IPS sensors in the network is also crucial. Whether it is in tap mode, span mode, or in-line mode is dependent on the organizational security and network policy. In order to deploy in in-line mode, one should have more experience in configuring IDPS to have different prevention modes thereby avoiding too many false positives and blocking genuine packets. Also, for in-line mode, the sensors should support wire-speed processing capabilities. For example, if your network is 10 Gbps, the sensors should process at the same speed. Another important deployment strategy is location of IDPS – whether in DMZ, or before the DMZ, or immediately after the firewall or VPN (Virtual Private Network) concentrator. Since the traffic through VPN tunnels is encrypted, unless the IDS/IPS has keys, it may not be capable of conducting adequate analysis.

The most important is the remediation process. IDS can detect intrusions and send an alert to the security administrator but it has no control over the remediation. Similarly, IPS can take action to prevent intrusions but it has to be configured by the security administrator for each of the traffic and attack types. This is part of the process followed in an organization and cannot be automated. If the organization does not have means of responding to security incidents and alerts in a timely manner, having such systems may be useless.

In conclusion, firewall, anti-virus software, host-integrity system, and IDS/IPS technology complement each other. Having a firewall at the entrance of a network protects from unauthorized traffic entering and acts as a security guard; then IDS/IPS scrutinizes the traffic, acts as a surveillance system, and finally the anti-virus software keeps the system clean from further spreading of malicious software. It is crucial to have a layered defense in-depth strategy considering the threats being constantly created in the world of the Internet. The security is an overall process involving more than just technology. Technology can solve only a part of the problem but a process needs to be in place to protect the organization's assets from intrusion attacks.

Chapter Summary

- We first defined intrusion in lay terms. Then we mentioned that IDS helps to detect intrusions and differentiated it from a firewall. We also learned that IDS peels off the packet and inspects it to understand whether the packet has any malicious code or can lead to any malicious activities. We also mentioned that IDS complements a firewall by doing what a firewall cannot do.

- We looked at why we need to use IDS. We mentioned that IDS not only provides alerts on intrusions but also enables us to take appropriate actions including corrective actions, based on root causes, to eliminate such intrusions in the future. We looked into a few of the important terminologies like false positives, true positives, false negatives, and true negatives in the context of the results of IDS.

- We then explored both the important types of IDS: host-based IDS and network-based IDS/IPS. We went through the details of host-based IDS including how it monitors the access to the system, its application, and sends alerts for any unusual activities. We then explained that it constantly monitors event logs, system logs, application logs, user policy enforcement, rootkit detection, file integrity, and other intrusions to the system. We then explained how the changes in logs can be interpreted by IDS and alerts are provided by IDS against any intrusions. We looked into the context of network-based IDS/IPS in that it inspects the network packets and checks against the stored malicious signatures to determine whether a packet has been sent with a malicious intention or not. We then differentiated between IDS and IPS. We further explored the pros and cons of both host-based IDS and network-based IDS/IPS.

- We explained how the signature-based detection and anomaly-based detection are used by IDS to identify the intrusions and provide the alerts. We then explored Protocol Anomaly and Statistical Anomaly Detection. We also looked into the advantages and disadvantages of the Anomaly-based Detection.

- We then explored Stateful Protocol Analysis Detection and listed the pros and cons of this form of detection.

- We explored on the architecture of IDS/IPS. In this context, we looked into the functions of important components of the IDS/IPS like Appliance (Sensors), Database, Management Console, and Signature Update Server, including the need to keep the signatures updated so that the detection is appropriately ensured. We also looked into the important capabilities of the IDS/IPS of needing to have logging capabilities, detection capabilities, prevention capabilities, code viewing, and editing capabilities.

- We then discussed various attacks the IDS/IPS can detect and prevent. We further discussed the various responses of IDS/IPS, including blocking, denying, or dropping a packet; resetting the connection; or reconfiguring the firewall.

- We discussed various modes in which the IDS/IPS can be deployed like SPAN mode, TAP mode, and in-line mode. We also looked at how IPS needs to be supported by wire speed processing in in-line mode.

- We ended the chapter with a final note on how firewall, IDS/IPS, and anti-virus play complementary roles to each other.

▪▪▪

CHAPTER 12

Virtual Private Networks

Introduction

Business has changed in the last couple of decades. Companies now have to think about having a global presence, global marketing, and logistics. Most of the organizations have branches spread across different geographies of the world. Wherever you are located, all these branches need to be connected with their headquarters data center for information. With the changing culture and environment, the demand of the sales force to be able to connect to the headquarters data center from either their homes or hotels is increasing and seamless connectivity to the main data center has become a necessity. Hence, there is one demand that the companies are asking for from their network team: a fast, safe, secure, and trustworthy network that helps in communicating with all their offices wherever they are located.

When the companies want to connect their network with outside partners, external vendors, or even with external telecommuter and sales employees, there are two options: one private, dedicated lease line or share a part of bandwidth with an existing line such as the Internet.

Dedicated leased lines ranging from ISDN (144 Kbps) to Optical Carrier (192 Gbps) fiber enable the companies to connect a geographically dispersed office as shown in Figure 12-1. For example, X.25, Frame Relay, Asynchronous Transmission Mode (ATM), and MPLS (Multiprotocol Label Switching) are examples of private WAN networks.

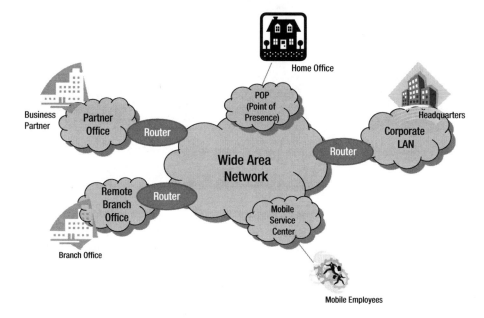

Figure 12-1. *Typical Business Scenarios*

For secured connection, it is always recommended to have your own private dedicated line between different points. However, this option is very expensive as you have to connect different places by different cables and laying cable across geographies is an expensive affair and maintaining these lines is even more expensive. Additionally, a leased line is not a viable option as the locations of the offices may change or for a mobile work force that is constantly on the go. The other option is to share the line with others which is cheap, but not always secure. To overcome this problem, the concept of Virtual Private Network (VPN) was developed. VPN creates a tunnel between the two end hosts and data is transmitted securely through this tunnel but on a public shared network.

A VPN is a private network, as shown in Figure 12-2 (similar to a leased line) but uses the public network (Internet) to connect to remote sites. VPN creates a "virtual" tunnel connection routed through the Internet from the company's trusted network to the remote office or to a mobile work force. With VPN, you can send data via the public network which emulates a private link between the two parties or two networks.

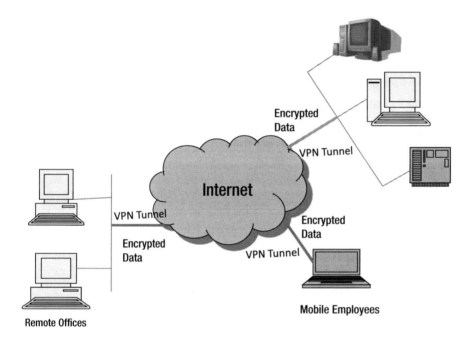

Figure 12-2. *Virtual Private Network scenario*

A secure VPN encrypts data before passing it through the tunnel to ensure privacy. Data integrity and authenticity are also maintained before the creation of the tunnel. Thus, VPN protects data with privacy, integrity, and authenticity. With VPN, you can provide many services such as the Internet, e-mail, applications, and database services to users in remote locations with secured communication.

Advantages of VPN

A Virtual Private Network (VPN) allows two computers to communicate securely over the public network such as the Internet. This allows for connecton of employees, partners, and other small branch offices to the corporate network securely and at low cost. For example, a sales person on the road can access a product database securely from a laptop or mobile device as if she is sitting in the office. A company's small branch office can connect to the corporate office using VPN across the Internet and access information on the network as if it is all in the same network. Following are some of the advantages of using VPN:

- **Cost savings:** Using private networks used to be the only solution for WAN connectivity. However, it was expensive and not always feasible, not easily scalable, and lacked security features. A VPN solution making use of the Internet is an inexpensive alternative, allowing the full advantage of cost savings of the Internet and providing a superior level of security.

- **Smooth and Seamless Integration:** VPN allows seamless integration with the existing network infrastructure. There is no need to change your network architecture or any network software component.

- **Secure Remote Access:** One of the primary objectives of the VPN is to provide remote users secured access to the organization's trusted network. VPN technology allows the same connectivity whether it is network to network, host to host, client to server, dial-up connections, or home office or mobile users.

- **Extranet Connections:** In today's global economy, most organizations have one or more partners for mutual growth and success of the business. Companies have to connect to their external partners to share certain information, sometimes even critical, confidential information. Hence, they need to have a secured connection between the two partners. VPN solutions allow secured connection between the two parties allowing even proprietary information to be shared.

- **Low Maintenance:** VPN eliminates much of the day-to-day maintenance such as key management and SNMP.

VPN Types

When data is routed through the Internet, it will pass through different service providers' network and equipment. The service provider may or may not provide any security. The customer data needs to be transported securely where the customer does not trust the service provider's network and prefers creating a "virtual" tunnel to pass the traffic securely. In such cases, the service provider merely acts as a transporter of IP traffic.[1]

Primarily, VPN supports two types of communication:

- Remote Access (host-to-site) VPN

- Site-to-site (intranet and extranet) VPN

Remote Access (Host-to-Site) VPN

Remote Access (Host-to-Site) VPN is a connection between a user and the LAN inside a company where the user is an employee who needs to connect to the corporate network from outside the company. This type of connection is used mainly by telecommuting or sales force employees who want to connect to the corporate LAN from remote locations. The remote employees, once they connect to the Internet, use their VPN client to connect to the corporate LAN. The VPN client first connects to the VPN gateway server, a network device located in the DMZ. The VPN gateway server authenticates the user and then creates a "virtual" tunnel between the remote host and the gateway for a secured connection. Once the virtual tunnel is created, the channel becomes secured and the remote host can connect to any server in the trusted network to start sending data. This type of Remote Access provides a secure, encrypted communication between two parties that are connected via the Internet. This is depicted in Figure 12-3, where a remote employee is accessing a corporate network from his house. He is authenticated at the corporate network level. Once he is inside the network, he can access any resources within the network. However, any data flows out of the network are secured and travel through the VPN tunnel.

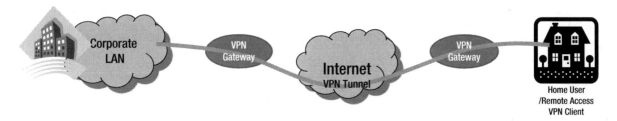

Figure 12-3. *Remote Access VPN*

Host-to-Host VPN

Some refer to host-to-host VPNs as remote access with one small change. In host-to-host VPN, two hosts are connected through a VPN tunnel. The tunnel is directly established between two hosts for a secured data transfer. Before the data transmission, the user is authenticated and the encrypted keys are exchanged between the two parties and then the transmission of data begins. The VPN tunnel ensures data authenticity, data integrity, and data confidentiality.

As shown in Figure 12-4, two hosts are connected over the internet. This type of connection is allowed when an employee or a partner wants to connect to a specific network resource (server/database) securely. He/she may not be allowed to access any other resources within the network.

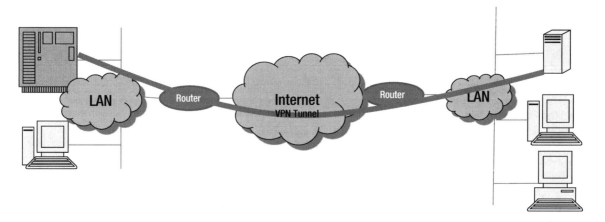

Figure 12-4. *Host-to-Host VPN*

Site-to-Site (Intranet and Extranet) VPN

Site-to-site VPN connects one network to another network over the Internet, such as connecting a remote branch office to the corporate headquarters LAN. In this setup, the tunnel is created between two VPN gateways. The VPN gateway of the remote branch negotiates a connection with the VPN gateway of the corporate headquarters network and establishes a secured tunnel. The remote hosts will not have any VPN clients but they send normal TCP/IP traffic through the VPN gateways. The VPN gateway is responsible for authentication of the user/network, encryption, and integrity of data. Once the VPN gateway receives the encrypted data, it strips the headers, decrypts the content, and relays normal data toward the target host inside the trusted network. Thus, the VPN tunnel is created between two sites allowing the company's network and resources available to the remote location. This solution is ideal for small offices located in remote parts of the world.

As shown in Figure 12-5, two networks are connected as if they are one. Any device on one network can communicate with the device on the other network securely as if the other device is part of the same network. Whenever the data leaves one network, it passes through the secured VPN tunnel.

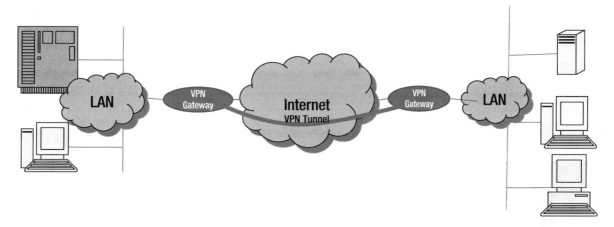

Figure 12-5. *Site-to-site VPN*

There are two types of site-to-site VPNs:

- **Intranet-based VPN** – A company with a small number of remote offices, wishing to connect all of them together to make it into a single network can use this type of connection. A seamless connection is established between all the remote branches of the company which helps in sharing of systems and network resources. This gives the feeling that all the different networks of the various branches are one single network.

- **Extranet-based VPN** – A company may wish to connect with its partner's network. One company's LAN is connected with another company's LAN to share certain information across the companies for better business relationships and processes. For example, in case of supply chain relationship, companies allow their partners to connect to their network to share the database and other relevant information. The extranet-VPN allows the companies to share certain information with their partners, such as just a customer database application and nothing else. If the team working on this database application consists of 10 people from one company and 5 people from the partner company, then a secure VPN is created only between this small network of 10 systems and the other 5 systems. No other network resources are shared except for the database application. It allows the companies to work together in a secure and shared environment while still allowing their internal network to be secure and available for only the internal users.

VPN and Firewall

A firewall is used to control the access into the network so that it can stop the spread of "fire" in the surrounding area whereas VPN provides the secured channel between the two parties who are exchanging information. A combination of VPN and Firewall would ensure only authorized applications and users are accessing the information. VPN Firewall, as shown in Figure 12-6, ensures that malicious intentions are impeded and only authentic traffic enters into the VPN.

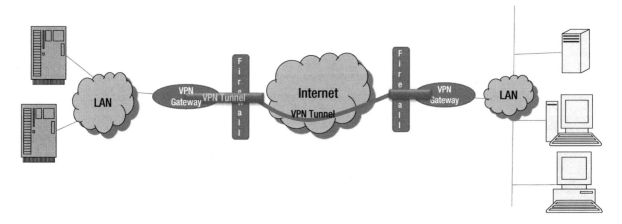

Figure 12-6. *VPN and Firewall Deployment*

VPN and firewall can be deployed separately. Normally VPN is deployed after the firewall. First check of entry is firewall. A firewall provides proper policy and access check and then allows the traffic to pass through the VPN tunnel. Some of the VPN gateway vendors are now providing firewall functions also. This has an added advantage of using a single device to configure both as VPN gateway and firewall.

VPN Protocols

VPN supports secured communication over a public network. Before the data transmission, the secured channel should be established. Each party should know how they securely communicate, how they encrypt the data, and how they exchange decryption keys so that each party can transmit information securely. VPN connection has two phases. In the first phase of connection, both parties establish secured connection by identifying themselves as genuine parties and exchanging the keys to support data encryption, decryption, and data integrity. In the second phase, actual data transfer happens with the encrypted data where only two parties know the keys. For secured connection, VPN protocols should support:

- Tunneling
- Data Authentication
- Data Integrity
- Data Encryption
- Anti-replay services

Tunneling

VPN Tunneling is the encapsulation of one type of data packet within another data packet. A specific data packet of one protocol is wrapped into another protocol and then transmitted between a VPN client and a server. For example, an IP packet is wrapped around a PPTP (VPN protocol) and transmitted. PPTP is a tunneling VPN protocol. PPTP protocol itself manages user authentication, data integrity, and data encryption.

Data Authentication and Data Integrity

Data authentication guarantees the authenticity of the two parties who are communicating with each other. It authenticates that the data is actually being received from a genuine user who has sent the data. Integrity means that the data received has not been modified during transmission.

Anti-Replay Services

Anti-replay services are services in which the receiver device can reject duplicate packets or late arrival packets in order to protect against replay attacks.

Data Encryption

Encryption is the mechanism commonly used for protecting confidentiality and privacy of data over the public network. The sender encrypts the data using a particular method, which is normally called a key, and the receiver decrypts the message using the same method and the same key.

The implementation of a VPN is based on one of the protocols listed in Table 12-1.

Table 12-1. *VPN Protocol Architecture*

Site-to-site VPN	Remote Access
Internet Protocol Security (IPSec)	Point to Point Transport Protocol (PPTP)
Generic Routing Encapsulation (GRE) Or IP Tunneling	Layer Two Protocol (L2TPv3)
Multi-Protocol Label Switch (MPLS)	Cisco L2F
	The Secure Socket Layer (SSL)

Point to Point Transport Protocol (PPTP) Tunneling Protocol

Point-to-Point Tunneling Protocol (PPTP), Layer Two Tunneling Protocol (L2TP), or Secure Socket Tunneling Protocol (SSTP) rely on Point-to-Point Protocol (PPP). PPP[1] was designed to provide a full-duplex communication between the two peers that is assumed to deliver packets in order. PPP is intended to support a wide variety of connections between routers, bridges, and hosts.

PPP first authenticates the users before the transmission of data. The PPP encapsulation supports multiplexing of different protocols simultaneously over the same link, thus allowing multiple vendor compatibility and supporting multiple applications and protocols.

PPTP protocol describes how a secure PPP link can be established over a TCP/IP connection. PPTP encapsulates the IP protocol packets inside PPP datagrams and transmits them over the Internet. PPTP requires IP connectivity between the server and the client. If there is already a connection between the server and the remote client, then a PPTP tunnel can easily be created and data transmitted over a secured channel across the LAN. If the remote client needs an Internet connection, then a dial-up can be used or any other services to connect to an ISP before establishing the tunnel.

PPTP was developed by the vendor consortium of Accend Communications, Microsoft Corporation, Copper Mountain Networks, 3COM, U.S. Robotics, and several other individuals. It was then submitted to the Internet community as an RFC 2637.[2]

PPTP allows PPP to be tunneled through the IP network as shown in Figure 12-7. It does not change any PPP protocol itself. PPTP uses Generic Routing Encapsulation (GRE) to provide a flow and congestion control datagram services for transporting PPP packets over the Internet connection.

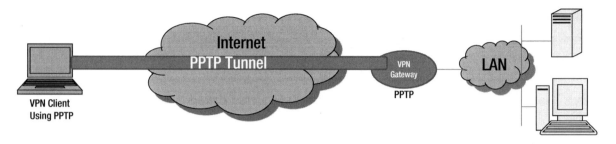

Figure 12-7. *PPTP Tunneling*

PPTP uses an enhanced GRE (Generic Routing Encapsulation) mechanism to provide a flow- and congestion-controlled encapsulated datagram service for carrying PPP packets. The PPTP Network server (NAS) runs on any operating system platform while the client, PPTP Access Controller (AC) operates on a PPP platform.

PPTP supports the Password Authentication Protocol (PAP) and the Challenge Handshake Authentication Protocol (CHAP) authentication methods:

- **PAP** – The Password Authentication Protocol (PAP) provides a simple method for the peer to establish a connection by simple two-way handshake as soon as the link is established.[3]

  PAP is not a strong authentication method. Passwords are sent over the link in a clear text (plain text) format, and there is no protection against playback or repeated packet attacks.

- **CHAP** – This is another protocol for authentication. The Challenge-Handshake Authentication Protocol (CHAP) is used to verify the identity of the remote user by a three-way handshake. After the link is established, the server sends the "challenge" message to the remote user, which becomes the first handshake. The remote user responds to the "challenge" using a one-way hash, which is the second handshake. If the response matches, then the authentication is acknowledged and a connection is established, which is the third handshake. Otherwise the connection is terminated. The CHAP protocol protects the network from playback or repeated packet attacks and controls the frequency and timings of the challenges.[4]

Other protocols include:

- MS-CHAP – Microsoft CHAP

- MS-CHAPv2 – Microsoft CHAP version 2 (and later versions)

- Extensible Authentication Protocol (EAP)

The PPTP protocol implementation is designed to use its own encryption algorithms, with an option to negotiate their own keys. However, DES (Digital Encryption Standard), triple DES, Rivest Cipher (RC)-4, and RC-5 are some of the other common encryption algorithms that are used by PPTP. The 128-key encryption algorithms are considered secure enough for VPN.

Layer Two Tunneling Protocol (L2TPv3)

A Layer Two Tunneling Protocol (L2TP) is an extension of PPTP protocol. It combines the features of PPTP and Cisco's L2F protocols. L2TP provides a transparent communication between the two end-users and applications across the intervening network. L2TP extends the PPP model by allowing Layer 2 protocol and PPP protocol to communicate with each other, interconnected by a packet-switched network. When a user sends the connection request, it first connects to an access device (L2TP Access Concentrator) such as a modem, ADSL, or DSLAM, and then the access device tunnels the PPP frames to the NAS (Network Access Server).[5]

Generic Routing Encapsulation (GRE)

Generic Routing Encapsulation (GRE) tunneling protocol encapsulates one IP datagram within another IP datagram and transports the encapsulated IP datagram. In other words, GRE encapsulates one network layer protocol with any another network layer protocol. The general specification is described in RFC 2890.[6]

A typical GRE datagram is shown in Figure 12-8. A network layer packet, called the "payload" packet is encapsulated in a GRE packet, which may include all the routing information of the network payload packet information. The resulting GRE packet is further encapsulated in some other network layer protocol, called "delivery protocol," and then forwarded to the transmission inside the VPN tunnel.[6]

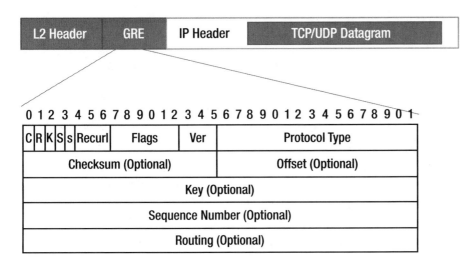

Figure 12-8. *Format of a GRE[6] encapsulated packet*

Internet Protocol Security (IPSec)

The goal of the IPSec is to provide security services for the IP layer, in both IPv4 and IPv6 protocols. *IPsec provides cryptographically designed security services for IPv4 and IPv6 protocol.* [7] IPSec security services cover data confidentiality, data integrity, authenticity, and anti-replay protection for the network traffic.

IPSec is a complex framework consisting of many protocols that provide a flexible set of security features. Toward this end, IPSec uses two main security protocols, the Authentication Header (AH) and the Encapsulating Security Protocol (ESP). The IPSec framework has two modes: the tunnel mode and the transport mode. In tunnel mode, an entire IP packet is encapsulated inside another IP packet. In transport mode, only the IP packet header is modified.

The Authentication Header (AH) supports data integrity, authentication, and optional anti-replay services. The Encapsulation Security Payload (ESP) provides data confidentiality (encryption). Together, AH and ESP provide the full set of security features for IP protocol and these are configured in a data structure called Security Association (SA). To summarize, the main functions of IPsec are Authentication, Encryption, and Key Management.

IPSec RFC 4301, Security Architecture for IP, consists of the following:[8]

- Security Protocols – Authentication Header (AH) and Encapsulating Security Payload (ESP)
- Security Associations – what they are and how they work, how they are managed, and associated processing
- Key Management – manual and automated (The Internet Key Exchange (IKE))
- Cryptographic algorithms for authentication and encryption

IPSec Tunnel and Transport Modes

IPSec is configured in two modes:

- Tunnel mode: is used between two gateways, or between a host and a gateway, with the gateway acting as a proxy for the host behind it.

Transport mode: is used between two end stations or two hosts.

The Authentication Header (AH)

The Authentication Header (AH) protocol provides authentication of the origin and integrity of the datagram transported between two systems. Data integrity in IPv4 is achieved through the CRC check. If a CRC error is detected at the destination, it means that the IP datagram has been changed during the transmission. The same concept is used in AH protocol, except, instead of using a simple algorithm, it uses a special hashing algorithm and a unique key known only to the sender and the receiver. This key is exchanged during the initial phase of connection establishment and Security Association (SA) is established between the two devices to know how to perform the computation of the algorithm using the unique key that has been exchanged during the initial phase, which none of the other systems can perform. On the source device, AH performs the computation and updates the results in the Integrity Check Value (ICV) field of the AH header and the datagram is transmitted. The destination device decrypts the message with the key, if there are no errors in the transmitted datagram.

Some fields of the IP header change during transmission (for example the fragmentation flag), and this change is not predictable during transmission. Hence, such fields are not covered as part of the AH authentication process. AH provides authentication for most of the fields of IP as well as the next level protocol data thus rendering protection provided by AH as partial.

It is important to note that the original data is not changed either by the checksum value or ICV value. Thus, AH performs only integrity check and not privacy (privacy is handled by ESP). The protocol header (IPv4 or IPv6) preceding the AH header SHALL contain the value 51 in its protocol (IPv4) or next header (IPv6) fields. Figure 12-9 illustrates the AH header format.[9]

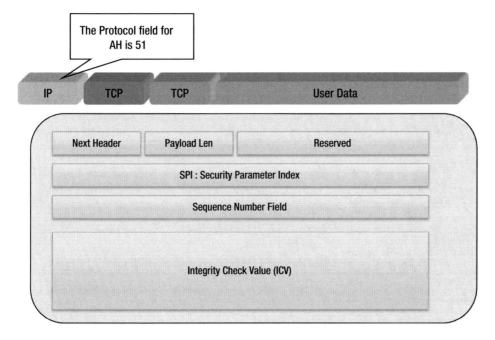

Figure 12-9. AH Format

With transport mode, the source IP address fields are not modified as shown in Figure 12-9. The authentication header is added after the original IP header. In tunnel mode, a new IPv4 header is encapsulated in the original IPv4 packet, as shown in the Figure 12-10.

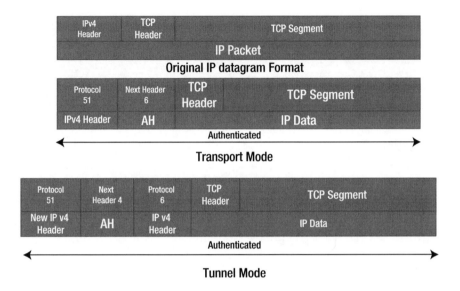

Figure 12-10. *AH Header*

AH uses Hashed Message Authentication Code (HMAC). VPN uses either HMAC-MD5 or HMAC-SHA. But SHA is regarded as more secure because of its large hash length. HMAC-MD5 is defined in RFC 2085, HMAC-SHA is defined in RFC 2404. The details of all the RFCs are given at `http://tools.ietf.org/rfc`.

The Encapsulation Security Protocol (ESP)

IPSec provides data confidentiality services through Encapsulating Security Payload (ESP). ESP may be applied alone or in combination with IP Authentication Header (AH) as described above. Confidentiality is provided by encryption algorithms and confidentiality of the data is between two hosts, two security gateways, or a gateway and a host.[10] The ESP header is illustrated in Figure 12-11.

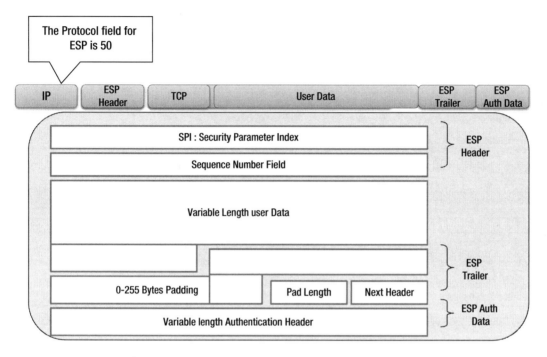

Figure 12-11. *ESP Header*

The encryption algorithms used by ESP are specified by the SA during the negotiation phase. ESP is designed for use with symmetric encryption algorithms. Since IP packets arrive out of order, each packet must have enough information to allow the receiver to establish cryptographic synchronization.[10] ESP uses a shared key for encrypting and decrypting the data, which is exchanged between the two parties.

Figure 12-12 shows the difference between the transport mode and the tunnel mode. In the transport mode, the IP payload is encrypted and the original headers are left intact. In the tunnel mode, the entire original IP datagram is encrypted. However, the new IP header is not included in the authentication mechanism.

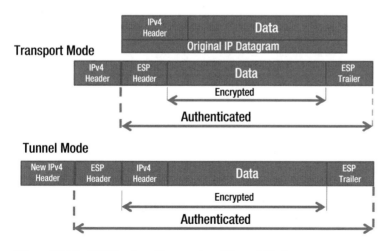

Figure 12-12. *ESP Header – Transport and Tunnel Mode*

ESP uses a symmetric key to encrypt and decrypt the messages. The standard symmetric key algorithm used in IPSec VPN are DES, triple-DES, RC5, RC4, or Advanced Encryption Standard (AES). Whatever the cipher being used, it should be interoperable among IPSec products. RFC 1829 defines DES, RFC 1851 describes 3DES. These RFCs can be downloaded at `http://tools.ietf.org/rfc`. Other algorithms are MD5 and DES-CBC (Cipher Block Chaining).

Internet Key Management (IKE)

Before a secure transmission can begin, both the sender and the receiver need to negotiate on the keys, which are defined in the Security Association (SA) document. The AH protocol is used for authentication and integrity, the ESP is used for privacy. In both the AH and ESP protocols, both the parties exchange "secret" keys. This exchange of keys happens through a protocol called IPSec Key Exchange (IKE) protocol as defined by RFC2409.

IKE is meant for establishing, negotiating, modifying, and deleting SAs. IKE performs authentication between the two parties and establishes Security Association (SA) by exchanging the secret key that can be used to establish SAs for both AH and ESP protocols and a set of cryptographic algorithm that is used by the SAs to encrypt and decrypt the messages (payload).[11]

MPLS (Multi-Protocol Label Switching)

MPLS is the latest core technology providing the next-generation WAN connectivity, in particular for the optical networks. As a packet travels from one network to another network, each router in that network makes an independent decision on how to forward the packet based on the routing table entries. As the packet enters the router, the router analyzes the packet header and based on its destination address, it looks at the routing table and forwards the packet to the designated interface (network). This process is repeated at each hop. The disadvantage of this process is that every time a packet arrives, the router has to repeat this "table lookup" and if there are more than two packets to the same destination network, the router still has to look up the routing table twice.

The router assigns the packets to the next hop, which can be thought of as a function of two components. The first component could be partitioning an entire set of packets into what is called as "Forward Equivalence Classes (FECs)" and the second is to map each FEC to the next hop. In conventional IP forwarding, each packet header is analyzed and a routing decision is made at each hop, which is time consuming and process intensive.

In case of MPLS[12], the assignment of FEC to a particular packet is done only once, as soon as the packet enters the network. MPLS-Label format is as shown in Figure 12-13. The FEC is given a short, fixed-length value known as a "label" and the label is forwarded along with the packet. When the packet enters the next hop, just the label is analyzed and no further analysis of header is done in subsequent routers. All forwarding is done using "labels." This has a number of advantages over the traditional network layer forwarding apart from faster processing and speed.

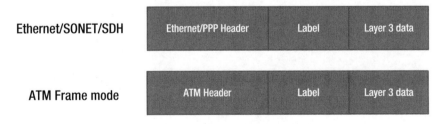

Figure 12-13. *MPLS – Label Format*

The advantages of MPLS networks include:

- MPLS forwarding can be done by L2 layer switches which have capabilities to read MPLS labels but are not capable of analyzing L3 (network) layer headers

- Quality of Service (QoS) - MPLS allows prioritization of traffic, allowing high-priority traffic first on the network then the lower-priority traffic. MPLS networks assign higher priority for latency-sensitive applications like voice and video over less-sensitive applications

- Improved performance, reliability, and efficiency of the network

- MPLS VPNs and VPLS services enable multiple sites to connect seamlessly

MPLS VPN

The main disadvantage of VPN networks is interoperability. The VPN connections are tied to one vendor or one Internet Service Provider (ISP). Many of the IP-based VPN solutions also require encapsulation of IP or double encapsulation of IP. This requires additional processing overhead at the entry and exit of ISP networks.

With MPLS networks, this can be overcome. Intermediate MPLS switches need not process the IP headers, in particular, the destination IP addresses in the packets are not examined, which enables MPLS to offer an efficient mechanism to forward the encapsulated data on the ISP backbone network. MPLS also has greater control over network parameters such as latency, bandwidth, and availability. Hence, MPLS VPN has emerged as a trusted WAN connectivity than the normal IP-based connectivity. One of the major advantages of MPLS VPN is that instead of managing point-to-point connections between multiple branch offices, now MPLS VPN customers need to provide only one connection from their corporate LAN to all other branch offices.

Traditional VPN technology depends on tunneling protocols such as GRE, L2TP, and PPTP whereas MPLS itself is a tunnel over public networks. Therefore, implementation of VPN over MPLS has better advantages. MPLS based VPNs connect geographically spread branch offices of a private network using LSP (Label Switch Path).[12]

Figure 12-14 shows the basic architecture of MPLS-based VPN. There are two components in the architecture, Customer Equipment (CE) and Service Provider Equipment (PE). A CE can be a router, switch, or host. PEs are part of the backbone network. PE is responsible for managing VPN connectivity, VPN users, and establishing MPLS LSP connections (VPN tunnel) between PEs and allocating routes among different branches of the same VPN.

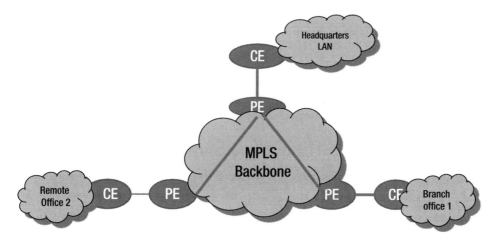

Figure 12-14. *MPLS-based VPN*

MPLS VPN Security

Customers expect their data to be secured across the VPN tunnel. VPN implementation based on ATM and frame relay provides secured VC (virtual connections) by virtue of connection-oriented network. However, IP based VPNs rely on cryptographic means to provide security and authentication. MPLS VPN security[13] is achieved through:

- Ingress SP router assigns a unique VPN ID to each destination thus ensuring private connection between two users

- Any other packet entering the MPLS backbone network without a label or a different label not in the MPLS network will be discarded

- SP routers can use the MD5 or similar technique to encrypt the labels of MPLS thus providing additional security

- If the customer wants to send data that is very sensitive and must be protected, then IPSec or similar protocol can be adopted

Important IETF Standards and RFCs for VPN Implementation

Some of the important Internet Engineering Task Force (IETF) standards and RFCs for VPN implementation are summarized in the Table 12-2. This is not a comprehensive list. For more details, you can refer to VPN consortium home page at `http://www.vpnc.org`.

Table 12-2. *Important IETF Standards and RFCs for VPN Implementation*

VPN Protocol Category	RFC No.	Description of RFC
Tunneling Protocol	2661	Layer Two Tunneling Protocol (L2TP)
	2637	Point-to-Point Tunneling Protocol (PPTP)
GRE	2890 (Obsolete 2784)	Generic Routing Encapsulation
ESP	4303 (Obsolete 2406)	Encapsulating Security Payload (ESP)
AH	4302 (Obsolete 2402)	IP Authentication Header
IPSec	4301 (updated 6301) (Obsolete 2401)	Security Architecture for the Internet Protocol
	2411	IP Security Roadmap
	2764	A Framework for IP Based Virtual Private Network
	4891	Using IPSec to Secure IPV6-in-IPV4 Tunnels
	5265	Mobile IPV4 Traversal across IPSec-Based Gateways
IPSec Key Exchange	4306	Internet Key Exchange Protocol (IKEv2)
	2408	Internet Security Association and Key Management Protocol (ISAKMP)
	RFC 2409	Internet Key Exchange (IKE)
	RFC 2412	OAKLEY Key Determination Protocol

(continued)

Table 12-2. (*continued*)

VPN Protocol Category	RFC No.	Description of RFC
MPLS	4381	Analysis of the Security of BGP/MPLS IP Virtual Private Networks (VPNs)
	4364	BGP/MPLS IP Virtual Private Networks (VPNs)
	4111	Security Framework for Provider-Provisioned Virtual Private Networks (PPVPNs)
Cryptographic Algorithm	2405	The ESP DES-CBC Cipher Algorithm With Explicit IV
	2104	HMAC: Keyed-Hashing for Message Authentication
	2403	The Use of HMAC-MD5-96 within ESP and AH
	2410	The NULL Encryption Algorithm and Its Use with IPsec
	3173	IP Payload Compression Protocol (IPComp)
	3051	IP Payload Compression Using ITU-T V.44 Packet Method
	3602	The AES-CBC Cipher Algorithm and Its Use with IPSec
	3686	Using Advanced Encryption Standard (AES) Counter Mode With IPsec Encapsulating Security Payload (ESP)
	4196	The SEED Cipher Algorithm and Its Use with IPsec
	4894	Use of Hash Algorithms in Internet Key Exchange (IKE) and IPsec
	4312	The Camella Cipher Algorithm and Its Use with IPsec
	4106	The Use of Galois/Counter Mode (GCM) in IPsec Encapsulating Security Payload (ESP)
	4615	The Advanced Encryption Standard-Cipher-based Message Authentication Code-Pseudo-Random Function-128 (AES-CMAC-PRF-128) Algorithm for the Internet Key Exchange Protocol (IKE)
	4634	US Secure Hash Algorithms (SHA and HMAC-SHA)
	4868	Using HMAC-SHA-256, HMAC-SHA-384, and HMAC-512 with IPsec.

A Few Final Thoughts about VPN

The Internet is not a safe place. It has every kind of network and every kind of system and every kind of people – good or bad. In order to keep your information safe while transmitting over the Internet, VPN technologies using PPTP, L2TP, IPSec, MPLS, SSL, or other protocols support the following:

- Confidentiality
- Authentication and Data Integrity
- Replay protection

Authentication is used to prevent unauthorized users gaining access to the secured network. Some of the common and traditional algorithms used for the authentication process are PAP (Password Authentication Protocol), CHAP (Challenge-Handshake Authentication Protocol). The newest authentication protocol is EAP, Extensible Authentication Protocol and an extension to EAP is EAP-TLS, EAP-Transaction Level Security. A "Replay" attack is when the attacker taps into the network, hears the conversation, and captures the packets and "replays" those packets to gain access. For example, if the packet is sent for authentication, then the attacker system captures the packet, reads the content, and identifies, say the password field, and the destination address, and then the attacker "replays" the same packet just by changing the source address and tries to gain access. To protect from such attacks, passwords also must be protected.

Encryption is meant to protect the confidentiality of data. A secret key is used to encrypt and decrypt the message. There are two types of encryption key mechanism - symmetric and asymmetric. In symmetric, the same key is used for encrypting and decrypting the messages. In asymmetric encryption, there are two keys – a public key and a private key. Using the public key, data is encrypted and the data is decrypted using the private key. The standard algorithms used for data encryption are the DES and the RSA. RSA is much faster than DES and has become a de-facto standard for high-speed data encryption.

VPNs allow remote sites, small offices, and branch offices to connect to the corporate network over a public network (Internet), while maintaining secure communications. VPN technologies are designed to address the current business needs and trends toward increased telecommuters and mobile and wireless users who are outside of the corporate network but need to connect over cell phones, smartphones, handheld devices, and notebooks distributed globally but at the same time providing a cost-effective solution. However, VPN may not be a good solution where latency and slow performance is not acceptable.

Recent years have seen the growth of several VPN technologies and services. With the advancement in Internet and Internet technologies, these new VPN services work on the same physical infrastructure as much as possible. Traditionally, the remote access services were built on dial-up. However, ADSL, cable modem, and wireless access have become more popular, making dial-up somewhat obsolete. Hence, to support these new access technologies, IPSec and SSL-VPN have evolved.

Service providers typically have a backbone network which is the ATM, Frame relay, or IP network based on MPLS technology. MPLS-based VPN technology has gained popularity because of MPLS's widespread deployment. MPLS-VPN has been deployed as a value-added service by the service providers to provide security services.

Mobile wireless technologies and Wi-Fi technologies are gaining momentum and the Internet can be accessed through your mobile device anytime, anywhere. Most hotels provide Wi-Fi hotspots. So, the corporations need to provide a technology to access their corporate network on these platforms but still need to keep the security in place. Most of the ISPs and the Wi-Fi hotspot routers allow very specific ports such as HTTP, HTTPS, POP3, and SMTP.

SSL-VPN/Web SSL VPN offers a complete, reliable replacement to IPSec remote access with its clientless, web-based architecture. SSL-VPN can offer connections restricted to a specific application by incorporating highly flexible authentication and authorization mechanisms and thus gaining wide acceptance.

While designing VPN technology, it is important to keep the following points in mind:

- VPN accelerator devices should support keys that are sufficiently long enough. A 128-bit key is certainly long enough but not all the devices support it.

- Even with the VPN technologies, it is possible for a hacker to insert bits into the data stream during transmission. IPSec has a mechanism to detect data integrity whereas others may have limitations in this area.

- It is important for the end devices to interoperate. IPSec at both ends should support the same type of AH and ESP algorithms and key length. Otherwise, communication itself may not be able to be established.

Chapter Summary

- The business need for connecting to organizational data centers securely from outside teams, such as sales and marketing and logistics, was explored. As most of the information that's transmitted needs to be secure, we looked into the option of having a dedicated line. We discussed how it is costly to have and maintain a dedicated line. We also discussed the disadvantages of having a dedicated line. Then we discussed a cheaper alternative, Virtual Private Network (VPN), which allows for the privacy, integrity, and authenticity of the data being transmitted by the internal team resources from outside the organization. VPN is a secure tunnel created between outside trusted partners including the internal workers working from outside the organizational boundaries and the internal networks.

- We looked into the benefits of VPNs, including cost savings, smooth and seamless integration, secure remote access, extranet connections, and low maintenance.

- We discussed the two important types of VPNs: Remote Access (Host to Site) and Site to Site. We discussed how Remote Access VPNs help the organizational work force operating from outside the organization to connect securely to the corporate LAN. We also looked into how this is implemented and how a secure tunnel is established to the external workforce and the organizational internal network, after authentication to the VPN gateway. Then we explored how site-to-site VPNs help one branch office to connect to the other branch office or headquarters and how this is established through the handshake between two VPN gateways at two ends. Then we looked into two types of site-to-site VPNs: intranet-based VPNs and extranet-based VPNs. We also looked briefly into how host-to-host VPNs work.

- We also discussed how VPN protocol architecture supports tunneling, data authentication, data integrity, data encryption, and anti-replay services. We then explored each of the protocols like point to point transport protocol (PPTP), layer two tunneling protocol (L2TPv3), generic routing encapsulation (GRE) tunneling protocol, and Internet protocol security (IPSec) in detail. We also looked into the need for Internet key management and how it is ensured.

- Finally, we highlighted some of the points to be kept in mind when designing the VPN technology.

CHAPTER 13

Data Backups and Cloud Computing

Introduction

Data backups and cloud computing can be treated as two separate subjects in one context and can be considered as complementary in another context. Data backups have been common since the inception of computers. Cloud computing, on the other hand, is a relatively recent phenomenon. The cloud infrastructure helps with effective data backups and is a low-cost disaster recovery option. Data backups help in ensuring restoration of data in case of data loss, data corruption, and data integrity issues.

As we have seen in previous chapters, "Availability" is one of the important aspects of information security. Data backups are the first line of defense against crashing of systems, corruption of data, exploits leading to data integrity issues, and accidental loss of data. Data backups stem from the fact that the disks on which the data is stored are prone to failures and can lead to a single point of failure. Data backups provide for continued operation by effective restoration of data and assure continued availability of the systems albeit the time taken for bringing up of the system by restoring the data for the corrupted or crashed part of the system. Although over the last few years, the reliability of the hardware and software systems has increased, there are still the risks of crash of the hardware, operating system, applications, and databases resulting in data loss or corruption. Hence, data backups are a must even today. The process of backing up your data has also progressed from manual backups to automated backups using mechanisms such as tape libraries, offline backups to online high speed mirroring, and in-house storage to off-site storage at third-party data custodians. However, one thing that has remained constant is that, even today, you cannot do away with the backups.

On the other hand, cloud computing has brought in new avenues of hope for low-cost use of applications, application development and deployment possibilities, and infrastructure acquisition. The cost effectiveness is evident in not only the reduction of the upfront investment, but also the reduction of financial burden in the pay-as-you-use model. Also, you can add or reduce computing power and storage based on the changing needs of your business. However, the cloud computing phenomenon also elevated the issues related to security and privacy. Even though most of the issues related to privacy and security are applicable to other platforms or applications too, there are some specific, additional privacy and security issues that arise with using a cloud.

Need for Data Backups

As we discussed above, even in today's world, the value of backups cannot be discounted and they are still the first line of defense against data loss, data corruption, or system crashes. Today, most documents and records are stored in computers and hence, if something happens to them, they could be completely lost forever without the correct backup system in place. Consider the following situations: A property has been registered in your name and the registration process was entirely handled through a computer. Now you find that the computer through which the registration was carried out has crashed or the server in which the registration details were held has crashed and the entire details were completely wiped off.

Similarly, imagine you concluded a big deal with another corporation electronically. The related computers crashed and the documents were lost or the bank's server and the database thereon has crashed, causing complete loss of all online transactions of the bank throughout the day.

In all these situations, unless the parties have other means of demonstrating / verifying that those transactions took place (such as through e-mails or written documentation), it will put the parties involved in very difficult circumstances. Nothing can replace the original information or transaction; thus, backups are the best and primary means of ensuring that the data is restored back quickly and effectively.

Not having backups is dangerous for the organization. Most of the transactions are initiated on the internet, pass through different network equipment, and are culminated in the relevant servers. Proof of such transactions may not be maintained by the individuals. Suppose I order a $1000 computer online but I do not save the order onto my system. The amount gets debited to my credit card but the order gets wiped off as the server of the online store crashes and they do not have a backup of my transaction. The only way I can convince them is through the debits to my credit card account. But, if they have lost the transactions from their server, my laptop may not be delivered to me even after 30 days because they have to verify that this transaction really did take place and they have received the amount from my end. Having a backup would have helped them restore the data and later ensured that the deliveries are made as promised.

Backups protect us against the availability and integrity aspects of information security. If the database gets completely corrupted, only the backups can make the availability of the corresponding systems possible. Similarly, if data integrity is compromised, only the recent backup enables us to bring back the application to its last state. As seen from these discussions, backups are an integral part of the information technology infrastructure which cannot be overlooked.

The various availability options like RAID (Redundant Array of Inexpensive Disks), Server Clustering, Electronic Vaulting, Remote Journaling, and Database Shadowing provide further alternative / complementary options to what backups can do and facilitate concepts like Online Mirroring and Hot Alternative Sites which are important constituents of Disaster Recovery and Business Continuity. These aspects have to be looked into, along with the backups, as an integral part of backup strategy. These are detailed as appropriate in subsequent sections.

Types of Backups

Backups can be categorized in different ways, as described in the following sections.

Category 1: Based on current data on the system and the data on the backups

The way backups are taken and the time delay between the current data and the data on the backups is one of the ways of such categorization. On the basis of this time delays, the backups can be categorized as Online Backups, Near-line Backups, and Offline Backups.

Online Backups

Online backups are taken in real time, and provide for high redundancy and fault tolerance. RAID Level 1, RAID Level 15, and RAID Level 51 are examples of online backups that provide high redundancy. Server Mirroring, Remote Journaling, and High-Speed Online Mirroring are other ways of enabling online backups and provide for high redundancy which does away with the single point of failure. These online backup mechanisms are required in highly critical systems where you cannot afford to lose even a small fraction of data, such as banking, data centers supporting various organizations, or organizations where different portions of the same work are being carried out by different centers.

Near-line Backups

Near-line backups are the backups taken at near real time but not at real time. There is a gap between the current system data status and that on the backup device. The electronic vaulting concept can enable this, if the batch transfer of data to another system or offsite alternative system can be carried out frequently. Electronic vaulting has been explained in detail in a subsequent section of this chapter. Often, offline backups are considered to be near-line backups.

Offline Backups

Offline backups are the most common form of backup used. These backups are taken on tapes or external hard disks or other media as relevant. Individual system's data can be backed up to external hard disks. Servers and other systems with huge data stored on them may be backed up on tapes using automated tape libraries on which the backups are scheduled. Sometimes backups taken when the systems are offline (not being used) are considered as offline backups, such as a backup taken when no transaction was happening on the database or the database was in offline mode.

Category 2: Based on what goes into the backup

Another way of categorizing the backups is on the basis of what goes into each backup and include full backups, incremental backups, and differential backups.

Full Backups

As the name suggests, full backups back up the entire system and are generally on external media like tapes or external hard disks. These consume a lot of time to back up depending upon the quantum of data to be backed up. Normally, these are taken during the weekends when there are hardly any transactions or very low number of transactions so that they do not adversely impact the performance of the system being backed up. This also ensures that most of the files are backed up. Most of the organizations take these backups weekly but occasionally businesses also conduct a full back up monthly or annually. Weekly backups are usually overwritten the following month. Once the backup is taken, the archive file attribute is set for all the backed up files to enable the system to know that these files are backed up.

Incremental Backups

Incremental backups complement the full backup, but only the files that have changed subsequent to the full backup are backed up as incremental backups. For example, on the Monday following a weekend full backup, only file Z has been changed. So during the incremental backup that occurs Monday night, only file Z will be backed up. Suppose on Tuesday, another two files X and A are changed, only these two changed files are backed up during the incremental backup process. Then again on Wednesday, if the file B is changed, only that file is backed up during the incremental backup process. This process will be carried on until the next full backup is taken.

Differential Backups

Differential backups also complement the full backup, but again only the files that have changed subsequent to the full backup are backed up as incremental backups. However, the difference between incremental backups and differential backups is that differential backups taken on Monday (taking the above example) will back up only file Z whereas on Tuesday it will back up the files Z, X, and A (i.e., all those files changed on Monday and Tuesday or subsequent to full backup). Accordingly, on Wednesday all the files (i.e., files Z, X, A, and B) will be backed up during the differential backup process. Here, the archive file attribute is not reset after the backup of these files is carried out so that they are backed up on the subsequent day also. This process will be carried on until the next full backup is taken.

Different types of backups, such as full backups, incremental backups, differential backups and the relationship among them, are illustrated in Figure 13-1.

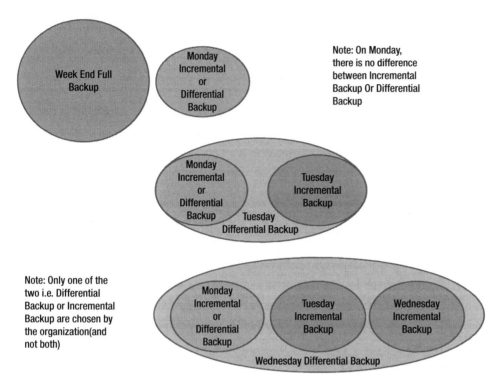

Figure 13-1. *Types of Backups*

Category 3: Based on storage of backups

On the basis of the storage of backups, two possibilities of storage are available: On-site Storage, Off-site storage.

- **On-site Storage:** Backups are stored / preserved on site. Such backups may be on tapes or external hard disks or another backup system where the backup files are dumped.

- **Off-site Storage:** Backups are stored off site. These off-site storage backups may be at some other office / branch of the same organization or with specialized records and data custodians.

Category 4: Based on the extent of the automation of the backups

Different levels of automation are used for backups. On the basis of the extent of automation of the backups, the backups may be categorized as follows:

- **Highly automated backups:** These are through online backup mechanisms like RAID Level 1, RAID Level 15, RAID Level 51, and Server Mirroring.

- **Scheduled and automated backups:** These are scheduled and automated through mechanisms like tape libraries.

- **Manual Backups:** These are manually taken as per a calendar of backups. For example, the month end, year end, and weekend calendar will specify the full backups, and daily calendars will specify the daily incremental or differential backups as per the backup strategy of the organization.

RAID Levels

The following RAID Levels are the most important:[1]

- **RAID Level 0:** This level uses the technique known as Striping and stores data on one large virtual disk consisting of several physical disks. It spreads the data onto several disks. Even though this improves the performance, it does not create redundancy. If any of the constituent disks fails, the entire system fails.

- **RAID Level 1:** This level uses the technique of online mirroring. As transactions happen, while the application writes the data onto a disk or a set of disks, it also mirrors the same data onto another disk or another set of disks. This provides for complete redundancy in the sense that if one disk fails, the system automatically switches onto the corresponding mirrored disk. This is a costly option but works well for critical systems that have zero or minimal tolerance for downtime.

- **RAID Level 2:** This level is hardly used now.

- **RAID Levels 3 & 4:** RAID Levels 3 and 4 are similar except that Level 3 is implemented at byte-level and Level 4 is implemented at block-level. While data is written to several disks constituting one large volume like in Level 0, the parity bit is written to a separate parity drive. This enables redundancy as the data can be reconstituted using the information from the parity drive. However, the risk here is that if the parity drive crashes the entire redundancy is lost. Further, as the parity information is written onto a single parity drive, performance is negatively impacted.

- **RAID Level 5:** This level is almost similar to RAID Levels 3 and 4 except that there are many drives onto which the parity check bits are written, rather than onto a single parity drive. This uses the technique of interleave parity. This provides for higher redundancy, lower single point of failure and higher performance. The crashed disks are possible to be swapped online while the system is still working without the need for the system to be brought down.

- **RAID Level 6:** This level is the same as RAID Level 5 except that this uses two-dimensional parity checks.

Various other RAID Levels have been designed as necessary. Popular among them are RAID Level 10 which uses both the concepts of mirroring as well as spreading or striping of the data across multiple pairs of disks; RAID Level 15 which uses mirroring technique of RAID Level 1 with interleave technique of RAID Level 5; and RAID Level 51 which ensures that all the disks including the parity information is mirrored.

Other Important Fault Tolerance Mechanisms

Some of the other important tolerance mechanisms are:[1]

- **Server Clustering:** A group of servers are clustered to provide high performance as well as provide redundancy. While in good health, all the servers complement each other to provide a better performance. But when one of these servers crashes, the others continue with the work, thus appearing the same as usual to the users, albeit with a reduced performance, which may not be perceivable by the end users most of the time. This system balances the load as well as provides for redundancy in case of failures of individual servers. Server Clustering is illustrated in Figure 13-2.

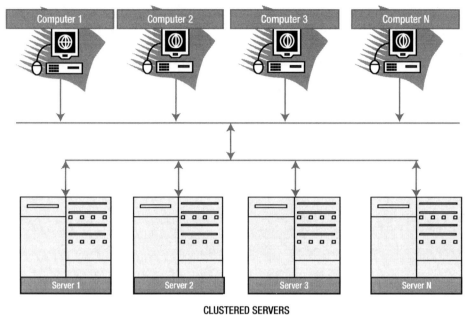

Figure 13-2. *Server Clustering*

- **Electronic Vaulting:** Here the data is transferred to an alternative system (usually at an alternative site) using the batch mode.

- **Remote Journaling:** This is almost similar to Electronic Vaulting except that the transfer of data is not carried out using batch mode, but is done online as and when the transactions happen, so that the alternative site can take over at any point of time if the main site or main server fails, either due to natural disasters or because of other reasons. These sites are connected usually through high speed links to keep both these sites always in sync.

- **Server Mirroring:** Here another server known as the secondary server is deployed. This will help in taking over the running of the system if the primary server fails. The data is usually mirrored between these two systems (i.e., the primary server and the secondary server) using high-speed links. It is possible to roll over to the secondary server without the users being aware of it or the users may be redirected to the secondary servers when the primary server fails. This depends upon the strategy of the organization. Server Mirroring is illustrated in Figure 13-3.

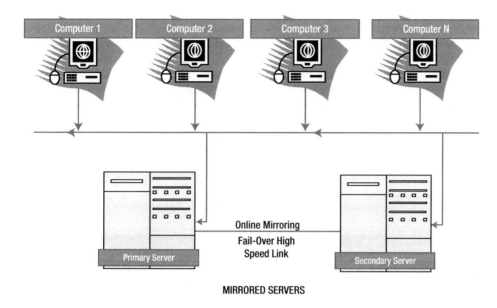

Figure 13-3. *Server Mirroring*

Role of Storage Area Networks (SAN) in providing Backups and Disaster Recovery

Storage Area Networks (SANs) can complement traditional backups as they provide both for backup and recovery. These are high speed, special purpose network devices. They provide for disk mirroring and enable sharing of the data between different servers, thus enabling effective disaster recovery in case of failure of one of the servers or by providing for replication of stored data. Further, the data can be easily migrated from the SANs to other systems. SANs may be relatively costly, but offer an effective and efficient mode of backup and restoration, as well as disaster recovery capability.

Cloud Infrastructure in Backup Strategy

Cloud infrastructure provides for an easy and low-cost backup option to organizations as the cost of public cloud infrastructure is low and continues to decrease as more players enter the field. Organizations need not invest highly in backup hardware, software including tape libraries, tape media, tape storage space, off-site tape storage custodian services, and backup personnel. They now have the option of backing up or replicating the data on to the cloud infrastructure. However, to be successful, the organizations require substantial bandwidth and network speed to connect to the cloud. Further, the correct replication and data backup has to be verified periodically to ensure that the backups of the data are being carried out appropriately. Any issues identified have to be promptly addressed or the data may not be replicated or written to the cloud in case of network connection failures, in which case you need to manually sync the data between the clouds and the current data on the systems. Further, you need to ensure that the backups on the cloud are protected from malicious attacks.

Database Backups

Most of the database systems have provisions for replication of data, physical database backups, and logical database backups. They also provide for cold (offline) and hot (online) backups. Each type of backup has some advantages and some disadvantages. The organization has to effectively study the backup methods available, for each database management system that is deployed and enable only those methods which suit the organization and its backup objectives well. The criteria for such a decision depends upon the size of the database, the transaction load, the criticality of the function performed by the database system, and whether the database has any idle period. Similarly for appropriate data recovery, the methods suggested by the database vendor have to be used.

Backup Strategy

Each organization has to decide on its backup strategy based on the systems it has, the criticality of its business, the criticality of its functions, the criticality of the data it has, and the data loss tolerance an organization has.

Some organizations like banks, financial institutions, e-commerce sites, and online reservation / booking systems may not be able to lose even a single transaction or a portion of the data with respect to their critical systems. If looked at from the availability aspect, this can adversely impact the business of the organization in a significant manner or if taken from the perspective of the integrity of the system, this can bring down the reputation of the organization or can lead to serious confusion. Hence, high availability may be a requirement in those cases.

An organization with no tolerance for data loss or loss of integrity of data must implement such strategies as online mirroring using the relevant RAID technologies, Server Mirroring, or Database Shadowing. Mirroring or Remote Journaling to an alternative hot site can enable a highly critical business to resume business from an alternative site without any business lag.

Again the backups cost money. The cost components are that of backup hardware, backup software, backup media, personnel involved in taking the backups, backup storage costs including the physical and/or logical space used, backup restoration verification costs, and backup offsite storage costs. Hence, the backup strategy has to be worked out by comparing the benefits of backup with respect to the costs. This is not to mean that you need not have backups. But, investments in backups have to be commensurate with the risks the organization is trying to avoid.

Most organizations follow this typical backup strategy:

- They conduct weekly full backups using tapes. These are normally completed on the weekends. These tapes are normally recycled the following month during the corresponding week.

- They also conduct monthly and/or yearly backups which are preserved perpetually.

- In addition to this, they conduct the differential or incremental backups during the week days. The tapes used for the incremental or differential backups are recycled in the subsequent weeks.

Typically backup software (e.g., Acronis True Image, Genie Backup Manager, Symantec Backup Exec – Recovery Manager, etc.,) is used for conducting a backup in a reliable way. There are also many good backup managers available for free. The important part of the backup process is the verification process which checks that the backup has been completed successfully. The backup software should also throw up messages to notify the system administrators about errors, if any, so that these can be handled effectively.

Backup reliability is further ensured through periodic checks on the backup media for their continued usability, as these media are also likely to be prone to faults / issues due to ageing/repeated use or due to environmental conditions to which they are exposed to. As backup media are written on again and again over a period of time, every organization should understand the reliability of such media and for how many 'write' cycles it can be effective or for how long it can be used. This leads us to an effective retirement of aged / faulty media and a program of planned restoration of the media to test the backup and the said media's continued usability.

Primarily, even though backup is that of data which changes as the systems or applications are used, it may also be of system software or application software. Backup may not be effective by simply copying the files. Different types of data, like databases or configuration management system data may have to be backed up using a different method as specified by the corresponding database or utilities, tools, or vendors. Additionally, some of these backups may have to back up the logs internal to these systems. These aspects have to be kept in mind to ensure that the backups are useful for restoration when required.

Restoration Strategy

Restoration from backups may not be effective if the media is not readable when required. It may not be effective if all the files were not backed up during the backup process. This may be due to a faulty backup or media fault. Hence, every organization needs to have a planned restoration strategy to understand the effectiveness of its backups.

The above strategy should be planned and may be carried out on a quarterly basis by identifying which types of backups and which media will be checked into for restoration during this planned exercise. This ensures the following benefits, such as checks for continued suitability and effectiveness of the media used, the continued effectiveness of the backup method, and completeness and correctness of the backups. This strategy should ensure that all the backups work when required for restoration/recovery.

Restorations are also carried out on user requests. Normally a user may accidentally delete a file. Many of us have made a similar mistake. Of course, sometimes recycle bin can come to our rescue but we may realize later that we have accidentally deleted a file that even recycle bins would have emptied. Sometimes, the files may be overwritten by mistake. It is also possible that the file was corrupted because of system issues like abnormal behavior of the system, sudden shutdown of the system, or because of a virus. The only way to restore such files is to go back to the system administrators and request them to restore the files from appropriate backups. This may require the system administrators to go back in the history and locate the appropriate backup file.

If during the week, a file has been accidentally deleted, overwritten, or corrupted, then the file may be possible to be restored through the full backup of last weekend or differential / incremental backups of the current week days depending upon when the file was last modified. If the file was last modified prior to the previous weekend, then the previous weekend's full backup should help. If it was modified during this week, then the differential / incremental backup as applicable should help. If a file created last month was found to be untraceable now and was possibly deleted during this month's first week's abrupt system corruption, the system administrators may have to trace back for the file in the last month's month-end full backup.

Online backups also have to be audited periodically for effectiveness of the backups, including the completeness and correctness. In my experience, backup tools have confirmed that the backups have been completed successfully, but there have been no files physically found on the tapes. This is often due to defective tape.

Important Security Considerations

We highlight here (even though some of them would have been mentioned in the earlier sections) some of the important information security aspects to be considered:

- Backups have to be in encrypted mode (at least for corporations) so that they are not tampered with or misused either by internal employees or by external off-site data custodians or by others during data transmission between on-site and off-site.

- Backups are never missed for any reason.

- The completeness and the correctness of backups are verified invariably and reliably by the backup process so that the backups are useful when required to be used.

- Backups have to be protected against fire threats by preserving them in fire proof cabinets when they are on-site. Similar care has to be taken by the off-site data custodians.

- Backups have to be protected from adverse environmental impacts, such as leaked water, strong electromagnetic field, fungus, and dust.

- Backups have to be protected through appropriate handling from issues such as static electricity (in case of backups in external hard disks, etc.), vibrations / shocks, and dropping.

- Backups have to be securely transferred from on-site to off-site and vice versa.

- Wrong overwriting has to be avoided by appropriate labelling.

- Backup media have to be accounted for so that none of the media are missed; backups are stored and arranged appropriately so that they can be traced easily.

Some Inherent Issues with Backups and Restoration

The following are some of the inherent but important issues with backups and restoration:

- Most of the backups on tapes and other media (other than through online mirroring and high speed storage area networks) are very slow and take significant time to complete the backup. Similarly, these types of backups on tape and similar media also take significant time for restoration. Your disaster recovery efforts have to factor in this restoration time.

- Most of the backup strategies, other than online instant mirroring and high-speed storage area networks, may not be able to restore the data completely in case of data corruption or data loss as there is always time lag between the last backup and the server crash leading to data corruption.

- In case of server crashes, including operating system crash and / or application crash, it is not enough that you have data backup but must also have a clean (non-infected and genuine) copy of the operating system and / or a clean (non-infected and genuine) copy of the application software. You also need to ensure that before the data is restored, the system is brought up-to-date by applying relevant updates / patches both to the operating system and / or to the application, as relevant.

- While restoring, ensure that appropriate data backups are selected and restored from. Otherwise, it will lead to an unnecessary waste of time; particularly after restoration (which takes significant time), you find that you have restored the data from an old backup and not from the one which you were supposed to restore. Furthermore, it is very important to internally / externally label the media appropriately, so that there is no issue in correctly identifying them.

Best Practices Related to Backups and Restoration

We suggest the following best practices in respect to backups and restoration:

- Have a written Backup Policy and Strategy which is understood by all, particularly by the system administrators who are responsible for the backups

- Make it clear to the users as to what information they need to pass on to the system administrators to ensure that the backups do not miss critical systems, files to be backed up (as some of the systems may be deployed at the departmental level too like HR or Finance or some of the directories or file backups are carried out only on a request basis).

- Have the Backup Policy and Strategy after considering the criticality of the business data and systems and after weighing the benefits and the costs of backups. This also takes into consideration the tolerance of the business to the down-time of the systems or adverse impact on business of not having system availability.

- Once the Backup Policy and Strategy is decided, ensure that it is executed without fail. If the systems crash and you lose the data and realize that the backup has not been taken for the past month, your backups taken earlier will be useless and you may not have much recourse.

- Have a periodic restoration plan (like quarterly restoration plan) that specifies which backups have to be restored and which media have to be tested. Again ensure that these plans are invariably executed and the outcome of these plans is recorded. If any media is found to be not readable then it has to be substituted with a good media. Usually the entire restoration has to be carried out or the files selected by the data owners have to be restored to ensure that the backup is effective and restoration is possible.

- Backup policies and strategies are to be revisited and modified as appropriate whenever new systems or applications are added to the organizational IT infrastructure.

- The Backup Management Software has to be configured and used appropriately. The errors thrown up by the backup management software have to be handled appropriately.

- Periodically, the backup media have to be reconciled to ensure that no backup media are missing. If any of the backups are missing, it may lead to an information security breach, as the data can be misused by others if it is not in encrypted properly.

- The transfer of the data backups between the on- and off-site storage facilities should be carried out securely. Usually locked boxes with the key available at the other centers are used for such transfers.

- Media have to be recycled periodically to avoid risks posed by expiration.

- All the media have to be appropriately labelled to understand what it contains, when it was last written on, and a media number to enable the traceability of the media at on-site or off-site facilities.

- Critical backups are to be held in an appropriate environment that is not exposed to high heat, high humidity, or high magnetic field as relevant to the media. The critical backups are to be held in fire-proof cabinets to protect them from fire disasters.

- Permanently archive, into a reliable external media, the currently not required files or files not required for future usage but which may be required from the perspective of the organizational data retention policies because of legal and audit purposes and held securely, thus eliminating the need to unnecessarily store them in the current systems and unnecessarily back them up regularly.

- Carry out regular periodic audits of the backup and restoration practices and identify the weaknesses in the current backup policies. Ensure that the policies are modified appropriately to address the issues found.

Introduction to Cloud Computing

Clouds or cloud computing are the hotly debated topic of late, drawing divergent views, with many people strongly supporting them because of their benefits. At the same time, many oppose them or not accept them because of the apprehensions related to security and privacy. Cloud technology itself is evolving and many of the aspects are yet unclear. Visibility into many of the cloud infrastructure and significant transparency related to them is yet to be achieved. All these have led to prime concern among the organizations that want to go on to cloud but are holding back because of these concerns.

Of course, the world is excited about the prospects of cloud computing. Individuals, enjoy the benefits of cloud computing as they are not very worried about the security concerns or may not be aware of the security issues as they presume that the cloud provider, being a professional entity, would have taken care of all these aspects. However, corporations and legal entities must weigh the benefits against the risks cautiously as they are accountable to their shareholders, customers, and partners. Despite the hype around cloud computing, it has not become as popular as expected as many experts are highlighting the security, privacy, and other concerns which need to be addressed effectively.

What is Cloud Computing?

In lay terms, cloud computing is the provision to use applications, platforms, and infrastructure from a third party without upfront investment but with the provision to pay as you use, while at the same time, providing for flexibility to increase or decrease the usage depending upon the organizational necessities or requirements. Definitely, the outright benefits are that you need not put up a huge upfront investment to create the infrastructure or purchase the tools for development. You can acquire the rights to use them without any initial investment, but pay for them based on the usage. You can also increase the usage by opting for additional infrastructure, additional tools for development, or an additional number of applications or facilities for adding more users to use the current applications.

The beauty of cloud computing is that the users can make use of the services from the cloud using their web browsers, thin clients, or even equipment like smartphones and tablets. They do not require any sophisticated tools or complicated environment or utilities to utilize the cloud services.

Cloud computing can definitely be a boon for small organizations carrying out non-critical business, where there is little sensitive information and few transactions. They may be okay with the occasional non-availability of connectivity, or occasional breaches of data, as the benefits outweigh the risks. Hence, security may not be of much concern for such smaller organizations. However, they also need to be concerned and cautious about the storage of privacy and personal information related to their customers, as they too have to follow the laws and regulations of the region and cannot shirk their responsibility in this regard. Further, organizations can choose to use cloud infrastructure only for those applications and those data which are not sensitive.

However, most of the corporations who engage with their competitors for better market share, who have lots of confidential proprietary or intellectual property rights information, cloud computing is unacceptable in its current form. The risks related to security and privacy issues including confidentiality, integrity, authenticity, authorization, privacy, and availability need to be weighed against the benefits cautiously. None of these issues can be taken lightly, in spite of the cost effectiveness or the flexibility accorded.

Therefore, it is necessary for the organizations to study the offering by the cloud providers in detail, considering the following information:

- the scope and benefits of the offering, and how it impacts their business, customers, and partners,

- the terms and conditions of the offer, including the responsibilities the cloud provider is undertaking and the responsibilities the cloud provider is passing on to the cloud consumer,

- the legal implications of the usage of cloud,

- the technology employed by the cloud provider,

- the transparency provided by the cloud provider,

- how the cloud provider fulfils the demands of his consumer base,

- how the cloud provider governs or manages the infrastructure,

- how the changes are managed, and

- how the transition from one cloud provider to the other is possible.

There are many more questions to be evaluated based on the needs of the organization.

Fundamentals of Cloud Computing

What is cloud computing? "Cloud computing is a model for enabling ubiquitous, convenient, on-demand network access to a shared pool of configurable computing resources (e.g., networks, servers, storage, applications, and services) that can be rapidly provisioned and released with minimal management effort or service provider interaction".[1]

Some of the words in the above definition are very interesting. Most of the words in the definition are self-explanatory except possibly the word "ubiquitous" that means all pervasive or universal. Yes, as we can find the real clouds everywhere, so the cloud infrastructure can be anywhere. While the words "ubiquitous," "convenient," "on-demand," "configurable," "rapidly provisioned or released," and "minimal management effort or service provider interaction" highlight the benefits of the cloud, according to our opinion, the words to be watched carefully are "ubiquitous," "shared pool," "configurable resources," and "minimal management effort or service provider interaction" as these also indicate the need for higher security consideration.

Cloud computing can be discussed around its three Service Models and four Deployment Models.[1] The three Cloud Service Models are:[1]

- Software as a Service (SaaS)

- Platform as a Service (PaaS)

- Infrastructure as a Service (IaaS)

The four Deployment Models are:[1]

- Private Cloud

- Public Cloud

- Community Cloud

- Hybrid Cloud

Cloud Service Models

As mentioned previously there are three different Cloud Service Models: Software as a Service (SaaS), Platform as a Service (PaaS), and Infrastructure as a Service (IaaS). The details of each of these and the interaction among them are explained in the following section.

Software as a Service (SaaS)

Software applications or products are developed by different vendor organizations by investing substantially in the conceptualization, research, design, development, and testing. The development process would not have been smooth. They would have gone through many dilemmas in the process, including:

- whether to go in for all functionalities planned upfront or to develop and release the product with features in phases;

- which technology to go in for – whether cheaper or costlier, whether simple or complicated;

- which operating system to be chosen as the platform for the application – whether open source like Linux or the popular one like Windows;

- who should be the targeted users; what factors like the usability, scalability, flexibility, response times, maintainability, portability, etc. to be considered (of course, unfortunately, most of the times security as a factor is hardly considered);

- whether to deploy the new resources to develop it or to hire experienced people to develop it.

Considering the infrastructure costs, development tool licensing costs, and human resources salary the total investment, often tends to be substantial. Hence, the pricing of the product will also be substantial unless the product is targeted for mass market. Added to that, the required marketing and sales efforts are huge and they cost significantly. At the end of all these, it is difficult to still say whether the product will be successfully sold and if successfully sold, whether it will be a successful product that will continue to be in demand or by the time the product comes out in the market, some other competitor has come up with a better product and may be, with even better pricing.

The cloud-based Software as a Service (SaaS) has become a handy tool for application providers to rent out their software applications by hosting them on the cloud. Through this, they can make the software application readily available to organizations and users on demand. They can also attract more users as the price per user comes down substantially. Further, enabling additional instances of the same application software or installation of software application additionally for a particular organization is very easy for the vendor organization. This brings down the total cost of marketing, sales, installation, and maintenance of the application software. Again, it is very easy for such vendors to patch / update the software applications in case of any security issues or bugs. Further, because of the pay-as-you-use mode which is applied to the customers, the vendor organizations get a steady stream of revenues instead of the ups and down in the revenue realization because of the traditional sales efforts.

For the users, it is cost effective as the cost of renting is comparatively less than the cost of outright purchase. Further, they will pay as they use and not upfront. They can also increase and decrease the number of users as they scale higher thus not locking up funds in unused software application licenses. More importantly, they need not have dedicated servers and other infrastructure to install and use such software applications in-house. In addition, most of the time, the consumer just has to provide the user with a web browser or a thin client interface. The end user platforms can be, for the most part, smartphones or tablets. This makes the entire proposition very attractive to the consumer organizations.

Software as a Service (SaaS) is defined as: "The capability provided to the consumer is to use the provider's applications running on a cloud infrastructure. The applications are accessible from various client devices through either a thin client interface, such as a web browser (e.g., web-based email), or a program interface. The consumer does not manage or control the underlying cloud infrastructure including network, servers, operating systems, storage, or even individual application capabilities, with the possible exception of limited user- specific application configuration settings".[1]

The advantage of SaaS is that the control on the appropriate configuration of applications lies with the cloud consumer. Other than this, most of the control, from the network to the servers to the operating systems, lies with the cloud provider. Some of the examples of SaaS are SalesForce.com, QuickBooks, Zoho Office Suite, justcloud.com, Dropbox, and many more similar applications.

Platform as a Service (PaaS)

PaaS is "The capability provided to the consumer is to deploy onto the cloud infrastructure consumer-created or acquired applications created using programming languages, libraries, services, and tools supported by the provider. The consumer does not manage or control the underlying cloud infrastructure including network, servers, operating systems, or storage, but has control over the deployed applications and possibly configuration settings for the application-hosting environment."[1]

Many of the organizations in the IT industry are in the business of developing software frameworks or software application products, utilities, or tools. They require the infrastructure to develop these software applications, design and development tools, and testing tools to test their output. All these are costly and when added to the cost of human resources, add up to a significant cost to organizations. This has sometimes led companies to use pirated developmental tools which in turn have led to bugs in the outputs, security issues, and violation of laws.

PaaS allows organizations to rent the design, development, and testing platforms, software, and utilities at significantly less cost and often in a pay-per-use structure of payment, At any point of time, depending upon the need, they can move from one platform to another platform if they change course. This would have been possible only at additional cost in a traditional scenario where the organizations have to purchase the design and development frameworks / tools. Also, the number of resources using such tools can be increased or decreased on an as needed basis.

Another significant advantage is that some of the design and development tools which are new and which could not have been used by the organizations because of the exorbitant costs now become affordable to the consumer organization. These advantages are significant particularly for smaller organizations with limited funding and resources.

As mentioned in the definition, PaaS may also be used to deploy acquired applications in addition to the consumer created applications. Here, the application developer does not have much control over the underlying environment except for setting configurations on application hosting environment and full control over deployed applications. All other controls on the entire underlying infrastructure, including the storage, lie with the cloud provider. Sometimes, this may constrain the designers and developers to use the provided infrastructure and thus compromise even though they wanted a better underlying infrastructure.

Some of the examples of PaaS are Force.com platform, Windows Azure Platform, Google Apps, and Google Apps Engine.

Infrastructure as a Service (IaaS)

IaaS is defined as: "The capability provided to the consumer is to provision processing, storage, networks, and other fundamental computing resources where the consumer is able to deploy and run arbitrary software, which can include operating systems and applications. The consumer does not manage or control the underlying cloud infrastructure but has control over operating systems, storage, and deployed applications; and possibly limited control of select networking components (e.g., host firewalls)."[1]

Every organization usually invests heavily in data centers wherein servers are installed, servers are connected through networks, desktops and laptops are installed with the corresponding client software, other infrastructure like physical security, logical security including access control is implemented. The required support infrastructure like IT Managers to System Administrators to support vendors to support systems like generators, UPS, and other backup mechanisms are deployed. All these come at a significant capital expenditure upfront and even more cost to maintain.

IaaS comes in handy here as it eliminates the investment in the infrastructure in data centers, servers, high-end network equipment, storage equipment, and supporting utility infrastructure including physical security like access control. Again, the pay as you use comes in handy to the users. In the traditional scenario, once the investment is made by the organization, it is stuck to it even when the business decreases whereas in the cloud infrastructure scenario, it can requisition additional infrastructure on an as needed basis and release unused or additional infrastructure if the business decreases. This provides for significant financial leverage to the organization. Further, you need not have sophisticated personnel to maintain your IT infrastructure, physically and logically support your systems. You are also less likely to be hit by malicious infections as you have very lean IT infrastructure on your premises. Further, most of the infrastructure management headache is taken over by the cloud provider. On the other hand, if the cloud gets a malicious infection you are hit significantly as such infection can spread quickly to your internal organization unless the cloud provider has significant security controls built into the infrastructure.

With IaaS, organizations have very limited control over the underlying core infrastructure except the operating systems, the applications deployed thereon and related storage most of the times. Virtualization has enabled the entire game of cloud infrastructure (IaaS) provision. A single physical server (i.e., hardware) is logically partitioned to many different virtual servers and provisioned to various consumer organizations depending upon their requirement. A high number of servers are horizontally deployed to provide for large requirements of customers, at the same time, catering to the smaller requirements from smaller organizations, thus building a huge capacity by the cloud provider.

Basically, in this type of cloud provision, the control over Virtual Machine Monitor (VMM), underlying hardware (i.e., physical infrastructure), and network infrastructure lies with the cloud provider. However, depending upon the cloud deployment models chosen by the organization, controls that are available with the consumer organization may vary substantially.

Some of the examples of IaaS are: Amazon Elastic Compute Cloud, RackSpace Cloud, Eucalyptus, and GoGrid.

The various types of cloud service models, namely SaaS, PaaS, and IaaS, and the relationship among them from the control perspective of both customer and vendor, are illustrated in Figure 13-4.

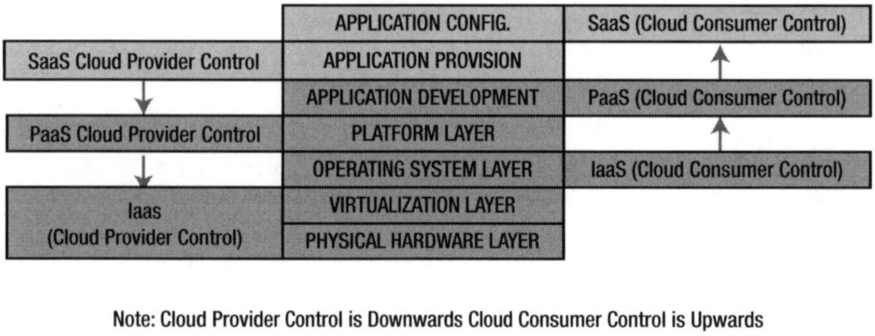

	APPLICATION CONFIG.	SaaS (Cloud Consumer Control)
SaaS Cloud Provider Control	APPLICATION PROVISION	↑
↓	APPLICATION DEVELOPMENT	PaaS (Cloud Consumer Control)
PaaS Cloud Provider Control	PLATFORM LAYER	↑
↓	OPERATING SYSTEM LAYER	IaaS (Cloud Consumer Control)
Iaas (Cloud Provider Control)	VIRTUALIZATION LAYER	
	PHYSICAL HARDWARE LAYER	

Note: Cloud Provider Control is Downwards Cloud Consumer Control is Upwards

Figure 13-4. *Cloud Computing Service Models Structure*

Important Benefits of Cloud Computing

Cloud computing offers plenty of important benefits. We discuss just a few of them here in the following section.[2]

Upfront Capital Expenditure (CAPEX) versus Pay as you use Operational Expenditure (OPEX)

In the cloud environment, the consumer organization is not required to make huge capital investments or payments upfront. The payment is made by the consumer organization depending on the services it needs and hence the payment is staggered and is made periodically, allowing for significant financial advantages to the organization.

Elasticity or Flexibility

The organizational business and transaction load increases or decreases over time. In the cloud environment, the consumer organization has the flexibility to increase or reduce the usage, demand additional infrastructure, storage, or application usage as their needs change. This flexibility eliminates the need for the organization to provide for the infrastructure to cater to the peak loads or predicted increased business. Further, changes can be made by the consumer in the cloud environment (often without the intervention of the cloud provider) whereas the additional infrastructure ramp up in the traditional way would take substantial lead time.

Reduced need for specialized resources and maintenance services

In the traditional setup, the organization requires expert staff like IT managers and system administrators to run the data centers and relies on outside vendors for maintenance. However, in the cloud environment, most of these are the responsibilities of the cloud provider (of course, the extent depends upon the cloud type used by the consumer organization), which saves the organization time and money.

On-Demand Self-Service Mode versus Well-Planned Time-Consuming Ramp Up

In the traditional setup, the addition of a new facility or capability required significant planning, which is often stressful and necessitated extensive collaboration with internal and external resources. However, in the cloud environment, the additional infrastructure, storage, or other capabilities can be requisitioned on demand, through self-service, without even the intervention of the cloud provider.

Redundancy and Resilience versus Single Points of Failure

Traditional IT infrastructure is mostly prone to single points of failure as most of the applications are deployed on a server and backups are taken in a traditional way through costly mechanisms like online mirroring or server mirroring. In cloud environment, the virtualization across many VMs and the usage of storage equipment with better capability can provide for better redundancy and resilience than the traditional systems.

Cost of traditional DRP and BCP versus the DRP & BCP through Cloud Environment

Traditional IT infrastructure requires elaborate arrangements for DRP & BCP including costly hot / warm / alternative sites, equipped with relevant infrastructure depending upon the business criticality and infrastructure criticality. Further, these have to be revisited and maintained to be effective in case of need. However, cloud environments permit cheaper, more reliable, and easier to implement and use DRP & BCP mechanisms.

Ease of use on the Cloud Environment

Access to and use of the cloud environment is available through simple mechanisms like Web browsers, thin client interfaces, or simple interfaces provided by the cloud provider, whereas traditional client server applications require significant learning on the part of the users for most of the applications.

Important Enablers of Cloud Computing

Many technological developments have enabled cloud computing. Some of the important ones are:[2]

- **Internet:** Most of the recent advances in technology can be attributed to the Internet which enables connectivity from one system to any other system across the globe. This connectivity has enabled any organization from anywhere to connect to the cloud infrastructure deployed somewhere else.

- **Network Bandwidth and Reliability:** The next important advancement is the availability of higher network bandwidth at a lower cost. This has enabled the organizations to connect to the cloud environment using web browsers and thin clients, yet supporting the required performance across the network in spite of requests being pumped into the cloud and output being pumped down the network channel. Further, high speed and highly reliable network equipment provide requisite support to this end.

- **Server Virtualization:** Server virtualization is the most important enabler of the cloud. The slicing of the physical hardware into virtual machines and enabling different users to use the same physical equipment transparently and without impacting each other is the biggest contribution of the virtualization. Cloud computing would not have been possible without the virtualization. These are assisted by virtual network communications.

- **Cheaper and reliable equipment:** The cost of hardware, including the servers to hard disks to solid state devices to memories to peripherals has gone down year after year. At the same time, reliability of this equipment has gone up significantly. These two have enabled a huge cloud infrastructure to be created at a cheaper cost and made available at a cheaper price to the users.

- **Standardization:** Tremendous standardization efforts have been carried out across the globe to ensure better interoperability of hardware. Protocols have been well defined to enable hardware / communication / network equipment manufacturers to appropriately design their equipment. This standardization effort has led to significant interoperability among different hardware, leading to the possibility of large-scale deployment of the cloud infrastructure.

- **Advancement in Technology:** Advances in technology include: clustering of the computers enabling higher computing power; increased storage capability enabled through network technologies like Storage Area Networks (SANs); high-speed links enabling online mirroring; and Web technologies like Web 2.0 and Web services have propelled cloud computing capability.

Four Cloud Deployment Models

Organizations have different needs for cloud services based on the criticality of the applications, sensitivity of data, speed of servicing the requests, safety related aspects, customer requirements, and security requirements. One organization may have two different types of deployment of cloud models applicable to different segments or groups or for different applications within their organization running at the same time.[2&4]

The four Cloud Deployment Models are: Private Cloud, Public Cloud, Community Cloud, and Hybrid Cloud. Each of these deployments is discussed in the following sections.

Various Cloud Deployment Models and how they relate to other types of Cloud Deployment Models are illustrated in Figure 13-5.

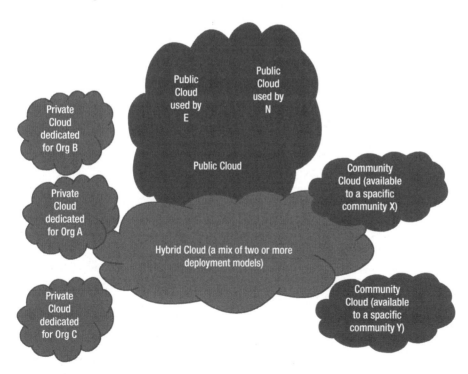

Figure 13-5. *Deployment Model Options*

Private Cloud

A private cloud is dedicated and set up for a particular cloud consumer based on their unique high-security needs. However, private cloud comes only at high capital investment as well as high maintenance cost. A private cloud ensures high availability, confidentiality of the data, and complete integrity of the data. A private cloud allows the user to realize the benefits of cloud computing, such as avoiding upfront high capital expenditure, pay as you use model, best in class applications, high end technology, and large and fast storage capability without the security risks of a public cloud environment.

Of course, as this private cloud is dedicated to the cloud consumer and designed as per the requirements / specifications of the cloud consumer, it is relatively costly compared to the other cloud deployment models.

The advantage of this model is that the cloud consumer still has significant control over the cloud infrastructure and can negotiate and agree on clear terms and conditions with the cloud provider, including the security level requirements. The security in this type can be demanded by the cloud consumer and can be provided by the cloud provider.

Public Cloud

Unlike the private cloud, the public cloud is the cheapest option available on the cloud infrastructure and it is available to everybody. Here, the cloud provider leverages upon the huge infrastructure which he can share with a large number of customers as he deems fit. While these are cheaper, the terms and conditions are mostly unilaterally decided by the cloud provider and the cloud consumer has very little say in this. The cloud consumer does not have much control over the cloud provider. Little significant responsibility is assumed by the cloud provider either on the availability or on the security of the information. Hence, the cloud consumer is at the mercy of the situation or the cloud provider most of the time. A public cloud is best for new organizations with no critical data that are looking for a cost-effective solution. Of course, cloud consumers can request higher service levels and higher assurance but these come at a higher cost and still may not be appropriately serviced. The advantage this provides for the smaller organization is the expertise of the cloud provider which a smaller cloud consumer may not have.

As multiple customers co-exist on the cloud, it may be difficult to monitor the activities of each of these individual customers and hence it is highly difficult and impractical for the most part for the cloud provider to assure high security in this type of deployment model.

Community Cloud

These clouds are set up for collaborative work between the organizations belonging to a particular community like health care, government organizations, or social service organizations with shared objectives. These clouds are set up by the community for use by the organizations within the community. These may be managed by one or more of the organizations belonging to the community or may be managed by a designated outsourced agency or a third-party cloud provider. The collaborative set up of such a cloud brings down the cost of such an infrastructure to each organization while bringing the benefits of cloud to all the participants. However, information security may be still a concern as many organizations will be using the cloud and the cloud provider may not have the necessary security expertise. Also, the capability and strength of such a cloud depends upon the capability of those who design and maintain it and the infrastructure they chose to support it.

Hybrid Cloud

An organization may use a hybrid cloud, which is a combination of any of the above three deployment models (Private Cloud, Public Cloud, and Community Cloud). Depending upon the different purposes for which the cloud infrastructure is to be used, different deployment models may be used by a cloud consumer. These may be requisitioned from different cloud providers. Highly critical and highly confidential applications may go on to private cloud while non-critical, non-sensitive, generic applications may go on to public cloud and community collaborations may be serviced through community clouds.

Main Security and Privacy Concerns of Cloud Computing

While the benefits are very attractive, security concerns are also significant. Some of the important security concerns are described in the following section.

Compliance

Various countries have various privacy, statutory, and regulatory requirements. These, when it comes to IT and related fields, are still being strengthened. Nobody can afford to violate the laws of the land (both the laws of the land to where it belongs and from where it operates). Violations of these legal requirements can lead the organizations to severe penalty and may also risk the closure of their business. These may be in addition to the loss of reputation and other risks. For example, think of a situation: US export laws prohibit a nuclear reactor design, high end encryption technology to be exported to trade restricted countries. In a public cloud environment, you may not know where the data will reside. If the capacity is requisitioned from China, your data which is not allowed to be exported to the trade restricted country China, is residing in China on the cloud!! Your employees, your third-party service providers may abuse the cloud infrastructure and use it for their own or unethical or immoral purposes like pornography, racial abuse, or extortion. As the monitoring, either by the cloud provider or by yourself, may be very less, this may risk your organization as a violator of the laws!!

Lack of Segregation of Duties

In case of in-house systems, most of the duties are well segregated. For example: the accounting personnel or payment authorizers are never the system administrators, application developers are not the system administrators, and so on. In the cloud environment, you do not know who is taking care of what responsibility. It is possible that the same resource is responsible for many aspects. This provides or exposes the cloud consumer to a significant risk. Many of these frauds, if committed by such resources, may come to light only very late or may not come to light at all!!

Complexity of the Cloud Computing System[2]

The cloud computing system is a system of interconnected systems and a large number of components and sub-components. This leads to high complexity. Any infection anywhere or any system or subsystem or component failure because of any reasons, including security flaws or malfunctioning etc., can lead to substantial impact on the availability, confidentiality and integrity of the cloud computing services itself. Further, a cloud computing system is provisioned by a cloud provider by using the services from many other parties. Some part of the entire system would have been further outsourced. This may vary from one cloud provider to the other. The failure or negligence or mistake of one party can also trigger substantial impact on the availability, confidentiality and integrity of cloud computing facility itself. Further, even though significant standardization efforts are being driven, there may still be known or unknown interoperability issues between various systems or subsystems or components. Also, the proprietary application programming interface provided by the cloud provider can also throw up the challenge of understanding and implementing the security.[2] All these can put the cloud consumers in a disadvantageous position if any anticipated or unanticipated lapse / failure / disruption / issue happens.

Shared Multi-tenant Environment[2]

The cloud computing environment provides for usage of the same physical environment by multiple unrelated organizations. One consumer infrastructure is separated from the other consumer infrastructure only virtually / logically. With the increased or newer means of malicious attacks being explored and brought up day-in and day-out and any attackers with cloud tenancy, intentionally trying to exploit the loopholes / flaws / errors, they can create significant availability, confidentiality and integrity issues to other consumers. Again, the cloud providers may not be able to monitor all the activities happening within the cloud, thus risking other consumers.

Internet and Internet Facing Applications[2]

The access to the cloud is through the internet. The availability or non-availability of internet link or degradation of the internet link performance can pose problems for the cloud consumers. These may degrade the performance of access or deny the access to the required services on the cloud. Further, each cloud consumer organization uses many internet facing applications to manage the cloud like configuring the applications or setup on the cloud or to transact on the data on the cloud or to provision for additional services / additional infrastructure etc. One of the important components of such access is Client Web Browsers. Unless these or any other internet facing applications are very secure and maintained very securely by conscious and appropriate configuring / patching / updates, there is a high chance of the cloud consumer being least protected. Further, if the cloud provider himself uses the remote administrative facilities to service clients or to maintain the infrastructure, this also can pose substantial threats to the cloud consumers unless appropriate care is taken by the cloud provider.

Control of the Cloud Consumer on the Cloud Environment[2]

On the cloud computing environment, the control of the cloud consumer depends upon the cloud service model as well as cloud deployment model. The lowest control lies with the cloud consumer when he is opting for SaaS on the public cloud. When he is opting for the IaaS on the private cloud, he has the highest control. The organizational objectives of the usage of cloud computing, organizational security requirements including those imposed on them, by their customers, and through the legal requirements have to be evaluated appropriately and made by the cloud consumer.

Types of Agreements related to Service Levels and Privacy with the Cloud Provider

There may be various agreements signed off between the cloud provider and the cloud consumer. Some of them are Service Level Agreements (agreeing on some service levels assured by the cloud provider to the cloud consumer), privacy agreements, and acceptable use policy (which usually detail do's, and don'ts on the part of the cloud consumer and their users). Data ownerships also have to be explicitly agreed between the cloud provider and the cloud consumer to avoid any confusions / issues. This is absolutely required to ensure that the intellectual property rights and proprietary information of the cloud consumer organization. There may be many more agreements depending upon the context. In case of public cloud, normally, the agreements between the cloud provider and the cloud consumer provides for unilateral conditions imposed by the cloud provider. These conditions can also be unilaterally modified by the cloud provider at any time. The cloud consumer has to specifically request for and agree on the service levels, privacy requirements and other security requirements at a higher cost if the cloud consumer wants them absolutely. This has to be understood clearly by the cloud consumer organizations and has to be appropriately handled by them. Otherwise, the cloud consumer may be at the mercy of the cloud provider and may not be protected appropriately.

Data Management and Data Protection[2]

In the cloud computing environment, the same infrastructure is allocated / assigned to another cloud consumer when released by the earlier cloud consumer. If the data is not sanitized and cleaned up completely, which can lead to the retrieval of the data through advanced technologies, there is a potential threat of sensitive data theft / misuse by others. Further, a cloud consumer's data may be concentrated on the cloud, providing for an appropriate attack surface to the attackers. Also, because of the technical complexities, the data isolation between various cloud consumers may be at risk and one cloud consumer's data may be exposed accidentally to another cloud consumer. This is to be explicitly checked with the cloud provider so that the cloud consumer is assured of the relevant controls.

Insider Threats

Insider threats are still one of the significant risks in any system which should not to be discounted. However, it can get accentuated on the cloud computing environment because of the lack of effective organizational control over the services or control mechanisms like review of logs / audit trails etc. On the cloud computing environment, there is possibly more need for the cloud consumer organizations to ensure logging of the user / administrative activities and audit trails to the applications. Further, these logs / audit trails have to be analyzed to understand if there are any insider threats.

Security Issues on account of multiple levels

A cloud infrastructure is built up of multiple levels and work through interfaces between them. This may pose additional threats and to counter this issue, multiple security layers may have to be deployed, as appropriate, to provide for adequate security.

Physical security issues related to Cloud Computing environment

As discussed earlier, the cloud infrastructure is spread over multiple data centers and multiple locations. All these centers and the infrastructure have to be physically protected. A compromise in one of the centers can potentially nullify the physical security controls exercised at other places.

Cloud Applications Security

The cloud applications used by the cloud consumers have to be tested for all the vulnerabilities that may exist like SQL Injection, and Buffer Overflows as these are still relevant on the cloud computing environment. Secure Design and Development practices on the part of the application creators and applications providers have to be checked, ensured either directly or through a third-party assurance provider mechanisms like certification agencies. Otherwise, while you may be saving cost, you may be prone to more issues related to availability, confidentiality and integrity which also risk the reputation of your organization and place your customers in an awkward position.

Threats on account of Virtual Environment[3]

The virtual machine (VM) instances created by the cloud provider to service its cloud consumers may itself create the risks. It may be possible to monitor and spy one of the virtual machines by another. Also, it may be possible to monitor and spy on the virtual machines from the host. Malicious infection of one VM may spread to the other. Data transfer between one VM to the other related VM itself may be attacked. There may be a possibility of a back door on VM affecting the security adversely because of covert channels between guest operating system and the host. Further, the VMMs like Hypervisor and Xen are so complicated that they may have some flaws which may compromise the security of the cloud environment. Bugs, defects, and other security flaws in any component of the host system including the VMM or VM or the guest operating system etc. can compromise the overall security of the cloud computing environment.

Encryption and Key Management

Most of the communications between consumer interfacing tools or mechanisms to the cloud computing environment is encrypted. However, encryption is only as good as the encryption method used and the strength of the encryption keys. If the keys are not strong or if the secrecy of the keys is not maintained, it exposes the cloud consumer to high risks. Further, most of the applications require the data to be decrypted before further processing or computing, which may increase the possibility of exposure of sensitive data.

We have highlighted the above risks which are primarily applicable to the cloud computing environment. This list may not be exhaustive and comprehensive. Further, many other risks, vulnerabilities which are applicable to VMs, Operating Systems, Host Hardware, Networks, and Application software are still applicable to the cloud computing environment and need to be considered appropriately. These may be malware infection threats, man-in-the-middle attacks, sniffing, spoofing, session hijacking, command injection, buffer overflows, credentials hacking, and password cracking. Similarly, defects / bugs and errors in any of these can always expose the cloud computing environment to compromises / attacks.

Some Mechanisms to address the Security and Privacy Concerns in Cloud Computing Environment

The cloud providers, as well as the cloud consumers, are learning from current issues / concerns and current deployments of the cloud computing environment. Many standardization efforts and best practices are being formulated and put in place. However, there are still plenty of risks / vulnerabilities which can adversely impact security, privacy, and legal requirements and affect the cloud consumers significantly. Following are some of the mechanisms which need to be addressed to handle / contain the security, privacy and legal concerns:[2]

Understand the Cloud Computing environment and protect yourself

Each Cloud Consumer has to understand the services provided by the cloud provider thoroughly, including how the security, privacy and legal considerations are handled effectively by the cloud provider organizations. Further, the data ownership issues, privacy, security, and legal issues have to be explicitly agreed upon through comprehensive legal agreements between the cloud provider and cloud consumer.

Understand the Technical Competence and segregation of duties of the Cloud Provider

The cloud consumer has to make efforts to understand the technical competence of the cloud provider and ensure that they have experienced staff not only in technical expertise related to infrastructure, but also have competent staff related to information security. Further, segregation of duties among the cloud provider staff is very important to ensure that all the powers are not concentrated with the same role, so that there is no possibility of misusing a client's data for malicious purposes. Such expectations / requirements can explicitly be agreed with the cloud provider by the cloud consumer and made part of the agreement between them. As per our views, this should also be considered by the cloud provider, to safeguard their reputation, even when not explicitly requested by the consumers.

Protection against Technical Vulnerabilities and Malicious Attacks

Each cloud consumer has to be aware of the mechanisms the cloud provider has put in place to understand the technical vulnerabilities, keep track of the ongoing technical vulnerabilities and malicious attacks, and proactively take such actions that are required to ensure security and privacy of the data of the cloud consumer. Another related aspect is that the cloud providers need to be transparent to the cloud consumers, without delay, about the security and privacy breaches observed by them at any point of time. This will enable them to gain the confidence of the cloud consumers. Also, appropriate Incident Response Mechanisms have to be instituted and followed by the cloud providers.

Regular Hardening and Appropriate Configurations of the Cloud Computing Environment

Depending upon whose responsibility it is (depends upon the cloud computing services used and the cloud service deployment model) both the cloud provider and the cloud consumers have to take comprehensive steps to ensure appropriate settings / configurations, hardening of the environment, appropriate design and development, appropriate interoperability, and adequate testing. These should include right from Virtual Machine Monitor to Virtual Machines to Guest Operating Systems to Applications. Further, all cloud interfacing mechanisms, including Web browsers, have to be well configured and well protected against malicious attacks. The cloud providers have to ensure that the back to back commitments from other providers / other vendors, including outsourced vendors / other partners, are ensured so that availability, confidentiality, and integrity of the cloud consumer data including authentication, authorization are achieved.

Data Protection

Cloud providers have to ensure that sufficient steps are built in their systems and procedures to ensure that the data of different cloud consumers are well insulated / isolated from each other and the data is sanitized appropriately when the reallocation of resources are made from one cloud consumer to the other. The cloud consumers also have to ensure that all their valuable data is not consolidated at one place on the cloud so that it becomes a target for the attackers.

Encryption

Appropriate encryption mechanisms have to be used with strong encryption keys while authenticating to the cloud infrastructure and also while getting the response back. The mechanisms have to be built by both the cloud provider and the cloud consumer to ensure that the encryption keys are held secret. Similarly, the data stored on the cloud computing environment has to be held encrypted. When decrypted for usage or processing purposes, the data needs to be well protected by appropriate complementary mechanisms.

Good Governance Mechanisms

Both the cloud providers and the cloud consumers have to set up good governance mechanisms to ensure that there is visibility, transparency, and mutual trust within their individual organizations and all other stakeholders.

Compliance

Compliance requirements have to be well understood and well-articulated by the cloud consumer organizations and ensured by the cloud providers. The transparency and visibility to the cloud consumer has to be provided by the cloud provider in this regard, including the location of the storage of the data of the cloud consumer (as applicable). Otherwise, compliance will be a big issue for the cloud consumers.

Logging and Auditing

Logging of various important activities including those of the administrators has to be logged / audited by those who are responsible for the same. It is not enough that these are only logged, but also are analyzed to ensure that there are no malicious activities / attacks already perpetrated or are being planned.

Patching / Updating

All the components of the cloud computing environment, including the host systems to the network components to the operating systems to applications have to be patched and maintained daily by those who are responsible.

Application Design and Development

All the applications which are provided or deployed on the cloud computing environment have to be appropriately designed and developed using secure design and development concepts. All the typical vulnerabilities like non-validated inputs leading to various attacks, possible defects / bugs have to be avoided by secure design, development and comprehensive testing, configuration management, release, and deployment practices.

Physical Security

All the cloud computing facilities have to be physically secured with appropriate measures throughout the cloud computing facilities.

Strong Access Controls

Strong access controls need to be built by the organizations that have their applications and data on the cloud computing environment. Depending upon the risks, these may be through multi-factor authentication or through other relevant mechanisms. Otherwise, security of the applications and data will only be a myth.

Backups

There should be well planned backup mechanisms deployed to ensure availability in case of exigencies. They still cannot be done away with.

Third-Party Certifications / Auditing

The cloud providers have to obtain third party certifications or agree for / arrange for strict third-party auditing of their cloud computing environment. The transparency has to be provided to the cloud consumers and strict and immediate actions have to be taken, without fail, on any findings.

Chapter Summary

- We introduced the data backups and cloud computing. We looked into how both these topics, even though they can be treated as distinct subjects, complement each other. The cloud computing environment provides for backups and backups can be enabled through cloud computing. We also highlighted as to how the data backups provide for availability while cloud computing brings out new avenues of hopes as far as cost reduction is considered, etc.

- We examined the concept of data backups, highlighted the need for backups, and discussed the dangers of not conducting regular data backups. We looked at how the data backups help us out in case of issues like crash of servers, loss of integrity of data, and corruption of data.

- We explored various categorization of the data backups. We differentiated between online backups, near-line backups, offline backups, on-site backups, off-site backups, automated backups, and manual backups. We also looked into some of the enablers of these backups. In this context, we explored RAID, server mirroring, and electronic vaulting, remote journaling. We also highlighted the fact that there may be different methods of data backups required in the context of database systems.

- We went on to explore the backup strategy and restoration strategy. We also highlighted the importance of these strategies and what considerations have to be accorded to them.

- We then explored further the security considerations related to the data backups and highlighted the important security considerations which need to be invariably taken care of.

- We then went on to explore some of the possible issues with data backups and then detailed the important best practices related to backups and restoration.

- We introduced the cloud computing concept and then went on to identify and define the cloud computing environment through the delineation of three service models and four deployment models.

- We explored each of the cloud computing service models: Software as a Service (SaaS), Platform as a Service (PaaS), and Infrastructure as a Service (IaaS). We highlighted how SaaS enables organizations to have cost-effective applications, how PaaS enables the access to the software design, development, testing, and deployment tools to the software vendors, and how IaaS provides beneficial infrastructural facilities like servers and storage.

- We elaborated on the benefits provided by the cloud computing environment and the enablers of cloud computing.

- We explored in detail each type of cloud deployment model: Private Cloud, Public Cloud, Community Cloud, and Hybrid Cloud. We also differentiated between them and highlighted their applicability to various organizations during the course of discussions.

- We discussed the important security, privacy, and legal concerns on using the cloud computing environment.

- We addressed important security, privacy, and legal concerns.

PART V

■ ■ ■

Physical Security

This section examines one of the important layers of security: physical security in general and biometrics in particular. We also explore the information security particularly from the perspective of how human beings are conned or duped or misled to perpetrate attacks through the mechanisms of social engineering.

Chapter 14 describes "Physical Security and Biometrics". The term physical security refers to the measures taken to protect the physical environment and the infrastructure against physical threats such as theft, fire, water, and floods, which is housing the information system resources, such as hardware, software, and other networking devices. Physical security is as important as other technical security measures that are provided for the information. Since all the system resources are placed inside a physical facility, the environment around and within this facility should be safeguarded from both natural and unnatural events. Some may be thinking that if we move our infrastructure on to cloud we would not be impacted by physical security. It is only partially true. We may not be required to take care of physical security but somebody who provides the infrastructure facilities for the cloud needs to ensure the physical security as the servers and the infrastructure are still located in some physical facility somewhere.

The physical and environmental security mechanism should protect the above said threats either by automatic controls or driven by a set of manual processes. Normally organizations have standard policies and procedures to protect the facility including the data/computer center. These may be general management policies and procedures to secure the facility or IT security policies and procedures to guard against unauthorized access to restricted areas such as server rooms, control and privileges of administrator, password policies, remote access policies, and access card privileges. Also, we need to ensure environmental controls required for the server/data farms/centers such as temperature, humidity, static controls and dust controls. Though physical security deals with all aspects of physical environment and other hazards associated with nature, IT physical security should provide the protection of computer systems and other IT systems. The controls are generally classified as physical controls, technical controls, and administrative controls.

There are a number of physical security controls available in the market that the organization should consider for implementing physical access controls both inside and outside of the facility. Some of the controls include: Security Guards at each of the entry and exit points; ID cards and badges to all employees, and contractors; Electronic Access cards for all the major doors; Electronic monitoring and Surveillance cameras; Metal Detectors; Electric Fencing; Alarms and Alarm systems; Specialized access to computer labs, data centers, server rooms, and R&D labs; Biometrics; and Automatic Locks and keys. We explore ID cards and badges, locks, and keys.

We then describe how the electronic monitoring and surveillance cameras help in ensuring physical security. We then describe how these passive devices are supported effectively by alarms and alarm systems. We then explore biometrics, which is a technology for measuring and analyzing biological data of the human body such as fingerprints, eye retinas, irises, voice patterns, facial patterns, hand geometry and vascular patterns, and DNA. Biometrics is mainly used for authentication purposes. Biometrics technology is used to prevent frauds, enhance security, and to reduce identify theft. The biometric systems work on the basis of the behavioral traits of the users or the physical traits of the users or a mix of these. Behavioral biometric systems use methods like voice recognition, signature verification, keystroke recognition, and gait. Physical biometric systems use methods like fingerprint biometrics, facial biometrics, hand biometrics, iris biometrics, retina biometrics, and vascular pattern biometrics. We then describe each of these. We then explore how the biometric systems work through the mechanisms of enrollment and recognition. We also explain how the matching is carried out by the biometric systems and how the features are extracted during the enrollment as a template and then used during the matching process which is part of the recognition. We then explain how the performance is important in case of biometric systems and how the modern day computers with higher CPU power and memory are helping out in this regard. We also discuss that when the data to be matched against is huge then the system may experience lower performance. We then look into five important characteristics of a good biometric system i.e. unique, repeatable, accessible, universal, acceptable; false acceptance rate, false rejection rate should be low; and true acceptance rate and true rejection rate should be high. Then we look into the possible security issues with the biometric systems.

Then we discuss how multi-modal biometric systems can help to overcome some of the limitations of unimodal biometric systems. Then we list the advantages of biometric systems compared to the traditional access system with simple passwords and IDs viz. users do not need to remember passwords; users need not have to carry an ID card; unless the person is physically present, access is denied; no impersonation of identity is possible; Biometric traits cannot be stolen or duplicated; Biometric systems are hard to break; Biometric systems have good accuracy; with the advent of the computers, the declining cost of computers, the cost of the biometric systems have significantly reduced.

Then we discuss some of the administrative controls like fire safety factors. In this context we discuss some of the precautions to be taken with regard to fire. We then highlight some of the issues related to fire safety and fire control. We then explain how the physical security has to ensure proper protection of data from interception of data. We also explore how physical security of organization owned mobile and portable devices should be ensured including such personal devices used by the employees in the execution of office work. In this context we discuss the proper care of laptops during travel, locking up of these devices with proper passwords when not in use, remote wiping up of the data in case of theft of these devices, and encryption of these device disks. We then highlight the need for visitor control like escorting them during their visits, not allowing them to bring in unwanted devices like USBs, not allowing them to connect to the organizational LAN, and not allowing them to photograph any sensitive document/area.

Chapter 15, "Social Engineering," targets human beings. These social engineering attacks are based on the following premises - human beings are helpful by nature and want to help out people in distress or in difficult situations; human beings by nature trust others; human beings by nature obey the orders of their superiors or persons with authority in their organization; human beings by nature are afraid of consequences of not doing something company wants them to do, particularly losing the job. Social engineering attacks can be initiated by attackers personally or through the use of computers. These attacks are targeted at individuals or through individuals in the organizations. In the case of attacks on the individuals, the target of exploitation are their banking accounts or financial accounts and the intention is mostly monetary gain. In the case of attacks on the companies, it may be to benefit the competitors or to take revenge or to initiate distrust in such companies by leading to their loss of reputation. The means used may be leaking of sensitive information, modifying the integrity of the information, or leaking the strategic and confidential information to the competitors. The initial information collected can be used to initiate physical security attacks and/or network security attacks and/or host security attacks depending upon the information at the hands of the attackers. Even after somebody is duped or conned to provide the information pertaining to himself/herself or others or organization, the person so duped or conned may not even know that he/she has been so duped and the information so collected may be misused. This is the beauty of the social engineering attacks as the authority or trust or fear is used most of the time for ensuring the effectiveness of such attacks. Social engineering attacks have much less propensity to be dealt with through technical countermeasures.

Policies, awareness, and training are the only major means of ensuring that the people are not easily duped or conned through social engineering attacks. Social engineering attacks start mostly as passive foot printing activities and mostly culminate in active social engineering/technical attacks. The risks of social engineering is high as you cannot monitor each employee in the organization, you also cannot monitor the transactions carried out by each employee, and you cannot analyze the logs of all the activities carried out by each employee.

We then explore how human nature, namely helping nature, trusting nature, obeying the authority, and fear are exploited during social engineering attacks. These are carried out by the attackers by impersonation as an employee or contractor or vendor – mostly pretending to be in distress, difficult situation or urgency – calling the technical help desk or calling any specific targeted department or person; by exerting authority as a superior or management person; by exerting authority of a management person by invoking the authorization of such a person; by posing as a very important person like a customer or a legal authority or an outsourced entity doing a critical job for the company. Next we explored the attacks using computers or automated means like through fake websites, through popup windows, and through emails with links or attachments. In this context, we also provide some examples as to how such attacks may be carried out. We then explain the common attacks used in social engineering, such as pretexting, phishing, spear phishing, vishing, baiting, tailgating, and e-mail attachments.

We explain each of these for the better understanding of the readers. We also describe some other methods of social engineering attacks employed like inducting some person into the competitor organization, identifying a disgruntled employee, blackmailing targeted employees of the company using their background information, and other forms of attacks once the employee is inside the organization.

We then explore various measures that organizations can take to avoid falling prey to social engineering attacks.

Chapter 16 describes "Current Trends in Information Security". We thought of including this chapter at the end of the book even though logically it does not fit into Physical Security as these are of interest to the readers of this book. The three current trends of interest to all are Wireless Security, Mobile Security, and Bring Your Own Device (BYOD). In this chapter, we describe two of them namely Wireless Security and Mobile Security.

Wireless communications are carried out through Radio Frequency carriers. They can connect to the other Wireless network or to the wired network. Even though they remove some of the difficulties of the wired network, are relatively easy to use and relatively cost effective, they are also prone to information security issues. Some of the security concerns related to wireless security are weaknesses with the encryption mechanisms employed, rogue access points, SSID capturing, and the cracking of pre-shared keys. War-walking and War-Driving are some of the methods used to collect information related to the wireless access points and to initiate attacks. We also mention that WPA2 Personal and WPA2 Enterprise usage is more effective and recommend the usage of MAC filtering. We also describe some of the best practices to be followed so that the potential for attacks on wireless infrastructure is reduced significantly.

We further describe Bluetooth Security. Even though the chances of misusing bluetooth security are less because of the short range of communication it cannot be ruled out. We look at the security issues related to bluetooth and also discuss the best practices to be followed by all to ensure bluetooth security.

We then discuss Mobile Security. The publishing of SSID with the real names, malicious mobile apps, the weaknesses of the underlying operating system, losing or stealing of the mobiles which expose the data thereon, downloading of malicious games (sometimes disguised as freeware), etc. are some of the important security issues related to mobile devices, such as tablets. This is compounded by the lack of protection enabled through anti-virus software by most mobile users. We discuss in detail the security issues related to mobile devices, and also specify the best practices that users should follow to avoid facing such security issues.

■ ■ ■

CHAPTER 14

Physical Security and Biometrics

Introduction

Physical security refers to the measures taken to protect the physical environment and infrastructure that is housing the information system resources, including hardware, software, and other networking devices against physical threats such as theft, fire, water, floods, and so on.

Physical security is as important as other technical security measures that are provided for the information. Since all the system resources are placed inside a physical facility, the environment around and within this facility should be safeguarded from both natural and unnatural events. People may be thinking that having moved their infrastructure on to the cloud, they would not be impacted by physical security. It is only partially true. They may not be required to take care of physical security but somebody who provides the infrastructure facilities for the cloud needs to ensure the physical security as the servers and the infrastructure are still located in some physical facility somewhere.

Spilling water or a cup of hot coffee on the computer has the potential to destroy the electronic component of the computer and make the system dysfunctional. An unauthorized person entering into the electrical control room and switching off the power to the server room could lead to a complete shutdown of the data center. Someone can sneak into the facility and photograph or take video and hand it over to a competitor. All these are physical security related threats that need to be curtailed. Deliberate acts of sabotage or vandalism of the facility, employees stealing computers, computer accessories, confidential data, and passwords from the facility are all physical threats and need to be addressed. Natural calamities such as fire and floods, can also destroy the data including physical backup tapes inside the facility. Water leakages and power surges also represent physical threats and appropriate measures need to be taken to protect these assets.

Table 14-1 summarizes the security threats based on the CIA triad.

Table 14-1. *Security Threats Based on the CIA Triad*

Threat	Description
Physical damage	Availability
Theft	Confidentiality and Availability
Unauthorized entry to the facility	Confidentiality and Integrity
Natural Disasters (Fire, Flood, Earthquakes, and so on.)	Availability
Human Intervention (Sabotage, Vandalism, Strikes)	Availability, Confidentiality
Emergencies (Fire, Smoke, Building collapse, Explosion, Water leak, Toxic material release)	Availability

Seven major sources of physical loss have been identified as:[1]

- Temperature: Extreme variation of temperature

- Gases: War gases, commercial vapors, humidity, dry air, and so on. Examples would be transformer explosion gas, air-conditioning failures, smoke or smog, printer's liquids and toners, and cleaning liquids

- Liquids: Water and chemicals. Example would be water pipe leakages, sanitary leakages, fuel leaks, spilled drinks, acids, and chemicals used for cleaning

- Organisms: Viruses, bacteria, people, animals, and insects

- Projectiles: Tangible objects in motion such as moving vehicles, cars, trucks, and explosions

- Movements: Collapse, shearing, shaking, vibrations, and so on.

- Energy Anomalies: Electric surges, failures, magnetism, static electricity, radiation, sound, light, radio and microwaves. Examples include static electricity or carpets, cosmic radiation, explosion, and decomposition of magnetic tapes

The physical and environmental security mechanism should protect the threats either by automatic controls or driven by a set of manual processes. Normally, organizations have standard policies and procedures to protect the facility including the data/computer center:

- General management policies and procedures to secure the facility. Includes security guards, allowing visitors inside the facility after proper vetting, escorting visitors, building access, and surveillance cameras at each and every important location, both outside and inside of the facility.

- IT security policies and procedures to guard against unauthorized access to restricted areas such as server rooms, control and privileges of administrators, password policies, remote access policies, and access card privileges. Also, environmental controls required for the server/data farms/centers such as temperature, humidity, static, and dust controls.

Though physical security deals with all aspects of physical environment and other hazards, IT physical security should provide the protection of computer systems and other IT systems from the following:

- Physical damage of hardware/software as an act of sabotage, theft, unauthorized access to the server/computer rooms, or labs with the intention to damage physical assets

- Unauthorized access to server rooms/data center/labs

- Physical theft of equipment, systems, and other accessories

- Bringing personal storage devices and injecting viruses, worms, and other malicious software into the trusted networks

There have been instances of labor unions being used as a conduit by the competitors to create havoc on the premises of the target organization and physically damage the infrastructure.

Physical and Technical Controls

Physical access controls restrict the personnel access to the office buildings, labs, server rooms, data centers, or computer operation rooms where critical assets related to IT operations are operational. It should also restrict access to the locations where wiring is passing through to connect the systems, patch panel rooms, electric supply rooms, UPS rooms, the air conditioning or heating plant, data backup storage place, telephone and data lines connected area, and any other area which has IT or IT related operations.

Apart from the technical controls, enhanced corrective actions can reduce the risks. Higher levels of screening, reorganizing traffic patterns at some key locations, not displaying names of important buildings, and R&D facilities, can reduce the physical threats. Closed-circuit television cameras, motion detectors, and other devices can monitor the activities of the people and detect any intrusions.

There are a number of physical security controls available in the market that the organization should consider for implementing physical access controls both inside and outside of the facility. Some of the controls include:

- Security Guards at each of the entry and exit points

- ID cards and badges to all employees, and contractors

- Electronic Access cards for all the major doors

- Electronic monitoring and Surveillance cameras

- Metal Detectors

- Electric Fencing

- Alarms and Alarm systems

- Specialized access to computer labs, data centers, server rooms, and R&D labs

- Biometrics

- Automatic Locks and keys

ID Cards and Badges

ID cards and badges are a common method for physical access to the premises. Photo ID and digital smart cards are two common types.

Photo ID cards

Photo ID cards are simple identification cards with a photo of the personnel who is identified to provide access to the facility. Every organization provides to its employees a photo ID card for the purpose of identification and this should be worn by the employee at all times within the premises. Any violations of rules or policies within the facility by an employee can be easily identified through his/her ID.

Digital-coded cards contain chips or magnetic encoded strips on the photo ID card, which also contains all the information related to a person/employee. These types of cards are generally used in credit cards, ATM, and debit cards.

Magnetic Access Cards

Magnetic access cards are programmed by the security personnel for an entry into specific location. All the major entry and exit points of an office premise may have access points where one needs to flash this magnetic access card so that the door opens automatically. Otherwise, the access is restricted. For example, a server room or an R&D facility in the campus have special access to only few people. The door opens only when they swipe the access card at the door entrance. This will prevent any intrusions, even within the organization.

Other Access Mechanisms

Other access mechanisms that are prominently used include:

- **Wireless proximity readers** do not require users to physically swipe the card. The card reader senses the card automatically and allows the user who is in possession of the card to enter the door, which opens automatically. **Radio Frequency Identification** (RFID) technology is the one typically used by wireless proximity readers. Figure 14-1 shows one example of a RFID reader that is used for access control.

Figure 14-1. *RFID Reader*

One of the inherent weaknesses of such systems is **tailgating**. Tailgating is a method / technique used by an unauthorized person who enters the premises by following the authorized person. As soon as the authorized person swipes his/her card and the door opens and he enters the room, just behind this authorized person, another person enters before the door closes, who may or may not be authorized.

Locks and Keys

Locks and keys are probably one of the oldest access control methods ever used besides security guards. There are two types of locks:

- **Preset locks:** These are normal locks used in the houses and door locks. They are preset and the keys are fixed, you cannot change the keys.

- **Programmable locks:** These are either mechanical or electronic. A mechanical lock is generally an electromagnetic lock where a combination of numbers has to be entered to unlock. Common mechanical type programmable locks can be found in earlier labs and office doors. These are the common five-key pushbutton lock that requires users to enter a combination of numbers. This is a very popular lock for IT operations, server rooms, and so on. Nowadays, the mechanical locks have been replaced by electronic combinations, where the user is required to punch in a code on a number pad to get the access. This type of lock is known as a cipher lock or keypad access control.

Electronic Monitoring and Surveillance Cameras

Electronic monitoring controls such as Closed Circuit Television (CCTV) Cameras are used to monitor areas where either guards or dogs are not watching. These CCTV cameras may also complement the guards and the dogs. Also, the facilities are monitored 24/7 from a central location. The video footage of the CCTVs are normally recorded and stored for future investigations.

The main drawback of the electronic monitoring system is that it is a passive device. It can only monitor the intrusion but it cannot prevent intrusions. People who are monitoring the activities from the central location have to trigger an alarm in case they detect intrusion. In case the people who are monitoring the systems are not alert, intrusions cannot be stopped and later the recorded videos have to be viewed to identify the intruders and the intrusion activities.

Alarms and Alarm Systems

Alarm systems are closely related to electronic monitoring systems. But, alarms will notify whenever there is an unauthorized access. Alarms are very similar to Intrusion Detection System (IDS) that can detect any physical intrusion or any other events such as a fire, burglary, smoke, or environmental disturbance such as flooding.

Motion sensors are sensors that monitor the motion within a confined area using infrared, microwave, or optical technology. Sensors are widely used in current-day scenarios. Sensors are also additionally used in data centers to alert about temperature changes, water leakages, humidity increases, and so on.

Biometrics

We have watched in many movies how various kinds of complicated physical security measures are easily broken by intelligent planning and executing by spies and others. We have also watched in movies how various kinds of biometrics are used by military and other organizations. We have seen these biometrics systems being defeated by the severed finger of an authorized but slain officer, through static pictures of iris, through forged fingerprints. While biometrics has advanced over a period of time, additional aspects are being envisaged to be considered along with the main traits like pressure exerted or lack of pressure exerted during the fingerprint scan, and so on.

Biometrics is a technology for measuring and analyzing biological data of a human body such as fingerprints, eye retinas, irises, voice patterns, facial patterns, and hand geometry, and vascular patterns and DNA. Biometrics is mainly used for authentication purposes. Biometrics technology is used to prevent fraud, enhance security, and reduce identify theft.

There are several applications of biometrics in both government and commercial fields. Biometrics have been in use in forensic analysis for over 100 years. Biometrics have aided in criminal investigations, identification of missing children and people during disasters. Biometrics provides a higher degree of accuracy which would not be possible by human experts and has helped to solve many problems.

Governments constantly make use of biometric measures to prevent passport fraud hence preventing intruders getting inside the country by using fake VISAs and passports. Most international airports have adopted iris, fingerprint, or face recognition systems to prevent terrorists or illegal immigrants entering the country using false identity. In some developed countries, biometrics identities are included even in the driver's license (smart chips) for extra security. In India, the Aadhaar card (a unique identity for every citizen) has adopted biometric identity of all 10 hand fingerprints, face, and iris of both the eyes.

Many commercial organizations are using biometrics to protect customers' identity theft and secure commercial transactions. Most of the ATMs in developed countries have face recognition and fingerprint identity as passwords to withdraw money. Low cost biometric sensors and technology have led to the deployment of many biometric systems at ATMs, grocery stores, smartphones (iPhone 5s), laptop computers, and so on.

Apart from commercial applications mentioned above, many organizations are using biometric access control. These biometric access controls are installed and connected to door locks. When the biometric identity, such as fingerprints or retina or irises are matched with the data already captured during the enrollment process in the central database, lock systems unlock the door so that the person can enter.

Biometrics allows employees to access facilities based on the following methods:

- Acquiring data

- Extraction of features

- Encryption of template so that it is not tampered with

- Capture of data and matching

- Access is allowed or denied based on the match or no-match.

Some of the important biometric mechanisms

The biometric systems work on the basis of the behavioral traits of the users or the physical traits of the users or a mix of these.

Behavioral biometric systems use methods such as voice recognition, signature verification, keystroke recognition, gait, and so on.

- **Voice Recognition**: Voice patterns differ from person to person. The pitch value and frequency value are unique to each person and hence voice patterns are easily used for identity / authentication / verification purposes. Input voice is captured and the features are extracted from this using suitable training methods and the voice sample is stored as a template in the database. Training the voice samples is an important step. When the actual voice has to be tested, it is processed, the features out of the same are extracted and compared with the templates saved in the database. When there is a match the person is verified. Cleaning up the voice sample for noise is an important step and is carried out during preprocessing.[2]

- **Signature Patterns:** Keystrokes, the style of writing, orientation of writing, and the pressure applied while writing are the features of writing which differ from one person to the other. Hence, for a long time, banks and financial systems are relying upon the signature verification against the lodged signatures for authenticating a person or the documents signed by a person. Various government agencies also use this method effectively and extensively.

Physical biometric systems use methods such as fingerprint biometrics, facial biometrics, hand biometrics, Iris biometrics, retina biometrics, and vascular pattern biometrics.

- **Fingerprint Biometrics:** It is well known that fingerprints are most used in criminal investigations. In many countries fingerprints were taken as additional authentication to the signatures during the registration of properties, deeds, and so on. Fingerprint biometrics has almost percolated to most of the fields including companies to passport authorities to immigration authorities to many other fields. This is one of the comparatively cost effective, easy to use, and easy to implement systems available for identification and authentication or verification. The fingerprint biometrics uses the minutiae like arches, whorls, loops, ridges, valleys, and furrows which allow one fingerprint to be differentiated from the other.[2] Figure 14-2 shows an example of a fingerprint reader device.

Figure 14-2. *Fingerprint Reader Device*

- **Facial Biometrics:** Facial features like distance between two eyes; geometry of eyes, nose, lips, ears, and so on are the features used to differentiate one face from the other. Faces are captured and the facial features are extracted and used as a template. When the face is to be matched, again the same process is used to extract the features, the features so extracted are matched with the stored templates and when there is a match that means that the person is authenticated or verified. Some people have privacy reservations about this method.

- **Hand Biometrics:** Here the hand features such as size, length, width of the hand; lengths and angles of the fingers, bones, muscles, and ligaments of the hand are used to identify a person. Even the pressure applied by the hand on the scanner is one of the features that may be used.[2,3]

- **Iris Biometrics:** The use of Iris biometrics is picking up in critical and sensitive areas which require better entry controls. Iris differs from person to person significantly. Even iris may differ from left eye to right eye of the same person. Iris is the area surrounding the pupil in the eye of a human being. This is the area of the eye that determines eye color such as blue eyed, black eyed, and so on. The ring structures, furrows, and freckles pertaining to the iris are used as the features. This is easy to implement but requires specific readers and the eye has to be positioned appropriately for effective reading and is relatively costly to implement. Some people still express it as a privacy invasion.

- **Retina Biometrics:** Retina is the area within the human eye that reflects the image. This has different blood vessels flowing through it. These are captured as features as these differ from person to person significantly. This is difficult to capture as it requires appropriate lighting and exposure for a sufficiently long time span.

- **Vascular Pattern Biometrics:** Here the thickness and location of veins in a person's hand are used as features. These differ from person to person. Scanning the hand is easy and also does not involve privacy issues.[2]

How the biometric system works

Biometric system is a pattern recognition system where a biological pattern is analyzed, matched, and processed for further actions. This process has two stages:

- Enrollment stage
- Recognition stage

A basic biometric system is illustrated in Figure 14-3.

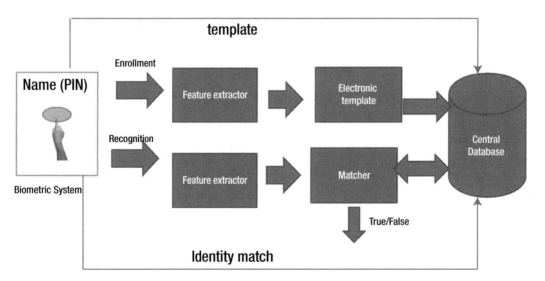

Figure 14-3. *Biometric Access System*

Enrollment

During the enrollment, a user's biological traits are captured with a scanner, camera, or appropriate reader. The captured data is preprocessed to remove any noise. The features are extracted from the captured data and the extracted features are then placed in an electronic template which is stored in a secured database in a central location for future recognition.

Recognition

During recognition, a sensor captures a user's biometric data. The data that is captured is analyzed with an algorithm that extracts only relevant features. Then this information is compared with the previously captured electronic template. If the match is found, further actions take place or else an alert is generated.

Performance of the Biometrics System

In order to be successful in commercial implementation, performance of the biometrics system has to be good. With the cost of memory and processors having come down significantly, there is more computing power available at less cost. This has propelled the usage of the biometrics systems in identification or authentication or verification processes. However, when the number of templates stored in the database increases significantly, the performance can start declining. The enrolment and matching and each of their constituent steps can take significant memory and processing time. However, as specified above, the advances in the field of computers have brought down the response time considerably.

The test of a good biometric system

A biometric system is considered good only if the following five characteristics are fulfilled:

- Unique: The feature being captured for matching purposes should be unique to each person.

- Repeatable: If again, after time lapse, the same characteristics are captured, the features extracted should be the same as that of earlier time, that is, it should be repeatable over a period of time. It should not change from one period of time to the next period of time.

- Accessible: The characteristics should be easy to be captured, such as through a simple scanner.

- Universal: Any biometrics system is not useful if it can be applied to only a portion of the target group. It should be easy to apply to all the target personnel. It should not require having some other alternative system for certain people as the system in question is not possible to be used by them.

- Acceptable: The method of biometrics should be acceptable to all. People should not have any objections about the same, like privacy related objections.

Furthermore, the following rates of acceptance and rejection by a good biometrics system should be at the minimum:

- False Acceptance Rate (FAR): A person's biometric characteristics match with somebody else's from the template database. This should not be the case as this can allow access to somebody else in the place of the genuine person. This is also known as False Match Rate.

- False Rejection Rate (FRR): A person's biometric characteristics do not match even though his feature template is already captured in the corresponding template database. This should not be the case as the person who requires genuine access may be denied access. This is also known as False Non-Match Rate.

Finally, the following rates need to be "high" for a good biometrics system:

- True Acceptance Rate (TAR): This is rate of correct match, that is, the person's identity is established correctly.

- True Rejection Rate (TRR): This is the rate of non-match correctly established, that is, if the person is falsifying the identity, that is correctly found by the biometrics system and the match is rejected correctly.

Possible information security issues with the Biometric Systems

The following information security breaches are possible with biometric systems:

- Possibility of forging the fingerprint by molding or fabricating it

- Possibility of false acceptance match

- Leakage of biometrics data may raise privacy and misuse concerns

- If not stored in encrypted mode, it may be possible for hackers to substitute the template and hence get unauthorized entry into an organization

- Possibility of the registration of a wrong person instead of a genuine person during the enrolment process without verifying the identity of the person being enrolled

It is strongly suggested that the biometrics data are not shared with others and also are not duplicated in some other systems even within the organization. Further, the biometric data has to be held encrypted so that it is not copied or replaced fraudulently by others.

Multimodal biometric system

Unimodal biometric systems, that is, biometric systems which use single characteristic like fingerprint biometrics or retina biometrics or iris biometrics have been found to have some limitations like propensity for attacks, noise in sensors, improper usage of the sensors for scanning or improper way of scanning or inadequate lighting provided (in case of iris scan), and improper exposure during retina scan leading to the noise in the traits captured for matching, and so on. Multimodal biometric systems use more than one biological trait of a person for recognition and access. For example, retina and fingerprint both can be used for establishing a person's identity. This enhances the security and also reduces the difficulties faced during recognition phase which the user experiences sometimes. It is also possible to collect data from different sensors, use different algorithms, use multiple samples, and so on.

In multimodal biometric systems the captured data can be fused at different levels and match or no-match is established. Multimodal biometric systems provide higher accuracy levels.[2]

Advantages of Biometric systems

Biometric recognition has several advantages compared to the traditional access system with simple passwords and IDs.

- Users do not need to remember passwords

- Users need not have to carry an ID card

- Unless the person is physically present, access is denied. No impersonation of identity is possible

- Biometric traits cannot be stolen or duplicated

- Biometric systems are hard to break

- Biometric systems have good accuracy

- With the advent of the computers, the declining cost of computers, the cost of the biometric systems have significantly reduced

Administrative Controls

In addition to the physical and technical controls, administrative controls are also very important from the perspective of ensuring totality and effectiveness of the controls. Some of these administrative controls are detailed in the following section.

Fire Safety Factors

Fire is an important risk each organization has to protect against. The fire risk arises from electric short circuits, gas leakage, consequential fire / fire mishaps on the premises, friction / malfunctioning of machinery leading to fire, and so on. Fire can turn uncontrollable within a few minutes depending upon the location of the fire, if not contained immediately. Fire can burn the organizational infrastructure including cabling, computers, and network equipment leading to an almost complete shutdown of the organization unless the organization has a well thought out and well-structured Disaster Recovery and Business Continuity Plans.

Some of the precautions that need to be taken to reduce the threat of fire are:

- Do not stock any inflammables like oil, old papers, and chemicals within the office premises. If you need to store them, store them separately in a secluded area and ensure that the area does not have any fire threats.

- Have smoke detectors installed at all the important places and high risk fire prone places within the organization.

- Have a good fire alarm system installed which has the capability to identify the zone in which the fire has originated and provide sufficiently audible strong alarm across the place impacted by fire.

- Have appropriate fire extinguishers installed at all the strategic and important locations within the organization, in sufficient numbers.

- Train your security guards, Emergency Response Team members, other staff members on effectively using the fire extinguishers.

- Maintain, test, and understand continued effective working of the smoke detectors.

- Ensure that the fire extinguishers have the requisite pressure maintained, the contents have not expired.

- Ensure that the electrical wiring and the switches used are of high quality and adhere to the product specifications.

- If there is an in-house canteen, ensure safe fire handling precautions. Also, have the fire extinguishers installed in sufficient numbers in that area.

- Get water sprinklers installed across the organization so that in case of huge fires the water sprinklers are activated and can control the fire.

- Train all the Emergency Response Team members in effectively handling emergency responses, effective evacuation of the employees. Carry out periodical fire-drills and ensure that the staff members understand the do's and don'ts to be followed during any fire emergency. Record the learnings of the fire drill and ensure that the Emergency Response Plans (in most of the organizations part of Disaster Recovery & Business Continuity Plans) are updated to reflect the applicable learnings.

- Ensure that the electrical earth points are well maintained.

- Emergency exits to be clearly marked and the path to the nearest emergency exit clearly specified.

During audits that we have carried out, we have discovered some of the following issues:

- Security guards and others did not know how to handle the fire extinguishers.

- Security guards did not know the priority of evacuation. When the security guards were asked, they mentioned that the computers which are costly have to be evacuated first as they are costly and surprisingly not human beings!!

- Fire Alarm Panels were not working.

- Smoke detectors were not working.

- Fire extinguishers had expired / did not have the requisite pressure.

- Fire exits were physically locked and they had a difficult time locating the key.

- Fire drills were carried out for the sake of complying with certain certifications. The learnings were not recorded and acted upon.

- Earth pits were not maintained.

- Electrical wiring was substantially old and was patched up at many places. Electrical panels were not well maintained.

- Old papers and inflammables were stored very near to the canteen area.

- Sufficient care was not exercised during the fire drills and some of the laptops were stolen by somebody when all the doors were opened automatically!!

Fire requires important consideration like other parameters by the organization. Otherwise, the organization will be at substantial risk.

Interception of Data

Data cables running within the organization, particularly in infrequently used areas, should be completely concealed so that they cannot be tampered with and to avoid the possibility of anybody fixing a monitoring / sniffing device to them. Data cables running outside the organization should be completely concealed and should be well protected so that there is no possibility of tampering by anybody.

In case of wireless devices, it should be seen that there is hardly any possibility of anybody using any rogue wireless router from outside the perimeter of the organization. The communication from the wireless devices needs to be encrypted through a strong encryption mechanism so that they are not interfered with and tampered with.

LAN points should not be normally provided in the visitor area or discussion rooms where the visitors are allowed so that there is no possibility of any visitors connecting to the LAN and manipulating the network.

Mobile and Portable Devices

Mobile phones and portable devices like laptops are highly prone to theft. Along with the theft of this system, substantial confidential data of the organization is also at risk. Particularly, mobile phones and laptops are issued to senior people within the organization and the loss of these systems can lead to substantial information security risks to the organization.

The following best practices apply to laptops:

- When not in use and needs to be left unattended, lock it to the desk using the locking cable

- While travelling, ensure that the laptop is held securely by you. Do not leave the laptop unattended at airports. Do not leave your laptop in your car when you are away from the car. Data on a laptop should be always held in encrypted form.

- Do not leave your mobile phones unattended anywhere. Ensure again that the organization has the policy to encrypt the data on the mobile. In case of loss of mobile, the organization should have the capability to wipe out the data on the mobile remotely.

- Always keep as little data as required on the mobile devices. If you are storing some content on these while not being connected to the office servers, ensure that the data is appropriately transferred back to the office servers once you are back at office or able to connect to the office servers; and delete the data from your mobile device.

As far as employee personal mobile devices are concerned, these have to be controlled as per the organizational policies. Nowadays, these mobile devices like mobile phones have high resolution cameras and have the capability to store documents and other data. Hence, a considered decision has to be taken by the organization after analyzing the risks and the benefits. If employee mobile phones are allowed to be used for official purposes, then appropriate controls as above have to be implemented so that they are not stolen placing the organization at risk. Further, employees should be strictly instructed about the do's and don'ts of the use of mobile phones within the office if personal mobile phones are allowed within the organization (e.g., not to photograph any confidential document or client sensitive data, etc.).

Visitor Control

Control over visitors is often neglected but is an important control from the perspective of physical security. Visitors normally have to be restricted to the reception area and any discussion rooms which are around the reception area but outside of the working area. If any visitor is required to come inside the organizational working area, they have to be necessarily escorted by a responsible person from the organization. Visitors should not be allowed to wander at will within the organization and have to be always escorted by a responsible person from the organization.

Visitors should be required to declare all their personal belongings including mobile phones, laptops, and pen drives. The details have to be written down in the Visitor Personal Belonging Register and have to be allowed inside the organization only on an as needed basis. Normally visitors are allowed to bring their mobile phones inside the organization. In such cases, the escort has to ensure that the mobile phones are not used to capture any sensitive document or sensitive work area. Further, while entering highly sensitive zones, they may be made to deposit the mobile phones with the security outside the area. Normally USB devices and memory cards should not be allowed within the organization.

Staff members have to follow the "clear screen" policy when the visitors are at their desk, so that even unintentionally, they do not allow the visitors to understand some sensitive information.

Chapter Summary

- We looked at the importance of physical security and at some of the threats and how they impact the information security aspects like confidentiality, integrity, and availability. We also briefly looked into the necessity of having physical security in the context of cloud infrastructure. We also looked into the need for IT physical security.

- We looked into the physical and technical controls. We described ID Cards and Badges, Locks and Keys, Electronic Monitoring and Surveillance Cameras, and Alarms and Alarm Systems.

- We explored what Biometrics is, and the different types of biometric systems in use such as behavior trait based and physical trait based systems. We looked into various behavior trait based and various physical trait based biometric system details. We explained how the biometric systems work through enrollment and recognition phases. We explored the performance of biometric systems and the characteristics of a good biometric system in detail. We looked into the security issues related to biometric systems. We then explored the value of multimodal biometric systems over unimodal biometric systems.

- We elaborated upon the administrative controls like fire safety controls, protection against interception of data, controls required over mobile and portables devices, and visitor control.

CHAPTER 15

■ ■ ■

Social Engineering

Introduction

Social Engineering attacks are increasing in our well-connected world. One of the main reasons for this is the availability of personal information on the Internet. For example, social media websites such as Facebook are used by attackers to collect information about people, which in turn can be used in their attacks, or can be used to initiate attacks. Hackers can uncover significant information about their targets—be they people or companies—by simply searching the Internet, or by searching social media sites such as Facebook or LinkedIn. Many of the images posted on social media, like family photos or photos of the company picnic, can reveal lots of information that is otherwise unavailable to the outside world. Using the information collected about the individuals, further information can be collected from their relatives and friends. The bits and pieces of the information collected from all such means can become substantial information about people and companies, which can be effectively used by attackers to initiate the attacks. Unlike in other attacks, the targets here are not primarily computers but human beings.

These social engineering attacks are based on the following premises:

- Human beings are helpful by nature and want to help out people in distress or in difficult situations

- Human beings by instinct trust others

- Human beings tend to obey the orders of their superiors or persons with authority in their organization

- Human beings by nature are afraid of consequences of not having followed the rules/orders of the company, particularly of losing their jobs

Social engineering attacks are initiated typically in two ways:

- By the attackers personally

- Through the use of computers[1]

Such attacks often may be initiated by attackers personally and once they are successful in collecting significant and sufficient information; further attacks may be initiated through computers. Both these types of attacks are part of social engineering attacks.

Such social engineering attacks may be targeted at:

- Individuals

- Organizations

In the case of attacks on individuals, the target of exploitation is their banking accounts or financial accounts and the intention is mostly monetary gain. Sometimes, it may be to initiate attacks on people, with some ulterior motives. In the case of attacks on companies, it may be to benefit their competitors, to take revenge, or to initiate distrust in such companies by leading to their loss of reputation, and so on. The means used may be leaking of sensitive information, modifying the integrity of the information, leaking strategic and confidential information to the competitors, and so on.

The initial information collected can be used to initiate physical security attacks and / or network security attacks and / or host security attacks depending upon the information at the hands of the attackers. This depends upon the intentions of the attackers and the information available to them through social engineering to further initiate attacks. The auto dialing facility using computers, other such utilities, and so on, have made the use of telephonic lines one of the easier methods to be used to connect to people from anywhere anonymously.

Even after somebody is duped or conned to provide the information pertaining to himself / herself or others, the person so duped or conned may not even know that he/she has been duped and so the information collected may be misused. This is the modus operandi of social engineering attacks as authority, trust, or fear is used most of the time for ensuring the effectiveness of such attacks. Technical attacks can be understood and avoided using technical countermeasures. However, social engineering attacks have much less propensity to be dealt with through technical countermeasures. Policies, awareness, and trainings are the only major means of ensuring that the people are not easily duped or conned through social engineering attacks.

Social engineering attacks start mostly as passive foot printing activities and ultimately culminate in active social engineering / technical attacks. The risks of social engineering are high as you cannot monitor each employee in the organization and the transactions they carry out and you cannot analyze the logs of the activities carried out by each employee. It requires concerted efforts on the part of the organization to reduce these risks. Security Policies and awareness and trainings on information security on a regular basis are the main means of reducing the risk. However, this risk cannot be completely avoided.

The typical Social Engineering Attack Life Cycle is illustrated in Figure 15-1.

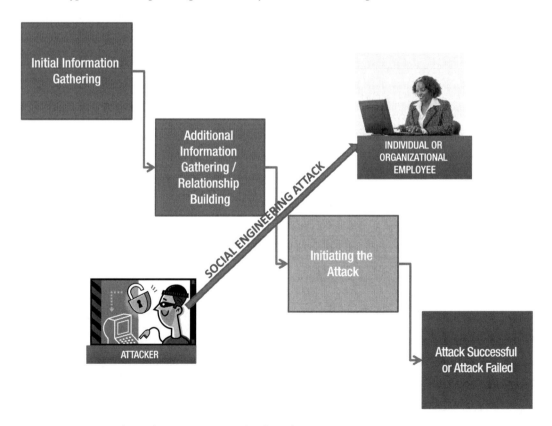

Figure 15-1. *Typical Social Engineering Attack Life Cycle*

Social Engineering Attacks: How They Exploit Human Nature

As discussed social engineering is an attack on / through human nature; attackers exploit this nature in several ways in order to collect the information, which subsequently may be used by them to initiate the attacks:

- Helping nature

- Trusting nature

- Obeying the authority

- Fear

The only thing the attacker needs to do is to imagine the scenarios through which he can exploit the above nature, such as those described in the following sections.

Helping Nature

Imagine you are working in the technical support function of your organization which is a big multi-national company. You get a call on your support desk number from an international number. The scenario goes something like the following:

Caller: Hi, I am Robin from Sales & Marketing department. I work for Tim.

You at technical help desk: Hi, I am Fred. How can I help you?

Caller: Thanks. I am working on a new proposal to acquire a multi-national prospect and millions of dollars are at stake. The prospective client had just now called me and wants some urgent information. I need to connect to the sales server to get the information. I am in Paris and I need to catch my flight in 30 minutes. I am required to send the information to the prospect before boarding my flight. But, my password is not working. Can you help me out by quickly resetting my password? Hurry up fast. Otherwise, I will be fired by Tim.

You at technical help desk: Ok. Ok. I understand. You are....

Caller: Robin, Robin Hogg from the Sales & Marketing. The fat man. Hurry up, please.

You at technical help desk: Ok. Now, your password is reset. It is RoSe123!! – Capital R for Rome, small o for orange, capital S for Sweet, small e for English, numerals 1 2 3 and exclamation mark two times. You need to reset the password upon first login.

Caller: Thanks a lot Fred. You saved my day. (Hangs up the call)

Precursor to the call: the attacker had understood through the social media account that Robin Hogg works in the Sales & Marketing department of the company. He also knows from the social media that Robin Hogg is known as "the fat man" within his company because of his huge body size. He had some other credible information about Robin Hogg from the social media if Fred had asked him. He also knows from the social media that his boss is Tim who is a very strict disciplinarian. The attacker had easily obtained the help desk number from the website of the company.

The following things worked in favor of the attacker:

- Fred had been chosen to work on the help desk as he was very helpful and was quick at solving other's problems.

- Fred did not go beyond verifying the basic details like name of the employee, boss's name in the database as there was an "urgency" in the attacker's voice as he did not have much time at his disposal.

- The additional details provided by the attacker like he works for Tim, that he will be fired by Tim, and that he is known as "the fat man," made Fred believe that the caller is a genuine employee. He had heard about some fat man in the Sales & Marketing department and he knew that Tim who headed the department was a strict disciplinarian.

- The fear that the new prospect and the millions of dollars of business may be lost also added to the fear and responsibility Fred felt not wanting to be responsible for losing the deal.

Even though other factors did help the attacker, in this case the primary factor that worked in his favor was the "helpful nature" of Fred which is also true with most of us as we want, by nature, to be helpful.

Trusting Nature

Imagine you are the receptionist at a medium-sized company and are at the desk. You get a call on your mobile number. The scenario goes on like the following:

Caller: Hi, I am Rose Mary, Secretary to the CEO.

You: Good Morning, Rose Mary. Jennie here. How can I help you?

Caller: Good Morning, Jennie. As you may be aware, my boss, Mr. Smith is at SFO today. He has forgotten his Standard Chartered Bank card CVV. It is written in my diary which is available on the side cabinet. You can get the key to the cabinet from Thomas or any of the security guards on duty. I am on vacation and the boss called me. I need to pass on this information urgently to him. I will hold for the information.

You: Ok. Sure. I will do it right now.

Jennie walks across to the security guard and informs him that Rose Mary had called her for some information and she needs to open Rose Mary's side cabinet. The security guard trusts Jennie, even though she has been the receptionist only for the past 6 months, as she is known for hard and sincere work. He hands over the key to Jennie.

Jennie opens the side cabinet, gets the CVV number and passes it on to the caller trusting that the caller is Rose Mary.

Precursor to the call: The attacker had met Rose Mary at her desk as a person representing one of the professional bodies of secretaries. She had interviewed Rose Mary on the best practices she follows to ensure that her boss is supported effectively. During this conversation, the attacker had understood that Rose Mary has a practice of noting all the important details about her boss including the credit card, debit card, and CVVs in a diary. Further, through the social media, the attacker also knew that Rose Mary is on a vacation.

The following things worked in favor of the attacker:

- Jennie trusted people easily

- Security guards trusted Jennie

- Jennie knew that Rose Mary was on vacation and that was confirmed by the caller who posed as Rose Mary

- The mention of the diary and the availability of the information therein, made the call more authentic

Even though other factors helped the attacker, the primary factor which worked in her favor in this scenario was the "trusting nature" of Jennie as well as that of the security guard. But, this normally would be applicable to most of us as most of us, by nature, trust others easily.

Obeying the Authority

By nature, human beings are obedient to their superiors and obey their orders without hesitation / much thinking. Imagine a situation where you are one of the trusted and loyal seniors in the finance and accounts department. You are well respected and the management people, including your boss, the CFO, rely on you for most of the information, including historical information / records of the company, or during the audits. Your boss was recently fired by the company and you had just started reporting to the COO. You also like to be respected, and get elated by this respect.

It is 10am in the morning. Your phone rings. The conversation goes as follows:

Caller: Hi David. Good morning. This is Parker, your COO.

You: Good Morning Mr. Parker. What can I do for you?

Caller: David, listen to me carefully. This is most important. There is an important external audit a customer wants us to undergo. Mr. King from Management Consultants X & X will be there at our office in another half an hour. You need to provide him with all the information and connect him to other departments as required. You are empowered by me to do this. I need not tell you, but ensure that the auditor is respected. Remember, he is representing one of our important customers.

You: No issues Sir. I will take care of it.

Caller: Ok. Thanks. I need to move on to another meeting. I will be busy in meetings throughout the day.

About one hour after the above call, a tall, smart gentleman in professional attire arrives at the reception and introduces himself as Mr. King from X & X and is warmly welcomed and led to Mr. David of the finance and accounts department. David warmly welcomes him. Mr. King mentions that he is acting on behalf of M/s. XYZ Inc., one of the large customers of the company and that he is provided with the charter to study the information security practices of the company. Mr. King praises the loyalty of David and mentions that the COO had high praise for David. David provides Mr. King with all the information required by him as well as connects him to the other departments as required by Mr. King. Mr. King has detailed discussions with the IT Manager and leaves by 6 pm. While leaving, Mr. King congratulates David again for being an asset to the company and appreciates his loyalty.

Precursor to the call: The attackers had collected the details of the board members and the executive management from the web-site which had more details about them than required. Most of them maintained a presence on social and other media, and it was easy to learn the COO's "voice." David, on social media, had highlighted his achievements at the company and the awards he had won. They had understood that he is working in the finance and accounts department. In discussion with some of the employees during some of the recent conferences, the attackers had corroborated on the fact that David at the finance and accounts section is well respected, is well recognized for loyalty and has been working there in the company for a long time and is also well known in Management circles of the company. The attackers also had details about the customers of the company and the services with which they are being provided from the website of the company. Another important fact was that the CFO was recently fired by the company and it was well published in all the newspapers.

The following factors worked in favor of the attackers:

- The authority with which the order was conveyed to David. There was no other option for David but to carry out the orders.

- Lots of details about the company and the customers available on the website of the company and social media

- The details posted by David about his achievements on the social media

- The fact that Mr. King appreciated David at the outset elated David and led to his cooperation

- Very familiar and reputed name of the Management consultancy organization

- The internal network created by David and the respect he earned because of his knowledge and loyalty helped him connect to the other departments easily

Even though other factors helped the attacker, the primary factor which worked in favor of the attackers in this scenario was the "nature of obeying the superior" of David. But, normally this will be applicable to most of us as most of us, by nature, are obedient to our superiors.

Fear

Fear of losing a job or fear of being reprimanded by the boss later on is one of the reasons to act on any requests, even though one may become suspicious of such requests. Sometimes, the employees may be blackmailed by the attackers using their personal knowledge about certain unwanted behavior or relationships of the employee outside the business. For example imagine the following scenario:

You are part of the purchasing department and handle important contract negotiations. You report to the CFO directly. You get a call at around 2 pm.

Caller: Good afternoon, Betsey. I am Stewart King, Senior Partner from AXYZ Consultants. We have been directed by your CFO to conduct a quick study of the current contracts in the pipeline and suggest strategies for better negotiations as the board has directed the CFO to cut some costs. Your CFO called us this morning from SFO where he is on vacation and instructed us to make this exercise a top priority this week. Please print out of all the current contracts under negotiation. Your CFO has instructed us to keep this work highly confidential.

You at Purchase department: Good afternoon, Mr. King. I understand your request for these details, but how can I send these details without authorization?

Caller: Betsey (voice is hardened, stern), I do not think you have any other options. Your CFO has ordered us today from SFO where he is on vacation. You can imagine the urgency. This work has to be completed this week and we do not have much time. He has specifically authorized us to collect the details from you. Consequences of not honoring his orders may be grave for you. You may be fired once he returns from vacation if you do not follow his instructions. And, you know very well that your boss does not like anybody who does not take their work seriously. Further, the board also may not take your disobedience lightly as this work is at their request. It is up to you. Anyhow, in an hour's time, our person will be at your reception. Please hurry up.

You at Purchase department: Ok, Mr. King. Your person can collect the printouts in an hour.

Precursor to the call: The vacation of the CFO is well published by him on social media. He is also posting the photos as he moves from one place to another. His tour program is also published on social media by him. Further, the details of the purchasing department contacts including Betsey is well known to all the vendors. The attackers have found the details about Betsey from one of the vendors of the company without raising any doubts.

The following factors worked in favor of the attackers:

- The fact that the CFO was on vacation

- The urgency of the work highlighted by the attacker

- The fear created by the attacker in Betsey

- Reputed name of the consultancy organization

- The weight in the voice of the caller as a senior person with lots of knowledge

Even though other factors helped the attacker, the primary factor which worked in favor of the attackers in this scenario was the "fear" incited by the attacker in Betsey. But, normally this will be applicable to most of us as most of us, by nature, are afraid of what can happen to us, particularly we dread the thought of losing our job.

Social Engineering: Attacks Caused by Human Beings

Most social engineering attacks are initiated and carried out by the attackers personally (i.e., without the use of computers).

Some of the attacks that are perpetrated by using human beings are:

- By impersonation as an employee or contractor or vendor – mostly pretending to be in distress, a difficult situation, or urgency – calling the technical help desk or calling any specific targeted department or person

- By exerting authority as a superior or a management person

- By exerting authority of a management person by invoking the authorization of such a person

- By posing as a very important person like a customer or a legal authority or an outsourced entity doing a critical job for the company

Let us look into some of the probable scenarios related to the above. In the earlier section 1.1, we looked at how an impersonation works. We have looked at impersonation as an employee and as a top management person. We also looked into the scenario where a third party calls as authorized by the top management person. We will look at some more relevant scenarios here in the following section.

You are working in the technical support department and you are manning the technical help desk and your phone rings (it is late in the evening and most of your staff are away from work).

Caller: Good evening. This is Michael, IT Manager from XYZ Ltd., which is, as you know, one of your privileged customers (commanding voice, hurry and anxiety evident in the voice).

You at technical help desk: Good evening, Michael. I am Rajan. How can I help you out?

Caller: (commanding voice, hurry and anxiety in the voice continues) We have a major information security incident at our end. We have a serious virus attack. This virus is known to use existing user ids and passwords. We need to reset all passwords. Please reset all the user credentials belonging to persons from our organization on your systems. This is urgent. Otherwise, there is a risk that virus may spread to your network too. As my official id is at risk, please change the passwords and send them to following personal id …

You at technical help desk: Ok, Michael. Thanks. We'll get right on this. However, before that I have to get permission from my IT Manager.

Caller: Rajan, listen (commanding voice, anxiety continues). No need to get additional permission. I have already informed your IT Manager, Mr. Johnson, and he is fine with it. We do not have much time to salvage the situation. Please do this immediately. You know we have provided huge business to your organization.

Precursor to the call: The attacker obtained the number of the technical help desk from the company website, and details about the client from publicly available brochures. Further details about the client company, including the name of the IT Manager, are obtained from the client company's website. Additional details about the IT Manager were obtained by the attacker from social media. The attacker had further details about the current ongoing projects from the website of the client company and also from some resources within the client company.

These characteristics worked in favor of the attacker:

- Commanding voice of the attacker

- Importance of the customer and the quantum of business they provide to this organization

- The possibility of virus spreading to this organization if not acted upon immediately

- Additional details known by the attacker like the IT Manager's name of this organization

- Main factor which acted in favor of the attacker was the importance of the customer and the quantum of business they provide to this organization

Consider another situation. You are the second in the finance and accounts department. Your department head is on leave and you are at your desk. A heavy weighed voice announces:

Caller: Good Morning, Mr. Alexis. I am John Madtha from Export Control Office of the Department of Commerce. Listen to me carefully. I am directed by the President to carry out a highly confidential urgent investigation, on some of the export irregularities on behalf of the federal government. The probe covers many companies. We know that your department head Mr. Joseph is not available, which is why we're calling you directly.

Alexis: Good Morning, Mr. Madtha what can I do for you?

Caller: (continues) The probe is not on your company but covers some of your customer companies. We will be faxing you an authorization letter from our department in the next 5 minutes. We want certain details regarding some of your customers. Keep in mind, it is highly confidential and nobody else should know about it. You need to fax me the details within the next hour.

Alexis: Ok, Sir.

Caller: Thanks, Alexis. But, remember. This is highly confidential and you need to keep this confidential.

Alexis: Ok, Mr. Madtha. I will. (call cut from the other side)

In next five minutes he gets an authorization letter from the Export Control of Department of Commerce (on the surface nobody can make out that it is fake). As an obedient citizen Alexis faxes the details required to the number provided on the fax received by him.

Precursor to the call: The attacker has studied the details of the customers of the company through their website. Some of those companies are big names and the company was providing them certain critical services as mentioned in the website of the company. The attacker knew through various accounting forums that Alexis is working there in the accounts department as second in command. The attacker had chatted with Alexis on one of those forums and understood that he was a law-abiding loyal citizen with a mild personality. Additionally, the attacker through one of the persons known to him from the company understood that the department head is on leave.

What worked in favor of the attacker:

- Attacker's commanding voice which sounded like that of the senior officers from the government

- Attacker reached Alexis's desk directly and addressed him as Alexis which confirmed the belief of Alexis that because the call is from law enforcing department they should know his name

- The department head who was handling the legal matters was on leave

- The letter of authorization faxed was a look alike of any government letter with all the appropriate formatting, symbols, and so on.

- Law-abiding nature of Alexis

But what worked the most was the law-abiding nature of Mr. Alexis in this specific context. This applies to most of us as we are all law-abiding citizens and consider it is a privilege to be of use to the government at any point of time.

Social Engineering: Attacks Caused by Computers or Other Automated Means

The other ways of perpetrating social engineering attacks are by using computers or automated means.[2]

One way of attacking is through fake websites, which are easily created. Websites which look like the legitimate sites also can be created very easily. One very popular type of social engineering attack is done by offering free downloads or very high discounts and encouraging them to use their official ids. The persons may be lured and provide substantial details in the process. Sometimes, the employees may reuse the same password as that of their official ids. The information collected will be used for further attacks.

Through Popup Windows: Interesting popup windows with irresistible offers can again lure the people to share substantial but unwanted details requested to be keyed in. These popup windows may announce that you have won a lottery or laptop or jackpot and may want you to provide details about yourself including sometimes your banking details so that the amount can be credited to your banking account or the gift can be sent to you.

Through E-mails: Again, interesting and irresistible offers can be made to you through e-mails. These e-mails may again request urgent intervention on a technical glitch as a user of e-mail, verification of credit card details, banking account details, and so on due to technical issues or resetting of credentials required on account of the upgrade of the systems of the bank to make them more secure for the customers, and so on. These e-mails provide the links to fake websites. Sometimes, these e-mails can have attachments which can download malicious software like keyloggers or screen capture tools or viruses, and so on which will make all the details keyed in by the users available to the attacker. Such e-mails also sometimes declare that the attachments or the links are to anti-spyware whereas they may be in fact installing spyware. Similarly, they may lure you with useful software while they may install actually useful software they may additionally install malware without your knowledge. Such e-mails can bring to you so called useful utilities, interesting games, and interesting reports and entice you to download them leading to malware infection of your system [Ref 5]. Such attacks are many times targeted at you knowing your specific interests.

Again the scenarios which can be created are only limited by the imagination of the attacker. Let's consider a hypothetical situation.

One recent—and highly publicized—attack on a retail giant during the holiday season resulted in the compromising of the details of millions of credit card accounts. Your bank name is also part of the list of the banks whose card details were leaked out. You get an e-mail message purported to be from your bank (with all the logo and style similar to that of the e-mails you normally get from your bank) that in order to ensure the security of your credit cards you need to reset your PINs. You click the link, provide your old PIN and then create a new PIN. You provide all the details sought in the process without observing whether they are required or not as you feel the urgency and necessity to be secure. When you complete the process you feel secure but actually your PIN is compromised and lots of details about you are in the hands of the attacker. You do not even know that you are attacked and the attack was successful.

Let's consider another scenario.

You get a job interview call from one of the African countries through an e-mail (it can come through other means like telephonic calls also). The position and the compensation offered sound very lucrative (it also sounds unreasonable – but because it has come to you, you do not believe so as you believe that you deserve such a position and compensation and feel happy somebody has noticed your talent). The link is provided to the company website. You go to the link, the company is a great company with excellent spread of branches and with great performance. You feel happy that you are privileged to be considered for the position. You anticipate the interview and prepare well. On the date and time mentioned, the interview is telephonically conducted. There may be some technical questions but the questions also remotely ascertain your or your parents' monetary status. You have done well in the interview.

Promptly after the interview, you get a communication that you have been selected and you get your offer letter. You are excited as you got an offer which is five times your current salary and there are also additional perquisites. But, they have also requested a good amount of money be remitted to them towards Resident Permit / VISA charges, and so on. But, it does not sound very big when compared to the potential salary! You do not waste time, you go to your bank and remit the amount promptly. The recruiter is in touch with you either through phone or through e-mail. They come back to you again and inform you that there are some issues with your Resident Permit / VISA and to clear the issues you need to remit some more amount to them expeditiously. The amount is specified in the message or communication from your recruiter. You are excited to join the company as early as possible (not a surprise if you already resigned from your current job) and hence expeditiously remit the amount.

Then these requests may be followed by similar requests citing one reason or the other but the amount requested to be remitted may be smaller than the earlier one but still substantial. You will continue to remit the amount till you feel something is "fishy". Now you start exploring. You do not find anything "fishy" in the website. You go through the offer letter, everything sounds fine. However, you may find, if you observe closely that either they have not provided any telephone number or address of the office in the offer letter or the number provided does not exist or is a wrong number. You go to the local police and file a complaint. They inform you that this may be fraud.

Now, if you had written to either your embassy at that country or that country's embassy at your country, you may have been fortunate to get a reply that "The Company does not have an office at the address and location specified in the letter." Again, such a reply will also caution you not to fall prey to fraudulent attacks. Now, you realize that your craze to get huge compensation has not only made you lose your current job, but also has made you spend a substantial amount without any return. Maybe you would have borrowed those funds from others. Now, your excitement turns into sorrow.

Some of the other scenarios are:

- You get an e-mail announcing that you have won a lottery or jackpot of a huge sum like Euro 2,500,000. This also has a request to send your details. Once this information is provided by you, you may get the request to send your bank account details. Along with this request you may also be requested to remit them a sum of for example: Euro 10,000. Compared to the amount you are going to get you feel the amount to be remitted is nothing. You pool all your savings or borrow from others and arrange for this amount and remit it to them. You may get further messages citing some trouble in processing and requesting additional money to clear the hurdle, and so on.

- You get an e-mail from somebody that she came to know of you through one of your common friends and that she has bequeathed a huge sum of money from her husband after his death and that she is ready to share that huge amount with you, but in return she wants a small favor. She wants you to send her an amount to fight the legal hurdle to repatriate the amount to your country. You believe her and remit the money. Subsequent requests will follow for additional money citing some more unanticipated hurdles which need to be cleared before being able to get the amount released. As you have already invested some amount you may remit the amount as requested the second time. But, as more and more requests for remittances pour in, you start getting doubts. When you enquire with friends, one of your friends informs you that these are all fraudulent messages.

Many more instances can be cited but, the variety of social engineering is only limited by the imagination of the attacker!

Social Engineering: Methods that are Used for Attacks

Different methods are used by the attackers when it comes to social engineering attacks. However, use of some of these methods depends upon the completion of collection of contextual data or building based on the currently collected contextual data. The initial attacks will be to collect useful data like bank account details including user id, password or bank account number, or collection of personal information like name, social security number, address, and date of birth. If the primary attacks to collect useful data do not fetch the expected details, using the details collected during the initial attacks, subsequent calls or attacks will be used to try to collect further data. Hence, the required data to initiate a strong attack may be collected in one or more attacks by the attackers.

The following methods are commonly used:

- Pretexting
- Phishing
- Spear Phishing
- Vishing
- Baiting
- Tailgating
- E-mail attachments

Pretexting

Pretexting originates from the word "pretext". "Pretext" means "for some reason" and most of the times a reason which is not genuine. This involves the use of intelligently thought out well-crafted lies with the bad intention of collecting information about an individual or organization to initiate the attacks. These pretexting attacks build on information already available to the attacker, or through multiple, gradual attacks that continue until the intended objective is achieved.

Pretexting for privacy information or financial / banking information is prohibited by the acts of law in some of the countries of the world.

Phishing

Phishing is possibly the most heard of terminology particularly among those who use online means of dealing with the banking and financial related transactions. The bankers or financial institutions keep on cautioning their customers against the "phishing" activities. "Phishing" typically means "fishing," that is, "fishing" for useful personal information about the user which will be used by the attacker for identity theft.

Phishing attacks are usually carried out through links in the email attachments. E-mail seems to be from the legitimate bank or financial institution or electronic payment organization or similar organization but is not actually from the legitimate bank or financial institution or electronic payment organization. These attacks target primarily the obtaining of login credentials of the users like user ids and passwords, and so on or other personal information like social security number, banking account number, credit card / debit card details, and so on. Some of the reasons that are cited in such e-mails are:

- Crash of one of the servers or corruption of data which necessitates resetting of the passwords and allows for resetting the passwords (in the process capturing your current login credentials)

- Security reasons like suspicious transactions noticed in your account and the need to verify your current credentials (in the process capturing your current login credentials). These may be related to your bank accounts or credit or debit cards.

- Overcharge on the account which need to be reversed and to carry out the same they want the account details to be verified (in the process seeking such information which will lead to identify theft).

The logo of the bank or financial institution, style of the contents are typically copied from or are in close resemblance to that of the bank and therefore does not induce the thinking in the minds of the users that these may not be genuine. Further, the words like "to ensure security of your account" introduce the anxiety / urgency in the minds of the users to act on them. As such most of the users blindly believe such e-mails and act on them.

Even though banks and financial institutions keep on advising their customers not to fall prey to phishing attacks still many do not understand what phishing is and the implications of the phishing, and fall prey to such e-mails.

As more people have started using their mobile smartphones for carrying out their financial or banking transactions the risk of the phishing has also grown. People who use mobile devices without ever having used a computer may not be aware that computer security issues are equally applicable to mobile devices. Furthermore, sometimes these phishing messages seem to originate from trusted mobile apps. Because you trust these apps, your natural inclination is to assume these messages are genuine, and to divulge personal or banking credentials when prompted by them. This leads to further identity theft.

Most of these links take you to a URL that, again, looks like a legitimate website, and asks you to enter not only your user credentials, but also other personal data such as your social security number and mailing address, which is already on file with your financial institution. A genuine bank / financial institution never asks for the information it already has unless as a part of the telephonic verification to ensure that the person contacting them is the person who owns that particular account or credit card or debit card the details of which he is trying to obtain or on which he is transacting upon. Any website which asks for such details should be suspected.

Unfortunately to the disadvantage of the user, the user goes by the words mentioned in the mail like "if you do not respond operations on your account may be suspended." Ideally, when any user gets a message which looks like a phishing message he has to promptly delete it or forward it to the concerned authorities in their countries. They should not act on the instructions in such mails or even click on the links in such mails. Still in case of doubt that it may be from the bank or financial institution or electronic payment organization, the person should directly contact them at the original contact numbers available with him or on their official websites and confirm that the concerned organization has not sought such details and it is likely most of the times it has not.

These phishing e-mails are normally spams which are sent to large numbers of users. The target list may also have the users who are not customers of the bank or financial institution who is spoofed. Normally most of them will ignore such e-mails. Some of the knowledgeable or information security aware users may ignore them even though they have accounts in such bank or financial institution. Some others who are not well aware of phishing or who are normally "anxious" or who become easily "weary" are the persons who will fall prey to such attacks. Attackers are fine even if they get the required information from some of the mailers sent as they can use such information to initiate further attacks.

Spear Phishing

Spear phishing differs slightly from phishing. The intention of the phishing attack remains the same. However, the phishing message is normally not from outside organizations, but from somebody with sufficient seniority and position, normally who is well respected and considered to be a reliable person in the organization. The attack is directed at a particular target organization. The spear phishing mails request the employees to update certain critical personal details or reset some critical user ids and passwords. Again, such mails are drafted very intelligently by the attackers. As the mail seems to be from the legitimate person many employees are likely to act upon the request and in the process lots of personal data which can lead to identity theft or banking or financial frauds are made available to the attacker.

Vishing

Vishing is short for "Voice Phishing." Here, normally the call is made to the number of the user instead of sending an e-mail with the link and a message is left to the user to call a particular number. These calls seem to be from the legitimate organizations like banks or financial institutions. These calls are normally initiated through automated means. When you call the number specified in the recorded message, you will be redirected to a voice response system and you are led to provide the information like in the case of the normal phishing attacks. These may be passwords and other personal information. The intention of the attacker is the same as that of the normal phishing attacks, such as identity theft and use of the information gathered for further attacks.

Baiting

Baiting is an attack where physical drives like CDs, DVDs, or USB drives are used instead of the emails. These drives are loaded with malicious software by the attacker. Intention of the attack is to maliciously infect the computers which use them and then the network, thus providing access to all the information on the computer and network to the attacker.

Normal scenarios of baiting works like this: usually a few copies of the CDs, DVDs, or USB drives infected with malicious software are placed by the attacker in such places as rest rooms or walkways or reception area or elevators or parking lots, and so on. These CDs, DVDs, or USB drives are labeled intelligently with interesting name / content tags. Such CDs, DVDs, or USB drives are then placed or dropped outside / nearer to the target company premises including many times at reception or waiting lounges. The employees who find them normally want to explore what is there inside the drives and when they insert them into their computers, without their even being aware of it, their systems are infected with malicious software which does the further part of the work required by the attacker like passing on the targeted information to the attacker. Even if these are found by a good employee and returned to the company IT staff, again when the IT staff inserts them into his / her computer or other authorized person takes possession and analyses the same by inserting into his computer, his computer is highly likely to get infected. As the malicious software is intentionally written by the attacker, it may not be even detected by the anti-virus software on the machine where it is used.

Tailgating

Tailgating is also sometimes known as "piggybacking." When this occurs, a legitimate user is followed by an attacker through authenticated gates like the ones where access is allowed by using access cards or fingerprints. Normally most of the employees do not want such an employee (because the person is entering they feel that he is also an employee – sometimes such attacker may wear a fake badge so that they are not doubted) closely following them struck by the doors and hold the doors open for them to come in. Sometimes such attackers may request other employees to allow them inside in the pretext that they have forgotten to bring their ID card or they have lost the card and requested a duplicate card and the other employee may open the door for them. Once within the organization such attackers can initiate attacks like inserting malicious software through USB drives on unlocked unattended computers (user may be away temporarily) or by shoulder surfing or by dumpster driving find out useful information like passwords, and so on. Again the courteous nature of human beings and the nature which does not like to see colleagues in distress help out the attackers, in good faith but with negligence.

E-mail Attachments

E-mails with interesting subjects always bring an urge in the employee to open them. Normally these have attachments with interesting names. The employee opens the attachments and malicious software is downloaded even without his knowledge. The attachment may also contain sometimes the matter of interest to the employee. However, it also does infect the user's system and in turn the network. Now, the user's system and other infected systems can be accessed easily by the attacker. Sometimes, the emails seem to have originated from government authorities and again carry serious subjects like mistake in the return filed by him which forces the employee to open the attachment and again his system is infected with malicious software. Some of these e-mails also may warn the employee that there is a virus attack and the solution is provided in the attachment, if he clicks and installs the solution his system will be trouble free and a virus will not attack it. Obviously to avoid any virus issues, he clicks and installs the so-called solution which is nothing but the malicious software.

Social Engineering: Other Important Attack Methods

In addition to the previous descriptions of attacks, there are also important attack methods that are often employed by the attackers:

- Find an employee in the target organization who hates his organization strongly: It is easy to find out through other employees remotely as to who in their organization always talks negatively and does not like the management. The reasons for that employee's hatred of the companies may be many, such as repeatedly denied promotion, continual recognition as low performer, sidelined by the management even though good at performance, intentionally one or more of the management persons ridicule his views, and so on. Such an employee when offered either some monetary benefits or alternative job may be ready to carry out any work you tell him particularly anything he has to do against his current company which he hates. He will be ready to carry out such attacks even though he knows that he is not doing something ethical or good but at that point in time the only thing that prevails upon him is that he has to take revenge against his company which has not taken care of his aspirations or has not looked after him well.

- Plant your person as an employee of the target company by getting him recruited by the target company and for a crucial position. Once he is within the target company get the credentials required for the attack through him and carry out the attacks or get him to carry out the attacks intelligently like malicious infection of the computers of one of the key employees, and so on. This person may instead identify a disgruntled employee and get the work carried out through such a person.

- The attacker may identify the weaknesses of some of the employees from the information collected through various sources like neighbors, and other employees and collect relevant information to blackmail such employees and use them to collect the information required by the attacker to initiate attacks.

- Look for the notebooks wherein the employees take notes as some people have the habit of writing their passwords in the first or last pages of their notebook. When the employee is not around and the notebooks used by the employee are around, the attacker may search into these notebooks or steal these notebooks and later check for the written passwords, if any.

- Once the attacker is inside the organization the attacker may use shoulder surfing to learn the password when the password is typed by the employee. There are even instances wherein a PIN entered by an ATM user is observed with the help of binoculars or telescopes and is copied.

- Once the attacker is inside the organization he may also check the dustbins for any written down passwords.

- Once inside the organization the attacker can listen to the conversations going on around gathering some of the confidential information or be able to read the files or messages from the systems switched on but unattended at that point of time.

- Today we are in the world of mobile smartphones and tablets. Some of the malicious apps may be sold through online stores with the same name or similar name to that of a popular mobile app. Users downloading and using them will get infected with malicious software which will perform the activities intended by the attacker.

Social Engineering: How to Reduce the Possibility of Falling Prey to Attacks

In a real and practical sense, it is very difficult and nearly impossible to eliminate social engineering completely as no software or hardware can stop these types of attacks. Further, human nature, particularly of every employee differs from that of the other and is very difficult to make out and devise countermeasures. However, that does not mean that we should not do something. Definitely organizations as well as the individuals should consciously work against social engineering attacks and try to avoid falling prey to them.

Some of the important measures that need to be taken by the organization in this regard are:

- Clearly define, document, and describe your organization's security policies. Make it clear in these policies what is expected from the employees, vendors and customers in the organization. Also, specify clearly what is not acceptable from the employees, vendors and customers in the organization. Circulate these policies among all the employees, vendors and customers (as applicable) so that they are aware of them.

- Include important do's and don'ts with respect to information security and the expectations from the vendors related to information security in the contracts / agreements with them and clearly mention the consequences of the breach of these. Also, again ensure that the vendors in turn, train their staff, who are involved in dealing with / working for your organization, about these information security related responsibilities.

- Include important do's and don'ts and adherence to the security policies as a mandatory aspect in the employee agreements with the organization (like employee appointment letter or Terms and Conditions of Employment) and make the employees sign such undertakings after consciously understanding the information security related responsibilities. Include in these also the responsibilities which will survive beyond the termination of their service.

- Carry out regular and detailed information security awareness trainings with clearly specified do's and don'ts related to information security with clear information as to what can go wrong if they do not follow the good practices of information security. They should also be informed of the consequences of the breach of information security by them and how it attracts disciplinary action. Such trainings are to be conducted first during the joining of the employee and then whenever key changes are made to the security policies or information technology infrastructure / tools as the risks undergo change. Also, periodical and regular refresher trainings need to be carried out at least at a minimum of once a year. Also, again when the employees leave the organization they should be apprised of the continuation of some of their information security responsibilities which survive beyond their termination. Such information security awareness trainings also should cover social engineering attacks and how to avoid them.

- Information security awareness trainings as described above have to be provided to the contract employees as well as vendor employees.

- Clearly defined information security event and incident reporting mechanism which is easy to use should be set up. All the information security events have to be regularly analyzed and if turned out to be incidents have to be analyzed further for the causes and appropriate corrective actions have to be drawn up. It is most necessary to ensure that drawn up corrective actions are actually executed too within the targeted timeframe. Corrective actions, if require employee training, the same has to be ensured across the organization.

- All access control / authorizations have to be periodically reviewed and revised on need-to-do and need-to-know basis. Authorizations have to be kept at the lowest level possible, but it has to be ensured that the work of the employees is not adversely impacted. Where such reviews throw up issues such as people granted temporary access to some of the folders or applications are still holding them, the access has to be removed immediately. Some of the authorizations earlier valid but are not required in view of the current role and responsibility of the employee have to be removed accordingly. The need for change of the authorizations during the promotions, and transfers have to be considered during such changes and authorizations have to be appropriately set. Earlier permissions if not required being continued have to be removed.

- All the highly confidential data has to be secured appropriately and authorizations should be strictly controlled. Access to such data has to be monitored. If possible, such confidential data is also segregated appropriately.

- All the data needs to be appropriately classified and labeled so that all are aware of the sensitivity and know whether there are restrictions on them being shared with others.

- All the employees should be sensitized to ensure that they do not divulge under any circumstances their passwords or PINs or such other credentials including the badges, smart cards etc. to anybody else even to a co-worker. All should use their own badges. They should be clearly made to know that their user ids and passwords are not required by technical help desk for any work.

- Background checks of all the employees including those of outsourced contractors have to be conducted. The background checks have to be assigned to an organization with repute and capability. Some of the organizations do not carry out the background checks of key resources like outsourced security guards, outsourced housekeeping personnel, outsourced IT resources, and so on. This can turn out to be a serious omission on the part of the organization.

- The systems should force employees to use only strong passwords. Weak passwords should not be accepted by the systems. The access to the systems should be barred after a specified number of failed login attempts.

- Areas within the organizations have to be additionally secured depending upon the sensitivity of the information handled. For example, data centers have to be additionally secured with the lock and key or additional layer of access control so that only few authorized persons are allowed inside.

- All the employees should be invariably issued badges and it should be made mandatory that they display the badges on their person invariably when they are within the organization. This enables somebody to differentiate an employee from an external visitor.

- Visitor Policy should be clear. Visitors should be always escorted by an employee when he / she is within the organization.

- All the unwanted papers have to be shred invariably. They should not be allowed to be dumped in the dust bins.

- Strict policies on clear screen and clear desk should be issued and employees should be made aware of the same.

- Employees should be trained as to how to ensure that the voice is kept low when they take confidential calls from their desks. Or, they should be advised to take such calls from closed rooms.

- Multi-factor authentication can be introduced for sensitive servers or network equipment so that password compromise does not lead to any issue.

- All permissions for additional access have to be reviewed thoroughly and should be considered only as per the Access Control Policy and based on the need for such information access to such an employee, vendor, or customer.

- Strong anti-virus software with strong anti-spyware / strong anti-malware capability should be installed by the organization. Organization should always ensure that the signatures are maintained up-to-date.

- Ensure that the organization follows all the employee exit procedures. Where an employee has administrative access to some of the applications or servers, such rights are revoked and the administrative passwords known to such employee are modified invariably. Also, all his access / authorizations are disabled.

- Employee registration / de-registration process is strictly followed to ensure that access systems do not allow any ex-employee to still authenticate and get into the organization.

- Carry out regular internal audits on the adherence to information security policies. All the issues found need to be fixed immediately.

- At least once a year carryout Penetration Testing on Social Engineering, understand the vulnerabilities and take appropriate corrective actions.

Some of the measures that individuals have to take to avoid becoming prey to social engineering attacks are:

- Do not publish any of your personal information

- Do not give your personal information over the phone unless you know for sure the other party to whom you are talking. Look at the need for the other party to know your personal information. Banks for example have all your information with them and may require little information to validate you if you have called them.

- Do not believe in any request for your personal information. When in doubt, notify the bank or financial institution named in the request via an official phone number gleaned from a verified legitimate source.

- Always create strong passwords. Never have same passwords for various systems. Ensure that you invariably change your passwords periodically.

- Do not write down your passwords anywhere.

- Ensure to cover up if you have to type your passwords / PIN in front of others. Ensure that your screen is clear or is locked when you have to discuss with strangers at your desk.

- Verify regularly your banking account statement or credit card statement to ensure that no unauthorized transactions are reflected thereon.

- Ensure that any personal information written down by you or unwanted copies of the applications with personal information are completely destroyed.

Chapter Summary

- We introduced social engineering and specified how social engineering attacks are carried out by taking disadvantage of the human nature like helping nature, trusting others, obeying the orders of the superiors, and fear of losing a job. We also talked about the social engineering attacks initiated personally and social engineering attacks initiated through computers. We also classified the attacks as attacks on the organizations and attacks on the individuals. We explored the risks of social engineering and mentioned that the risks of social engineering are high but are difficult to easily contain the same. We highlighted the importance of security policies, building awareness and conducting information security related trainings as most important aspects to reduce the extent of social engineering attacks.

- We offered different suitable scenarios as to how social engineering attacks exploit various aspects of human nature like helpfulness, trusting nature, superior's order obeying nature, and fear. In this section, we explored as to how these are exploited by other human beings (attackers) personally. For each of the scenario we also gave precursor information and analyzed as to how and why the attack was made possible.

- We discussed how social engineering attacks are carried out using computers. We looked into how through fake websites, through popup windows and through emails with links or attachments these attacks are carried out. Again we explored some of the relevant scenarios.

- We described various methods used in social engineering attacks like pretexting, phishing, spear phishing, vishing, baiting, tailgating, and e-mail attachments.

- We explored other social engineering attack possibilities such as attacks by planting an employee in the target organization (through recruitment process) or identifying a disgruntled employee from the target organization who hates the organization. We also looked at how such attacks can be carried out.

- We provided an approach and measures that organizations and individuals need to take to ensure that their propensity to fall prey to social engineering attacks is substantially reduced. We highlighted the necessity to have strong information security awareness training focus among others.

CHAPTER 16

■ ■ ■

Current Trends in Information Security

There are several trends in information security that are gaining in relevance. Three of these trends are:

- Wireless Security
- Mobile Security
- Bring Your Own Device (BYOD)

In this chapter, we discuss Wireless Security and Mobile Security briefly.

Wireless Security

Wireless communications use radio frequency carriers which carry the information. These may be direct communications between two wireless devices or these communications may be routed through a wireless network, such as through intermediate communication devices. Personal computers, laptops, smartphones, mobile phones, and tablets communicate with each other through a wireless network. Modulators, transmitters, wireless networks, receivers, and demodulators ensure that the messages initiated at one place are received and understood at the intended place.

Wireless communication has gained more prominence in the last five to ten years even though it has been in place for more than 100 years. Increasingly more organizations have started using wireless communication as it is easy to set up and removes some of the limitations of the wired communication structure. It does not require extensive cables to be laid through the walls, ceilings, or floors. In many instances, it is also cost effective compared to the cost of a wired structure. Further, access points are also movable easily. Systems can be moved from one place within the organization to the other and yet can access the network through wireless access points. Further, wireless communication can be used to complement or extend the wired communication structure. Wireless is used primarily in the context of the organizations and homes as wireless local area networks and is popularly known as Wi-Fi. The base standard or specification for this is IEEE 802.11. Various devices connect to the other network resources including the internet through wireless access points. Wireless access points connect you to a wired network or directly to the internet. The systems and the devices which connect to the wireless access point are known as stations. The stations need Wi-Fi adapters to communicate with the wireless access point. Wireless access is also possible through 3G or 4G USB based data cards which can be used as a hotspot by other connecting client devices. Further, it is also possible to connect two or more LANs using a wireless network. Worldwide Interoperability for Microwave Access (WIMAX) and Bluetooth are other wireless technologies which provide wireless access.

While it has provided ease of use, cost effectiveness, and ease of implementation it also has certain information security issues which have to be considered. While there has been extensive work carried out to improve the information security scenario of wireless communication, there are many concerns and limitations at this time. Wireless networks support limited bandwidth and when more computers use the access points, the performance suffers. Also, improvements to the wireless technology may require the equipment to be replaced. Further, plain

text communication through wireless is prone to sniffing, eavesdropping, man-in-the-middle attacks, and the like. Misuse of your wireless network for illegal activities by others including hacking other systems
is dangerous.

One of the solutions provided for some of the information security issues on wireless is encryption. Even though encryption of wireless communication is implemented by most, some of these are still prone to information security breaches. The two Wi-Fi encryption standards are Wired Equivalent Privacy (WEP) and Wi-Fi Protected Access (WPA). While WEP can be easily cracked, WPA has been found to be more effective. The biggest issue with WEP is the use of weak initialization vectors, among others, including password cracking and lack of effective key management mechanisms. WPA2 Personal and WPA2 Enterprise are the most widely used versions of WPA protocol. These use Temporal Key Integrity Protocol (TKIP) or Advanced Encryption Standard (AES) and CCMP or Extensible Authentication Protocol (EAP) for encryption and authentication mechanisms. While WPA2 Personal uses a pre-shared key, the WPA2 Enterprise uses Extensible Authentication Protocol (EAP) or RADIUS server for centralized authentication of the clients. Pre-shared key should be strong enough to avoid the possibility of dictionary attacks or cracking through brute force mechanisms. In order to increase the security of the communications in corporate organizations, virtual private network (VPN) technology can be additionally used. Further, ensuring strong encryption mechanisms like WPA2 Enterprise with appropriate settings on the client machines will aid in avoiding the attacks complemented by strong authentication mechanisms provided through an authentication server.

Each Wi-Fi network is identified through a Service Set Identifier (SSID). It is advised that this SSID is changed to a name that is neutral in representation and does not unnecessarily attract attackers / hackers. This is the identifier among the access point and the clients. The Wi-Fi network broadcasts the SSID as a part of the frame-header. Even if the broadcast of SSID is disabled it can be still be found out easily by the attackers using the frames, which clients use when they associate with the access point.

Wi-Fi authentication can happen using a centralized authentication server, open system authentication, or shared key authentication by the access point. It is strongly advised to use either shared key authentication or authentication through a centralized authentication server. Corporations are advised to always use the centralized authentication server. Further, to strengthen the authentication process MAC filtering may be enabled.

Various discovery and analysis tools are available for free or for a price. These enable the analysis of the wireless frames and man-in-the-middle attacks, including denial of service attacks, by sending fake packets or sending fake Clear to Send (CTS) signals in the name of a fake client making other clients wait indefinitely for their turn.

War-Walking and War-Driving are two popular methods wherein the attackers / hackers walk around or drive around with their laptops with Wi-Fi identification / analysis tools, connected with powerful antennas. They will identify open wireless networks and can use such networks for malicious activities, for sniffing the communications thereon, or initiate attacks on others using such networks including the connected networks. The tools like NetSurveyor, NetStumbler, WiFi Hopper, and Meraki WiFi Stumbler allow for easy network discovery. Additionally, mechanisms like MAC spoofing, unauthorized association, and adhoc association are the ways in which wireless networks can be attacked. Similarly, various client and access point misconfigurations allow for attacks by the attackers. Further, wireless traffic analysis may be carried out by the attackers to identify wireless vulnerabilities which may be exploited by them.

Another big issue with wireless networks is the use of rogue access points. These may be setup with the same SSID as that of the organization, but just outside the boundaries of the organization. These may be used by the organization's personnel who think they are genuine access points. The unfortunate result of rogue access points is they provide the attackers with the means to capture the information flowing through them. Similarly, the attackers can set up access points with renowned SSIDs that users may think are legitimate; users may expose information flowing through the access points to the attackers.

Powerful jamming signals can be used to jam the entire Wi-Fi network of an organization and thus ensure denial of service. Many of the jamming devices are available easily in the market.

We sum up the discussion above with some of the best practices to avoid / reduce the propensity for wireless attacks:

- Ensure that the default SSID is reset at the beginning into a neutral name so that it does not have the corporate entity name etc. which may entice or attract the attacker.

- Ensure that the MAC filtering is enabled on the router or the access point.

- Enable a firewall between the access point and the internal network for corporations.

- Ensure that the encryption is enabled.

- Ensure that the pass-phrase is periodically changed.

- Ensure that a strong access password is set on the router.

- Ensure that the strength of the wireless signal is not high so that it cannot be accessed from the outside of the organization.

- Use VPNs additionally for secure communications for corporations.

- Use better encryption mechanisms like WPA.

- Ensure that you use a centralized server for authentication for corporations.

- Do not allow access points to be accessed by others. Secure them.

- Ensure that the drivers are up-to-date.

- Use Wireless Intrusion Prevention Systems if possible.

- Carry out periodic audits of your wireless systems and fix any issues found.

- Carry out a penetration testing at least once a year on your wireless network system and ensure that the issues found are fixed appropriately.

Bluetooth Technology and Security

Bluetooth is the wireless communication technology that is used for short range communication (usually about 25 feet). This technology is used for transferring the files between one mobile device to the other (e.g., from mobile phone to the laptop or laptop to the mobile phone, etc.). As the range of communication is short the possibility of hacking it is less but cannot be denied. Bluetooth can be set to discoverable, limited discoverable, or non-discoverable mode. It can also be set as pairable mode or non-pairable mode. For the communication to be established, the two devices that want to connect with each other need to be paired. The Bluetooth devices communicate with each other using adhoc networks and hence are prone to attacks, such as denial of service, pumping of unwanted and unsolicited messages to the connected devices, and copying of the files from the connected devices.

It is advised that the users set the Bluetooth to off and enable it only when required. Otherwise, by default they need to configure it as non-discoverable and non-pairable and enable them to be discoverable and pairable only when required to provide access to or from other devices. If the Bluetooth is enabled and the configuration is in pairable mode, then other devices are able to connect and copy the files or information from the connected device. Mobile phones of others may be used by the attackers of Bluetooth to send messages to others. Similarly, malicious code that can control the mobile phones may be installed by the attackers using the Bluetooth technology and then the attacker can have complete control over the phone of the victim. Contact details can be stolen and misused. Other mobile phones can be used for making phone calls or for connecting to the internet. Further, Bluetooth protocol related vulnerabilities can be exploited by the users.

Some of the best practices to ensure security of the Bluetooth communication are as follows:[1]

- Have the devices securely with you or store them securely when not used.

- Ensure use of pre-shared key authentication and encryption for the Bluetooth communication.

- Enable Bluetooth only when required to communicate. Ensure that the Bluetooth is set to non-discoverable and non-pairable mode. Use discoverable and pairable mode only when you need to connect to other devices or vice versa.

- Remove stolen or unwanted devices from the list of paired devices.

- Carry out the pairing of the devices only in a secure area. Have the paired device as near as possible to the other device with which it is pairing.

- Ensure that anti-virus systems are in place.

- Ensure that the device firewall is active.

- Ensure regular patching of the Bluetooth devices.

Mobile Security

Mobile phones, smartphones, and tablets are being widely used now-a-days. Various operating systems are used in these mobile devices. Mobile devices are being used for transacting on the web, sending e-mails, instant messaging apps / tools, gaming, and various official / personal purposes. Mobile apps are being used heavily by the users of these devices as most of them are free or are available at very low cost. Mobile devices have made the lives of users easy and more active; however, at the same time they have created a number of security issues and all of us need to be concerned about them because many of us may be using the same mobile phone for both personal and work use.

The primary security concern is that mobile phones and the information they contain can be easily forgotten somewhere or stolen, allowing for unauthorized access to personal information such as login ids, credit card details, and passwords.

Additionally, the security of the various games or apps we download is questionable. They may have been created with malicious intent and can infect your mobile device in a manner that allows it, or the information it contains, to be misused by attackers. Additionally, these apps could be tracking your activities, further exposing you to theft and fraud by the attacker.

Many of the underlying operating systems themselves may have multiple security issues. These security issues / vulnerabilities may be misused by the attackers. Many of these may be found out by the attackers / hackers themselves and may not be known to the genuine users even though some of them may be known to the vendors of those operating systems concerned.

Unfortunately, many of us do not have anti-virus software installed on our mobile phones. It is advisable to install good anti-virus software that can reasonably protect your mobile phones from malicious attacks, such as Eset, AVG, Avast, Norton, or McAfee. Furthermore, each of us needs to review all the settings and see that they are appropriately set. Unnecessarily enabled settings / features need to be disabled.

Some of the best practices for information security of mobile devices are:

- Do not carry out rooting or jailbreaking of your operating system.

- Ensure encryption of the device.

- Ensure to download apps from only authorized stores. Do not download unknown apps or even known apps from other untrusted stores or web sites.

- Ensure regular updates and patching of the mobile operating system and the apps, particularly those with security implications.

- Ensure that the mobile devices are always held with you and are not handed over to others in your absence. Do not leave them in public places. Always keep them locked with a strong PIN.

- Do not open links from unknown sources on your mobile.

- Use strong encryption mechanism while using Wi-Fi.

- Transfer confidential data and other sensitive information from your mobile phone to other secure devices or secondary storage devices under your control. Have only limited data on your mobile at any point of time.

- Do not access secure websites using unsecured Wi-Fi connections. It is possible in such cases that your credentials are captured or sniffed by others.

- Ensure that your phones are configured to be locked after a certain amount of idle time.

- Enable remote wiping so that the data on the mobile can be wiped-off if it stolen or lost. In cases of phones used by corporate employees enable Mobile Device Management software.

- Disable unwanted settings. Enable them only when required.

Chapter Summary

- We highlighted three important current trends related to information security: Wireless Security, Mobile Security, and BYOD.

- Wireless communication uses radio frequency carriers. Wireless communications can occur between two wireless devices, or over a wireless network when a wireless device connects to a wired network.

- Ease of use including the mobility of access points and no need for extensive cabling, comparatively lower cost of installation and administration, connectivity to wired network or internet and ability to work on multiple types of networks like 2G/3G etc. have provided fillip to the wireless networks.

- Wireless networks also bring out a few security issues like possible compromise of the encryption provided by the protocols like WEP. The ease of capturing SSID or learning communication details from clients when they associate with an access point is a matter of concern. WPA2 Personal and WPA2 Enterprise are the most used encryption mechanisms by wireless networks.

- War Walking and War Driving are the mechanisms used by the attackers to understand the presence of and weakness of the wireless networks / access points, and exploit them by sniffing, eavesdropping, or misusing them. Rogue access points misleading genuine users and sniffing / capture of wireless communication contents is another important threat to corporations. Additionally, mechanisms like MAC spoofing, unauthorized association, and adhoc association are ways in which wireless networks can be attacked.

- We also discussed some of the best practices that may be used to reduce the potential for attacks on wireless networks.

- We explained Bluetooth Technology and its Security. Bluetooth technology is a wireless technology for short range communications and is used to transfer data / files between two mobile devices. Even though propensity for misuse of the Bluetooth technology is less it cannot be denied.

- Pairing is an important aspect to enable data transfer. Bluetooth switched off, not paired and non-discoverable Bluetooth devices are not prone to security issues. Some of the best practices like keeping the Bluetooth in off-mode when not required, removing the pairing when the work for which the other device was paired is over, making the device not discoverable when not required, etc. allow better Bluetooth security. Otherwise, files can be copied, contacts and addresses can be stolen, malicious software can be installed thus leading the attacker to have control over the other device by using the Bluetooth technology. Also, credit card data, login ids and passwords, and other confidential information stored thereon may be misused by the attackers.

- Then we discussed Mobile Security. Mobile phones, smartphones and tablets are widely used now. They have made the life of people lively and active. They have many uses to people. However, usage of the mobile devices for both personal and official purposes exposes them to higher security risks.

- The potential for mobile devices to be forgotten, lost, or information on the mobile devices to be stolen, the potential for stealing of the information on these mobile devices through malicious apps or by exploiting the weaknesses of the underlying operating system or by exploiting inappropriate or improper settings leading to security vulnerabilities, and not having the protection of anti-virus software are some of the security issues which should be addressed by all.

- We provided a list of best practices that users of mobile devices can use to have better mobile security.

Bibliography

Chapter 1

Footnotes

1. MIMOSO, MICHAEL & THREATPOST, THE KASPERSKY LAB SECURITY NEWS SERVICE. (2013). *BREACH Compression Attack Steals HTTPS Secrets in Under 30 Seconds.* [Online] 5th August 2013. Available from: http://threatpost.com/breach-compression-attack-steals-https-secrets-in-under-30-seconds/101579.

2. FISHER, DENNIS & THREATPOST, THE KASPERSKY LAB SECURITY NEWS. (2013). *Most Surprising NSA Capability: Defeating the Collective Security Prowess of Silicon Valley.* [Online] 30th December 2013. Available from: http://threatpost.com/the-year-in-nsa/103329.

3. SYMANTEC CORPORATION. (2014). *2013 Norton Report.* [Online] Available from: http://www.symantec.com/about/news/resources/press_kits/detail.jsp?pkid=norton-report-2013

4. INTERNATIONAL ORGANIZATION FOR STANDARDIZATION. (2014). *Management System Standards.* [Online] Available from: http://www.iso.org/iso/home/standards/management-standards.htm

References

5. ABBATE, JANET ELLEN. (1994*). From ARPANET to Internet: A history of ARPA-sponsored computer networks, 1966–1988.*

6. CORBATO FERNANDO, J. & VICTOR A. VYSSOTSKY. (1965). Introduction and overview of the Multics system. *Proceedings of the November 30–December 1, 1965, fall joint computer conference, part I.* ACM.

7. BERNERS-LEE, TIM., CAILLIAU, R., GROFF, J.F., & POLLERMANN, B. (1992). World-Wide Web: the information universe. *Internet Research* 2.1. pp. 52–58.

8. BERNERS-LEE, TIM, ET AL. (1993). *The World Wide Web initiative.* [Online] Available from: http://info.cern.ch/hypertext/WWW/TheProject.html

Chapter 2
Footnotes

1. LEESON, PETER T. & CHRISTOPHER J COYNE. (2005). The Economics of Computer Hacking. *Journal of Economics & Policy*, p. 511.

2. CERT, SOFTWARE ENGINEERING INSTITUTE, CMU, TIMOTHY J. SHIMEALL & JONATHAN SPRING. (2014). *Introduction to Information Security: A Strategic-Based Approach.* [Online] Available from: http://resources.sei.cmu.edu/library/asset-view.cfm?assetid=88289

3. GARFINKEL, SIMSON. (2002). The FNI's Cybercrime Crackdown. *Technology Review: Manchester NH 105.9* pp. 66–75

4. KAHN, DAVID. (1996). *The Codebreakers – The Comprehensive History of Secret Communication from Ancient Times to the Internet.* Revised ed. New York: Scribner.

5. MENKE, RICHARD. (2000). Telegraphic Realism: Henry James' In the Cage. *Publications of the Modern Language Association of America* pp. 975–990.

6. AGNEW, JAMES B. (1973). *The Great War that Almost Was: The Crimea, 1853-1856, pp. 83–102.* Birkhauser Basel.

7. RAKUS-ANDERSSON, ELISABETH. (2003). The Brains Behind the Enigma Code Breaking Before the Second World War. *Mathematics and War.* Birkhäuser Basel, pp. 83–102.

8. KRUH, LOUIS & DEAVOURS, CIPHER. (2002). The commercial Enigma: Beginnings of machine cryptography. *Cryptologia 26.1* pp. 1–16.

9. DIRK RIJMENANTS. *Photograph - The German Wehrmacht Enigma Cipher Machine.* [Online] Available from: http://users.telenet.be/d.rijmenants/en/enigma.htm

10. SHORT, KRISTI & DAGAN, AHARON. (2013). An Examination of the Components and Mathematics of the Enigma Electromechanical Rotor Ciphers. *Journal of Young Investigators, May 2013, Vol 25, No.5, pp. 33–40.*

11. COLIN SMITH. (2011). *Photograph - Alan Turing Statue near to Stoughton, Surrey, Great Britain.* [Online] Available from: http://www.geograph.org.uk/photo/2597296

12. CORBATO, FERNANDO J. & VYSSOTSKY, VICTOR A. (1965). Introduction and Overview of the Multics System. *Proceedings of the November 30-December 1, 1965, Fall Joint Computer Conference, Part I. ACM, 1965.*

13. BAKER, W.E., DUDONIS, R.M. & KEE, J.H. (1978). Transaction Network, Telephones and Terminals. *The Bell System Technical Journal, Vol. 57, No.10, December 1978.*

14. LAPSELY, PHIL. (2013). *Phreaking Out Ma Bell.* [Online] Available from: http://spectrum.ieee.org/telecom/standards/phreaking-out-ma-bell

15. BREEN, C. & DAHLBOM, C.A. (1960). Signaling System for Control of Telephone Switching. *The Bell System Technical Journal, Volume 39, November 1960, Number 6.* [Online] Available from: https://archive.org/details/bstj39-6-1381

16. BEATRICE COMPANIES, INC. *About Bell System Memorial, Photograph of John Draper.* Copyright of The Porticus Centre, Beatrice Technologies. [Online] Available from: http://www.beatriceco.com/bti/porticus/bell/about.html

17. SIMPSON, IAN & ROSHAN, MEDINA. (2013). *U.S. Soldier Manning Gets 35 Years for Passing Documents to WikiLeaks.* [Online] Available from: `http://www.reuters.com/article/2013/08/21/us-usa-wikileaks-manning-idUSBRE97J0JI20130821`

18. WIKILEAKS. (2013). *Statement by Julian Assange on today's sentencing of Bradley Manning.* [Online] Available from: `https://wikileaks.org/Statement-by-Julian-Assange-on,267.html`

19. A&E Television Networks, LLC. (2014). *Edward Snowden Biography.* [Online] Available from: `http://www.biography.com/people/edward-snowden-21262897#synopsis`

20. DEMOCRACY NOW. (2010). *Is WikiLeaks' Julian Assange a Hero? Glenn Greenwald Debates Steven Aftergood of Secrecy News.* [Online] Available from: `http://www.democracynow.org/2010/12/3/is_wikileaks_julian_assange_a_hero`

Additional References

- LUDLOW, PETER. (2010). WikiLeaks and Hacktivist Culture. *The Nation, October 4th, 2010.*

- BURGHARDT, TOM. (2013). ECHELON Today: The Evolution of an NSA Black Program. *Global Research.*

- A&E TELEVISION NETWORKS, LLC. *Edward Snowden, Biography.* [Online] Available from: `http://www.biography.com/people/edward-snowden-21262897`

- KARHULA, PAIVIKKI. (2011). *What is the Effect of WikiLeaks for Freedom of Information?* [Online] Available from: `http://www.ifla.org/publications/what-is-the-effect-of-wikileaks-for-freedom-of-information`

- NAKASHIMA, ELLEN. MARKON, JERRY, & WASHINGTON POST STAFF WRITERS. (2010). WikiLeaks Founder Could be Charged Under Espionage Act. *Washington Post: November 30th, 2010.* [Online] Available from: `http://www.washingtonpost.com/wp-dyn/content/article/2010/11/29/AR2010112905973.html`

- TAYLOR, MARISA. (2014). U.S. Spy Agency's Push for Secrecy Seen as Another Failing of Obama's Transparency Pledge. *McClatchy Washington Bureau.* [Online] Available from: `http://www.kansas.com/2014/01/15/3228179/us-spy-agencys-push-for-secrecy.html`

- ROSENBAUM, RON. *Secrets of the Little Blue Box.* [Online] Available from: `http://www.webcrunchers.com/crunch/esq-art.html`

- WESOLKOWSKI, SLAWO. (2009). The Invention of Enigma and How the Polish Broke It Before the Start of WWII. *University of Waterloo.*

- GOODELL, JEFF. (1996). *The Cyberthief and the Samurai: The True Story of Kevin Mitnick and the Man Who Hunted Him Down.*

Chapter 3
Footnotes

1. PERRIN, C. (2008). *Understanding layered security and defense in depth by Chad Perrin in IT Security.* [Online] Available from: http://www.techrepublic.com/blog/it-security/ understanding-layered-security-and-defense-in-depth/

2. INTERNATIONAL ORGANIZATION FOR STANDARDIZATION. (Various). *Information technology—Security techniques—Information security management systems–Requirements (ISO/IEC 27001:2013) Standard; Information technology—Security techniques—Code of practice for information security controls (ISO/IEC 27002:2013); Standards/Guidelines from International Organization for Standardization.* [Online] Available from: www.iso.org/

3. NATIONAL INSTITUTE OF STANDARDS AND TECHNOLOGY. (2011 & 2013). *Special Publication 800-39: Managing Information Security Risk: Organization, Mission, and Information System View & 800-53 Rev. 4: Security and Privacy Controls for Federal Information Systems and Organizations.* [Online] Available from: http://csrc.nist.gov/publications/nistpubs/.

4. THE SABSA INSTITUTE, John Sherwood, Andrew Clark & David Lynas. (2009). *SABSA® White Paper on Enterprise Security Architecture.* [Online] Available from: http://www.sabsa.org/white_paper

5. ORAM, A. & JOHN VIEGA. (2009). *Beautiful Security.* First Edition. Sebastopol, CA: O'Reilly Media, Inc.

6. NATIONAL INSTITUTE OF STANDARDS AND TECHNOLOGY. (2007). *Special Publication 800-100: Information Security Handbook: A Guide for Managers–Chapter 8.* [Online] Available from: http://csrc.nist.gov/publications/nistpubs/800-100/SP800-100-Mar07-2007.pdf

7. INTERNATIONAL ORGANIZATION FOR STANDARDIZATION. (2014). *ISO/IEC 27000:2014 -Information technology—Security techniques—Information security management systems—Overview and vocabulary.* [Online] Available from: http://standards.iso.org/ittf/PubliclyAvailableStandards/c063411_ISO_ IEC_27000_2014.zip

8. INFORMATION SYSTEMS SECURITY ASSOCIATION & DONN B. PARKER. (2010). Our Excessively Simplistic Information Security Model and How to Fix It. Volume 8 Issue 7, July 2010. *ISSA Journal.* [Online] Available from: http://www.bluetoad.com/ publication/?i=41813&page=1

9. SOFTWARE ENGINEERING INSTITUTE. (2005). *OCTAVE–S Implementation Guide, Version 1.* [Online] Available from: http://resources.sei.cmu.edu/library/asset-view.cfm?assetid=6795

10. INFORMATION SYSTEMS AUDIT AND CONTROL ASSOCIATION. (2009). *Risk IT Practitioner Guide.* [Online] Available from: http://www.isaca.org/Knowledge-Center/ Research/ResearchDeliverables/Pages/ The-Risk-IT-Framework.aspx

11. (ISC)². (2011). *2011 Frost & Sullivan Market Survey Sponsored by (ISC)2 and prepared by Robert Ayoub, CISSP Global Program Director, Information Security carried out in the fall 2010.* [Online] Available from: http://searchsecurity.techtarget.com/news/1527643/ ISC2-survey-reveals-need-for-secure-application-development-skills

12. NATIONAL INSTITUTE OF STANDARDS AND TECHNOLOGY. (1996). Special Publication 800-14: Generally Accepted Principles and Practices for Securing Information Technology Systems. [Online] Available from: http://csrc.nist.gov/publications/nistpubs/800-14/800-14.pdf

Chapter 4
Footnotes

1. NATIONAL INSTITUTE OF STANDARDS AND TECHNOLOGY. (2014). *Special publication 800-162: Guide to Attribute Based Access Control (ABAC) Definition and Considerations.* [Online] Available from: http://csrc.nist.gov/publications/PubsSPs.html

Chapter 5
Footnotes

1. NATIONAL INSTITUTE OF STANDARDS AND TECHNOLOGY. (2004). *Standards for Security Categorization of Federal Information and Information Systems, FIPS PUB 199.* [Online] Available from: http://csrc.nist.gov/publications/PubsFIPS.html.

2. NATIONAL INSTITUTE OF STANDARDS AND TECHNOLOGY. (2012). *Special Publication 800-30 Rev. 1 Guide for Conducting Risk Assessments.* [Online] Available from: http://csrc.nist.gov/publications/PubsSPs.html.

3. NATIONAL INSTITUTE OF STANDARDS AND TECHNOLOGY. (2012). *Special Publication 800-61 Rev. 2 Computer Security Incident Handling Guide.* [Online] Available from: http://csrc.nist.gov/publications/PubsSPs.html.

4. NATIONAL INSTITUTE OF STANDARDS AND TECHNOLOGY. (2010). *Special Publication 800-34 Rev. 1 Contingency Planning Guide for Federal Information Systems.* [Online] Available from: http://csrc.nist.gov/publications/PubsSPs.html.

Chapter 6
Footnotes

1. NATIONAL INSTITUTE OF STANDARDS AND TECHNOLOGY, DOLORES R. WALLACE & D. RICHARD KUHN. (2014). *Failure Modes in Medical Device Software: An Analysis of 15 years of Recall Data.* [Online] Available from: www.scholar.google.com

2. THE SYDNEY MORNING HERALD TRAVELLER. (22nd March 2014). *Air India Dreamliner flight from Melbourne makes emergency landing due to 'glitches.'* [Online] Available from: http://www.smh.com.au/travel/travel- incidents/air-india-dreamliner-flight-from-melbourne-makes-emergency- landing-due-to-glitches-20140206-322wh.html

3. HINDUSTAN TIMES, NEW DELHI. (5th Feb 2014). *AI flight makes emergency landing in Kuala Lumpur.* [Online] Available from: `http://www.hindustantimes.com/india-news/ai-flight-makes-emergency-landing- in-kuala-lumpur/article1-1180854.aspx`

4. GOLEM TECHNOLOGIES. (2014). *Shell Injection & Command Injection.* [Online] Available from: `https://www.golemtechnologies.com/articles/shell-injection`

Additional References

- BOYD, STEPHEN W. & ANGELOS D. KEROMYTIS. (2004). SQLrand: Preventing SQL injection attacks. *Applied Cryptography and Network Security.* Springer Berlin Heidelberg.

- YODER, JOSEPH & JEFFREY BARCALOW. (1998). Architectural patterns for enabling application security. *Urbana 51 (1998): 61801.*

- YIP, ALEXANDER, ET AL. (2009). Improving application security with data flow assertions. *Proceedings of the ACM SIGOPS 22nd symposium on Operating systems principles.* ACM, 2009.

- MCGRAW, GARY. (2004). Software security. *Security & Privacy, IEEE 2.2 (2004): 80–83.*

Chapter 7
Footnotes

1. KNAPP, M. (2014). *Hacked: Apple's Helpful Security Service Turned Harmful – By Mark Knapp dt. 27-May-2014.* [Online] Available from: `http://wallstcheatsheet.com/technology/hacked-apples-helpful-security-service-turned-harmful.html/`

2. USENIX – THE ADVANCED COMPUTING SYSTEMS ASSOCIATION, EVAN COOKE, FARNAM JAHANIAN & DANNY MCPHERSON. (2014). *Technical Paper The Zombie Roundup: Understanding, Detecting, and Disrupting Botnets.* [Online] Available from: `https://www.usenix.org/legacy/event/sruti05/tech/full_papers/cooke/cooke_html/`

3. KERNER, S.M. (2013). *Internet of Things Could Bring On Attack of the Killer Toaster Botnet.* [Online] Available from: `http://www.eweek.com/blogs/security-watch/internet-of-things-could-bring-on-attack-of-the-killer-toaster-botnet.html` (Posted 2013-10-10)

4. EWEEK. (2002). *Trail of Destruction: The History of the Virus.* [Online] Available from: `http://www.eweek.com/c/a/Web-Services-Web-20-and-SOA/Trail-of-Destruction-The-History-of-the-Virus/` (Posted 2002-03-22) & SEAN MICHAEL KERNER. (2013). *eWEEK 30: Computer Viruses Evolve from Minor Nuisances to Costly Pests.* [Online] Available at: `http://www.eweek.com/security/eweek-30-computer-viruses-evolve-from-minor-nuisances-to-costly-pests.html` (Posted 2013-11-15)

5. SYMANTEC CORPORATION. (2013). *Symantec Corporation's Symantec Threat Report 2013 - Volume 18.* [Online] Available from: `http://www.symantec.com/about/news/resources/press_kits/detail.jsp?pkid=istr-18`

6. MCAFEE LABS. (2014). McAfee Labs Threats Report – Fourth Quarter 2013. [Online] Available from: `http://www.mcafee.com/in/security-awareness/articles/mcafee-labs-threats-report-q4-2013.aspx`

7. MCAFEE LABS. (2013). McAfee Labs 2014 Threats Predictions Report. [Online] Available from: http://www.mcafee.com/in/security-awareness/articles/the-top-internet-security-threats-for-2014.aspx

8. SYMANTEC CORPORATION. (2014). *Norton Antivirus Product Details.* [Online] Available from: http://in.norton.com/360/ (accessed on 30th March 2014)

9. MCAFEE, INC. (2014). McAfee Antivirus Product Details. [Online] Available from: http://home.mcafee.com/store/total-protection (Accessed on 30th March 2014)

10. KASPERSKY LAB ZAO. (2014). Kaspersky Antivirus Product Details. [Online] Available from: http://www.kaspersky.co.in/kaspersky-pure

11. TECHMEDIA NETWORK | INTENDERS. (2014). *Top Ten Antivirus Reviews.* [Online] Available from: http://anti-virus-software-review.toptenreviews.com/

12. BITDEFENDER.COM. (2014). Bitdefender Antivirus Product Details. [Online] Available at: http://www.bitdefender.com/media/html/launch2014/?pid=in_nocover&sem_region=IN&utm_source=Google&utm_campaign=IN_Bitdefender&sem_type=search&sem_placement=&utm_content=38150774619&utm_term=bitdefender%20antivirus&gclid=CJnei73TvLOCFeIb4god6VoAYw & HERMAN STREET. (2014). [Online] Available from: http://store.hermanstreet.com/index.php?p=np&page_id=bitdefender-antivirus&ICID=bitdefender-2013-10-16&ofm

13. AVG TECHNOLOGIES. (2014). AVG Antivirus Product Details. http://www.avg.com/in-en/internet-security & HARMAN STREET. (2014). [Online] Available from: http://store.hermanstreet.com/pc-software/avg-anti-virus-2014-download/?&ICID=pin-AVG%20AntiVirus%202013-9-17bas&ofm (both accessed on 30th March 2014)

14. GRAVES, KIMBERLY. (2010). CEH Certified Ethical Hacker Study Guide. New Delhi: Wiley India Pvt. Ltd.

Chapter 8
Footnotes

1. INTERNET ENGINEERING TASK FORCE. (1998). *RFC 2440 - Open PGP Message Format.* [Online] Available from: http://www.rfc-editor.org/info/rfc2440

2. KAHN, DAVID. (1996). *The Codebreakers. The Codebreakers – The Comprehensive History of Secret Communication from Ancient Times to the Internet.* Revised ed. New York: Scribner.

3. NATIONAL INSTITUTE OF STANDARDS AND TECHNOLOGY. (2001). *Advanced Encryption Standard.* [Online] Available from: http://csrc.nist.gov/publications/fips/fips197/fips-197.pdf

4. INTERNET ENGINEERING TASK FORCE, C. Adams of Entrust Technologies. (1997). *RFC 2144 - The CAST-128 Encryption Algorithm.* [Online] Available from: http://www.rfc-editor.org/rfc/rfc2144.txt

5. INTERNET ENGINEERING TASK FORCE, C. Adams & J. Gilchrist of Entrust Technologies. (1999). *RFC 2612 - The CAST-256 Encryption Algorithm.* [Online] Available from: http://www.rfc-editor.org/rfc/rfc2612.txt

6. INTERNET ENGINEERING TASK FORCE, R. Rivest of MIT Laboratory for Computer Science and Data Security, Inc. (1998). *RFC 2268 – A description of the RC2(r) Encryption Algorithm.* [Online] Available from: `http://www.rfc-editor.org/rfc/rfc2268.txt`

7. INTERNET ENGINEERING TASK FORCE, R Baldwin of RSA Data Security, Inc & R Rivest of MIT Laboratory for Computer Science and RSA Data Security, Inc. (1996). *RFC 2040 - The RC5, RC5-CBC, RC5-CBC-Pad and RC5-CTS Algorithms.* [Online] Available from: `http://www.rfc-editor.org/rfc/rfc2040.txt`

8. SCHNEIER, BRUCE. (1994). *The Blowfish Encryption Algorithm.* [Online] Available from: `https://www.schneier.com/blowfish.html`

9. SCHNEIER, BRUCE. (1998). *Twofish.* [Online] Available from: `https://www.schneier.com/twofish.html`

10. INTERNET ENGINEERING TASK FORCE, M. Matsui & J. Nakajima. (2004). *RFC 3713 - A description of the Camellia Encryption Algorithm.* [Online] Available from: `http://www.rfc-editor.org/rfc/rfc3713.txt`

11. INTERNET ENGINEERING TASK FORCE, H Ohta & M Matsui of Mitsubishi Electric Corporation. (2000). *RFC 2994 - A Description of the MISTY1 Encryption Algorithms.* [Online] Available from: `http://www.rfc-editor.org/rfc/rfc2994.txt`

12. INTERNET ENGINEERING TASK FORCE, H.J. Lee, S.J. Lee, J.H. Yoon, D.H. Cheon, J.I. Lee of KISA. (2005). *RFC 4269 - The SEED Encryption Algorithm.* [Online] Available from: `http://www.rfc-editor.org/rfc/rfc4269.txt`

13. INTERNET ENGINEERING TASK FORCE, J. Lee, J. Lee, J. Kim, D. Kwon, C. Kim of NSRI. (2010). *RFC 5794 - A Description of the ARIA Encryption Algorithm.* [Online] Available from: `http://www.rfc-editor.org/rfc/rfc5794.txt`

14. INTERNET ENGINEERING TASK FORCE, M. Katagi & S. Moriai of Sony Corporation. (2011). *RFC 6114 - The 128-bit Blockcipher CLEFIA.* [Online] Available from: `http://www.rfc-editor.org/rfc/rfc6114.txt`

15. INTERNET ENGINEERING TASK FORCE, S. Kiyomoto & W. Shin of KDDI R&D Laboratories, Inc. (2013). *RFC 7008 - A Description of the KCipher-2 Encryption Algorithm.* [Online] Available from: `http://www.rfc-editor.org/rfc/rfc7008.txt`

16. THE SANS INSTITUTE. (2001). *The GSM Standard.* [Online] Available from: `http://www.sans.org/reading-room/whitepapers/telephone/gsm-standard-an-overview-security-317`

17. MITSUBISHI ELECTRIC CORPORATION. *Cellular Algorithms-Encryption Algorithms.* [Online] Available from: `http://www.etsi.org/services/security-algorithms/cellular-algorithms`

18. INTERNET ENGINEERING TASK FORCE, J. Jonsson & B. Kaliski of RSA Laboratories. (2003). *RFC 3447 - RSA Cryptography Specification.* [Online] Available from: `http://www.rfc-editor.org/rfc/rfc3447.txt`

19. NATIONAL INSTITUTE OF STANDARDS AND TECHNOLOGY. (2014). *RSA Validation List.* [Online] Available from: `http://csrc.nist.gov/groups/STM/cavp/documents/dss/rsanewval.html`

20. INTERNET ENGINEERING TASK FORCE, D. McGrew of Cisco Systems, K. Igoe & M. Salter of National Security Agency. RFC 6090 - Fundamental Elliptic Curve Cryptography Algorithm. [Online] Available from: `http://www.rfc-editor.org/rfc/rfc6090.txt`

21. INTERNET ENGINEERING TASK FORCE, B. Kaliski of RSA Laboratories. (1992).
RFC 1319 - The MD2 Message-Digest Algorithm. [Online] Available from:
http://www.rfc-editor.org/rfc/rfc1319.txt

22. INTERNET ENGINEERING TASK FORCE, D. Eastlake 3rd, T. Hansen of AT&T Labs. (2006).
RFC 4634 – US Secure Hash Algorithms (SHA and HMAC-SHA). [Online] Available from:
http://www.rfc-editor.org/rfc/rfc4634.txt

23. NATIONAL INSTITUTE OF STANDARDS AND TECHNOLOGY. (2012). *SHA-3 Competition (2007-2012)*.
[Online] Available from: http://csrc.nist.gov/groups/ST/hash/sha-3/index.html

24. TIMBERLINE TECHNOLOGIES. (2009). *Alphabetical List of Public Key Infrastructure Products*.
[Online] Available from: http://www.timberlinetechnologies.com/products/pki.html

25. INTERNATIONAL TELECOMMUNICATION UNION. (2012). *X.509: Information
technology - Open Systems Interconnection - The Directory: Public-key and attribute
certificate frameworks*. [Online] Available from: https://www.itu.int/rec/T-REC-X.509/en

26. NATIONAL INSTITUTE OF TECHNOLOGY AND STANDARDS. (1993). *Capstone Chip
Technology*. [Online] Available from: http://csrc.nist.gov/keyrecovery/cap.txt

27. ELECTRONIC PRIVACY INFORMATION CENTER. (1993). *The Clipper Chip*. [Online]
Available from: http://epic.org/crypto/clipper/

28. NATIONAL INSTITUTE OF STANDARDS AND TECHNOLOGY. (Various).
Federal Information Processing Standards. [Online] Available from:
http://csrc.nist.gov/publications/PubsFIPS.html

29. NATIONAL INSTITUTE OF STANDARDS AND TECHNOLOGY. (2008). *FIPS 198-1:
The Keyed-Hash Message Authentication Code (HMAC)*. [Online] Available from:
http://csrc.nist.gov/publications/PubsFIPS.html

30. SOURCEFORGE. (2014). *TrueCrypt – Migrating from TrueCrypt to BitLocker*. [Online]
Available from: http://truecrypt.sourceforge.net/

Additional References

- DIFFIE, WHITFIELD, & MARTIN E. HELLMAN. (1976). New directions in cryptography.
Information Theory, IEEE Transactions on 22.6 (1976): 644-654.

- ODED, GOLDREICH. (2001). *Foundations of Cryptography, Volume 1: Basic Tools*. Cambridge
University Press.

- MERRIAM-WEBSTER. *Cryptology (definition). Merriam-Webster's Collegiate Dictionary*. 11th
edition. [Online] Available from: http://www.merriam-webster.com/dictionary/cryptology.
Retrieved 2008-02-01.

- SCHNEIER, BRUCE. (1996). *Applied Cryptography*. Second Edition. J. Wiley and Sons.

- STALLINGS, WILLIAM. (2003). *Cryptography and Network Security, Principles and Practice*.
Third edition. Prentice Hall.

- JOHNSON, J. & B. KALISKI. (2003). *RFC 3447 - Public-Key Cryptography Standards (PKCS):
RSA Cryptography Specifications Version 2.1*. [Online] Available from:
https://www.ietf.org/rfc/rfc3447.txt

- NATIONAL INSTITUTE OF STANDARDS AND TECHNOLOGY. (2001). *Federal Information Processing Standards (FIPS) 140-2 - Security Requirements for Cryptographic Modules.* [Online] Available from: http://csrc.nist.gov/publications/fips/fips140-2/fips1402.pdf

- INTERNET ENGINEERING TASK FORCE. (2008). An Open Specification for Pretty Good Privacy (openpgp). [Online] Available from: http://datatracker.ietf.org/wg/openpgp/charter/

- SCHNEIER, B. (1996). *Applied Cryptography.* 2nd edition. New York: John Wiley & Sons.

- SCHNEIER, B. (2000). *Secrets & Lies: Digital Security in a Networked World.* New York: John Wiley & Sons.

- STALLINGS, W. (2014). *Cryptography and Network Security: Principles and Practice.* 6th edition. Dorling Kindersley (India) Pvt. Ltd.

Chapter 9
Footnotes

1. INTERNATIONAL ORGANIZATION FOR STANDARDIZATION. About ISO, What are Standards? [Online] Available from: http://www.iso.org/iso/home/about.htm

2. INTERNATIONAL TELECOMMUNICATION UNION. (1994). *X.200: Information technology - Open Systems Interconnection - Basic Reference Model: The basic model.* [Online] Available from: http://www.itu.int/rec/T-REC-X.200-199407-I/en

3. INTERNET ENGINEERING TASK FORCE, R. BRADEN. *RFC 1122* - Requirements for Internet Hosts - Communication Layers. [Online] Available from: http://www.ietf.org/rfc/rfc1122.txt

4. INTERNET ENGINEERING TASK FORCE. *RFC 791 – Internet Protocol – DARPA Internet Program Protocol Specification.* [Online] Available from: http://www.ietf.org/rfc/rfc791.txt

5. INTERNET ENGINEERING TASK FORCE. *RFC 793 – Transmission Control Protocol – DARPA Internet Program Protocol Specification.* [Online] Available from: http://www.ietf.org/rfc/rfc793.txt

6. MICROSOFT CORPORATION. *TCP/IP Protocol Architecture.* [Online] Available at: http://technet.microsoft.com/en-us/library/cc958821.aspx

7. CBS INTERACTIVE (ZDNET). (2012). *HSBC banking websites recover from DoS attack.* [Online] Available from: http://www.zdnet.com/uk/hsbc-banking-websites-recover-from-dos-attack-7000006063/.

8. PCMAG DIGITAL GROUP, JAY MUNRO. (2004). *MyDoom.A: Fastest Spreading Virus in History.* [Online] Available from: http://www.pcmag.com/article2/0,2817,1485719,00.asp

9. INTERNET ENGINEERING TASK FORCE, W. EDDY OF VERIZON. *RFC 4987 – TCP SYN Flooding Attacks and Common Mitigations.* [Online] Available from: http://www.ietf.org/rfc/rfc4987.txt

Additional References

- STEVENS, W.R. (1994). *TCP/IP Illustrated, Volume I: The Protocols.* Addison-Wesley.

- MILLER, M. (1999). *Troubleshooting TCP/IP.* John Wiley & Sons.

- CAPPELL, L.A. & E. TITTEL. (2004). *Guide to TCP/IP.* Second Edition. Thomson Course Technology.

- FEIT, S. (2000). *TCP/IP: Architecture, Protocols, and Implementation with IPv6 and IP Security.* McGraw-Hill.

- COMER, D. (1991). *Internetworking with TCP/IP, Vol. I: Principles, Protocols, and Architecture.* Second Edition. Prentice-Hall.

Chapter 10

Footnotes

1. [Online] Available from: `http://postscapes.com/internet-of-things-market-size`

2. [Online] Available from: `http://www.cisco.com/c/en/us/td/docs/solutions/Enterprise/Campus/HA_campus_DG/hacampusdg.html`

3. INTERNET ENGINEERING TASK FORCE. *RFC 791 – Internet Protocol – DARPA Internet Program Protocol Specification.* [Online] Available from: `http://www.ietf.org/rfc/rfc791.txt`

4. INTERNET ENGINEERING TASK FORCE. *RFC 793 – Transmission Control Protocol – DARPA Internet Program Protocol Specification.* [Online] Available from: `http://www.ietf.org/rfc/rfc793.txt`

5. INTERNET ENGINEERING TASK FORCE, K. EGEVANG of Cray Communications & P. FRANCIS of NTT. RFC 1631 – *The IP Network Address Translator (NAT).* [Online] Available from: `http://www.ietf.org/rfc/rfc1631.txt`

6. INTERNET ENGINEERING TASK FORCE, Y. REKHTER of CISCO Systems, B. MOSKOWITZ of Chrysler Corp, D. KARRENBERG of RIPE NCC, G. J. DE GROOT of RIPE NCC & E. LEAR of Silicon Graphics, Inc. *RFC 1918 – Address Allocation for Private Internets.* [Online] Available from: `http://www.ietf.org/rfc/rfc1918.txt`

Additional References

- CISCO SYSTEMS. *Cisco Firewall best Practices.* [Online] Available from: `http://www.cisco.com/web/about/security/intelligence/firewall-best-practices.html`

- THE SANS INSTITUTE. *SANS Security Consensus Operational Readiness Evaluation, Firewall Checklist.* [Online] Available from: `http://www.sans.org/score/checklists/FirewallChecklist.pdf`

- DARBY, R. (2012). Cyber Defence in Focus: Enemies Near and Far–or Just Behind the Firewall: The Case for Knowledge Management. *Defence Studies, 12(4), 523-538.*

- NICHO, M. (2012). Incorporating COBIT Best Practices in PCI DSS V2.0 for Effective Compliance. *ISACA Journal, 1, 42.*

- SINGH, A. N., PICOT, A., KRANZ, J., GUPTA, M. P., & OJHA, A. (2013). Information Security Management (ISM) Practices: Lessons from Select Cases from India and Germany. *Global Journal of Flexible Systems Management, 14(4), 225-239.*

- ROBERTSON, R. A. (2012). Security Auditing: The Need for Policies and Practices. *Journal of Information Privacy & Security, 8(1).*

- WEEK, J., IVANOVA, P., WEEK, S., & MCLEOD, A. (2011). A Firewall Data Log Analysis of Unauthorized and Suspicious Traffic. *Journal of Information System Security, 7(3).*

Chapter 11

Footnotes

1. SANS INSTITUTE – INFOSEC READING ROOM, ALLISON HRIVNAK. *Host Based Intrusion Detection: An Overview of Tripwire and Intruder Alert.* [Online] Available from: http://www.sans.org/reading-room/whitepapers/detection/host-based-intrusion-detection-overview-tripwire-intruder-alert-353

2. MCAFEE NETWORK SECURITY TECHNOLOGIES GROUP, DR. FENGMIN GONG. (2002). *Next Generation Intrusion Detection Systems (IDS).* [Online] Available from: https://www.mcafee.com/japan/products/pdf/IntruVert-NextGenerationIDSWhitePaper_en.pdf

3. MCAFEE NETWORK SECURITY TECHNOLOGIES GROUP, DR. FENGMIN GONG. (2003). *Deciphering Detection Techniques: Part II Anomaly-Based Intrusion Detection.* [Online] Available from: https://secure.mcafee.com/japan/products/pdf/Deciphering_Detection_Techniques-Anomaly-Based_Detection_WP_en.pdf

4. NATIONAL INSTITUTE OF STANDARDS AND TECHNOLOGY, KAREN SCARFONE & PETER MELL. (2007). *Special Publication 800-94: Guide to Intrusion Detection and Prevention Systems (IDPS).* [Online] Available from: http://csrc.nist.gov/publications/nistpubs/800-94/SP800-94.pdf

Additional References

- MCAFEE NETWORK SECURITY TECHNOLOGIES GROUP & DR. FENGMIN GONG. *Deciphering Detection Techniques: Part III Denial of Service Detection.* [Online] Available from: http://www.mcafee.com/japan/products/pdf/deciphering_detection_techniques-dos_detection_wp_en.pdf

- MUKKAMALA, SRINIVAS & ANDREW SUGAND AJITH ABRAHAM. Designing Intrusion Detection Systems: Architectures, Challenges and Perspectives. *Department of Computer Science, Oklahoma State University, USA.* [Online] Available from: http://wstst05.softcomputing.net/iec.pdf

- BACE, REBECCA GURLEY. (2000). *Intrusion Detection.* Macmillan Technical Publishing.

- BRACKNEY, R. (1998). Cyber-Intrusion Response. *Reliable Distributed Systems.*

- THE SANS INSTITUTE. (2008). *Network IDS & IPS Deployment Strategies.* [Online] Available from: http://www.sans.org/reading-room/whitepapers/intrusion/network-ids-ips-deployment-strategies-2143

- GARCIA-TEODORO, PEDRO, ET AL. (2009). Anomaly-based network intrusion detection: Techniques, systems and challenges. *Computers & Security 28.1 (2009): 18-28.*

- THE SANS INSTITUTE. (2001). *Understanding Intrusion Detection Systems.* [Online] Available from: http://www.sans.org/reading-room/whitepapers/detection/understanding-intrusion-detection-systems-337

- THE SANS INSTITUTE. (2004). *Understanding IPS and IDS: Using IPS and IDS together for Defense in Depth.* [Online] Available from: http://www.sans.org/reading-room/whitepapers/detection/understanding-ips-ids-ips-ids-defense-in-depth-1381

Chapter 12
Footnotes

1. INTERNET ENGINEERING TASK FORCE, W. SIMPSON of Daydreamer. (1994). *RFC 1661 - The Point-to-Point Protocol.* [Online] Available from: http://www.ietf.org/rfc/rfc1661.txt

2. INTERNET ENGINEERING TASK FORCE, K. HAMZEH of Ascend Communications, G. PALL of Microsoft Corporation, W. VERTHEIN of 3Com, J. TAARUD of Copper Mountain Networks, W. LITTLE of ECI Telematics & G. ZORN of Microsoft Corporation. (1999). *RFC 2637 - Point-to-Point Tunneling Protocol (PPTP).* [Online] Available from: http://www.ietf.org/rfc/rfc2637.txt

3. INTERNET ENGINEERING TASK FORCE, W.SIMPSON of Daydreamer. (1994). *RFC 1661 - The Point-to-Point protocol (PPPP).* [Online] Available from: http://www.ietf.org/rfc/rfc1661.txt

4. INTERNET ENGINEERING TASK FORCE, W.SIMPSON of Daydreamer. (1996). *RFC 1994 - PPP Challenge Handshake Authentication Protocol (CHAP).* [Online] Available from: http://www.ietf.org/rfc/rfc1994.txt

5. INTERNET ENGINEERING TASK FORCE, W. TOWNSLEY & A. VALENCIA of Cisco Systems, A. RUBENS of Ascend Communications, G. PALL & G. ZORN of Microsoft Corporation & B. PALTER of Redback Networks. (1999). *RFC 2661 - Layer Two Tunneling Protocol "L2TP".* [Online] Available from: http://www.ietf.org/rfc/rfc2661.txt

6. INTERNET ENGINEERING TASK FORCE, G. DOMMETY of Cisco Systems. (2000). *RFC 2890 - Key and Sequence Number Extensions to GRE.* [Online] Available from: http://www.ietf.org/rfc/rfc2890.txt

7. INTERNET ENGINEERING TASK FORCE, S. KENT of BBN Corp & R. ATKINSON of @ Home Network. (1998). *RFC 2401 - Security Architecture for the Internet Protocol.* [Online] Available from: http://www.ietf.org/rfc/rfc2401.txt

8. INTERNET ENGINEERING TASK FORCE, S. KENT & K. SEO of BBN Technologies. (2005). *RFC 4301 - Security Architecture for Internet Protocol.* [Online] Available from: http://www.ietf.org/rfc/rfc4301.txt

9. INTERNET ENGINEERING TASK FORCE, S. KENT of BBN Technologies. (2005). *RFC 4302 - IP Authentication Header.* [Online] Available from: http://www.ietf.org/rfc/rfc4302.txt

10. INTERNET ENGINEERING TASK FORCE, S. KENT of BBN Technologies. (2005). *RFC4303 - IP Encapsulating Security Payload (ESP).* [Online] Available from: http://www.ietf.org/rfc/rfc4303.txt

11. INTERNET ENGINEERING TASK FORCE, C. KAUFMAN, Ed. of Microsoft. (2005). *RFC 4306 - Internet Key Exchange (IKEv2) Protocol.* [Online] Available from: http://www.ietf.org/rfc/rfc4306.txt

12. INTERNET ENGINEERING TASK FORCE, E. ROSEN of Cisco Systems, Inc., A. VISWANATHAN of Force10 Networks, Inc. & R. CALLON of Juniper Networks, Inc. (2001). *RFC 3031 – Multiprotocol Label Switching Architecture*. [Online] Available from: `http://www.ietf.org/rfc/rfc3031.txt`

13. INTERNET ENGINEERING TASK FORCE, E. ROSEN of Cisco Systems, Inc. & Y. REKHTER of Juniper Networks, Inc. (2006). *RFC 4364 - BGP/MPLS IP Virtual Private Networks (VPNs)*. [Online] Available from: `http://www.ietf.org/rfc/rfc4364.txt`

Additional References

- GLEESON, B., A. LIN, J. HEINANEN, G. ARMITAGE, A. MALIS & INTERNET ENGINEERING TASK FORCE. (2000). *RFC 2764 - A Framework for IP Based Virtual Private Networks*. [Online] Available from: `http://tools.ietf.org/html/rfc2764`

- HANKS, S., T. LI, D. FARINACCI, P. TRAINA & INTERNET ENGINEERING TASK FORCE. (1994). *RFC1701 - Generic Routing Encapsulation*. [Online] Available from: `http://tools.ietf.org/html/rfc1701`

- HANKS, S., T. LI, D. FARINACCI, P. TRAINA & INTERNET ENGINEERING TASK FORCE. (1994). *RFC1702 - Generic Routing Encapsulation over IPv4 networks*. [Online] Available from: `http://tools.ietf.org/html/rfc1702`

- SHENKER, S., C. PATRIDGE, R. GUERIN & INTERNET ENGINEERING TASK FORCE. (1997). *RFC2212 - Specification of Guaranteed Quality of Service*. [Online] Available from: `http://tools.ietf.org/html/rfc2212`

- PERKINS, D. OF CMU & INTERNET ENGINEERING TASK FORCE. (1990). *RFC 1171 - The Point-to-Point Protocol for the Transmission of Multi-Protocol Datagrams Over Point-to-Point Links*. [Online] Available from: `http://tools.ietf.org/html/rfc1171`

- HAMZEH, K., ET AL., & INTERNET ENGINEERING TASK FORCE. (1999). *RFC 2637 - Point-to-Point Tunneling Protocol (PPTP)*. [Online] Available from: `http://tools.ietf.org/html/rfc2637`

- SIMPSON, W., OF DAYDREAMER & INTERNET ENGINEERING TASK FORCE. (1994). *RFC 1661 - The Point-to-Point protocol (PPPP)*. [Online] Available from: `http://tools.ietf.org/html/rfc1661`

- ZORN, G., OF MICROSOFT CORP & INTERNET ENGINEERING TASK FORCE. (1999). *RFC 2484 - PPP LCP International Configuration Option*. [Online] Available from: `http://tools.ietf.org/html/rfc2484`

- TOWNSLEY, W., ET AL, & INTERNET ENGINEERING TASK FORCE. (1999). *RFC 2661 - Layer Two Tunneling Protocol*. [Online] Available from: `http://tools.ietf.org/html/rfc2661`

- DOMMETY, G., & INTERNET ENGINEERING TASK FORCE. (2000). *RFC 2890 - Generic Routing Encapsulation (GRE)*. [Online] Available from: `http://tools.ietf.org/html/rfc2890`

- KENT, S., R. ATKINSON & INTERNET ENGINEERING TASK FORCE. (1998). *RFC 2401 - Security Architecture for the Internet Protocol*. [Online] Available from: `http://tools.ietf.org/html/rfc2401`

- KENT, S., & INTERNET ENGINEERING TASK FORCE. (2005). *RFC 4302 - IP Authentication Header.* [Online] Available from: http://tools.ietf.org/html/rfc4302

- KENT, S., R. ATKINSON & INTERNET ENGINEERING TASK FORCE. *RFC 2406 & RFC4303 - IP Encapsulating Security Payload (ESP).* [Online] Available from: http://tools.ietf.org/html/rfc2406

- HARKINS, D., D. CARREL & INTERNET ENGINEERING TASK FORCE. (1998). *RFC 2409, RFC 4306 - The Internet Key Exchange (IKE).* [Online] Available from: http://tools.ietf.org/html/rfc2409

- KENT, S., K. SEO & INTERNET ENGINEERING TAKS FORCE. (2005). *RFC 4301, RFC 2401 - Security Architecture for the IP.* [Online] Available from: http://tools.ietf.org/html/rfc4301

- ROSEN, E., A. VISWANATHAN, R. CALLON & INTERNET ENGINEERING TASK FORCE. (2001). *RFC 3031 - MPLS Architecture.* [Online] Available from: http://tools.ietf.org/html/rfc3031

- ROSEN, E., Y. REKHTER & INTERNET ENGINEERING TASK FORCE. *RFC 4364 - BGP/MPLS VPNs.* [Online] Available from: http://tools.ietf.org/html/rfc4364

- INTERNET ENGINEERING TASK FORCE. (2006). *RFC 4364 - BGP/MPLS IP Virtual Private Networks (VPNs).* [Online] Available from: http://tools.ietf.org/html/rfc4364

- CHANDRA, R., P. TRAINA, T. LI & INTERNET ENGINEERING TASK FORCE. (1996). *RFC1997 - BGP Communities Attribute.* [Online] Available from: http://tools.ietf.org/html/rfc1997

- CHEN, E., T. BATES & INTERNET ENGINEERING TASK FORCE. (1996). *RFC1998 - An Application of the BGP Community Attribute in Multi-home Routing.* [Online] Available from: http://tools.ietf.org/html/rfc1998

- WAITZMAN, D., C. PARTRIDGE, S. DEERING & INTERNET ENGINEERING TASK FORCE. (1988). *RFC1075 - Distance Vector Multicast Routing Protocol.* [Online] Available from: http://tools.ietf.org/html/rfc1075

- INTERNET ENGINEERING TASK FORCE. (2005). *IP Security Protocol.* [Online] Available from: http://www.ietf.org/html.charters/ipsec-charter.html

- RAJA, P. & F5 NETWORKS, INC. (2006). *Rolling out New SSL VPN Service.* [Online] Available from: https://www.f5.com/pdf/white-papers/sslvpn-sp-wp.pdf.

Chapter 13

Footnotes

1. NATIONAL INSTITUTE OF STANDARDS AND TECHNOLOGY. (2011). Special Publication 800-145: The NIST Definition of Cloud Computing. [Online] Available from: http://csrc.nist.gov/publications/PubsSPs.html

2. NATIONAL INSTITUTE OF STANDARDS AND TECHNOLOGY. (2011). Special Publication 800-144: Guidelines on Security and Privacy in Public Cloud Computing.[Online] Available from: http://csrc.nist.gov/publications/PubsSPs.html

3. KRUTZ, L. & RUSSELL DEAN VINES. (2010). *Cloud Security – A Comprehensive Guide to Secure Cloud Computing.* New Delhi - Wiley India Pvt. Ltd.

4. NATIONAL INSTITUTE OF STANDARDS AND TECHNOLOGY. (2012). *Special Publication 800-146: Cloud Computing Synopsis and Recommendations.* [Online] Available from: http://csrc.nist.gov/publications/nistpubs/800-146/SP800-146.pdf

References

1. KRUTZ, R.L. & RUSSELL DEAN VINES. (2004). Second Edition. The CISSP Prep Guide. New Delhi - Wiley dreamtech India Pvt. Ltd.

Chapter 14

Footnotes

1. PARKER, D.B. (1998). *Fighting Computer Crime.* New York: John Wiley and Sons Inc. pp. 250–251.

References

2. SINHA, G.R. & SANDEEP B PATIL. *Biometrics: Concepts and Applications.* New Delhi: Wiley India Pvt. Ltd.

3. GREGORY, P. & MICHAEL A. SIMON. (2008). *Biometrics for Dummies.* Hoboken, NJ: Wiley Publishing, Inc.

Additional References

• NATIONAL INSTITUTE OF STANDARDS AND TECHNOLOGY. *Special Publication 800-12: Introduction to Computer Security: The NIST Handbook – Chapter 15.* [Online] Available from: http://csrc.nist.gov/publications/nistpubs/800-12/800-12-html/chapter15.html

• JAIN, A. K., A. ROSS, & S. PRABHAKAR. (2004). An Introduction to Biometric Recognition. *IEEE Trans. on Circuits and Systems for Video Technology, Special Issue on Image and Video-Based Biometrics, vol. 14, no. 1, pp. 4-20, January 2004.* [Online] Available from: http://ieeexplore.ieee.org/iel5/76/28212/01262027.pdf

Chapter 15

Footnotes

1. GRAVES, KIMBERLY. (2010). CEH Certified Ethical Hacker Study Guide. New Delhi: Wiley India Pvt. Ltd.

Additional References

- LUO, XIN (ROBERT), RICHARD BRODY., ALESSANDRO SEAZZU., & STEPHEN BURD - ALL OF THE UNIVERSITY OF NEW MEXICO, USA. (2011). Social Engineering: The Neglected Human Factor for Information Security Management. *Information Resources Management Journal, 24(3), 1-8, July-September 2011.* [Online] Available from: http://scholar.google.co.in/scholar?q=social+engineering+neglected+human+factor&btnG=&hl=en&as_sdt=0%2C5&as_ylo=2010/IRMJ2011.pdf

- DIMKOV., T., WOLTER PIETERS, PIETER HARTEL OF UNIVERSITY OF TWENTE, THE NETHERLANDS. (2010). *Two methodologies for physical penetration testing using social engineering.* [Online] Available from: http://scholar.google.co.in/scholar?q=social+engineering+two+methodologies+for+physical+penetration+testing&btnG=&hl=en&as_sdt=0%2C5&as_ylo=2010

- MAAN., P.S., MANISH SHARMA. OF DAV INSTITUTE OF ENGINEERING AND TECHNOLOGY, PUNJAB TECHNICAL UNIVERSTIY, INDIA. (2012). Social Engineering: A Partial Technical Attack. *IJCSI International Journal of Computer Science Issues, Vol. 9, Issue 2, No 3, March 2012.* [Online] Available from: http://scholar.google.co.in/scholar?q=social+engineering+a+partial+technical+attack&btnG=&hl=en&as_sdt=0%2C5&as_ylo=2010

- HASAN, M., NILESH PRAJAPATI, & SAFVAN VOHARA OF BVM ENGINEERING COLLEGE, INDIA. Case Study On Social Engineering Techniques For Persuasion. *International journal on applications of graph theory in wireless ad hoc networks and sensor networks.* [Online] Available from: http://scholar.google.co.in/scholar?as_ylo=2010&q=case+study+on+social+engineering&hl=en&as_sdt=0,5

Chapter 16

Footnotes

1. NATIONAL SECURITY AGENCY, UNITED STATES OF AMERICA - SYSTEMS AND NETWORK ANALYSIS CENTER, INFORMATION ASSURANCE DIRECTORATE. *Bluetooth Security.* [Online] Available from: http://www.google.co.in/url?sa=t&rct=j&q=&esrc=s&source=web&cd=10&sqi=2&ved=0CFQQFjAJ&url=http%3A%2F%2Fwww.nsa.gov%2Fia%2F_files%2Ffactsheets%2FI732-016R-07.pdf&ei=d294U9XHB8aLuATj_YJ4&usg=AFQjCNFc2CXHzjfl27QVF7gBZuZonc9tKQ

Index

▓ D

▓ E

■ X, Y, Z

Made in the USA
Middletown, DE
07 September 2015